James D. Moore
Literary Depictions of the Scribal Profession in the Story of Ahiqar and Jeremiah 36

Beihefte zur Zeitschrift für die alttestamentliche Wissenschaft

Edited by
John Barton, Reinhard G. Kratz, Nathan MacDonald,
Sara Milstein, and Markus Witte

Volume 541

James D. Moore

Literary Depictions of the Scribal Profession in the Story of Ahiqar and Jeremiah 36

—

DE GRUYTER

ISBN 978-3-11-075254-0
e-ISBN (PDF) 978-3-11-075304-2
e-ISBN (EPUB) 978-3-11-075312-7
ISSN 0934-2575

Library of Congress Control Number: 2021942886

Bibliographic information published by the Deutsche Nationalbibliothek
The Deutsche Nationalbibliothek lists this publication in the Deutsche Nationalbibliografie;
detailed bibliographic data are available on the Internet at http://dnb.dnb.de.

© 2021 Walter de Gruyter GmbH, Berlin/Boston
Printing and binding: CPI books GmbH, Leck

www.degruyter.com

For scribes and outsiders.

Preface

This manuscript is a revision of my Brandeis dissertation, "'I Am Unable to Do My Job': Literary Depictions of the Scribal Profession in the Story of Ahiqar and Jeremiah 36" (2017). That study included a long appendix containing a new edition of the narrative portions of the Elephantine Aramaic Ahiqar manuscript and an extensive philological and historical commentary. Because more unpublished fragments of that manuscript have come to light, it seemed fitting to separate the edition from the social and historical study of its content. Although there are many unpublished fragments, they are small and difficult to read and to place. They will be of value for understanding the papyrus's physical qualities and the manuscript history of the tale more than for what they add to our understanding of the manuscript's narrative content. It is possible that as work on those fragments continues to develop, the narrative content may change slightly, but as the one tasked with the job of publishing those new fragments, care has been taken to ensure the longevity of the arguments in this book after the new edition is published. All translations of the Ahiqar manuscript in this book are my own, but the reader should consult the Aramaic and English edition found in Bezalel Porten and Ada Yardeni, *Textbook of Aramaic Documents from Ancient Egypt*, vol. C no. C1.1. for the most used version of the full text, as it now stands.

A project of this magnitude has afforded me the privilege to be advised and helped by many along the way. Foremost, this work, and many key moments in my career, are owed to the steadfast support of Professor David P. Wright. Over the years he has modeled for me the value of comparative research and has taught me how to approach ancient data with fastidious attention to detail, all the while using the exploratory and creative approaches that make the humanities human. The readers of the original dissertation: Tzvi Abusch, Jacqueline Eliza Vayntrub, and Edward Silver provided me with challenging and perceptive feedback that helped me to produce a clearer and more precise work.

I am also indebted to my past teachers who have invested in me, especially Marc Brettler, in whose classes seeds of the ideas herein began to sprout. Dozens of other professors and colleagues met with me throughout this project or corresponded by email, and I thank them for their insights and time, especially Bezalel Porten, Aaron Demsky, Gillian Greenberg, and Jack Lundbom. With them and others, I was able to articulate and fine-tune my ideas. Lastly, I would like to thank those with whom I studied years ago. They and others have been both teachers and friends to me.

Many organizations and institutions made it possible for me to complete my research for this study. The Tauber Institute for the Study of European Jewry, The Mellon Foundation, The Near Eastern Judaic Studies Graduate Student and Faculty Research Fund at Brandeis University, and the Graduate Student Affairs Ph.D. Research Grant at Brandeis University all provided me with much needed funding. The Albright Institute of Archaeological Research, the École Biblique, the British Library, the Cambridge University Library, the Israel Antiquities Authority, and the Staatsbibliothek zu Berlin provided me with resources and access to manuscripts to conduct my research. Lastly, this work would not have been possible without the help and support of Verena Lepper and her team at the Ägyptisches Museum und Papyrussammlung of the Staatliche Museen zu Berlin. In 2016, she allowed me the privilege of serving as a Gastwissenschaftler on her ERC-funded Elephantine project (ID no. 637692) and granted me access to the Elephantine manuscripts, in particular the Ahiqar manuscript, on which this study is based. With the support of the ERC grant along with a grant I wrote for the Fritz-Thyssen Foundation under Bernd Schipper and Verena Lepper, I have been able to continue my work on the Ahiqar manuscript's unpublished fragments, which will come to light in the future.

Content

Preface —— vii

1 Introduction —— **1**
1.1 The Story of Ahiqar —— **1**
1.2 The Tale of Jeremiah and Baruch's Scroll —— **11**
1.3 Thesis —— **16**
1.4 Trends in the Study of Scribal Culture —— **17**
1.5 Approach —— **30**
1.5.1 The Comparative Perspective —— **30**
1.5.2 Textual Criticism and Manuscript Studies as Part of Reception History —— **31**
1.5.3 Literary Anthropology and The Sociology of Literature —— **33**
1.6 Summary of Chapters —— **37**

2 Allusions to the Aramaic Scribal Profession in the Story of Ahiqar —— **39**
2.1 Scribal Features in the Story of Ahiqar —— **41**
2.2 The Prologue to a Scribe's Tale (A.1–2) —— **43**
2.3 Acquiring a Scribal Student (A.2–7) —— **48**
2.4 Scribal Succession and Retirement (A.7–B.6) —— **57**
2.5 Scribal Conspiracy and Defamation (B.6–14) —— **65**
2.6 The Consequences of a Scribe's Rebellion (C.1–8) —— **70**
2.7 The Collusion of Courtiers (C.8–D.i.15) —— **75**
2.8 Concluding Remarks —— **81**

3 Allusions to the Hebrew Scribal Profession in the Tale of Jeremiah and Baruch's Scroll —— **84**
3.1 Training and Conspiring in the Scribal Workshop (MT 36:1–8 / LXX 43:1–8) —— **87**
3.2 Professional Scribal Characters in the Temple Complex (MT 36:9–11 / LXX 43:9–11) —— **99**
3.3 Courtly Scribal Interactions in the Palace (MT 36:12–19 / LXX 43:12–19) —— **104**
3.4 Courtly Scribes in the Royal Chamber (MT 36:20–26a / LXX 43:20–26a) —— **114**
3.5 Regrouping in the Scribal Workshop (MT 36:26b–32 / LXX 43:26b–32) —— **121**
3.6 Concluding Remarks —— **129**

4	**The Story of Ahiqar and the Tale of Jeremiah and Baruch's Scroll in Comparative Perspective —— 135**
4.1	The Story of Ahiqar, the Tale of Jeremiah and Baruch's Scroll, and the Court Tale Genre —— 136
4.2	Shared Motifs between the Story of Ahiqar and the Tale of Jeremiah and Baruch's Scroll —— 139
4.2.1	Introductory Focus on the "Word(s)" of the Scribal Protagonist —— 139
4.2.2	The Succession of Kings —— 140
4.2.3	Imparting Knowledge to a Student or Apprentice —— 141
4.2.4	Protagonist's Confessed Inability to Perform his Scribal Duty —— 143
4.2.5	Professional Conflict Brought on by the Scribal Student's Actions —— 145
4.2.6	An Angry King Who Commands a Prince to Capture/Kill the Protagonist —— 146
4.2.7	Courtly Characters Intervene in the Protagonist's Fate —— 147
4.2.8	Scribal Colleagues Encourage the Protagonist(s) to Hide —— 148
4.2.9	Discussion of the Shared Motifs —— 150
4.3	A Possible Explanation for the Evolution from First- to Third-Person Narration in Jeremiah Manuscripts in view of the Transmission History of the Story of Ahiqar —— 153
4.4	Differences between the Allusions to the Scribal Experience —— 164

5   **Conclusion —— 169**

Appendix: Syriac Ahiqar Manuscripts Cited —— 173

Bibliography —— 175

Indices
Ancient Sources Cited—— 192
Foreign Words Discussed——204
Abbreviations——209
Sigla——210

1 Introduction

At first glance, the Aramaic Story of Ahiqar and the Hebrew Tale of Jeremiah and Baruch's Scroll in MT Jer 36 (LXX Jer 43) have little in common, and this study begins with the presumption that the two are fundamentally different. The Story of Ahiqar is about the tribulations of a courtier who falls from the king's grace, but is later rehabilitated. The Tale of Jeremiah and Baruch's Scroll concerns a prophet of Yahweh, Jeremiah, who, with Baruch, writes prophecies on a scroll, which king Jehoiakim burns, and which Jeremiah and Baruch then rewrite. But closer examination reveals that these two ancient sources are written in narrative form and recount turbulent events in the lives of scribal characters who interact with each other in a king's court. These two mid-first millennium BCE Northwest Semitic narratives contain detailed descriptions of the scribal craft and of the role it played in the professional lives of scribes working within a politically charged context. Unlike, Egyptian, Anatolian, Mesopotamian, or Greco-Roman scribal cultures, little is known about the social dynamics of the professional scribal experience among ancient Aramaic or Hebrew writers. The Story of Ahiqar and the Tale of Jeremiah and Baruch's Scroll are two of the only Aramaic or Hebrew sources to survive that reflect on the scribal experience. These two tales are first and foremost literary works, that were written about scribal figures for scribal readers. It should not be assumed, however, that these works are historical. As such, this study will discuss to what degree—if at all— are the allusions to the Aramaic and Hebrew scribal professions embedded in the stories reliable reflections of the scribal ethos in the constructed historical settings of their narratives. Despite the specific differences in narrative setting, characterization, and plot, the two tales share a number of thematic similarities that will be fleshed out in chapter four of this study.

1.1 The Story of Ahiqar

The Story of Ahiqar was written in Aramaic in or before the early 5th century BCE, and depicts a teacher-student relationship between its main characters, Ahiqar and his nephew Nadin (Nadan in Syriac).[1] The tale is set in the Assyrian court of

---

1 Early discussion of the tale suggested that there may have been an Akkadian "original," but the discovery of the Aramaic manuscript with its standard Aramaic usage have convinced scholars that the tale was originally composed in Aramaic (see Harris, Story, 2nd ed., xcii). I also

Esarhaddon immediately after he succeeded his father Sennacherib, whom we know from historical sources was assassinated. Under the new regime of Esarhaddon, Ahiqar, the old "wise scribe" and "counselor of all of Assyria," contemplates who might succeed him in his prestigious scribal office, and Esarhaddon later has the same concern. As his replacement, Ahiqar presents to Esarhaddon his nephew Nadin, whom he had adopted and had been training in the scribal art, and, after a short interview, Esarhaddon approves the appointment. Ahiqar, wishing to take advantage of the king's good graces, requests in this moment that he might retire. The king grants the request, and Ahiqar returns to his country estate to spend time in his vineyards. In a new episode, Nadin shifts from a co-protagonist to the plot's central antagonist; he defames his uncle at the Palace Gate in which he worked. Nadin brings charges against Ahiqar before the king, and Ahiqar's purported actions are deemed treasonous. The king sends a courtier, Nabûsumiskun and two companions, to find and to kill Ahiqar as punishment for his alleged crimes. In a backstory, the reader learns that Ahiqar had banked social capital with Nabûsumiskun by saving his life from a similar fate, and thus Ahiqar convinced this courtier to hide him rather than to kill him. At this point, the oldest manuscript of the tale breaks, and later, more expansive, editions describe how the Assyrian king received an ultimatum from the Egyptian Pharaoh: the Assyrian king must help solve an architectural riddle that Pharaoh's courtiers could not in order to receive tribute. Nabûsumiskun reveals that Ahiqar is alive and that he could solve the problem. The king jubilantly welcomes Ahiqar back and sends him to Egypt to solve the riddle. Upon Ahiqar's return, the king hands Nadin over to him for punishment. Ahiqar kills Nadin for his insolence, apparently while lecturing to him. In most of these later manuscripts, one or more lists of maxims, which Ahiqar taught to Nadin are edited into the narrative or appended to it. Likewise, the narrative of the Elephantine manuscript is followed by a list of maxims.

The Story of Ahiqar is one of the most disseminated texts in the history of literature. In the ancient world the text was internationally known. The tale spread as far West as the Greek-speaking world, as far south as the Nubian-Egyptian border (and later into Ethiopia), and potentially as far East as India.[2] The Story of Ahiqar is thought to have inspired Aramaic and Hebrew writers of the book of Esther, the Joseph Story in the book of Genesis, the book of Daniel, and the book of Tobit, as well as the characterization of Ezra. The Story of

---

espouse this view, but do not reject the possibility of an Akkadian version of the tale at some point in its manuscript history.

2 See Krappe, "Story," 280–284.

Ahiqar's maxims may have influenced sections of the book of Proverbs. The tale was a source for ancient fictional (auto)biographical works, such as a scene in the Life of Aesop which appears to have directly borrowed from the Story of Ahiqar and to have simply replaced the tale's characters.[3] Sections of the book of Tobit can even be seen as ancient fan fiction that transforms the character of Ahiqar into an ancient Jew/Judean[4] and gives him a supportive role in Tobit's autobiographical life story. In the Common Era, the tale continued to inspire composers, even as late as the Arabic writers of *Alf laylah wa-laylah* (i.e. 1001 Arabian Nights) and perhaps the Quran sura 31 (*Luqman*). The Story of Ahiqar is one of the few original first millennium BCE Mesopotamian sources to have been continuously copied and read in the Near East since its inception.[5]

The oldest manuscript of the Story of Ahiqar is a fifth century BCE Aramaic papyrus, found on the southern Egyptian Nile island of Elephantine, where it appears to have been read and used by Aramaic speaking expatriates living there. Along with the Elephantine Aramaic manuscript, dozens of other manuscripts of the Story of Ahiqar or lists of maxims ascribed to Ahiqar are known in Syriac, Armenian, Ethiopic, Old Turkish, Greek, Slavonic, Karshuni, and Arabic.[6] These were published in the first two decades of the twentieth century.

---

3 See Wills, *Jew*, 193–204 and Holm, *Courtiers*, 47–53.
4 In this book, "Judahite" refers to a citizen of the kingdom of Judah. "Judean" refers to those who are natives from the region of Judah after the fall of its kingdom in 586 BCE. "Ancient Jew" refers to the religious identity of (mostly) Judeans living during the Second Temple period up to 70 CE. "Jew/Jewish" is a socio-religious identity that developed after 70 CE and in response to the Roman destruction of the second Jerusalem temple. "Israelite" is reserved specifically for a citizen of the ancient kingdom of Israel. For a discussion of the historical and terminological problems, see Brettler, "Judaism," 429–447.
5 Not even the famous Epic of Gilgamesh or the Enuma Elish has this honor. Even though he is a polytheist, Ahiqar was held in high esteem among eastern Christian writers.
6 When these texts were collected and published in Conybeare, Harris, and Lewis, *Story* (1898, second edition 1913, hereafter Harris, *Story*), only sayings of Ahiqar were known in Ethiopic and Greek. Since then multiple copies of an Ethiopic narrative, without the sayings have been discovered (Lusini, "Ethiopic;" Schneider, "L'histoire"). Harris' main Syriac manuscript for the complete tale was Camb. Cod. Add 2020, though he was aware of Sachau 336 and three modern transcriptions from Urmia (Harris, *Story*, xxii–xxiii), one of which is Houghton 80 = transcription of Urmia 230 (mistakenly marked no. 270) with variants to Urmia 117. For the lost Urmia documents see Coakley, "Manuscripts" and an unpublished discussion accompanying Houghten 80 in the library's documentation. In addition, BM Or. 2313 attests to the same Syriac tradition, but was written by a less skilled copyist; this may be Nöldeke, *Untersuchungen* ms. "M." Other manuscripts have varying degrees of peculiarities which may be identified as unique recensions e.g., BM 7200, Graffin and BnF 422, Mingana 433, Sachau 162, JerMkl 162, Sachau 336, Dom. Fr. Mosel 430, or Dayro d-Mor Gabriel 192, though a complete study of them

Today, manuscripts are also known in Turoyo, Sogdian, and Demotic Egyptian.[7] At the turn of the twentieth century, scholars had begun to compare the manuscripts to understand how they relate, and they concluded that most stem from Syriac originals,[8] yet an unknown Greek,[9] which has affinities with the Syriac, must lie behind the tangled connections and variants between the Slavonic and Armenian recensions.[10]

As Rendel Harris admitted over a century ago, no individual scholar possesses the expertise to effectively study the Ahiqar manuscripts.[11] Fortunately, since it appears that the later editions derive from early Syriac core texts, the present study will limit its purview to mostly the Aramaic and Syriac manuscripts. Passing references may be made to Demotic Egyptian or the derivative editions when necessary. No study has yet been made that convincingly explains, in detail, how different Syriac manuscripts may be organized into recensions, much less has a study been made that negotiates all the variations between the Syriac and Aramaic versions.[12] The present study will not perform a comprehensive assessment of the Syriac manuscripts, but will negotiate the relationship among manuscripts for points in the tale deemed relevant.

---

has not been made. Other unpublished manuscripts exist, but I did not have access to them. I am thankful to Luca Koronli and Simon Birol for sharing their references with me.

7 Karshuni is a form of Arabic written in Syriac script. For a list of five Karshuni manuscripts see Ferrer and Monferrer, *Historia*, 20–22. The Turoyo (also known as "Modern Syriac") version is known from StaBi Sachau 339, which remains unpublished; it includes both an Arabic and Turoyo version. For Sogdian, an Eastern Iranian language written in Syriac script, see Sims-Williams, *Biblical*, 107–124 and plates. This version only appears as sayings. For a discussion of the Demotic recension, see Quack, "Interaction" and "demotischen."

8 Harris, *Story*, lxxxiv.

9 Some consider the Life of Aesop to preserve a lost Greek original and have used it to reconstruct older structural episodes in the tale, see Strugnell, "Problems," *204–*211. Two unpublished Syriac manuscripts refer to Ahiqar using Greek loanwords, Dom. Fr. Mosel 430, which uses satrap and notary, and Mingana 433, which uses philosopher and prefect. At present these seem to be best explained as later edits by Syriac copyists who saw Ahiqar within the larger world of philosophical and wisdom literature.

10 Harris, *Story*, 174–184, esp. 184. Those working in this hypothetical recension must now consider the Sogdian version as a control in their analysis since it is a witness to an early Syriac recension but not a Greek text. See Sims-Williams, *Biblical*, 108–109.

11 Harris, *Story*, "Preface."

12 For early discussions of the various recensions see, in addition to Harris' introduction, Charles, *Apocrypha*, 719–725 and Nau, *Histoire*, 78–86, 281–285. For recent studies see Brock, "Notes," 205–206 and "Ahiqar," 11. I am also indebted to Sebastian Brock for his communications with me about the subject. See also Denis et al, *Introduction*, 2:993–1036.

Although this study will not consider them in detail, additionally, the Ethiopic manuscripts exhibit developments that are worth mentioning. They contain unique narrative features, such as resetting the tale in the Persian (perhaps Parthian or Sassanid) court of an unnamed king, rather than in the Assyrian court. They exhibit the appropriation of the character of Ahiqar along with his tale, rather than replacing the character with a cultural hero, as the Aesop tradition and *Alf laylah wa-laylah* have done. The Ethiopic manuscripts, which recast the tale in a Persian court, are the only examples of the character's appropriation into a new cultural and historical setting other than the Judean appropriation of Ahiqar in the book of Tobit. Although the Ethiopic manuscripts are thought to derive from Arabic sources, it remains unknown if the Ethiopic is a product of a unique Egyptian reworking of the tale or a daughter of those coming from Syria-Mesopotamia or the Levant. Certainly, Late Antique Persian-isms can be found in some Syriac manuscripts,[13] but to recast the historical setting in such a drastic way as does the Ethiopic tale exhibits the types of extreme developments one must be on guard for when discussing the historical evolution of the narrative.

While the Ethiopic Ahiqar merely reminds one to be analytically cautious, the Demotic Egyptian fragments as well as the paraphrase of the Story of Ahiqar known from the book of Tobit are directly relevant to this study. Late Demotic Egyptian fragments of the Story of Ahiqar (Pap. Ber. P. 23729, P. 23730(?), P. 23829, P. 23830, P. 23831, and Cairo National Library 3122) contain unique readings, but resemble the Syriac narrative more than the Aramaic.[14] Since the Demotic predates the earliest known Syriac manuscripts by nearly a millennium, yet appears to resemble Syriac, rather than Aramaic, narrative features, it becomes an important witness to the antiquity of the core narrative elements in the Syriac manuscripts as well as the order of the sections of narrative and maxims.

Lastly, the first century BCE Aramaic Dead Sea Scroll manuscripts of the book of Tobit contain references to the character of Ahiqar (≈ Tob 1:22; 2:10), and fragmentary references to a paraphrase of the Story of Ahiqar are known

---

13 E.g., the use of ܡܘܒܕ "mobed" in BnF 422 and Graffin p. 1 §I.1. Even Camb. Cod. Add. 2020 refers to Parthians.
14 Quack, "demotischen," forthcoming. Based on a fairly standardized composition known as the Book of the Temple copied on the verso of the Berlin and Vienne fragments, the relationship between Demotic Ahiqar's narrative and maxims is clear: "Demnach stehen die erhaltenen narrativen Fragmente vom Rekto am Anfang des Textes, darauf folgen die Weisheitssprüche" (ibid.).

from the book of Tobit's long recension.¹⁵ Jonas Greenfield has convincingly argued that the paraphrase of the Story of Ahiqar draws on allusions known from the Syriac manuscripts and not the Elephantine text.¹⁶ As with the Demotic Egyptian fragments, the fragments of the Aramaic book of Tobit attest to the antiquity of the Syriac's narrative features, and provide grounds for critically comparing the Elephantine and Syriac manuscripts.

While a study that works out the relationship and trajectory of development among the many recensions is long overdue, such a difficult enterprise will not be attempted in this book in a comprehensive way. Instead, this study will focus on the Elephantine Aramaic manuscript and consult the later manuscripts when it is necessary to build an argument about how the reader can understand the story's scribal characters.

Until recently, the trend was to see the Story of Ahiqar as an ancient Syrian text that was brought to Egypt, but some now consider that the tale may have been composed in Egypt.¹⁷ Regardless of its place of origin, I maintain that an Aramaic writer who had intimate knowledge of Neo-Assyrian scribal culture composed the narrative portions of the Story of Ahiqar. This knowledge derives from the long standing and co-developing Akkadian and Aramaic scribal cultures of the 8th–5th centuries BCE.¹⁸ Chapter two will elaborate on the socio-

---

15 DJD 19 pp. 1–76. The papyrus manuscript 4Q196 (paleographically dated to the first century BCE) contains the description of the character of Ahiqar (frag. 2.5–8 ≈ Tob 1:14), and potentially a reference to his trip (corvée service) to Elam (frag. 4.1 ≈ Tob 2:10). The phrase "who went to Elam" ^{uru}mātu Elianda illiku is a Persian period phrase identifying corvée service which was even undertaken by Judeans in Babylonia, see CUSAS 28 no. 41 and BaAr 6 no. 4. For a discussion of why people traveled to Elam, see Waerzeggers, "Babylonians," esp. 800–813. For examples of this tax obligation see, Jursa and Waerzeggers, "Aspects," 237–269. The parchment manuscript 4Q198 (paleographically dated to the first century BCE or CE) retains a portion of the Ahiqar paraphrase (frag. 2.1–5 ≈ Tob 14:10). The parchment manuscript 4Q199 (paleographically dated to c. 100 BCE) clearly retains a reference to Nadin (frag. 2 ln. 1 ≈ Tob 14:10).
16 Greenfield, "Ahiqar," esp. 333–334.
17 See Bledsoe, "Wisdom," 57–58 for a review of the scholarship. Notably, Holm, "Memories," 304 states, "[I]t is possible that the Story of Aḥiqar was composed in Egypt where it was connected to the Syrian proverb collection. The setting of Aḥiqar and perhaps some of the rivalry is drawn from the Assyrian court as a mere literary frame," and she cites evidence of Assyrian scholarly rivalries from the Neo-Assyrian scholarly letters. Holm does not directly claim that *an Egyptian writer* composed the tale in Egypt. One can interpret her work to mean that a writer of (As)syrian origin, with intimate knowledge of the history of the Assyrian court, wrote the tale in Egypt (see her discussion on 307). An aberrant view is held by Chyutin, *Tendentious*, 32–33 which claims that a Jew living in Elephantine composed the Story of Ahiqar.
18 This topic has been the thesis of a number of works. Most notably Muffs, *Studies*, who finds idiomatic evidence that connects legal verbiage in some Elephantine documents with Neo-

historical circumstances of the Aramaic writer who knows and critiques the elitism of Neo-Assyrian scribal culture. To be sure, the few surviving literary Aramaic sources from Egypt, which date to the Persian period, exhibit a strong interest in Neo-Assyrian history and culture.[19] The Darius Inscription (*TAD* C2), which is the only other Aramaic literary work to come from Elephantine, certainly came from Akkadian-Aramaic scribal interactions. The Mesopotamian focus in the story of Ahiqar and its discovery at the same site as the Aramaic Darius Inscription, suggests that it is more than coincidence.[20] A more precise date for the composition of the story is not possible, nor is it necessary for the present study (see §5.3 below).

Elite Neo-Assyrian scribal culture is attested firsthand by the Neo-Assyrian scholars, themselves, the *ummânū*. Simo Parpola has studied dossiers of hundreds of the surviving letters sent from the *ummânū* to the late Neo-Assyrian kings.[21] His work has shown that the term *ummânu* literally means "master" and appears in the letters as an elite class of five professions: *ṭupšarru* "astrologer/scribe," *bārû* "haruspex/diviner," *āšipu* "exorcist/magician," *asû* "physician," and *kalû* "lamentation chanter."[22] According to Parpola, these five scribal positions were associated with the concept of "wise men" and thus can be called "scholars."[23] The five disciplines of these scholars constitute the areas of Mesopotamian scholarship and demonstrate how the Neo-Assyrians saw "the

---

Assyrian sources. A similar study was conducted on many Aramaic letters by Fales, "Aramaic Letters." He has also discussed the relationship between some Aramaic dockets and the Neo-Assyrian texts they are found on (Fales, *Aramaic Epigraphs*). Recently the Aramaic curse formulas from Iron Age sources and what they may reveal about the interactions between the two scribal cultures were in focus in Quick, *Deuteronomy*. Sanders, *Adapa*, discusses the issue on the conceptual level of intellectual transmission. There are ample studies on the general social and textual discussion of Akkadian and Aramaic scribal interactions, notably Beaulieu, "Official;" Fales, "Multilingualism;" and Röllig, "Aramäer," the latter of whom sees Ahiqar as the beginning of Aramaic literature (185).

19 Moore, "Review," 5–6; Holm, "Memories," 297–323.
20 Moore, *Aramaic*, forthcoming.
21 Parpola, *LAS*. Five letters in the dossier were sent to the crown prince, four to the queen mother, three from the king to a scholar, and three among scholars (SAA 10 p. xxv).
22 Parpola, SAA 10 p. xiii. This list derives from SAA 10 no. 160. One list (SAA 10 no. 7) includes *dāgil iṣṣūrī* "augurs" and not the *kalû*, and another (SAA 7 no. 1) includes *dāgil iṣṣūrī* and *kalû* in addition to Egyptian magicians and scribes (xiv). See also Kvanvig, "Advisors" 689–690.
23 Parpola, SAA 10 p. xiv. Parpola notes that not every individual who bore one of these titles was considered among the *ummânū*.

supernatural or numinous" to be "the greatest wisdom of all."[24] The role of these court scholars was to interpret divine signs and to direct the king's conduct in order to keep him from sinning. While each scholar may have held his own position, all were trained in the five fields of Mesopotamian scholarship.[25] The *ummânū* saw themselves as the intellectual heirs of the gods. Their knowledge was passed from the gods to the mythical sages, whom the scholars saw as their forefathers.[26] According to Parpola, these scholars worked in a "professional team, each headed by an eminent 'chief.' The most important of these, the chief scribe, held a position in the Assyrian cabinet as the king's personal scholar (*ummânu*)."[27] Parpola has organized the mostly undated texts into chronological order from c. 680–621 BCE [28] and concludes that there was an "inner circle" of 17 Ninevite scholars and an "outer circle" of mostly Babylonian scholars who corresponded with the king in this period.[29]

Parpola's work on the Neo-Assyrian scholarly letters helps to reconstruct the social setting of the Neo-Assyrian court portrayed in the Story of Ahiqar. For example, in the publication of one scholarly letter (SAA 10 no. 294),[30] Parpola notes the similarities between the circumstances suffered by Ahiqar and the professional perils of an exorcist named Urad-Gula, who was the son of Adad-šuma-uṣur, the personal exorcist of Esarhaddon and Ashurbanipal. Historical data, such as this, is used in this study to determine the accuracy of historical allusions embedded in the Story of Ahiqar, and to serve as a control in distinguishing social reality from literary artistry. These documentary sources are important historical data, but are by no means textual data which the various writers and editors of the Story of Ahiqar directly relied on.

The literary features of the Story of Ahiqar also have antecedents in Neo-Assyrian documentary and literary works. The autobiographical style of the Elephantine narrative resembles Akkadian fictional autobiographical texts as

---

24 Parpola, SAA 10 p. xv. Parpola sees the Assyrian "tree of life" as a concept that informed their worldview. See also Parpola, "Tree," 161–208.
25 Parpola, SAA 10 pp. xiv, xvii, xxii.
26 Parpola, SAA 10 pp. xviii, xxi.
27 Parpola, SAA 10 pp. xxix.
28 Parpola, *LAS*, xi and SAA 10 pp. xxviii–xxix.
29 Parpola, SAA 10 pp. xxv–xxvii.
30 First published in Parpola, "Forlorn," 257–278. Von Soden, "Unterweltsvision," 11–13 previously drew connections between Nadin and Urad-Gula and saw his father Adad-šuma-uṣur as the "Urbild" of Ahiqar.

noted by Tremper Longman III and Joan Westenholz.³¹ The court tale genre to which the Story of Ahiqar belongs is attested across the ancient Near East, but as Stephanie Dalley has argued, "The tale has developed out of a thoroughly Mesopotamian genre of wisdom literature" though it was influenced by Egyptian material.³² The Mesopotamian literary tradition is a pool of cultural idioms, traditions, and ideas that influenced the literary development of the Ahiqar narrative, but finding direct dependency on a particular Akkadian literary source is difficult to argue and prove. This is owed to the fact that while Akkadian-Aramaic bilingualism has a long history in the scribal circles that produced Neo-Assyrian through Late Babylonian sources, the vast majority of the Aramaic evidence needed to prove direct dependency between similar Aramaic and Akkadian literary sources is lost. Recent efforts have been made, notably by Laura Quick and Seth Sanders, to shed light on this problem,³³ but the most significant evidence for this discussion are the Aramaic literary compositions from the Persian period, which remain understudied by those working on the issue of scribal cultural interactions.

Without direct evidence of textual dependence, one must turn to correspondences on the basis of genre, theme, motif, and the like. The Story of Ahiqar shares motifs and narrative features with Akkadian literary works, notably with the Underworld Vision of the Assyrian Prince (SAA 3 no. 32) and a short folktale known from a wisdom text (K4347+16161 ii 50–63). Wolfram von Soden was the first to publish an edition of the Underworld Vision of the Assyrian Prince. He uses the letters of the *ummânu* Adad-šuma-uṣur and his son Urad-Gula as well as the Story of Ahiqar to inform his reconstruction and interpretation of the badly damaged Akkadian tale. He sees the shared details of these various sources to be instructive for his reconstruction.³⁴ Similarly, Erica Reiner found in a bilingual Sumerian-Akkadian proverbial tablet published by W.G. Lambert (K4347+16161 ii 50–63),³⁵ a fourteen line folktale that corresponds with the narrative frame of the Story of Ahiqar.³⁶ In view of both the documentary and literary Akkadian similarities, Parpola has proposed that the Story of

---

31 Longman, *Fictional*, esp. 118–119; Longman, "Israelite," 177–195; and Westenholz, *Legends*, esp. 16–24.
32 Dalley, "Assyrian," 154. For the Story of Ahiqar's maxims see Bojowald, "Bespucken," 17–21.
33 Quick, *Deuteronomy* and Sanders *Adapa*.
34 Von Soden, "Unterweltsvision," esp. 10–13.
35 Lambert, *BWL*, 239–250.
36 Reiner, "Etiological," 7–8.

Ahiqar was a product of the political circumstances of the Neo-Assyrian court during the 7th century BCE.[37]

The detail by which the Story of Ahiqar alludes to a Neo-Assyrian scribal experience is surprising since the narrative portion of the Elephantine manuscript is written in good Imperial Aramaic, like that known from the Persian period, with no clear examples of archaic forms or dialectical variation.[38] This poses a problem for dating the older and so far unattested versions of the narrative, which must have existed. The consensus is to see the date of an early Ahiqar narrative between a terminus ante quem of the Elephantine manuscript (between 475–399 BCE) and a terminus post quem of 660 BCE.[39] Assyriologists or those working with significant amounts of Neo-Assyrian sources tend to date the composition to the Neo-Assyrian period,[40] while others favor a date from the Neo-Babylonian period. In a recent study, I have shown that the Elephantine manuscript bears witness to two, or possibly three, Persian period Aramaic recensions (Ar–Hr, Jr–Lr [overwritten]; Lv^{pal}–Hv^{pal}; Gv$^{upside\ down}$), with a newly deciphered line Gv$^{upside\ down}$ that refers to an Ahiqar tradition other than that on the manuscript's recto; this line may use a pre-Persian Aramaic form, and resembles the introductory line found in various Syriac manuscripts.[41] Circumstantial evidence of the antiquity of an Ahiqar narrative tradition in Syria is found in Greek sources in which Clement of Alexandria cites Democritus, who claims to have translated Ahiqar from a stele in the 5th century BCE,[42] and the Story of Ahiqar does, in fact, retain an autobiographical narrative written in the form of inscriptions, both in Akkadian and Aramaic (as well as other NWS languages) well attested in the Neo-Assyrian and Neo-Babylonian periods. This point will be discussed in chapter four, but suffice it to say there is no way of

---

37 Parpola, "retroterra," 91–112.
38 A distinction between Eastern Aramaic (narrative) and Western Aramaic (maxims) long dominated the linguistic study of the Elephantine manuscript (Greenfield, "Wisdom," 49; Lindenberger, *Proverbs*, 16–20). But Holger Gzella has convincingly shown that the distinctions between so-called Western and Eastern Aramaic are not clear until the Hellenistic and Roman periods (*Cultural*, 265 and "Heritage," 85–109). That said, even though the Ahiqar manuscript is composed in good Imperial Aramaic, remnants of earlier forms and diction as well as evidence of multilingual cultural backdrops can be found in the document (see Briquel-Chatonnet, "L'histoire," esp. 22–29).
39 Niehr, *Ahiqar*, 11.
40 Parpola, "retroterra," 92–4, and references.
41 Moore, "'Ahikariana,'" *forthcoming*.
42 Harris, *Story*, xli; Nöldeke, *Untersuchungen*, 21–23

knowing, when between the 7th and 5th centuries BCE the narrative was composed.

Despite the rather obvious focus the Story of Ahiqar places on scribal characters, studies on ancient scribal culture have only made passing comments about the tale. While the scholarship on the Story of Ahiqar is quite vast, it focuses predominantly on manuscripts and source-critical issues.[43] Such works are incidentally used throughout this book, where deemed relevant.

1.2 The Tale of Jeremiah and Baruch's Scroll

The Tale of Jeremiah and Baruch's Scroll survives in two different ancient versions, MT Jer 36 and LXX Jer 43.[44] The story is described by scholars as a unique narrative episode that has a particular interest in the scribal craft.[45] It begins with a regnal date formula that establishes its historical setting in the fourth year of king Jehoiakim, the son of Josiah (605/4 BCE). Much like setting modern historical fiction during the iconic year of the declaration of American independence in 1776, a setting which evokes an assumed backstory, events, and characters, the fourth year of Jehoiakim became its own literary topos. To its writers and ancient readers it was a provocative setting for a historiographic tale. Jehoiakim's fourth year occurs immediately after the great Egyptian and Mesopotamian battle of Carchemish in 605 BCE and during the ascension of Nebuchadnezzar II that year.[46] MT Jer 36 claims that Jeremiah receives a prophetic word from Yahweh who instructs him to take a scroll and to write down a prophetic message during the unrest of 605/4 BCE. In response, Jeremiah summons Baruch, gives him a scroll, and Baruch writes down Jeremiah's words verbatim. After having done so, Jeremiah tells Baruch that he will be unable to enter Yahweh's temple, at which point the two concoct a plan to send Baruch in

---

43 Since the Story of Ahiqar is thought to have influenced a number of ancient works in many languages, and since it was one of the most translated works in antiquity, studies can be found across a number of academic disciplines, making it impossible to present a comprehensive history of scholarship. The finest survey of Ahiqar scholarship to-date can be found in Seth Bledsoe's dissertation in which he presents (predominantly English and German) studies from the last century in no less than 44 pages ("Wisdom," 29–73).
44 This study relies on the text of the Göttingen LXX of Jeremiah.
45 E.g., Muilenburg, "Baruch," 223 and van der Toorn, *Scribal*, 184.
46 There is no evidence outside of the Bible that Jeremiah or Baruch were historical figures. The bullae of Baruch that are often cited as evidence for a historical Baruch (and Jeremiah) are now known to be forgeries, see Goren and Arie, "Authenticity," 147–158.

Jeremiah's place and to have him read the scroll in the temple's outer courtyard. During a fast, which signifies a time of national distress, Baruch enters the temple complex, and from the chamber of Gemariah, a son of Shaphan the famous scribe of Josiah, Baruch reads his scroll to the people. Michaiah, Gemariah's son, understands the implications of Baruch's lecture and reports the event to the שָׂרִים, the high-ranking Judahite courtiers cloistered away in the palace's scribal chamber. They summon Baruch, who reads the scroll to them. At this point in LXX Jer 43 the courtiers debate the scroll's content, while in MT Jer 36 they respond to its content with trepidation. In both versions, the courtiers conclude that Baruch and Jeremiah should go into hiding before word of the scroll reaches the king. Baruch heeds their advice in LXX Jer 43, and he and Jeremiah go into hiding, while in MT Jer 36 Yahweh intervenes and hides the two. The chief courtiers enter the king's winter chambers, where one of the courtiers reads the scroll while slicing it to pieces and burning it on the king's hearth, at his approval. The scene turns to Jeremiah, who reacts with a second prophecy which predicts Jehoiakim's humiliating death. Jeremiah and Baruch then repeat their compositional process and produce a second and more exhaustive scroll.

The Tale of Jeremiah and Baruch's Scroll is unique for its information about scribal content, and because of this it holds a special place in scholarship.[47] Early scholars, such as Bernard Duhm and Sigmund Mowinckel, began to investigate the compositional history of the book of Jeremiah, and they speculated that Tale of Jeremiah and Baruch's Scroll may be the book's self-acknowledgement of how it was composed.[48] The core narrative section of the book, which Mowinckel refers to as the "B" source, became known as the *Baruchschrift* or Baruch Document because it was thought, based on the Tale of Jeremiah and Baruch's Scroll, that Baruch authored sections of the book of Jer-

---

47 To read all of the studies conducted on MT Jer 36 would be, in itself, a life's work. For this reason scholars summarizing the previous scholarship on the book of Jeremiah discuss trends in current research rather than the history of scholarship, e.g., Wilson, "Exegesis," 3–12.
48 Duhm, *Buch*, xvi. Duhm refers to the biographical sections of MT chapters 26–29 and 32–45 as "Das Buch des Baruch." Mowinckel presented a three-source hypothesis that he called "A" (≈ MT Jer 1–25), "B" (≈ MT Jer 26, 28, 29, 36–44), and "C" (many small passages in MT Jer 7–44; *Komposition*, 20–21, 24). He claims that MT Jer 46–52 is a later appendix (14). MT Jer 45, which makes direct reference to MT Jer 36, is problematic for Mowinckel, and he ascribes it to RJ, the redactor of MT Jer 1–45 (16). MT Jer 45 is commonly considered a colophon, to either MT Jer 36–44 or 37–44 depending on the view, see Lundbom, "Baruch," 89–114 and Leuchter, *Polemics*, 142–144. For a clear discussion of the *Baruchschrift* see Brueggemann, *Commentary*, 338–344.

emiah. Two later German studies generally support Mowinckel's broad claims.⁴⁹ A number of scholars follow Mowinckel's source and redactional divisions though they slightly alter the boundaries of the sources and redactional layers.⁵⁰ In 1986 William Holladay wed these earlier source/redactional theories with historical observations and produced a complex history of the composition of the book of Jeremiah. At the core of his argument lies the Tale of Jeremiah and Baruch's Scroll, which he, like previous scholars, saw as a historically reliable self-proclamation of the book's sources.⁵¹ A contemporary of Holladay, Robert Carroll, presented a counter view and proposed that the book of Jeremiah is a sophisticated and composite work, the final product of which is the result of a Deuteronomistic editor. For him, "the problems surrounding the composition and redaction of the book of Jeremiah persist and are unlikely to be resolved in favor of one overarching theory."⁵² Carrol follows a long tradition of seeing the book of Jeremiah as a product of Deuteronomistic redactional interests, but approaches the subject with a refreshingly historical skepticism. Since Carroll, some scholars look at the narrative portions of the book of Jeremiah, especially the Tale of Jeremiah and Baruch's Scroll, with reservations about its date and historical reliability, but others persist in reading the tale as a reliable historical account.⁵³ As a result the field remains splintered into a daunting array of theo-

---

49 Rudolph, *Jeremia*, xvii supports Mowinckel's views, but Rietzschel, *Problem* challenges Mowinckel's hypothesis. Wanke, *Untersuchungen*, significantly altered the boundaries of the so-called *Baruchschrift* and argued that it was made up of components that comprised much of Mowinckel's B and C sources (esp. 144).
50 See the discussion in Wilson, "Exegesis," 3–9.
51 Holladay, *Jeremiah 2*, 10–24. A similar view can be seen in Lundbom's many publications (see bibliography) that favor reading the book of Jeremiah as a reliable historical document. Recently, Leuchter, *Josiah's*, 146–168 maintains the idea that MT Jer 36 refers to a so-called *Urrolle* that can be recovered from the content of the present book. One should also compare Eggleston, *See*, which focuses on the book's self-reference as written work.
52 Carroll, *Jeremiah*, 50. A recent dissenting view is proffered by Fischer who believes that the book of Jeremiah was compiled in a relatively short period of time in the Persian period and is the product of a single author ("Understanding," 34–37).
53 Most notably the works by Leuchter, *Josiah's* and *Polemics*. For recent trends in Jeremiah Scholarship see Wilson, "Exegesis," 3–12, esp. 7–10, which (via Thomas Römer) observes that "[s]ome scholars, particularly in the United States, are still following versions of the approaches sketched out by Duhm and Mowinckel... Some scholars have heeded the cautions of Carroll and concentrated on producing various types of holistic readings that pay careful attention to the way in which the book's various types of literary materials relate to each other... Scholars are increasingly seeing throughout the book one or more Deuteronomistic editions... [And] a number of scholars have seen at work in Jeremiah the phenomenon of what in German is called *Fortschreibung*... [which is best understood as a form of interpretation of an existing text in

ries that ultimately rest on one's historical assumptions or one's intuitive understanding of the book's thematic relationships, both within the portions of the book of Jeremiah and between the book of Jeremiah and the so-called Deuteronomistic History.

The research surveyed so far mostly consists of Anglo-scholarship on the book of Jeremiah, and MT Jer 36 more specifically, that branches from early to mid-twentieth century German scholarship. While German scholarship on the book of Jeremiah has seen the emergence of new studies that introduce promising new lines of inquiry and tackle the difficult issue of the so-called Deuteronomistic redaction, German scholarship on the Tale of Jeremiah and Baruch's Scroll has taken a significant turn due to the many studies by Hermann-Josef Stipp. Stipp's writings are technical, dense, and point-by-point try to negotiate the relationship between the MT and LXX editions of the book, and he focuses significantly on MT Jer 36 ∥ LXX Jer 43.[54] His work carefully negotiates the textual evidence and concludes that the MT edition is secondary to the LXX edition at key moments in the plot.[55] He also goes beyond text-critical analysis, and central to his research are the role and characterization of the chief courtiers, the שָׂרִים. He develops a theory of redaction in which a *Patrizier* (i.e. "patrician" his translation of שַׂר) developed and expanded sections of Jeremiah, including the Tale of Jeremiah and Baruch's Scroll, with knowledge of the so-called Deuteronomistic redaction of the book of Jeremiah.[56] This "aristocratic" redactor's pen produced MT Jer 36,[57] and while his theory has not received substantial support, it should be commended for negotiating textual and hypothetical redactional developments in the book of Jeremiah.

Unlike studies on the Story of Ahiqar, a long and ongoing scholarly pursuit has been devoted to understanding the scribal and political characters found in the Tale of Jeremiah and Baruch's Scroll and the book of Jeremiah more broadly. An influential study by William McKane (1965) considered the "sages" (חֲכָמִים) and "scribes" (סֹפְרִים) of the book of Jeremiah as "wisdom teachers" and "apolo-

---

order to apply that text to the issues, experiences, and perceptions of a later community." For the Tale of Jeremiah and Baruch's Scroll, in particular, see Silver's survey of scholarship, "Prophet," 63–99.

54 Stipp, *Parteienstreit*; Stipp, *masoretische*; Stipp, "Prophetic;" and Stipp, "Baruchs."
55 E.g., Stipp, *Parteienstreit*, 73–95 goes so far as to often create an unattested Hebrew translation than in his more judicious work in Stipp, *masoretische*, esp. 71.
56 Stipp, *Parteienstreit*, esp. 115–121 lays the foundation for the idea, which culminates in Stipp, *Tempel*, esp. 34–38.
57 Stipp, *Tempel*, 34, "Die Herkunft von Jer 36 aus der Feder der PR wurde bereits andernorts ausführlich begründet." (See reference in previous note.)

gists of the law" who "imparted instruction," rather than the specific Deuteronomists responsible for Deuteronomistic Torah, as was previously thought.[58] Two decades later (1986) his commentary on Jeremiah pays considerable attention to the שָׂרִים found throughout the book.[59] Prior to McKane, others speculated that the "sages" and "scribes" were priestly figures[60] and paid little attention to the שָׂרִים. McKane shifts the discourse from an interest in the "divine instruction" (תּוֹרַת יְהוָה), which the sages and scribes wrote in MT Jer 8:8, to the social function of the sages and scribes themselves. This opens a new line of inquiry into the characters in the book of Jeremiah, including Jeremiah himself, who hails from a priestly lineage (MT Jer 1:1) and also has intimate knowledge of the activities of the so-called sages (MT Jer 8:8). There have been a number of studies on the sages, scribes, and courtiers over the years,[61] but none to my knowledge focus solely on the narrative of the Tale of Jeremiah and Baruch's Scroll or discuss the ways in which the scribal characters interact with the scribal props in that literary episode, as this study will do in chapter three.[62]

Jeremiah's literary episodes comprise an extensive ancient tradition of narratives and prophecies that evolved and changed. Not only are the MT and LXX editions of the books significantly different, but surviving Greek manuscripts vary drastically as do surviving Hebrew manuscripts—not to mention the so-called apocryphal Jeremiah-traditions that survive in other languages.[63] Unfortunately, no complete manuscript of Jeremiah survives from the Dead Sea Scrolls, and in fact among the many biblical and "apocryphal" fragments in that corpus, none have been identified as part of the Tale of Jeremiah and Baruch's Scroll or allusions to it. This is a rather puzzling fact, if the persona of Jeremiah was used at Qumran "for imbuing authority in texts and institutions," as Kipp Davis espouses.[64] It is simply not clear if the episode existed at Qumran, and there is no manuscript evidence to date the tale before the Common Era. This disconnect between ancient and modern interpretive interest in Jeremiah is rather curious: the Tale of Jeremiah and Baruch's Scroll is a linchpin in modern

---

58 McKane, *Prophets*, 106.
59 McKane, *Critical*.
60 See McKane, *Prophets*, 104 and citations.
61 E.g., Dell, "Scribes," 125–144; Demsky, *Literacy*, 131–168, esp. 152–154; Fox, *Service*; Gilbert, "Jérémie," 105–118; Grabbe, "Prophets," 43–62; McKane, "Jeremiah," 142–151; Perdue, "Introduction," in *Scribes*, 1–34, and various essays in the volume; Whybray, *Intellectual*.
62 Hartenstein, "Prophets," 70–91 and two responses in the same volume; Panov, "King," 92–97; and White, "Scribal," 98–102.
63 E.g., Mingana with Harris, "Jeremiah."
64 Davis, *Cave 4*, 302.

understandings of the book's development, but the surviving ancient sources paid little attention to it.

This study, as are many on biblical texts, is left with Late Antique and Medieval manuscript evidence, but it seems safe to assume that the Tale of Jeremiah and Baruch's Scroll was present in some ancient Jeremiah collections and that the late manuscripts retain the general narrative framework of the episode. Nonetheless, historical questions rest on the details of the surviving variants.

1.3 Thesis

The Elephantine manuscript's narrative portion of the Story of Ahiqar is set in the late Neo-Assyrian period and contains no overt allusions to or linguistic features of the Persian period Egyptian culture or context in which it was found. Therefore, this study will identify and interpret the allusions to the scribal craft found in the Elephantine manuscript's narrative portion of the Story of Ahiqar against the backdrop of Akkadian and Aramaic documentary and literary sources from the Neo-Assyrian period. It will be shown that regardless of whether Ahiqar was a historical figure, the surviving legend about him exhibits highly stylized literary features that blend realia with artistry. This literary complexity demonstrates that while on the surface the narrative may be studied as a tale about a scribe whose ungrateful student rebels against him, on a deeper level the story also provides an Aramaic critique on the social practices of Akkadian scribal culture.

Unlike the complex literary messages found in the Story of Ahiqar, it will be shown that the Tale of Jeremiah and Baruch's Scroll uses loci of scribal activity, expected scribal interactions, and the mechanics of the scribal craft to construct a subversive piece of literature. Although neither text is read as a historical account, both contain realistic depictions of the mid-first millennium scribal experiences of those serving in royal courts, particularly from the perspectives of Northwest Semitic writers and editors.

After studying each narrative independently, they we will be considered in comparative perspective. It will be argued that despite obvious differences in the literary expressions of each tale, they share eight literary motifs that resemble, in part, the well attested court tale genre. The scribal content of the motifs, however, points to the identification of a subgenre, which is coined here as the scribal conflict narrative. The use of first-person autobiographical style is shown as an effective (though not necessary) feature of the scribal conflict narrative, and this provides a new lens through which each tale may be interpreted. In the case of the book of Jeremiah, in particular, this observation provides a new criterion and framework for interpreting its diverse manuscript traditions.

1.4 Trends in the Study of Scribal Culture

The Google Books Ngram Viewer, which charts the history of terms and ideas in digitized publications dating from 1500 CE – 2008 CE, illustrates how the topic of "scribal culture" has drastically increased in English publications since the 1950's (accessed 16.02.21).[65] The phrase received marginal attention until the 1980's and 1990's, since when interest in the topic has grown across disciplines. The earliest use of the phrase (that I could uncover) appears in a reference to the distinction between oral and written transmission.[66] In this sense, scribal culture is used as a synonym for written culture and refers less so to culture and more to the mechanics of textual production and the formalities of the writing process.[67] This is not to say that scholars are uninterested in other cultural aspects of the lives of scribes, but, from its earliest usage in modern scholarship, it was associated foremost with the production of texts in contrast with spoken communication. The idea that the study of "scribal culture" refers to the production of written culture, which would naturally include education, has become a hallmark of the phrase, and even efforts to describe scribal education emerged.

Works that do not mention "scribal culture" play a significant role in the topic's history. For instance, Moshe Weinfeld's 1972 publication *Deuteronomy and the Deuteronomic School*, which attempts to shift source-critical discussions

---

65 Ngram does not include academic articles. One might assume that the ideas in book-length projects may have been fleshed out in slightly earlier academic journals. A search in JSTOR confirms this suspicion.

66 The phrase "Scribal culture" may derive from Old Testament studies. Anderson, "Some," 246 uses the phrase to describe aspects of Widengren's seminal work *Literary and Psychological Aspects of the Hebrew Prophets*.

67 As with most seminal works, Widengren's thesis was more complex than merely reducing scribal culture to the mechanics of textual production. For him "ancient scribal culture" referred to "the manner of" reading, writing, and psychologically conceptualizing written texts (*Literary*, 57; he uses the phrase "manner of" frequently). His work is a response to the theoretical work of Herman Gunkel, who focused on the underlying oral tradition of the Old Testament, and to the sociological work of Hugo Gressmann, who studied ancient Israelite practices in view of modern Arab cultural data (*Literary*, 5). Widengren ultimately concludes against Gunkel that oral tradition is not an acceptable model for explaining the ancient fixation on the written word and against Gressmann that modern sociological comparisons are inadequate for the types of literacy evident in the Hebrew Prophets (*Literary*, 91–93).

from theoretical sources and authors to the practices used in the composition of texts, is frequently cited in the study of scribal culture. Weinfeld discusses intellectual communities who were responsible for producing the various texts that had traditionally been assigned to abstract sources. He referred to these communities as schools.[68]

After Weinfeld's work, one can see many trends in the study of scribal culture of which I will focus on three branches. The first and most prominent direction was to a more detailed study of the production of texts. Along these lines, Michael Fishbane proposes in his 1985 work, *Biblical Interpretation in Ancient Israel*, a model of textual production based on the careful rewriting and exegetical practices that can be witnessed in post-biblical periods.[69] His approach became known as innerbiblical exegesis and provided a new way of thinking about the scribal practice that produced doublets or similar passages across the Hebrew Bible. Fishbane's student, William M. Schniedewind, brings the process of textualization into dialogue with other ancient Near Eastern cultural practices, as well as with archaeological data. By doing so, he is able to discuss "important periods" in which parts of the Bible were written down.[70] For Schniedewind, widespread literacy develops in the seventh century BCE, at which time it began to spread while writing moved from having been "essentially a prerogative of the state… to various non-scribal classes."[71]

After Weinfeld's publication, scholarship moved in a second direction in which a number of studies brought the discussion back to theoretical sources and redactors who were now thought to operate in schools and who used their versions of texts to promote their ideological perspectives. I would consider Philip R. Davies' 1998 work, *Scribes and Schools*, the culmination of this theoretical and abstract line of inquiry. Davies' work is interested in how the production of ancient sources might influence the way in which works were organized into a canon, especially in the Hasmonean period.[72] The unfortunate result of this trend in scholarship, and Davies' study in particular, is that it moved the already polyvalent term "school" into an abstract category that refers to a faction of theoretical scribes or redactors or to a theoretical framework that bound

---

[68] Weinfeld, *Deuteronomy*.
[69] Fishbane, *Biblical*.
[70] Schniedewind, *How*, vii.
[71] Schniedewind, *How*, 25, 111–2. In a more recent publication, he responds to Rollston's claims (see below) and reiterates that literacy was not limited to a scribal elite (*Social*, 104–105), and in his most recent study (*Finger*) he discusses scribal education, which I identify as a distinct trend below.
[72] E.g., Davies, *Scribes*, 47, 174–184.

those theoretical scribes and redactors together. In response, I will use the term school in this study only to refer to an institution, and when possible an identifiable location, in which education in literacy occurs.

It is fitting here to also discuss the work of Seth Sanders, which focuses on the origins of ancient intellectualism and scribalism. In a book titled *The Invention of Hebrew* (2009) Sanders discusses the social and political circumstances that led to the emergence of Hebrew from an undocumented vernacular to a written corpus. In a more recent study From *Adapa to Enoch* (2017) he looks at, among other things, the Akkadian and Aramaic scribal traditions to determine the modes of intellectual and scribal transmission from Mesopotamian political and intellectual spheres to (mostly later) Aramaic sources. Although his work is highly theoretical, in my view, Sanders accomplishes two feats. First, he provides a model approach to ancient data from a comparative perspective that focuses heavily on understanding sources as textual objects from which one may deduce larger social trends. For instance, in his discussion of the transmission of the Darius Inscription from a cuneiform scribal milieu to its Persian period Aramaic translation, he notes how striking it is that no surviving Aramaic literature from the Persian period preserves the memory of Aramean kings.[73] He concludes that this is ultimately owed to Aramaic and an invisible scribal culture that may have preserved traditions of Aramean characters and locations, but due to its imperial and cosmopolitan breadth, the Aramean heritage became diffused.[74] Sanders, must be applauded as one of the few to discuss the Aramaic scribal culture in sufficient detail, but his omission of a careful study of the Story of Ahiqar is glaring since it portrays the very social dynamics Sanders attempts to explain, as I will argue in chapters two and four of this book.

A final direction in which scholarship turned, and one that has taken the attention of most writing on the topic, was toward the study of literacy and of schools as actual institutions of education and learning rather than theoretical constructs such as those discussed by Davies. A seminal work on this topic is André Lemaire's *Écoles et la formation de la Bible dans l'ancien Israël* (1981). Lemaire considers the role of education in ancient Israel by studying Northwest Semitic epigraphic sources that he identifies as "exercices scolaires," particularly those from Kuntillet Ajrud.[75] He organizes the epigraphic data into eleven text-types that were "essentiellement du domaine de l'enseignement 'élémen-

---

73 Sanders, *Adapa*, 184.
74 Sanders, *Adapa*, chap. 5, esp. 195–196.
75 Lemaire, *Écoles*, 5, 25–32. Recently, Lemaire has discussed education at the better documented site of Elephantine ("Aramaic").

taire.'"⁷⁶ It can be argued that some of the surviving epigraphic sources are scribal exercise from lower levels of education, but without clear examples of advanced educational texts he turns to the biblical sources in search of didactic (as distinct from wisdom) texts. Lemaire synthesizes evidence of early education with what he identifies as didactic biblical literature and postulates that education could have taken place in both family and privately run apprenticeships or in more institutionalized settings. Tutoring also could have supplemented a student's curriculum in these settings.[77] The palace and temple were loci of education, but he further discusses the possible existence of prophetic schools (écoles prophétique), though he supplies no location for their activity, and instead, addresses the model of education used by prophets. He states that "il semble que la Bible nous présente deux types de formation possible pour assumer la fonction prophétique: d'une part, on pouvait se mettre au service d'un grand prophète avant de lui succéder, comme Elisée au service d'Elie, d'autre part, on pouvait faire partie d'un groupe de 'fils de prophètes' partageant une certaine vie communautaire."[78]

Lemaire's arguments are global in nature and hardly make reference to MT Jer 36. Most of his evidence is drawn from sociological observations, or even perhaps intuitions about sociological allusions imbedded in sources that were not previously thought to be "educational" in the strictest sense. One of the striking features of his work, is that despite critique, many of his intuitive interpretations have been shown to be reliable by more data rich studies. For example, Schniedewind also sees a vibrant and diverse school culture in the late Judahite period;[79] Carr, like Lemaire, sees education integrated into society and not an independent institutionalized system;[80] and Sanders has shown that scribal education was available at many locations outside of the palace and temple.[81] Lemaire's work

---

76 Lemaire, *Écoles*, 32.
77 Lemaire, *Écoles*, 44–45 and Lemaire, "Sage," 168.
78 Lemaire, *Écoles*, 51.
79 Schniedewind, *How*, 64–117.
80 Carr, *Writing*, 301.
81 Sanders, *Invention*, e.g., 129.

naturally led to new questions about literacy.⁸² In turn, the topics of literacy and education emerged, albeit slowly, as a subject of interest.⁸³

In the last fifteen years, one finds in current scholarship a noted increase in discussions on scribal culture, especially around the questions of access to literacy and its relationship to social elitism. Most are valuable advances in the trends of literacy and education or textual production. Unique among them is Christopher Rollston's short epigraphic study. While some like Lemaire put significant weight on paleographic analysis, Rollston made it the focal point of his method in *Writing and Literacy in the World of Ancient Israel* (2010). He surveys the paleographic character of Phoenician and "daughter" scripts, such as Aramaic and Old Hebrew, in order to deduce patterns of paleographic standardization and what a standardized script reveals about ancient literacy. He claims, "These three national scripts (Phoenician, Old Hebrew, and Aramaic) and their congeners (Ammonite, Edomite, and Moabite) were used in the Levant during various horizons of the Iron Age," and that "for each of these national scripts, there was a major scribal apparatus and that scribes were formally educated members of the elite class."⁸⁴ Because he sees these as "national" scripts, he concludes that the states were responsible for education.⁸⁵ Rollston's study is divided into two parts. In the first part he examines the content of the epigraphic record in order to illustrate the variety—of both medium and functions—of surviving (typically) mid-first millennium BCE epigraphic data.⁸⁶ In the second part of the book he discusses scribes, education, and literacy in ancient Israel. While Rollston's paleographic observations represent an excellent Northwest Semitic paleographic survey and his challenge to scholars to pay careful attention to the minutia of textual data are warranted, his description of literacy as an elite activity is problematic because he provides no evidence that writing correlates with elitism nor provides a clear defi-

---

82 Crenshaw, *Education* and Heaton, *School*. As Sanders, *Invention*, 22–24 shows, questions regarding literacy have long been part of modern biblical scholarship but usually in contrast with oral tradition or oral societies. Today, literacy in the field of scribal culture acknowledges the oral-written dichotomy of early studies but incorporates it into a broader lens of education, curricula, and textual production.
83 Educational training and literacy were of interest before the trends outlined in this introduction (e.g., Gadd *Teachers*), but Lemaire used a comparative approach that had not been tried before.
84 Rollston, *Writing*, 46.
85 Rollston, *Writing*, 113.
86 Rollston, *Writing*, 47–82.

nition of the meaning of the term "elite."[87] Like Davies' use of the word "school," Rollston's study mostly shows the dangers of using nondescriptive terms such as "elite" without ample justification. As a result, I try to avoid vague and socially load terminology in this study.

Other scholars see the Northwest Semitic textual evidence as incomplete and rely on comparative perspectives to analyze the social standing of Northwest Semitic writers by using archaeological or anthropological evidence from Egyptian and Mesopotamian sources. None have come to such a radical conclusion as Rollston; instead, most see Northwest Semitic writing as existing within a complex social world of varying degrees of literacy in different sectors of society.

William Schniedewind's study *How the Bible Became a Book* (2004) was one of the first recent works to propose that variable levels of literacy existed among Hebrew speakers in the Late Judahite period (e.g., Iron Age IIb). He shifts the discourse from the concerns of a written culture and its questions of authorship to a discussion of oral culture and its notions of authority.[88] For Schniedewind, orality and textuality are competing modes of authority in the act of textual production.[89] With this in mind, his thesis argues that biblical literature, though not the canonical texts, was written down in the eighth through the sixth centuries BCE, in the age of Isaiah and Jeremiah. In this period the urbanization of Jerusalem gave rise to guilds of scribes in the palace and temple that held control over the authority of the written word.[90]

Schniedewind marshals both textual and archaeological data to illustrate the urbanization of Jerusalem in the late Judahite period (from the reign of Hezekiah to its fall). He sees in the evidence clues to a rise in government administrative centers, such as at Ramat Raḥel, and the birth of a bureaucratic political machine in Jerusalem.[91] In this context, literacy increased and the social location of writing began to move from state sponsored centers "to various non-scribal classes," such as "the priests and the temple."[92] In this period of literary growth one finds the critique of MT Jer 8:8, which Schniedewind interprets as a

---

87 See in particular, Rollston, *Writing*, 131–133. He equates the knowledge and skill of writing with elitism, rather than viewing elitism as a social phenomenon defined by a person's rank, economic resources, or class.
88 Schniedewind, *How*, 7.
89 Schniedewind, *How*, 13. Compare above, Carr, who holds the opposite view and sees oral and written communication as complementary.
90 Schniedewind, *How*, 17, 22. Sanders also sees "urbanization" as an operative component in scribal activity (see above).
91 Schniedewind, *How*, 68–71, in the time of Hezekiah, and 96–98 in the time of Josiah.
92 Schniedewind, *How*, 111–112.

"protest against the authority of the written texts that were understood as subverting oral tradition and the authority of the prophets."[93] For him Jeremiah was among the literate "non-scribal" classes and functionally literate, at best. He further emphasizes this point in a subsequent study titled *A Social History of Hebrew* in which he claims that in the late Judahite kingdom, "writing was no longer restricted to highly trained scribal elite"[94] and sees passages in Jeremiah reflecting the social dynamics of what I would call the scribal experience.

Apart from Schniedewind's work, another recent study challenges the scholarly assumption of scribal elitism. Aaron Demsky's 2012 magnum opus *Literacy in Ancient Israel* blends theories of textual production, history, epigraphy, and archaeology, with theories of ancient education.[95] The core of the study was actually composed as a Ph.D. dissertation in the mid-1970's before Lemaire's publication,[96] but having been written in Modern Hebrew like the final published edition in 2012, it has received a limited audience. The study is a well-balanced comparative philological approach to literacy in the biblical period (mostly during the kingdom of Judah), and tries to negotiate levels of literacy given social needs, pressures, and institutions. He demonstrates that literacy was socially stratified in the eighth to sixth centuries BCE.[97] Most important to my study is Demsky's work on what he calls the Israelite scribal class.[98] He close reads the biblical literature with datable scribal evidence (e.g., seals) from the period and notices that the title "scribe of the king" first appears during the united monarchy and exhibits generational characteristics. The title became a social reference point, and the palace's שָׂרִים "chief courtiers," who were scribal characters, relied on a small network of junior scribal officials for intelligence.[99] The most prestigious scribal position in the Near Eastern courts, including Israel and Judah, were the חֲכָמִים "sages" as evidenced not only in the Story of Ahiqar and the socially comparable—though not etymologically comparable—positions in Mesopotamian courts. Demsky, in dialogue with McKane's enduring treatise, determines that social status is a central factor in the titles that scribal characters hold in biblical literature, and that those who held such status actively

---

93 Schniedewind, *How*, 117.
94 Schniedewind, *Social*, 104.
95 I thank Aaron Demsky for his insights and for providing me with a number of resources on the subject.
96 Demsky, "ידיעת."
97 Demsky, *Literacy*, 323.
98 Demsky, *Literacy*, chap. 3.
99 Demsky, *Literacy*, 148–152.

shaped the policies of the court.[100] Ultimately, Demsky argues for a stratified royal court in the last centuries of Judah's monarchy that consisted of three scribal classes: senior officials, sages, and junior scribes.[101] Demsky's stratification is heuristically valuable, but is not overtly found in the Tale of Jeremiah and Baruch's Scroll. I will argue in a similar vein that one can deduce a teacher-apprentice relationship between Jeremiah and Baruch as well as a vague hierarchy among the competing scribal associations of chief courtiers.

Demsky's study on literacy and close reading of the biblical texts are not as focused on the production of those sources as is the work of some others, especially David Carr. Carr has published extensively on the composition and evolution of passages in the Hebrew Bible, and his work has reshaped the way in which scholars might approach the textual data.[102] He has produced two studies on the ancient writing process. The first, *Writing on the Tablet of the Heart* (2005), is a comparative study on the nature of literacy and education in the ancient world, and the second, *The Formation of the Hebrew Bible* (2011), focuses on the composition and editing of biblical, particularly wisdom, texts. This former work, more than the latter, falls within the domain of "scribal culture" though it never uses the phrase.[103] In *Writing on the Tablet of the Heart* Carr synthesizes views on the production of texts, elitism, and literacy and education into a single argument. According to him,

> [T]he literacy that most counted in... ancient societies often was not a basic ability to read and write. Rather it was an oral-written mastery of a body of texts. Moreover, this "literacy" was something that separated the members of an elite from their contemporaries.[104]

For Carr, ancient scribal elitism was the product of advanced education, and thus his view sees a complex social stratification among the various types of literate Judahites. He does not deny that literacy could have been a craft used by many in the ancient Judahite population, but for Carr, a group of educated elites, whom he calls "tradents," stand apart from the average scribal craftsman. These tradents can be studied to understand the "nature of education in

---

100 Demsky, *Literacy*, 153–154.
101 Demsky, *Literacy*, 168 translation of "פקידים בכירים, חכמים, וסופרים זוטרים."
102 E.g., Carr, "Method," 107–140.
103 Carr, *Writing*, 13 makes reference to "'scribal' cultures" but sees the phrase as a technical distinction for the study of scribes using the complex and esoteric writing systems of Egypt or Mesopotamia. This is in contrast to literate cultures, i.e. those using alphabetic scripts (Greece or Israel).
104 Carr, *Writing*, 13.

general and the use of writing as a major cultural-religious medium."[105] This leads Carr to study a theoretical relationship between orality, memory, and textuality, as preserved by tradents responsible for maintaining corpora of advanced literary works, such as biblical manuscripts.[106]

Carr is one of the few to discuss the Tale of Jeremiah and Baruch's Scroll in some detail, and his ideas are pertinent to my study. For Carr, this passage addresses how Judahites conceptualized students, teachers, and the dissemination of knowledge. Baruch serves as evidence that "[n]onroyal scribes also appear in various ways in the Jeremiah-tradition, including the prominent, positive depiction of the scribe Baruch (MT Jer 36:1–32; 45:1–5; see 32:12–16; 43:3) and the vigorous attack on those who claim to be 'wise' and that the 'Torah is with [them]' when that Torah has been corrupted by the 'lying pen of the scribes' (ᶜṭ sheqer sopherim, Jer 8:8)."[107] Carr does not interpret LXX's data, which suggests that Baruch's scribal status was a later addition (see chapter three), but he is nonetheless correct that the position of "the scribe" existed outside of a royal context. He further claims that "[l]iteracy, however, was hardly confined to those labeled as *sopherim* ('scribes') or *shoṭᵉrim* ('literate officials')."[108] Along this line of argumentation, Carr sees pre-exilic texts referring to a group of "wise" people (i.e. חֲכָמִים) as a general title for highly educated institutional leaders. In this way, Carr sees the Israelite and Judahite sages as comparable with Mesopotamian and Egyptian literary elites.[109] According to Carr, "literary elites" relied on copies of texts that "were stored in a scribal workshop or temple sanctuary."[110] Admittedly, the Bible makes no reference to such formal libraries, but allusions to temple storage can be found in the Bible's description of the Ark of the Covenant, and in MT Jer 32:14 is found an explicit reference to storing written materials in earthenware outside of the temple.[111]

For Carr, MT Jer 36 is a paradigmatic text that illustrates the educational process of the prophets. Carr provides a fairly standard summary of MT Jer 36

---

105 Carr, *Writing*, 4.
106 Carr, *Writing*, 13. The major difference between Carr and Schniedewind is that the latter sees orality and textualization as competing modes of communication, while Carr sees them as complimentary and integral to the scribal craft.
107 Carr, *Writing*, 118. *Sic* (inconsistent use of ᵉ, *e*, and ø).
108 Carr, *Writing*, 118.
109 Carr, *Writing*, 119.
110 Carr, *Writing*, 160.
111 Carr, *Writing*, 160–161. He uses the storage of the Ark of the Covenant as an example of an allusion to a space in a temple where documents were collected, and presumably his reference to MT Jer 34:14 is an example of the storage of a document in a scribal workshop.

with one exception; he sees the story as an attempt to preserve Jeremiah's teachings and to combat criticism. According to Carr, "Jeremiah receives a divine command to write down his prophecies for a future generation because of opposition from his contemporaries (MT Jer 36:1–3)."[112] This transmission and preservation of knowledge is played out by Baruch, whom Carr sees as Jeremiah's "advanced student."[113] Following H.M.I. Gevaryahu's comparative observations on MT Jer 36,[114] Carr notes that "the data in the Jeremiah tradition resembles that included in some Mesopotamian colophons in recording not only the name of the originating master but also the name of Baruch, the scribe, and in emphasizing the fact that he received the tradition "by mouth.""[115] Here it must be noted that neither Carr (nor Gevaryahu) argue that MT Jer 36 includes colophons, but that the scribal data relegated to Mesopotamian colophons can be seen as components in the narrative of MT Jer 36 as well as in the related prophecy of MT Jer 45.[116] Unlike others, who see actual colophons in parts of Jer 36,[117] Carr's observation alludes to a scribal mentality, the processes of training, and the transmission of a scribal tradition that can be deduced from the tale's prosaic content. Carr's observations, although somewhat esoteric, resemble the prac-

---

112 Carr, *Writing*, 146.
113 Carr, *Writing*, 147.
114 Gevaryahu, "Baruch," 204.
115 Carr, *Writing*, 147.
116 Carr, *Writing*, 147 and Gevaryahu, "Baruch," 204–205.
117 E.g., Lundbom, "Baruch." Lundbom further develops his argument in *Writing*, 50–75. Others, especially Leuchter, *Polemics*, 68, 142–144, uphold Lundbom's view. The notion is compelling, at first glance, but upon closer examination the argument relies on a misunderstanding of comparative evidence. Lundbom, bases his argument on Leichty's form-critical study of (predominantly Neo-Assyrian) Akkadian colophons ("Colophon," 147–154). Leichty intended his article to "facilitate the reading of colophons for other Assyriologists" (147). It serves as a guide for those reading the otherwise difficult (and sometimes cryptic) signs and literary style of Akkadian colophons. The literary style of Akkadian colophons is generally terse and significantly different than the content—especially the literary content—of an Akkadian tablet. A comprehensive study of Elephantine administrative formula has not been made, but the terse formulaic language of contract dockets and letter addresses are noticeable. Furthermore, in Aramaic (and presumably in Hebrew) documents, dates do not appear in colophons; instead, regnal formulas introduce a text's content. The few identifiable Hebrew colophons known, also demonstrate the terse and formulaic style of Akkadian colophons and Aramaic administrative formulas, and like Aramaic sources, they do not include dates (e.g., Sirah 50:27–29). Lundbom claims that passages in the book of Jeremiah "expand the genre in that they are prose accounts just like one finds elsewhere in the book" (Lundbom, *Among*, 135). But are they an "expansion of the genre," or are they simply the types of information that one would expect to find in a *narrative*? Compare Gevaryahu's and Carr's views above.

tices of scribal characters that I will discuss in the Tale of Jeremiah and Baruch's Scroll, particularly the practices found in LXX Jer 43's edition of the narrative, which Carr does not study.

Unlike Carr's work, Karel van der Toorn's 2007 publication *Scribal Culture and the Making of the Hebrew Bible* returns the discussion of scribal culture squarely to the question of textual production with an approach that is based less on theories of intellectualism and more on comparative philological research. He uniquely claims, "The scribes who manufactured the Bible were professional writers affiliated to the temple of Jerusalem."[118] Later he states, "The epigraphic evidence suggests that training in rudimentary scribal skills was available throughout Palestine, but the formation of scribes who were 'expert and wise' required a program of study provided only in the temple school."[119] This view stands in contrast to that of Schniedewind, who claims that the state played a (very) significant role in the education of ancient Israel and Judah. Even more than Carr, van der Toorn includes an extensive study on the Tale of Jeremiah and Baruch's Scroll.

Unlike most Jeremiah scholars who see MT Jer 36 as a historical report by which Baruch explains how he composed a Jeremiah scroll,[120] van der Toorn looks at Jer 36's depiction of scribal interactions with some skepticism, yet appears to accept the accuracy of its historical setting in 605 BCE (MT Jer 36:1) and some of its allusions to the process of textualization. For instance, he deduces from this passage that "professional scribes" were responsible for writing compilations of prophetic collections, particularly the Jeremiah scroll that MT Jer 36 "authenticates,"[121] and that their sources were either from the temple archives,[122] or in the case of Jeremiah from the memory of a tradition.[123] That is, he sees MT Jer 36 as the product of a professional scribe, who composed from memory in the early Exilic period an account of the textualization of a pre-exilic Jeremiah scroll. The function of the text is to "authenticate" the pre-exilic Jeremiah scroll that was in circulation among the exiles.[124] On two occasions, it is clear that he favors MT's rendi-

---

118 Van der Toorn, *Scribal*, 1.
119 Van der Toorn, *Scribal*, 97. His reference to "expert and wise" derives from the Aramaic the Story of Ahiqar not from a biblical reference.
120 See discussion of Holladay above.
121 Van der Toorn, *Scribal*, 174–175, 184. He sees the Deir Allah inscription as a model for what a prophetic מְגִלַּת־סֵפֶר might contain (176) and emphasizes that these prophetic "collections" were of a composite nature (177).
122 Van der Toorn, *Scribal*, 178, 183.
123 Van der Toorn, *Scribal*, 184, 186.
124 Van der Toorn, *Scribal*, 174–175.

tion of the tale because he cites a reference to the use of ink, which appears in MT Jer 36:18 and not LXX.[125] Furthermore, he makes a substantial argument on the basis that Baruch was a professional scribe,[126] an identification given him in MT Jer 36:26 and 32 and not in the corresponding LXX passages.

Van der Toorn does not view prophets as responsible for the composition of their own words or collections of words. He sees prophets as figures who "belonged to the religious establishment on par with priests and sages."[127] Prophets were literate, but rarely did they compose their own sayings.[128] When they did write their own words, their purpose was not to preserve "their words for future generations,"[129] and they did not compile their own prophetic sayings in writing.[130] While he sees prophets, at least Jeremiah, on par with the literate sages, he only sees "professional scribes" responsible for prophetic books.[131] He follows the commonly held view that Jeremiah had a number of associates who were related to Shaphan, "the scribe" of Josiah, and implies that Shaphan's family members were "scribes" themselves.[132] Van der Toorn also elaborates on his view of a professional scribe by interpreting the characteristics of Baruch, as a "transcriber," "companion," and "collaborator."[133] Van der Toorn's study is a milestone in the field of ancient scribal culture, but it is difficult, in my reading, to flesh out his understanding of the social position of the "scribe." He groups, at times, presumably literate characters without scribal titles into the domain of "a scribe," such as the descendants of Shaphan, while at other times, he deemphasizes the role of the literate characters who perform the same "scribal" tasks, such as literate prophets. Although van der Toorn asks an important

---

[125] Van der Toorn, *Scribal*, 174. Van der Toorn discusses the relationship between LXX and MT in regard to more general scribal trends (199–203) and concludes that MT Jeremiah is generally an expanded text (200).
[126] Van der Toorn, *Scribal*, 185–186.
[127] Van der Toorn, *Scribal*, 178.
[128] Van der Toorn, *Scribal*, 178–182.
[129] Van der Toorn, *Scribal*, 182.
[130] Van der Toorn, *Scribal*, 182–188. Van der Toorn does not make note of Jer 51:60 which claims that Jeremiah wrote (וַיִּכְתֹּב יִרְמְיָהוּ) his own prophecies against Babylon in a single document (אֶל־סֵפֶר אֶחָד), nor does he account for the early and continued tradition that Jeremiah wrote his own prophecies, e.g., Josephus *Ant* 10.6.2 and A. Mingana with introduction by J. Rendel Harris, "A Jeremiah Apocryphon," 154.
[131] Van der Toorn, *Scribal*, 194.
[132] Van der Toorn, *Scribal*, 185–186, 337 n. 23. He does not account for the fact that these professional "scribes" who supported Jeremiah do not bear the title of הַסֹּפֵר, but rather he appears to assume that their lineage identifies them as such.
[133] Van der Toorn, *Scribal*, 185. Here he relies on MT and not LXX's older edition of the text.

question—who were ancient writers—his answer remains opaque, and to his credit so does the historical evidence. Besides, his ultimate objective is to describe the process of textual production, rather than the social groups of the texts' writers.

With an elaborate and nuanced discussion of the composition of the book of Jeremiah, Van der Toorn addresses a final question: what was the social setting of prophetic literature? He argues, that "once prophecy had become a written genre, new prophets employed writing as a principal means of disseminating their ideas." He sees this "scribalization" happening in the Exilic period, and that by the Persian and Hellenistic periods, "those wishing to emulate the prophets such as the author of the visions of Daniel (Dan 7–12), presented their work as a scribal activity."[134] The study of scribal culture is indebted to van der Toorn's study, and by building on it and the other sources surveyed above, nuanced questions can be asked regarding the experience of the scribal characters found in biblical literature.

My study aims to contribute to this evolving quest to understand ancient scribal culture. It is different from previous studies in two significant ways. First, as Sanders shows, scribal culture refers to more than the study of education or the production of texts. In fact, studies of the mechanics by which texts were produced are arguably some of the least significant issues in the study of scribal *culture*. Ancient writers were humans, who lived in a complex social world and used their mechanical skills in the scribal craft to negotiate their way through life's circumstances. Surely they were educated, but similar to Carr's argument, it is unlikely that students wrote the advanced literary works of antiquity, such as the Tale of Jeremiah and Baruch's Scroll or the Story of Ahiqar. Instead, ancient scribal professionals who had finished their education and moved into a professional position (that may have included a teaching component) composed literature, and all literature is a product of social, artistic, and philosophical factors. For this reason this study will explore two first millennium BCE literary depictions of scribal characters and compare them to scribal experiences found in documentary sources or to scribal characterizations found in slightly earlier Semitic sources. As a result, facets of scribal *culture* will be deduced from the limited depictions of scribal experiences portrayed in the Story of Ahiqar and the Tale of Jeremiah and Baruch's Scroll.

Second, unlike the sources surveyed above, this study will seek to place the depictions of the scribal experience into their literary contexts. For the first time, it will be shown that these two scribal tales share a number of similar

---

134 Van der Toorn, *Scribal*, 203.

literary motifs as well as a tendency to use an autobiographical literary style. The result leads to a conclusion that literary depictions of the first millennium BCE Northwest Semitic scribal experience are modeled on an archetype of sorts that reflects social circumstances of actual scribal professionals from a range of historical contexts, in the form of similar literary motifs. These literary depictions appear to draw on the well-known court tale genre, but represent a unique sub-genre of the type, which I call the scribal conflict narrative.

1.5 Approach

A study such as this does not follow a single methodology but, instead, uses various approaches and methodologies as the data requires. Generally, however, this study uses three methodological approaches: the comparative perspective, textual criticism, and social scientific approaches to the study of literature.

1.5.1 The Comparative Perspective

In biblical and ancient Near Eastern studies, the comparative perspective, sometimes called the comparative method, looks at text or phenomena from discrete societies and examines them together to elucidate one or the other text, or even to make judgements about their historical connection.[135] It is not, in my view, a formal method but rather a framework through which one can ascribe value by analogy to similar data in different contexts. The approach has gone through cycles of favorable reception and vehement rejection. Currently, some welcome comparative studies with an appropriate degree of skepticism. Because of the perspective's past critiques, recent researchers have employed perspectives and approaches from the fields of comparative literature or comparative anthropology to help curb the danger of making simplistic one-for-one equations between two texts that originate in different linguistic, geographical, temporal, and cultural contexts. It is now common to conduct independent textual, literary, and historical analyses of texts before moving to engage them comparatively. The modern comparative approach calls for the sources to be studied in dialogue

---

135 For examples of the comparative method used to study "phenomena" see Wright, *Disposal*, esp. 6–8 and Broida, *Forestalling*, esp. 12–14.

with each other only after contextualizing each source in its own right.¹³⁶ This is preferred over the structure of older comparative studies, which are generally topic-based and bring texts into dialogue with each other without contextualizing them. By studying each source independently one sees how different they are, thereby curbing the tendency to create unjustified connections between the sources.

The organization of this book follows the newer approach to the comparative method, but the reader must realize that this organization is an artifice. In fact, finding comparisons occurs early in the research process, even though the study reserves comparative observations for the end.¹³⁷ This is because the medium of writing, which requires a linear explanation of single data points, cannot sufficiently present comparative data. Comparative observations have been made throughout the process of composing this book, but it is hoped that by presenting one text at a time, this study will communicate clearly the analytical value of the comparisons made.¹³⁸

1.5.2 Textual Criticism and Manuscript Studies as Part of Reception History

The autographs of neither the Tale of Jeremiah and Baruch's Scroll nor the Story of Ahiqar survive, if they ever existed.¹³⁹ The surviving manuscripts of the book

---

136 This outlines the modern approach to the comparative method used in comparative literature. See Webber and Mullen, "Breakthrough," 213–216 and Domínguez, Saussy, and Villanueva, *Introducing*, 16–18, 72–75. To my knowledge, in biblical and ancient Near Eastern studies only Strawn has advocated for a similar approach ("Comparative," 117–142). Some influential comparatists in biblical and ancient Near Eastern studies have advocated for positivistic "empirical" comparison of literary data, e.g., Talmon, "Comparative," 381–419; Tigay, ed. *Empirical*; and Hallo, "Compare," 1–30.
137 See Weber and Mullen, "Breakthrough," 213–216.
138 See Weber and Mullen, "Breakthrough," 213–216.
139 The search for an *Urtext*, an "original text," of an ancient or modern literary work is often a futile pursuit. As a writer or a series of redactors develop ideas, the wording evolves on a continuum. The "final" wording at a given point on that continuum may deal with content that is different from the previous wording to such a degree that the start of the process looks nothing like what follows. In such a process, there is no discernible *Urtext*, but only a final *edited* composition. The assumption that a work is fully edited orally or cognitively then penned defies the reality of complex literary compositions. Such may be true for very short tales or other genres that have strict formulas that a writer may follow, like administrative or legal documents. In this view, there is no "original" book of Jeremiah or the Story of Ahiqar. For a more mechanical explanation, see, Tov, *Textual*, 172–174.

of Jeremiah demonstrate that it is the most complex literary composition in the Hebrew Bible, but its manuscript complexity pales in comparison to that of the Story of Ahiqar, which is attested by dozens of manuscripts and many recensions. This study views the diversity of manuscripts as a challenging, yet valuable factor.

Traditional textual criticism operates within a limited critical purview. Tov claims that "[t]extual criticism deals with the nature and origin of all the witnesses of a composition or text,"[140] but in practice this is far from the case. The study of the "nature and origin" of a witness is usually reserved for higher and more theoretical modes of research. Textual criticism, more traditionally, focuses on the mechanics and physical processes of textual production. In this way, it is similar in many respects to the study of textual production conducted by those working in the area of scribal culture, but textual criticism focuses on the minutia of changes in the linguistic data rather than relying on predominantly cross-cultural observations. Text-critical arguments often rely on editions rather than manuscripts to make their claims because text-critical focus rests on linguistic variation more than the spatial and material properties of and cultural influences on a manuscript.

Only in recent decades has the field of biblical studies begun to consider the materiality and archeological context of manuscripts as important data for understanding their content.[141] This study on the materiality of a manuscript is, in my view, a challenge to the sterile methodology of traditional textual criticism that relies on edited editions.[142] By discussing the materiality of a manuscript, one is forced to consider the archaeological context (if it is available) and to theorize about the social conditions that produced or maintained such a manuscript. This blend of manuscript studies and textual criticism explores the reception of a composition in antiquity. Even copying a manuscript in antiquity is an act of interpretation because the copyist is reading and reproducing the composition in a new social context—his or her own.[143] And as Jonathan Roberts explains, "The reception of the Bible comprises every single act or word of interpretation of that book (or books) over the course of three millennia."[144] This includes the copying of manuscripts in antiquity.

---

140 Tov, *Textual*, 1.
141 E.g., Tov, *Scribal*.
142 See "Addendum 1: Assessing Variants and the Value of the Dead Sea Scrolls" in Moore, *Leviticus*, xxvii–xxx.
143 Even modern editions of ancient works should be considered as part of the textual history of a source.
144 Roberts, "Introduction," 1.

My unorthodox perspective on textual criticism plays a significant role in this study. It allows for a more dynamic approach to reconstructing the missing portions of the Elephantine manuscript of the Story of Ahiqar. Scholars generally avoid using the more complete Syriac manuscripts to aid in the reconstruction of the Elephantine manuscript, but in order to deduce, as Tov puts it, the "nature and origin" of the tale, the material limits of the Elephantine manuscript combined with a close analysis of relevant lines in the various Syriac manuscripts can lead to reasonable reconstructions of the Elephantine manuscript, at least for the narrative episodes that the Elephantine and Syriac manuscripts share. Furthermore, such comparisons demonstrate the uniqueness of the Elephantine edition among the other surviving editions. Similarly, a text-critical analysis of the Tale of Jeremiah and Baruch's Scroll confirms that LXX's edition contains an older version of the tale which an editor in the MT tradition had altered. MT's edits, in this case, reveal how the story was received in an early ancient context. This provides a foundation for a socio-historical assessment of the content.

1.5.3 Literary Anthropology and The Sociology of Literature

In the 1970's and 1980's the social sciences and the humanities began to experience a "cultural turn" that rattled older views of the "meaning" of texts and that challenged the purpose of scholarly inquiry more generally.[145] Clifford Geertz cut to the core of the problem with two questions that, in the midst of the cultural turn, continued to unhinge assumed epistemologies about scholarly discourse. He asked, how is "'the author' made manifest in a text?" And "just what is [the text]--beyond the obvious tautology, 'a work'--that the author authors?"[146] He also raised the question: what exactly do modern scholars produce?[147] Questions such as these shifted critical paradigms; Geertz made scholarship just as much about the researcher as it was about the object of study.[148] When this revelation is applied to ancient studies, a researcher might consider if

---

[145] See Burke, *What*, chap. 6.
[146] Geertz, *Works*, 8–9. Foucault began this conversation nearly two decades earlier in his 1969 lecture "What is an Author?" (*Language*, 113–138).
[147] Geertz, *Works*, 8–9
[148] In anthropology a distinction is now made between the "ethnographic self" and the "personal self" (see Bruner, "Introduction," 1–26).

an ancient author would have asked the same or different critical questions of his own predicament as would the modern scholar asks of hers.[149]

Before the cultural turn took hold, anthropologists and sociologists began to venture into the world of literary theory and pioneered new approaches to the study of texts, which they referred to as "literary anthropology" and "the sociology of literature."[150] According to two proponents of this approach, Laurenson and Swingewood:

> [T]he 'true' meaning of great literature and the social groups involved in its production lies precisely in the quest and struggle for "authentic values", the values of a genuine human community in which human needs, aspirations, and desires are mediated through social interaction... The task of the sociologist is not simply to discover historical and social reflection (or refraction) in works of literature, but to articulate the nature of the values embedded within particular literary works.[151]

Literature reflects or refracts social and cultural phenomenon. However, this does not mean that literature should be taken as a reliable source of sociological or historical data. As Thomas G. Winner, another advocate of the approach, puts it "[T]oday we no longer accept the absurd assertion of the immanence of the literary work, and to deny a connection between the literary and the extra textual systems and their manifestations would be as serious an error as to read a literary text as a direct documentary source."[152] This warning can be applied to so-called "historical" or "historiographical" texts of antiquity, which, as scholars, we should be skeptical of, as Lester Grabbe has argued.[153] Anthropological and sociological perspectives on literature prompt literary critics to analyze the social allusions within a literary work by considering the text's level of realism.[154] The critic must attempt to tease out realistic social data from the artistry of a literary composition.

---

149 See Peck, "Literary," 13–20.
150 See Cohen, "Introduction," 1–25; Rogers, *Novels*, esp. "Literary Socialization" pp. 129–152. For a critique of literary anthropology see Reyna, "Literary," 555–581. For a socio-literary study performed on a set of known authors see Van Kley, "American," esp. 29–31.
151 Laurenson and Swingewood, *Sociology*, 16.
152 Winner, "Literature," 53. He also writes, "Literature is not a direct reflection of cultural phenomenon" (52). More recently see Doloughan, *Contemporary*, esp. "Intercultural Translation: Language and Culture as Narrative Resource" pp. 68–87.
153 Grabbe, "Biblical," 400–414.
154 See Milner, *Literature*, esp. his comments pertaining to the "sociology of the novel" (85–94 [1st ed.]), and its focus on realism (90–91).

I am not a social scientist and do not employ social science in this book. Historical sources, particularly literary sources, are not an easy dataset on which social scientific investigations can be made, as the scholars cited above have argued; such approaches are too precise for incomplete ancient datasets or focus on communicative mediums (e.g., oral report), which simply do not survive from antiquity. The sociologist and anthropologist of literature recognize this. Recently one of the foremost biblical scholars writing on history and the Bible, Grabbe has issued warnings on the use of social scientific theory. He writes that, first, social scientific theories are approaches based on analogies to be used, "then modified or discarded where necessary." Second, the textual sources must be critically assessed and not read as "anthropological reports" on their purported settings. Third, even in critical investigation one must negotiate the intensity of the critique; "hair-splitting interpretations—sometimes based on dubious linguistic analysis (see Barr 1961)—should be treated as the speculation they usually represent." Lastly, in line with the responsible self-reflections proffered by Geertz, theological (or ideological) bias should be checked to avoid presenting the object of inquiry "from the point of view of what a modern liberal, middle-class biblical scholar with a social conscience would consider acceptable."[155]

This speaks to the problem of writing history. As noted above, the textual artifacts that retain the Tale of Jeremiah and Baruch's Scroll do not come from the period in which the narratives are set. The overwhelming consensus in the field is that the episode was composed in writing near the time of its purported events, between the 604 BCE and the late Persian period, but this remains strictly a hypothetical presupposition. The situation regarding the Aramaic manuscript that contains the Story of Ahiqar is significantly better, but still not ideal. With a high degree of certainty, the copy dates to the 5th century BCE —squarely in the Persian period, and it comes from Elephantine in Egypt. The circumstances regarding its discovery, however, are lost, so there are no significant archaeological controls that can help establish its social context and use, especially since new research shows that the bulk of the manuscripts unearthed with it come from an ancient secondary (Ptolemaic) context.[156] While it seems best to interpret it as a document read, and perhaps edited by Judeans, this remains conjecture.[157] But this is ultimately the job of the historian: to make reasonable

---

155 Grabbe, *Ancient*, 4–5.
156 Moore, *Aramaic*, forthcoming.
157 Note the reserved conclusion in Moore, "'Ahikariana,'" forthcoming, "Admittedly, these observations rely on circumstantial evidence, but in lieu of more evidence it can be said that at least parts of P. 13446r may have been a uniquely Judean recension of the Story of Ahiqar."

conjectures based on surviving evidence, with the aim of reconstructing the story (in narrative form) of peoples, items, or circumstances. This book intends to tease out the social allusions to the scribal profession in the two tales, but given the manuscript evidence, a critic may wonder about the historical validity of this task. It is to this point that the Story of Ahiqar is of paramount importance. While the language used in the 5th century BCE manuscript differs from that in the later Syriac manuscripts, the general plot structure remains surprisingly similar. This tells us that there are ahistorical, that is, anthropological and sociological, features of scribal interactions that resonant in very different historical, linguistic, and cultural circumstances. Identifying and discussing these features are the very goal of the sociology of literature as Laurenson and Swingewood intimate (above). The richness of these features and the historical and cultural nuances of them are found in the discussion of manuscript variance through the ages. Chapter two will highlight important examples of different cultural sensitivities regarding the scribal profession as evidenced by differences found in the Aramaic and Syriac manuscripts at key moments in the plot development of the Story of Ahiqar. In chapter three, the same endeavor will then be tried on the variance between the MT and LXX editions of the Tale of Jeremiah and Baruch's Scroll. As discussed above, this approach best resembles the marriage of traditional textual criticism and reception history, but at its core it is a sociological investigation of literature.

In much the same way that manuscript variance can demonstrate unique historical and cultural reactions to otherwise anthropologically recognizable features of scribal culture, comparative ancient literature and the comparative study of documentary sources can test the historicity of the scribal experiences portrayed in the Story of Ahiqar and the Tale of Jeremiah and Baruch's Scroll. Throughout this study, sections of these tales will be scrutinized in view of ancient sources from the periods in which their narrative settings unfold. This is done not to deem the events historically accurate, but rather to bring the field closer to understanding the social realities of the scribal experience from the periods depicted in the stories to the periods of the surviving manuscripts.

Lastly, in line with the call from Geertz and the warning from Grabbe, it is important to admit my own biases so that the reader may fairly judge the lens through which I view these two tales and their depictions of scribal experiences. My interest in the story of Ahiqar began after reading it in an Aramaic course as a young graduate student. I was highly attracted to the character of Ahiqar, his cunning and his strategic ability. My personal interests in and experiences with the complexity of various social classes prompted me to explore Ahiqar's legend in more detail. This starting framework has evolved, and I must admit that the results are professionally rewarding but personally disappointing. After critical inquiry, it became clear that Ahiqar's cunning and strategic ability were tools by which he constructed a vicious form of professional survivalism. After contextualizing the social historical factors of the period in which his tale is set, it has become clear that he is a product of his constructed environment. The scribal experience of the mid-first millennium BCE is marked by savagery and professional desperation in the guise of social elitism. Throughout this study my impressions of a romantic ancient scribal experience were lost and with them my respect for a literary "hero."

By the same token my extensive experience outside the academy among circles of craftsmen prompted me to focus on the setting and environment in which the Tale of Jeremiah and Baruch's Scroll unfolds. I must admit, I never particularly liked the character of Jeremiah, whom I long saw as a loud, yet impotent, self-victimizing figure—the producer of a jeremiad, so to speak. While my impression of his character has not changed much, my criticism of him and Baruch has lessened. I now understand them also as products of their narrative environment, one that resembles that found in the Story of Ahiqar.

1.6 Summary of Chapters

The next chapter of this book argues that the Story of Ahiqar is a complex piece of Aramaic literature that contains an explicit and implicit message. Explicitly, the tale is royal propaganda couched in a convincing autobiographical style. It praises the loyalty of a scribal courtier in the face of unjust oppression. Implicitly, however, the tale is a social critique of the Mesopotamian Akkadian scribal culture from an Aramaic writer's point of view. Surviving Neo-Assyrian sources demonstrate that Ahiqar's worldview and actions resemble those of the Akkadian royal scholars. The conflict which Ahiqar suffers is brought about by his adherence to the social norms of nepotism combined with his unorthodox intention to retire rather than to serve in his post until he dies. As a result, this "wise scribe" who is known for his teachings about maneuvering through the politics of courtly life, chooses a student and replacement who turns on him and libels him. In order to rehabilitate his reputation as a loyal courtier, Ahiqar engages in cronyism and coerces another, non-scribal, courtier to be disloyal to the king. Ahiqar agrees to the murder of an innocent and young scribal figure in order to save his own life and reputation. Ultimately, in the process of proving his loyalty, Ahiqar fails to secure the legacy that he had set out to establish.

Chapter three turns to the Tale of Jeremiah and Baruch's Scroll which, like the Story of Ahiqar, depicts complex social interactions among its scribal characters, but it does so within various settings of scribal activity. The Tale of Jeremiah and Baruch's Scroll begins and ends within an undisclosed private scribal workshop in which Jeremiah and Baruch compose and recompose a scroll of Jeremiah's teachings. Within this workshop they engage in specialized scribal practices as Jeremiah, who is portrayed as a senior scribe, prepares Baruch, an apprentice, for advanced collegial interactions with other scribal characters. The heart of the tale takes place in three loci of scribal presentation, the temple's outer courtyard, the palace's scribal chamber, and the king's presence. In these three places, Baruch and other scribal characters engage in advanced professional practices by which they scrutinize Baruch's scroll. These scenes depict how scribal professionals used debate to understand a written document of national concern and began to form groups that take various political stances on the document's issues. Furthermore, the tale alludes to the intellectual process of scribal reasoning when it refers to characters who comprehend all of the words (שמע + כל הדברים) of Baruch's document. The text juxtaposes this scribal reasoning with that of non-scribal characters who are within earshot (באזן) of the reading of the scroll, yet do not comprehend it (לא שמע).

The final chapter is a comparative assessment of the two tales. It shows how the setting of the royal court produces similar narrative expectations for the scribal characters by studying eight shared motifs between the two sources. These shared features are discussed in view of their narrative differences. Specifically, the comparative perspective fleshes out the subversive message of the Tale of Jeremiah and Baruch's Scroll in which scribal outsiders function independently of the expected forums of scribal activity, the palace and the temple. Viewing the Story of Ahiqar in light of the Tale of Jeremiah and Baruch's Scroll demonstrates that the Story of Ahiqar's creative Aramaic wording alludes to the shifting political landscape of the professional experience of a courtly scribal figure.

2 Allusions to the Aramaic Scribal Profession in the Story of Ahiqar

As discussed in the introduction, the story of Ahiqar survives on many manuscripts written in many ancient or medieval languages. As Harris hypothesized and new discoveries are confirming, the surviving Syriac manuscripts, although late, retain narrative features of the tale that appear to be very ancient.[1] For this reason, some Syriac manuscripts will be brought into discussion with the Elephantine manuscript, throughout this study,[2] but the objective of this chapter is to understand the scribal allusions found in the Aramaic Elephantine manuscript.

The manuscript was found at Elephantine (Pap. Ber. P. 13446 plates A–H, J–L = *TAD* C1 1 and C3 7),[3] presumably among the large cache of Aramaic sources from what the original German excavators Otto Rubensohn and Fredrick Zucker labeled houses *m* and *n* during their three campaigns between 1906–1908.[4] Scholarship has generally assumed that this is a cache of Judean sources, and to be sure the majority of the corpus excavated by the Germans refer to Judeans, but not all. New research into the excavation reports and the papyri find-spots on the island has revealed that houses *m* and *n* were ancient secondary contexts from the Ptolemaic period.[5] Unfortunately then, the archaeological data is of little value when discussing which communities read the Ahiqar manuscript and for what purposes.

After extensive research on the manuscript, Ada Yardeni published the first discussion of the manuscript's palimpsest along with an extensive (and mostly reconstructed) edition of the palimpsest in the *TAD* (C3 7 with Bezalel Porten). The infrared photographs on which she based her readings clearly show that the manuscript contains large portions of an erased import account and account summaries that recorded taxes on Phoenician and Ionian ships. In addition, the

---

1 See Quack, "demotischen" and Moore, "'Ahikariana.'"
2 For a list of the Syriac manuscripts cited in this study, see appendix.
3 Plate J was deaccessioned in 1912 and repatriated to Egypt. It is now Cairo EM JdE 43502, but for simplicity it will be referred to as plate J in this study.
4 Honroth, Rubensohn, and Zucker, "Bericht," 28.
5 For a full discussion see Moore, *Aramaic*, forthcoming. The incontrovertible evidence comes from Rubensohn's diary which states, "Im aramäischen Viertel werden 2 gerollte, vollständige aramäische Papyri, viele große Fragmente und viel Kleinzeug gefunden. Zwischen den aramäischen Fragmenten finden sich einige wenige demotische Brocken aus Ptolemäerzeit (Rest der Datierung erhalten)" (Müller and Rubensohn, "Die Papyrusgrabung," 83 [10 Jan. 1906]).

manuscript contains significant export accounts of taxes levied on, what she argued to be the same, ships. Although many of the dates are restored, lines on the account clearly refer to stocks (Dv.ii.1) or wine vintage (e.g., Fr.ii.1) from "year 10" and wine vintage from "year 11" (e.g., Fr.ii.5). In three surviving instances, the import account entries also date to "year 11" (Gr.ii.14; Jr.i.1; Kr.ii.22). Porten calculated year 11 to Xerxes I (475 BCE),[6] but one cannot rule out the possibility of the reign of Artaxerxes I (year 11 = c. 454 BCE) or Darius II (year 11 = c. 412 BCE).[7] The overwritten copy of the Ahiqar composition found on the manuscript's recto must have been written after one of these three possibilities, when the account was no longer needed for archival purposes. At present, the last known date from the Aramaic manuscripts on the island is 399 BCE, and this serves as a terminus ante quem for the overwritten copy of the Story of Ahiqar.[8]

The manuscript contains three other compositional acts of note. Ahiq. plate Av (1) contains a broken column of Demotic text which appears to be an unrelated composition from a papyrus fragment used to repair the roll and (2) an upside down Aramaic line that reads ⌈מרא{נ|כ}⌉ "⌈{our | your (m.s.)}⌉[1] lord." Ahiq. plate Dv contains an upside down overwritten four-line composition which is damaged and illegible (see *TAD* C3 7 col. DVEx1 [= p. 184]). Ahiq. plate Gv contains (1) a faded or partially erased list (see *TAD* C3 7 GV4), (2) an overwritten כן on a sheet-join with an unknown meaning, and (3) an upside down introductory line to a different Ahiqar tradition. This upside down line is written in a different hand than the overwritten copy on the recto, and tentatively I have interpreted it as a title/incipit drawn from another, and perhaps better known, Ahiqar tradition placed on the manuscript's maxims to help a reader identify the roll.[9] The diversity of the manuscript's compositional acts show that we still do not completely know how the manuscript was used, and the newly discovered introductory line to a different Ahiqar tradition provides clues to the early history of the tale's development (see below).[10]

---

6 Yardeni, "Maritime," 77 n. 7.
7 See the discussion in Briant and Descat, "registre," 61–62.
8 It is important to note that the taxes levied in the account roll were most likely collected at the mouth of the Nile Delta and not at Elephantine. Furthermore, while I tentatively follow the assumption of Yardeni (and Porten) that the wine vintages refer to the imperial calendar, it is possible that the imports come from a region outside the imperial economic system, in which case "year 10" and "year 11" would refer to local regents, thereby making it impossible to date the references.
9 Moore, "'Ahikariana,'" *forthcoming* n. 50.
10 Moore, "'Ahikariana,'" *forthcoming*.

Ahiq. plates H and L appear to have been added to the larger roll, though it remains uncertain if this was to lengthen the original account or to lengthen the roll in order to finish the Ahiqar overwritten copy on the recto.[11] The verso of Ahiq. plates H and L contains a palimpsest of a copy of the Ahiqar narrative that is very close to, yet different from, that found on the overwritten recto of Ahiq. plates Cr and Dr. The variants on the palimpsest suggest that it may be an Ahiqar tradition that differs from that on the recto, but is part of the same recension.[12] The date of the Ahiqar palimpsest is contingent on the date of the overwritten copy, its relationship to the overwritten copy, and the point at which Ahiq. plates L and H were added to the roll. This new research into the physical and textual traits of the manuscript suggests that Judeans or a group associated with the Judeans produced some of the unique readings on the manuscript's overwritten copy.[13]

2.1 Scribal Features in the Story of Ahiqar

As for the content of the overwritten copy, previous studies on the Story of Ahiqar have shown that the tale "blends two literary themes: the disgrace and rehabilitation of a wise minister, and the treachery of an ungrateful kinsman."[14] Studies have also shown that it is a tale of survival that promotes an "ethic of caution."[15] This chapter contributes to the literary and historical discussions on the Story of Ahiqar by close reading the narrative portions of the Elephantine manuscript for its allusions to the scribal profession. The tale depicts interactions of scribal characters within the Neo-Assyrian court of Esarhaddon, and in

---

11 *TAD* C p. 23 holds that Ahiq. plates H–L were added for the copying of the Ahiqar overwritten text, but the palimpsest account on Ahiq. plates Hr and Lr is too effaced to determine what year it was written in or whether it corresponds in some way with the variety of account styles found on the other plates. See the initial discussion of variant accounts and styles in *TAD* C esp. p. xxi which notes that Ahiq. plates A and B differ from the major import account, but Porten and Yardeni hold that these plates were part of the roll when the overwritten Ahiqar text was copied.
12 Moore, "'Ahikariana,'" *forthcoming*. The two most significant data are a line of text found in the overwritten copy (Dr.i.15) but not the Ahiq. plates Hv^{pal}–Lv^{pal} and the variant spelling of the king's name as אסרחאריב "Esaraḥʾerîb" which, as first noted by Joseph Fitzmyer ("Review," 710), resembles the spelling אסרחריב "ʾEsar(a)ḥerîb" found on 4Q196 frag 2.8, a reference to the king under whom Ahiqar served in the Aramaic book of Tobit.
13 Moore, "'Ahikariana,'" *forthcoming*.
14 Lindenberger, "Ahiqar," 2:490.
15 Bledsoe, "Wisdom," 256–261, 375.

its simplest form, is royal propaganda that prizes the loyalty and cleverness of a scribal courtier in the face of opposition. The narrative establishes a context for the reader to understand and to value the wisdom of Ahiqar's maxims. On a deeper level, however, this complex piece of literature contains motifs that portray the status quo of the scribal profession in a negative light. It depicts royal scribes engaging in nepotism and cronyism, and the plot's central conflict highlights Ahiqar's failed attempt to secure his legacy. Clues to this subtle message about the professional scribal experience are found in the story's rhetoric and tone which are presented from Ahiqar's own autobiographical perspective.

Ahiqar's troubles begin when he convinces the king to allow him to retire rather than to fulfill a social expectation that he would remain in his post until he dies. Ahiqar made his unorthodox choice to retire after he had ensured that his nephew would replace him as the wise scribe. While away from the palace, his nephew acts treacherously against him and falsely charges him with treason. When confronted with these accusations, Ahiqar uses his cleverness and social connections to save his own life and to prove that he had been innocent and loyal to the king. The remaining portion of the Elephantine manuscript is broken, but in all other surviving manuscripts which continue to this point the king hands Nadin over to Ahiqar for punishment. Again, the obvious moral of the story is clear; those who are faithful to the king will be saved and rebels will be punished.

When read through a socio-historical lens, however, the complexity and difficulty of the tale comes into better view. First, the tale was composed in Aramaic but portrays Ahiqar as though he were the leading scholar of the Neo-Assyrian court. Historically, only an Akkadian scholar (i.e. an *ummânu*) held such a position. This cultural dissonance in the tale results in subtle, yet powerful critiques against Akkadian scribal culture by the tale's Aramaic composer.[16] Second, although Ahiqar resembles an Akkadian scholar in a predominantly Akkadian royal court, the language used to describe courtly positions and characteristics contains uniquely Aramaic terms in addition to Akkadian loanwords. Terms such as יעט, נגד, עזקה, and רביא, are not used in the other Elephantine papyri or, if used, not in the same way as they are in the Story of Ahiqar. Terms such as these suggest that the writer must have been intimately aware of a distinctly Aramaic court vocabulary as well as the common Akkadian lexicon of

---

[16] Likewise, Michalowski, "Biography," 203–210 tries to show that self-reference in the autobiographical portions of Neo-Assyrian through early Achaemenid royal inscriptions conveys an implicit critique that undermines a conventional idea.

courtly professions. At the core of the Story of Ahiqar is a linguistic and cultural tension.

With literary artistry the tale repeats, nuances, and spins the meaning of literary motifs in which are embedded reflections of the professional experience of courtly scribes. It does this by developing a literary motif in one scene then nuancing it and applying it to a different social situation in another scene. The plot connects dynastic succession to professional scribal succession. It portrays the advantages of nepotism and puts them at odds with the advantages of cronyism. It uses a historically known treasonous character and casts him as a literary foil for a self-proclaimed innocent character falsely charged with treason. It, also, justifies the murder of an innocent, enslaved, and young scribal character in order to save an accused, privileged, and old scribal figure. The composition achieves its depth of meaning because it uses a crafty and convincing autobiographical voice through which Ahiqar portrays himself as a victim and loyal royal scribe, though subtly he represents an aggressor manipulating those around him for the sake of self-preservation.

2.2 The Prologue to a Scribe's Tale (A.1–2)

The Elephantine manuscript begins with a third-person prologue that introduces the tale's literary content and its subject matter. Due to damage the opening lines have been difficult to interpret. I read them as follows:

Ahiq. Plate A.1–2
{*Prologue*}
[The account of]ʳthe words ofˡ the one named ²Aḥîqar, a wise and skilled scribe who educated his son ʳwhˡ[o …]said, "may I have the son." The beginning of [his] word[s]:
{*Autobiography*}
[I] am ²Aḥîqar

[ספר]ʳמליˡ אחיקר שמה ספר חכים ומהיר זי חכם
לברה ʳזˡיˡ …
[אמר ברא למ יהוה לי קדמת מל]והי אנ[ה
אחיקרˡ¹⁷

---

17 I find no reason for restoring the first word as [אלה] as *AP*, Lindenberger, *TAD* and others have done. Nöldeke, *Untersuchungen*, 7 proposes [מה לי] which is too short for the reconstructed area and anachronistic; the manuscript later refers to מלי (A.4). Kottsieper, "Geschichte," 324 also reads [ספר], but without justification. One can consider the Aramaic epigraphic evidence from *KAI* 312 A 1.1, בלעם[.ב]ספר[.]זנה "[This] is the account of [Ba]laam" (see also *KAI* 222 A 2.8). Furthermore, ספר matches the genre distinction of ܬܫܥܝܬܐ "history" or "account" found in the short third-person prologue of many Syriac manuscripts (e.g., Camb. Cod. Add. 2020 1.1). Last-

The prologue describes the tale as [ספר] ˹מלי˺[אחיקר שמה "[The account of] ˹the words˺ of the one named Ahiqar" (A.1). The phrase ספר מלי "The account of the words of" might be taken as a reference to the autobiographical narrative style in which the tale is composed, that is, this is the account that Ahiqar told in his own words. I do not prefer this interpretation because throughout the autobiographical portion of the tale, Ahiqar's words (מלין) refer specifically to his counsel (עטתה), which he gives to others (B.8, 12; D.i.12). Furthermore, if the restoration of Ahiq. plate C.12 is correct, [ומל]˹והי˺ עטתה "his counsel and [his] word[s]," it equates Ahiqar's counsel to his words, and therefore the references to Ahiqar's words are not strong enough in the narrative to indicate that the prologue refers to autobiographical style. By comparison, the incipit to the second recension of Ahiqar found on Ahiq. plate Gv[upside down] appears to also emphasize counsel and not "words."[18] It reads:

Ahiq. Plate Gv[upside down]
Saying: 24 years belong(ed) to (the) Lord of   למ ר̇ ו ̇ש̇ ו שנג למרא מלכנ סנח[אריב מ]˹לכא˺
Kings, Sennaḥ[ʾerîb]˹the˺[k]˹ing.˺ In Kalaḥ   בכלח ˹יעטת˺[19] מלוכת˺ אתור
˹I advised the kingdom/kingship of˺ ʾAtûr.

The speaker of this line is presumably Ahiqar, who begins this autobiographical narration similar to the way it begins in many Syriac manuscripts, with a regnal year followed by Ahiqar's role as a counselor in the Assyrian court. Although the verb is damaged, it either emphasizes Ahiqar's role as a counselor or prioritizes his place in the Assyrian royal court. Both introductory lines, Ahiq. plate Gv[upside down] and the overwritten recto text, set up a narrative in which the main character is known for wisdom, counsel, or influence.

It is better, I believe, to understand the term "words" in the prologue on the manuscript's recto as an ancient Aramaic genre marker and reference to the instructional maxims that are collected at the end of the document, rather than to the tale's first-person narrative style. The use of the term מלה "word" marks the beginning of an announcement in Aramaic (e.g., Amh 63 xix ln. 7; MT Dan 2:5), and therefore naturally becomes a marker for the "sayings."[20] In this sense,

---

ly, the book of Tobit, which knows the Story of Ahiqar (e.g., Tob 1:22; 14:10), also begins Βίβλος λόγων Τωβιθ "The book of the words of Tobit" (1:1).
18 For discussion see Moore, "'Ahikariana,'" forthcoming.
19 Alternatively, read ˹הוית˺ and translate, "Saying: 24 years belong(ed) to (the) Lord of Kings, Šenn[ahʾerîb]the[k]ing. I was in Kalaḥ. The kingdom/kingship of ʾAtûr (...)" al a Moore, "'Ahikariana,'" forthcoming.
20 While it is easy to understand references to "words" in the Sefire Inscription as a literal statement of the engraved linguistic units, Donner and Röllig have rightly interpreted, "Die

the statement "[The account of] ⌜the words⌝ of Ahiqar" denotes a narrative explanation (an account) that supplies a context for a collection of instructions (his words). In its grammatically genitive construction, the emphasis falls on "the words" and not on the "account," and therefore, the prologue suggests that the narrative portion of the tale supplies the origin for his maxims and the narrative context in which they can be interpreted.[21]

The prologue implies that Ahiqar's instructional maxims are valuable because he was ספר חכים ומהיר זי חכם לברה "a wise and expert scribe who taught his son." The phrase "a wise scribe" resembles Ahiqar's professional title, ספרא חכימא "the wise scribe," which appears multiple times throughout the tale (A.12; B.12; C.11). Notably, however, the prologue's grammatically indefinite form disagrees with Ahiqar's grammatically determined title found in the autobiographical section.[22] In the prologue, Ahiqar is not "the wise scribe" (ספרא חכימא) but merely "a wise scribe" (ספר חכים). This is one indication that the prologue was an addition to the tale.[23]

The grammatically determined title ספרא חכימא is a literary invention used as an all-encompassing title to refer to Ahiqar's various scribal attributes. The title is not found in other ancient Aramaic sources, but resembles the Akkadian phrase "wise scholar" (*ummânu emqu*), which is known from a short folkloric work found among a list of proverbs on K4347+16161 ii 50–63; this work resembles the narrative structure of the Story of Ahiqar (see below). A related construction *ṭupšarru emqu* "the wise scribe" is known from a seal on an Akkadian tablet from Ugarit (RS 16.142 ln. 16). Generally, in Neo-Assyrian texts an *ummânu em/nqūtu* refers to a skilled (royal) craftsman (e.g., RINAP 4 Esar no. 48 r. 70) and is closely connected to the *šitimgalla enqūta* "skilled (royal) architect," who together plan royal building projects (e.g., RINAP 4 Esar no. 105 iv

---

Inscrift ist magisch als Zeuge gedacht; sie kann nicht nur hören (Jos. 24, 26f.), sondern auch reden" (*KAI* p. 2:254). The term מלי in the Ahiqar prologue matches the term ܡܠܐ in the Syriac headings. See for instance the Ahiqar excerpt in JerMkl no. 162 which simply reads in red, ܡܠܐܘܗܝ ܕܐܚܝܩܪ "the sayings of Ḥîqar."

21 This provides textual evidence that supports the thematic arguments made by others, who see literary (e.g., Weigl, *aramäischen*, 6912–703) or social historical (Wigand, "Politische") connections between the narrative and proverbs.

22 Only one exception appears in the autobiographical portion of the tale: [ה]נבלו [אח]יק[ר] זך שבא ספר חכימ [סכיל] "[Why sh]ould this old [ʾAh]îqa[r,] a wise scribe [*be foolish*?]" (C.4–5). The context is one in which Esarhaddon makes a defensive statement intended to belittle Ahiqar, and therefore, does not refer to him as "*the* wise scribe" but rather "*a* wise scribe" who is foolish.

23 The identification of this emic genre marker provides textual evidence that the Story of Ahiqar may have been used as a learned text among those at the highest levels of educational training or simply for the educated professional to reflect on.

29–30). The degree to which the skilled craftsmen and the *ummânū* overlap is found in a slightly later Neo-Babylonian inscription of Nabonidus which uses the logogram DUB.SAR (*ṭupšarru*) "scribe" in a context where architects seem to be in view (RIBo 7 Nab no. 24 i 32). Furthermore, although there is no evidence that the riddle of Pharaoh's tower, which appears in the Syriac narrative, was present in the Elephantine manuscript, the Syriac narrative retains a tradition in which Ahiqar is known as a skilled architect using a loan title ܐܪܕܟܠܐ ܚܟܝܡܐ "a wise builder" (Camb. Cod. Add. 2020 5.2) from Akkadian *arad ekalli* "master builder" (lit. palace servant).[24] The Story of Ahiqar uses the title ספרא חכימא as an honorific and a literary umbrella to represent the diversity of Ahiqar's various roles, which in turn have close ties to Assyrian courtly officials, rather than the alphabetic scribes, who mostly served in lower ranking administrative roles.[25] The phrase "the wise scribe" functions as though it were a professional title in the world of the fictitious narrative. It is analogous to the one in charge of the "house of the seal" (בית עזקה; A.3), that is, the king's seal-bearer. The title "seal-bearer" (Aram. רב עזקן,[26] Akk. *rab unqāti*) was an official title and office in imperial courts,[27] but "the wise scribe" was a qualitative phrase used to describe the character of a given royal Akkadian scholar. The title ספרא חכימא is best explained then as a literary invention that parallels *ummânu emqu* or *ṭupšarru emqu*;[28] is an umbrella term that encapsulates all the scribal roles that Ahiqar

---

24 See also the Aramaic phrase ארדכל זי מלכא (*TAD* B2 6.2) and the discussion in Oppenheim, "*arad*," 227–235.

25 Frequently in Neo-Assyrian sources one finds ^{lú2}A.BA which is a reference to cuneiform *ṭupšarru* "scribe" and not an alphabetic scribe as some have argued (Bloch, *Alphabetic*, 12–13 n. 29). Bloch discusses the great administrative diversity of the *sēpirū* "alphabetic scribes" in the Neo-Babylonian period. While some were in royal service, most held administrative positions in various institutions throughout the empire (see especially the helpful summary 399–412).

26 This is the title given to Ahiqar in Tobit, 4Q196 frag. 2.7. In some Syriac manuscripts he is simply called ܥܙܩܬܐ "the seal(-bearer)" (e.g., Camb. Cod. Add 2020 3.8).

27 See Pearce, "*sēpiru*," 358 n. 7 for its connection to *sēpiru*.

28 It is unknown when Akkadian *ummânu* came into Aramaic as א(ו)מן, but it is clear from its meaning "craftsman" (e.g., *TAD* A6 10.3) that it is not a reference to its specific Neo-Assyrian courtly usage. Even in Syriac manuscripts the Neo-Assyrian meaning is lost on the writers/copyists, and the term ܐܘܡܢ and its derivatives refers to skilled crafts(men) (e.g., Graffin 27.7; Camb. Cod. Add. 2020 1.20 ܐܘܡܢܘܬܐ, ܚܟܡܐ "tools of the trade"). For a comparative etymological study of the term see Cazelles, "Ahiqar," esp. 50–1.

can take on; and is meant to emphasize the wise characteristics of Ahiqar the Assyrian.²⁹

Another indication that the prologue was an addition is its use of the word מהיר "skilled one." Unlike the phrase ספרא חכימא "the wise scribe," the term מהיר "skilled one" appears only in the third-person prologue of the Elephantine manuscript. The word is not otherwise found at Elephantine or in the Aramaic Dead Sea Scrolls; this is the earliest datable occurrence of the word.³⁰ The term is only otherwise known from a few occurrences in late Biblical Hebrew (MT Ps 45:2; MT Ezra 7:6; MT Prov 22:29). These later examples all refer to the quality of a scribe³¹ or a courtier,³² thereby limiting the domain of the word to a courtly and scribal context in a later period. But not much more can be said about the social meaning of מהיר from the data. J. Conrad sees סֹפֵר מָהִיר in MT Ezra 7:6 and MT Ps 45:2 as comparable to Akkadian *ummânu emqu*.³³ This seems to be a reasonable deduction, and therefore מהיר in the prologue of the Story of Ahiqar can be seen is a Persian period gloss that explains the phrase ספרא חכימא. The term מהיר would then interpret Ahiqar's position in the Neo-Assyrian court for Persian period readers.

After the prologue introduces Ahiqar, it focuses on a specific narrative element in the tale. Ahiqar, as a wise and skilled scribe with significant words, is said to have taught his son. Ahiqar's ability to teach correlates with his scribal character and with the fact that he is known for his instructional words. This

---

29 The prologue to manuscript Sachau 336 17b refers to him as ܐܚܝܩܪ ܐܬܘܪܝܐ "ʾAḥîqar the Assyrian." Note that the Uruk List of Kings and Sages (W.20030, 7) provides an Akkadian equivalent for his name, Aba-Enlil-dari (ᵐa-ba-ᵈNINNU-da-ri, ln. 19). It also calls him an *ummânu* and claims that the Arameans call him Ahiqar. It does not refer to Ahiqar as an Aramean! For the latest edition of the text see Lenzi, "The Uruk List."
30 *DNWSI*, 602. The root is also known from Ugaritic sources where it refers to a valorous character or "hero" (see *DULAT*, 536). In Ugaritic, these elite characters appear to be skilled with their hands, see *kp mhr* "palms of the *mhr*" (*UD/KTU* 1.3.iii.11) or in a broken context ⌈y⌉d mhr "hand of the *mhr*" (*UD/KTU* 1.10.i.11).
The Syriac term ܡܗܝܪܐ appears in many Ahiqar manuscripts. This adjective and the verb of the same root (ܡܗܪ) often refer to intellectual skill rather than dexterity. See examples in Sokoloff, *Syriac*, 720–721.
31 See MT Ezra 7:6 סֹפֵר מָהִיר בְּתוֹרַת מֹשֶׁה "a scribe skilled in the instructions of Moses," and Ps 45:2 לְשׁוֹנִי עֵט סוֹפֵר מָהִיר "my tongue is the stylus of a skilled scribe." According to Williamson, מהיר suggests more than merely the ability to write fast, as its etymological meaning from √מהר "to hasten" might imply (*Ezra*, 92), contra Blenkinsopp, *Ezra-Nehemiah*, 137 and Ringgren, *TDOT*, 8:141.
32 See MT Prov 22:29 יִתְיַצֵּב לִפְנֵי־מְלָכִים "stands before kings."
33 Conrad, *TDOT*, 10:325.

statement, however, serves a more important purpose than to merely explain Ahiqar's role as a teacher. The autobiographical portion of the tale describes how Ahiqar taught his nephew (A.6), but then refers to this event three more times as a rhetorical device used to emphasize the nephew's betrayal (B.3, 9; C.13). By referring to Ahiqar's and Nadin's relationship, the prologue primes the reader for the motif of a student who rebels against his teacher.[34]

No other surviving prologue alludes to the narrative's theme of rebellion and betrayal in this way. The prologues in the later Syriac manuscripts of the tale also emphasize the scribal or intellectual traits of Ahiqar, his words or sayings, and a narrative context in which those sayings can be interpreted, but only the Elephantine prologue on Ahiq. plate A mentions Ahiqar's adoption and the training of his nephew. The emphasis that the prologue places on the maxims and the training of a student, who will betray his teacher later in the story, serves a different function than do the prologues in the later editions because the maxims in the Elephantine document appear only at the end of the tale. The later Syriac editions of the tale contain a list of positive ethical maxims at the point in the narrative that Ahiqar trains his nephew, as well as a list of negative admonitions used to punish the nephew at the end of the tale.[35] So when these later prologues refer to Ahiqar's sayings, they refer to both the positive and negative attributes of instruction. In the Elephantine manuscript, however, the sayings only appear at the end of the tale and must serve only as admonitions and ethical warnings, foremost against betrayal. The prologue of the Elephantine edition, then, primes the reader to view the manuscript as a source of ethical teachings and admonitions of a wise royal scribe who wishes to curb and punish disloyalty. It is the prologue that spins a positive tone on an otherwise propagandistic tale.

2.3 Acquiring a Scribal Student (A.2–7)

The first-person prologue introduces the text, but the story begins in line 2, in which Ahiqar introduces himself in the first-person stating, אנ[ה אחיקר] "I am Ahiqar"; A.2).[36] The same autobiographical introduction starts the book of Tobit

---

34 The corresponding information is also broken in the tale itself (A.5–6).
35 Nöldeke, *Untersuchungen*, 5 conservatively holds that it is unclear if Nadin is punished in the Elephantine manuscript. Clues in both the narrative and the maxims leave the issue open to debate.
36 Only Halévy, "nouveaux," 37–38 (noted by Nöldeke, *Untersuchungen*, 7) correctly restored this phrase. Others restore רב[ה אחיקר "Ahiqar became [gr]eat" (*AP* p. 212, 226; *TAD* C1 1.2;

after its prologue, Ἐγὼ Τωβιτ "I, Tobit" (Tob 1:3). Furthermore, this construction, *anāku* PN, is a common form in Akkadian autobiographical texts (e.g., in Adad Guppi, Idrimi, The Marduk Prophecy). Ahiqar introduces himself based on his previous accomplishments as the seal-bearer (עזקה; A.3) under the last monarch and as the one on whose words the kingdom had relied (מ׳ל׳י וה׳וה; A.4).[37] This is contextualized in an age of monarchic transition during which Esarhaddon "replaces" (√חלף) his father Sennacherib.

Attention must be paid to the tale's autobiographical style before studying its motifs.[38] Autobiography draws the reader into the narrator's experience in a way that third-person narration does not. Autobiographical narration invites a reader to role-play with the narrator and to conceive of herself within the narrator's world.[39] The Story of Ahiqar is not a typical autobiography. The work adds an additional meta-level of significance to the narration because the narrator is a scribe, and thus evokes a scribal relationship between the narrator and the literate reader. In its present form, this tale was written by a scribe, who composed a fictional autobiographical scribal narrator, who, in turn, directly addresses a reader and draws that reader into the constructed historical context of the royal court of Esarhaddon. Because ancient readers were themselves literate scribal individuals, a deeper relationship is forged between the scribal narrator and the scribal reader who share a professional experience. This unique narra-

---

Kottsieper, "Geschichte," 324; Niehr, *Ahiqar*, 38; Grelot, *Documents*, 433), [∘∘]רה אחיקר (Ungnad, *Aramäische*, 63), or ה אחיקר... (Sachau, *Aramäische*, 148).

37 Similarly, Milik, "Modêles," 385. There is no direct evidence that Ahiqar was a historical figure though Parpola, "retroterra," 111 esp. n. 1 has brought new evidence to the debate. Oshima, "How," 144–145 has tried to expand the dataset by considering the name Arqu to be a hypocoristic form of Ahiqar. The recent decipherment of the Aramaic line on Ahiq. plate Gv[upside down] of the Elephantine manuscript provides some evidence that a courtly official found in CTN 3 99 i 15; CTN 3 108 ii 38 by the same name (Ahûqar) and based in Kalḫu in the Neo-Assyrian period could have been the inspiration for the tale (Moore, "'Ahikariana,'" *forthcoming*).

38 Egyptian and Akkadian literatures attest to many examples of fictional autobiography, and the subject has been discussed in Second Temple studies. For Egyptological studies, see Frood, *Biographical*, 1–30; Hagen, "Constructing," 185–209; and Suhr, *ägyptsche*, esp. 40–47. The most comprehensive study on the subject in Assyriology remains, Longman III, *Fictional*, esp. 43–48 which calls fictional autobiography a genre. Westenholz, *Legends*, 18–19 classifies fictional autobiography as a type of *narû* "inscriptional" text. For a more recent work see Glassner, *Mesopotamian*, 32–3 n. 95. The study of pseudepigraphic works in Greco-Roman Palestine is vast, but see in particular Smith, "Pseudepigraphy," 190–227. For Northwest Semitic royal inscriptions see Green, *"Undertook,"* esp. 285–319.

39 (Ancient) autobiographical narration beckons the critic to consider the existence of a real or perceived author, though the author and narrator are not the same cognitive entities, see Milner, *Literature*, 51.

tor/reader dynamic may help explain, in part, the popularity of the Story of Ahiqar, one of the world's first recognizable novellas.

In a recent article on postclassical narratology, Martin Löschnigg synthesizes the latest research on the study of autobiography in literary studies.[40] He concludes that autobiographies are valuable for their "discursive representation of the experiential;" their perspective on the "role of narrative in the formation of identity;" their cognitive function regarding the role of frames, scripts and "textual representation of memory;" and especially for their "fictionality."[41] The experience shared between the narrator and reader of the Story of Ahiqar is intimately tied to the shared scribal identity of the two; the reader may feel represented by the character of Ahiqar. Together they create a shared discourse of (socially defined)[42] frames and scripts that produce a fictional world founded on the professional scribal experience.[43] In this way, the autobiographical narration produces two stories: one that can be read literally as a description of events in the narrator's (i.e. Ahiqar's) experience as a victim of malfeasance. This surface reading serves as a cautionary tale against rebellion, but if the reader engages with the narrator, as the autobiographical style beckons her to do, then a deeper scribal experience can be fleshed out of the text. There exists an intimate exchange between the Aramaic writer of a tale about an Assyrian scholar and the literate (Aramaic) reader. This deeper reading, as will be shown, provides a number of critiques on the scribal experience of an Aramaic narrator in the constructed historical setting of Esarhaddon's Assyrian court. From this perspective an underlying critique against the nepotism and cronyism of Akkadian scholarly figures comes into view.

Ahiqar begins his first-person account by describing how Esarhaddon "replaced" ([ף]חל; A.5) his dead father, Sennacherib the king. This is immediately followed by a description of how Ahiqar adopted Nadin, his nephew; Ahiqar states, [י]אחʼת ילʼבר ןחתʼ[ק]ילʼ[כנ] "So]ʼI toʼ[o]ʼkʼ [my] nephʼewʼ" (A.6).[44] As

---

40 Löschnigg, "Postclassical," 255–274.
41 Löschnigg, "Postclassical," 256.
42 See Rogers, Novels, esp. her discussion and examples on 132–133. Rogers argues that autobiographical style is a literary artifice that helps to instruct and to socialize the reader to the world of the narrator.
43 Löschnigg, "Postclassical," 255. Löschnigg describes how past critics viewed autobiography as representing "an autonomous and homogeneous self" in which the author and the narrator were the same mind, but deconstructionists challenged this view in the 1970's through 1990's, and instead, saw autobiography as purely an "illusion of 'self.'"
44 The interlinear pattern of traces can only be read as ילʼ[ק]ʼחתʼ. Kottsieper, "Geschichte," 325 n. 6 correctly noticed this.

such, the text introduces the motif of dynastic succession then hints at a related motif of scholarly succession, which it will develop in the next scene. This pattern of developing a motif then expanding on it with an analogous motif is a central feature of the tale's narrative structure. There is, however, something unusual about this scholarly succession; Nadin is not Ahiqar's son but his nephew. This unexpected relationship serves as a narrative hook that draws attention to a father-son relationship, while recognizing that that relationship is peculiar. Their unnatural pairing will manifest as a dysfunctional professional relationship as the tale unfolds.

The reason as to why Ahiqar chooses to adopt Nadin is uncertain because the relevant lines (A.5–6) are too badly damaged, but in line 6 is found the start of a word with the letters שב. This is likely a reference to "old age." In the next scene, Esarhaddon asks Ahiqar who will replace him when he dies (A.7), and in that exchange Ahiqar admits, שב אנה "I am old" (B.1). The evidence suggests that Ahiqar is motivated to adopt Nadin in Ahiq. plate A lines 5–6 because he desires to secure a professional heir and to establish his legacy. However, he feels unable to do so without a biological son, hence he adopts his nephew. Securing an heir has two consequences for Ahiqar. First, an heir would ensure that Ahiqar's "words," that is his sayings (מלין; A.4) which proved to be useful counsel for social affairs (A.4, 12; B.12), would survive for future generations.[45] Ahiqar explicitly refers to his own instructions as "the good things" (ⸯטבתאⸯ; A.9), and thus worth preserving.

The second consequence of Ahiqar adopting his nephew and instating him in Ahiqar's office is that Ahiqar engages in overt nepotism. Surviving Neo-Assyrian documents show that nepotism, such as that practiced by Ahiqar, was common among Akkadian courtly scholars. For example, the scholar (*ummânu*) to Esarhaddon late in his reign was Nabu-zeru-lešir. His "son" (*māru*), Issar-šumu-ereš, became the scholar after him and continued into the reign of Ashurbanipal.[46] The Assyrian position of the *ummânu* was dynastic,[47] and clearly, the most prestigious scholars in the royal court practiced nepotism. Similarly, other esteemed scholarly positions in the royal court also appear to have been dynastic. Urad-Gula, an exorcist (*mašmaššû*) and scholar (*ummânu*) during the reign of Ashurbanipal, was

---

[45] This interpretation presumes that wise sayings were accompanied by an oral component, since the saying itself could have been written down and read by future generations. See by analogy the notion of education in MT Deut 6:1–10 in which teaching (√למד), listening (√שמע), and writing (√כתב) are all seen as components of passing down words (דברים).

[46] SAA 10 p. xxvi.

[47] Baker, "Scribes," 68–69 and Radner, "Decision-Making," 363.

the son of Adad-šuma-uṣur, the chief exorcist to Esarhaddon.[48] On more than one occasion, Urad-Gula found the king disapproving of his performance, and his father, Adad-šuma-uṣur, helped him keep his job.[49] These records indicate that those holding a scribal position were inclined to select and to appoint their heirs in scholarly positions, and as such the constructed Neo-Assyrian setting of the Story of Ahiqar bears a sense of social realia.

Furthermore, scholarly fathers taught their sons their craft and did not send them off to school in the Neo-Assyrian period, as was common to do in the earlier Sumerian and Old Babylonian periods. The famous early second millennium BCE Sumerian Schooldays texts paint a picture of education similar to that which we now consider normative: a student would go to school each day, his parents would encourage him in his education at home, but his teachers would educate him at school.[50] The school was an institution with a number of workers, each performing specific tasks integral to the function of the institution. The social structure of those schools was modeled on the family. The "teacher" was not the biological father of the students, though he was viewed as "a second father."[51] The student was called "son."[52] By the first millennium, however, the model of education appears to have changed to an apprenticeship structure that better favors nepotism, particularly among families that staffed the royal courts. The details and impetus of that change are still enigmatic and may forever be lost to history.[53] The scant evidence that survives for first millennium education demonstrates that some of the scholars and scribes working at the highest levels of the empire groomed their own children to take their positions. These "children," however, were not always biological offspring.

Some evidence indicates that at least a few royal scholars educated a variety of students to fill scribal positions in the empire in the Neo-Assyrian period.

---

48 SAA 10 p. xxvi.
49 Parpola, "Forlorn," 270.
50 Kramer, "Schooldays," 199–145 and Kramer, *Tablets*, 10–13.
51 Kramer, "Schooldays," 204.
52 Kramer, "Schooldays," 204, 206 (esp. ln. 81). The "son," i.e. "student," was probably shorthand for DUMU EDUBBA "son of the school." By comparison see the recent study by Scafa, "Continuity," 352 which concludes, "The comparison of the characteristics of a generation with the characteristics of the next generation seems to suggest that the fathers were not the teachers of their sons." I cite this with caution, however, as it may not be relevant if the educational model of the early first millennium turned into an apprenticeship model. But even within apprenticeships, the relationship between teacher and student need not be biological. Furthermore, most of the school tablets are known from Nippur, but there is growing evidence that other sites used a slightly different style of instruction, see Gadotti and Kleinerman, "Unfulfilled," 213.
53 Charpin, *Reading*, 46–53.

Marduk-šapik-zeri, a Babylonian astrologer who contracted a disease and appears to have been quarantined from his work, wrote a letter recommending his students for jobs in royal scholarly service (SAA 10 no. 160).[54] This astrologer[55] more than once refers to the profession of his own unnamed "father," which is an appeal to his own educational pedigree (ll. 36, 45), but this may not have been his biological parent. The students for whom he wrote this letter of recommendation come from a variety of backgrounds, and are clearly not his biological children.[56] One is an immigrant from Elam (ln. r. 1) and at least three are refugees (or defectors?) from Assyria (ll. 4, 10, 13, 25?). This writer's appeal to his unnamed father/teacher and his recommendations for his "apprentices" (*šamallû*)[57] suggests that nepotism may have been encouraged in the Neo-Assyrian period but may have also taken a secondary and analogical form based on the fact that the apprentice model of education used familial terms metaphorically for teacher and student. This is further supported by the scribal literature, in which a father/teacher teaches his advice to his son/student in the wisdom traditions.[58] The power of this familial metaphor for education and its social affinity to apprentice education (rather than institutionalized education) demonstrate that scholars saw themselves as parents. Perhaps taking on a son/student was akin to adopting, as the act appears to be in the Story of Ahiqar. This brief window into the historical context of the Neo-Assyrian period provides circumstantial evidence that Ahiqar's motives for securing a replacement for the position of seal-bearer are based on nepotistic ideas prevalent in the actual historical period in which the narrative is purportedly set. The fact that Ahiqar's son turns on him in a later scene suggests that the Aramaic writer may have been critiquing the role of nepotism in courtly scribal appointments of chiefly cuneiform experts.

---

54 For a historical and literary analysis of this letter see Hurowitz, "Tales," 68–71.

55 The text does not refer to him as an astrologer (see SAA 10 p. xiii), but the content suggests that he was well versed in the astrological series.

56 Letters of recommendation are hardly a form of nepotism or cronyism; the fact that there is a need to recommend an individual means that there is a healthy competition for employment. But within the context of a nepotistic system, recommendations become more meaningful than the ability of the recommended, as is the case with Ahiqar's recommendation of Nadin.

57 The etymology of the word ^{lú2}ŠAMAN.LÁ (Sumerian) literally means a "merchant's apprentice." Scribal training may have been comparable to trade craft.

58 Lemaire, *Écoles* 54, 57, 61–62 was the first to develop this observation in Northwest Semitic studies and to discuss apprenticeship models, which he saw as more personal in the prophetic apprenticeships than in the palace and temple models (71). In (especially Western peripheral) Akkadian, this is a well-known phenomenon, e.g., *Šimâ Milka* ll. 1–7 following the edition of Cohen, *Wisdom*, 81–128. See also Parpola, "retroterra," 97 n. 4.

Early in the narrative, Ahiqar is associated with the act of sealing. As part of Nadin's training, Ahiqar would have taught Nadin the social and political power of seals. Furthermore, a study of the titles given to Ahiqar in the Elephantine manuscript can be put in dialogue with those given to him in the book of Tobit and the known Akkadian evidence. Doing so reveals important features about the dating of the Elephantine's copy and about the literary features of Ahiqar's scribal titles.

I restore Ahiq. plate A.3 as ב[ית] עזקתה זי שנחאריב "[in] the house of the seal(-bearer) of Sennaḥ²erîb" and Ahiq. plate B.3 [בב]ית עזקה "[in] a seal(-bearer's) [hou]se."⁵⁹ AP's reconstruction [צב]ית and claim that it derives from Akkadian ṣābit has been perpetuated uncritically.⁶⁰ There are four problems with AP's reconstruction. First, one might expect the Aramaic spelling of the participle to be צבת, without yod serving as a mater lectionis.⁶¹ Second, high officials with compound titles mostly take רב (Akk. rab) "chief," which cannot be restored, especially in Ahiq. plate A.3, given the material limits of the manuscript. Third, Akkadian ṣabātu comes into Aramaic meaning "possessions" see צבות ביתא "the possessions of the house" (TAD A6 8.2), and there is no indication that a verbal form of the word was brought into Aramaic. Lastly, while AP's reading could be a descriptive term like that referring to the official act of keeping a tablet (ṭuppi ṣabātu, CAD Ṣ 18),⁶² recent Aramaic evidence shows that this act would have been expressed with the Aramaic verb אחז/אחד "to seize."⁶³

Seals played a significant role in the bureaucratic world of Mesopotamia. Their function has been well studied.⁶⁴ The Aramaic term for seal, עזקה, is comparable to Akkadian kunukku "cylinder seal" in function and meaning, but because surviving Aramaic seals were stamp seals, עזקה more closely resembles Akkadian unqu "stamp seal," which appears frequently in the Neo-Assyrian scholarly letters and later sources. Those who held the king's unqu-seal were

---

59 There is also an unpublished Ahiqar fragment in the Berlin museum that contains the word "seal." I had proposed in my dissertation that this belongs on Ahiq. plate A.9 or to a lost column of narrative. At present, this assessment still stands.
60 AP, 226–7. The only dissenting view regarding this word is Kaufman, Akkadian, 96 who merely finds the reading "dubious." The restored words in the Elephantine manuscript are the only recorded instances of Aramaic צבית "bearer" (DNWSI, 98).
61 Compare the participle יעט "counselor" used throughout tale (e.g., A.12).
62 Also Greenfield, "Studies," 292–5, 297–9 who unconvincingly argues that צבית may be an Egyptian or Achaemenid cultural term via Akkadian loaned into Aramaic.
63 See Lipiński, "Aramaic," 255–256 tab. 6 (= Lemaire, Nouvelle Tablettes Araméennes, no. 6) r. 5' ואחז ספרא "and the keeper of the document."
64 See RLA, "Siegel."

either chief courtiers[65] or high-ranking courtly military personnel.[66] Documents or buildings with the royal seal were sometimes assigned a guard.[67] In Neo-Assyrian, the term *unqu* refers to a seal, but is also used metonymically to refer to a sealed document, a sealed building, a bulla,[68] or perhaps even a seal-bearer,[69] but it was not until the Neo-Babylonian period that one finds the official title *rab unqāti* "chief of the seals" (CAD U–W, 171a).[70] Most relevant to the phrase בית עזק(ת)ה in the Story of Ahiqar are Persian period texts that refer to ˡᵘ²*sēpir ša bīt unqāta* "the (Aramaic) scribe of the house of the seals."[71] The house of the seals is a strange phrase, but may be a reference to the royal treasury as indicated by a Neo-Assyrian tablet that uses the phrase as an appositive to describe the treasury.[72] Furthermore, the Persian Aramaic imperial administration developed a consistent format for sealed provincial decrees that mandated "the scribe's" name, either acting alone or with a chancellor, appear on the document to indicate that he was responsible for enacting the decree.[73]

The Aramaic book of Tobit continues the tradition of Ahiqar as a seal-bearer; in fact, it contains five titles for Ahiqar. The relevant lines read:

---

65 E.g., a *rab ša-rēši* "the chief eunuch" (SAA 5 no. 98 ln. 4).
66 E.g., a *rab kiṣir* "the unit commander" (SAA 5 no. 234 ll. 4'–7'). See Aramaic רבכצר (*TAD* D 11.1.1). In SAA 1 no. 45, a unit commander delivers sealed royal correspondence and is under the charge of a *rab ša-rēši* "chief eunuch."
67 I.e. a *qurbūte* "bodyguard" (SAA 5 no. 98).
68 The learned recipients of sealed documents carefully scrutinized their bullae for forgeries. E.g., SAA 15 no. 125 is a letter to the king claiming that the sealed document that the writer previously received is a forgery because it does not look like the "1,000" other sealed documents from the king that he had received.
69 *CAD* does not attest to this meaning, but texts such as SAA 5 no. 98 r. 9'–10' refer to an *unqu* "walking" (*alāku*). In Syriac, Ahiqar is called the ܚܬܘܡܐ "seal(-bearer)." A similar semantic is known in Persian period Elamite sources, see Tavernier, "Multilingualism," 65.
70 See further, the discussion in chapter four. It is notable that the *rab unqāti* owned considerable amounts of land. Compare the "villages of Ahiqar" found in SAA 6 no. 287 ln. 7.
71 See discussion in Donbaz and Stolper, "Gleanings," 86 and Pearce, "*sēpiru*," 358 n. 7.
72 SAA 13 no. 127 ln. 13 refers to gold that is *ina nakkante bīt unqi* "in the treasury, the/a house of the seal." Notably, the book of Tobit also calls Ahiqar an "accountant" using the Persian loanword, המרכל.
73 Moore, "Persian," 51–52.

4Q196 frag. 2.7–8[74]
[ʾAḥî]ʿqar my brother¹ was ʿthe chiefʾ cupʿbearʾer and the chief of the seal(-bearer)s, ʿaccouʾntant [and] ʿexʾchequer before ʾEsar(a)ḥerîb, king of ʾAtûr. And ʾEsar(a)ḥiddôn appointed him deputy to him.

[אחי]ʾקר אחיʾ הוה ʾרבʾ שʾקʾה ורב עזקן ʾהמʾרכל
[ו]ʾשʾיזפן קדם אסרחריב מלך אתור ואשלטה
אסרחדון תנין לה

The passage refers to Ahiqar as holding the well-known Neo-Assyrian courtly title "chief cupbearer" (Akk. *rab šaqê*) but also the title "chief of the seals" (Akk. *rab unqāti*), which as noted above, is so far only attested in Late-Babylonian texts. It then ascribes him the Persian period title "accountant" (Old Per. *hamāra-kara*).[75] He also is given the title "exchequer," the origin of which is uncertain; the term is so far only attested in this reference.[76] Lastly, while תנין means in its most simplistic form "second," I interpret it as a calque on Akkadian ^{lu_2}2 (^{lu_2}*šanû*), an official title known in Neo-Assyrian and later texts meaning deputy (CAD Š1 397).

In view of the evidence from the Aramaic book of Tobit one may propose one of two reasonable reconstructions for a title given to Ahiqar in the broken context of Ahiq. plate D.i.12: רב [עז]קה "chief [se]al (bearer)" or רב [ש]קה "chief [cu]p bearer." He is furthermore referred to as "a counselor of Assyria" יעט אתור (discussed below), these titles, combined with the manifold evidence from Syriac (as architect) and from the book of Tobit, portray him as a man of many scribal traits, which were reinterpreted in various scribal contexts between Neo-Babylonian and Persian periods, and which may have stemmed from Neo-Assyrian references. Hence, the Elephantine manuscript ascribes him the literary title ספרא חכימא as a catch-all for his varied and evolving scribal personas. The Elephantine manuscript's emphasis on his role in the seal(-bearer's) house, in particular, marks it as a recension that uses Neo-Babylonian professional imagery known at the time the Persian period copy was made. The results, then, are evolving scribal allusions that reflect a variety of scribal cultures represented between the Neo-Assyrian and Persian periods.

---

74 I have collated the manuscript.
75 Eilers, *Iranische*, 43–59; Tavernier, *Iranica*, 424. Contra Dalley, "Assyrian," 154 who claims that there are no "anachronisms that might point to a post-Assyrian date of composition" for Tobit's account of Ahiqar.
76 See Schmitt, "Achikar-Notiz," 113. The best solution is to either see it as of Persian origin, or as a Š stem of the Semitic root יזף/י "to borrow;" see *waṣābu* in Akkadian.

2.4 Scribal Succession and Retirement (A.7–B.6)

The tale's second scene focuses on two plot points: the succession of the royal scribe and his retirement. Lines in this scene are badly damaged, but traces indicated that the scene opens with references to Esarhaddon ([לאס]רחאדן; A.7) and to Assyria (אתור; A.8). Ahiqar's response, [... אחר אנ]ה "Then I[...]" (A.8), follows these broken lines. At the start of this scene in the Syriac manuscripts, the king asks Ahiqar who will replace him when Ahiqar becomes old and dies (Camb. Cod. Add 2020 1.12; Graffin 2.3). Ahiqar explains to the king that he had adopted and has trained Nadin. He then presents Nadin to the king, and the king approves the appointment. The same general sequence of events unfolds in the broken lines of the Elephantine manuscript (A.7–14), but the surviving details of the scene describe a rigorous interview process not found in the Syriac manuscripts:

Ahiq. Plate A.7–14

L[...]H (belonging) to ʾEs[araḥʾiddin, the king of ʾAtûr. And he said ... The king of] ʾAtûr(./?) Then I[...] my son [the one named Nadin ...] I have taught him wisdom, and [I have giv]en good (things) [to him (so that) I|you may appoint him at] the [Ga]te of the Pa[l]ace with[...] his ⌈hi⌉gh ranking courtiers. I presented him before ʾEsaraḥʾiddin, the k⌈ing of ʾAtû⌉r. And he taught him [wise] w[ords... th]at he asked him. Then ʾEsaraḥʾiddin the king of ʾAtûr loved him and said, "The favor of Ša[maš is upon you.[77] You have been/become] the

ל[...]ה[78] לאס[רחאדנ מלכ אתור ...[79] מלכ] אתור
אחר אנ[ה ...]ברי[נדנ שמה ...] וחכמתה וטבתא
י[הבת לה {ת|א}קימה בב[ב הי]כ[לא עמ] [...]
ונ⌈גדוהי קרבתה קדמ אסרחאדנ מ⌉לכ אתו⌈ר[80]
וחכמה מ[לנ חכימינ ...[81] ז]⌈י שאלה אחר רחמה
אסרחאדנ מלכ אתור ואמר חינ ש[מש עלכ]⌈הוית
[ס]⌈פרא חכימא יעט אתור כלה זי הקימ לברה ...[82]

---

[77] Alternatively, "By the life of Ša[maš!]"
[78] This may be a reference to the Esarhaddon's interrogation, and if so, Graffin 2.3 may be instructive as a reconstruction: ܫܘܐܠܐ ܕܡܠܟܐ ܣܪܚܕܘܡ "the question of the king, Sarḥaddôm." Thus perhaps restore:

ל[∘∘∘ אחר שאל הו]ה לאס[רחאדנ מלכ אתור ואמר לי ...]

"L[∘∘∘ Then] ʾEs[araḥʾiddin, the king of ʾAtûr, had a question, and said to me ...]"
[79] Compare the equivalent scene in Camb. Cod. Add. 2020 1.13–14 where Ahiqar's death is on the horizon. The Aramaic line may have ended:

[כזי תמות למ למנ יעט]

[(said to me,) "When you die, who will counsel ([the king of] ʾAtûr)?"
Compare AP's reconstruction (pp. 212, 220):

[ומן יהוה]ל[ספר וצבית עזקת]ה לאס[רחאדן מלכא כזי אנה הוית לשנחאריב מלך] אתור

["and who shall be scribe and bearer of the sea]l to Es[arhaddon the king, as I was to Sennacherib, king of] Assyria?"

wise [s]cribe, counselor of all of ?Atûr who
appointed his son...

Before confirming the appointment, the king appears to interrogate Nadin by asking questions. Fortunately for Ahiqar, Nadin answers all of the king's questions, and the king "loved him" (רחמה; A.11).[83] This exchange suggests that royal scribes did not have full control over the appointment of their replacements. In this scene, the king, whether qualified or not, served as a check and balance to nepotism, which if left uncontrolled could turn disastrous for the monarchy. In this context the informed ancient reader may even have on his mind the failure among Sennacherib's counselors, some of whom assassinated him. The interview in this case serves a literary function by which it establishes the authority of the king in the story, but it also resembles the actual practices of Neo-Assyrian kings. Some Neo-Assyrian kings claimed to be versed in scholarly material, such as Ashurbanipal who prided himself in his ability to read and write,[84] and in so doing, would have become a formidable interviewer of new scribes.[85] Generally, however, kings in this period relied on the expert counsel of

---

80 Graffin 2.5 is strikingly similar to the line found here. It reads:

ܐܝܟ ܕܐܘܒܠܬ ܠܢܕܢ ܒܪܝ, ܠܘܬ ܡܠܟܐ ܣܪܚܕܘܡ ܐܥܠܬܗ ܩܕܡܘܗܝ,

So I brought Nadan, my son, to king Sarḥaddôm, and I presented him before him

81 Perhaps continue the Restoration as:

[וענן טב לכל]

[*And he responded well to everything*]

82 Perhaps חלפה "his replacement" follows. Compare Sachau 162 fol. 87a ln. 1:

ܘܢܩܘܡ ܒܕܘܟܬܟ

"and (Nadan) can stand in your place."

83 No parallel remark is found in the Syriac manuscripts, but the king's response is reminiscent of that known from Neo-Assyrian courtly realia. Consider, *annurig šarru bēlī râmu ša Nineva ana nāši uktallim ana rēšī mā mārkunu bilâni ina pānīya līzzizu Urad-Gula mārīya šū issêšunu-ma ina pān šarri bēlīya līziz anīnu ina nāšī-ma gabbu lū hadiāni nirqud šarri bēlī nikrub* "Now, the king, my lord, has displayed his love for Nineveh to the people, (when) he said to the magistrates: 'Bring your sons to stand before me!' Urad-Gula is my son; he too should stay with them in the presence of the king, my lord. We should, with all the people, be glad. Let us dance and bless the king, my lord!" (SAA 10 no. 226 r. 6–13).

84 Charpin, *Reading*, 54–61; Zamazalová, "Education," 318–320.

85 Postgate, *Bronze*, 333 discuss a similar phenomenon that he finds in Middle Assyrian Scribal culture. He claims, "Sons following their fathers in their professions is hardly a surprise in any early society, but it need not mean that they technically inherited an appointment... Some nepotism was surely practiced, but we should not assume a son had a claim to succeed his father which was strong enough to override the wishes of the king or of the state administrators more generally." Similar evidence is found in SAA 10 no. 175 (Parpola, *LAS*, no. 113), a letter from one scholar requesting that the king question the report of another scholar, but in this

their scholars,[86] and the text explicitly refers to Ahiqar as "the wise [s]cribe (who) counsels all of Assyria" [ס]פרא חכימא יעט אתור כלה (A.12). In the context of the Story of Ahiqar, the interview is a scribal performance designed to impress the king. Even though a king may have been knowledgeable of scholarly matters, he was not an expert. Therefore, the king's interview was an evaluation of whether the interviewee met the king's preferences.

The conditions of royal scribal employment are portrayed as fickle and stressful both in the Story of Ahiqar and in the surviving historical evidence, such as the previously cited letter from Urad-Gula (SAA 10 no. 294). In SAA 10 no. 294, Urad-Gula feigns a dumfounded response to the unfair employment (from his point of view) of an Ekallate exorcist who takes his position. Urad-Gula claims that the king had mistreated him after he had served the king faithfully since the king was a crown prince (ll. r. 16–17). Urad-Gula felt entitled to a position on the grounds that he held seniority. Although the letter is one-sided, it can be read as a royal scholar excused without cause. In reality, the king may have found the service of another scholar to be more to his liking, particularly since Urad-Gula had already disappointed the king in an earlier instance. Nepotism attempts to insulate a volatile scribe from dismissal and in the case of Urad-Gula, his father Adad-šuma-uṣur helped him to acquire his position and on occasion advocated for Urad-Gula to keep it (SAA 10 nos. 224, 226–228).[87] Likewise, in the Story of Ahiqar nepotism is the means by which Nadin receives an interview with the king which in turn leads to his appointment. In this scene one can infer that Ahiqar is close to the king and able to persuade him, and this inference is confirmed later in the tale when Ahiqar explicitly describes himself as the king's "acquaintance" (כמנדע; D.i.5). This later reference, which occurs while Ahiqar and Nabûsumiskun are colluding in an act of disobedience to the king, illustrates the social value of close relationships, especially with the king, for scholars working in the royal court. They can use these relationships to leverage power in their family's, their associates', or their own favor. It seems that the Story of Ahiqar accurately depicts how scribes were hired and the condi-

---

case the scholar in question holds an appointment and is not undergoing an interview, but rather a review.

86 See Radner, "Decision-Making," 363. In addition, SAA 4 nos. 149–173 are formulaic "appointment queries" in which a scholar performs a divinatory ritual in order to determine if a new hire will be faithful to Esarhaddon and not instigate rebellion. The scholars interpreting such queries had the advantage of persuading the king's decision for or against the new hire.
87 Parpola, "retroterra," 102–103 and Parpola, "Forlorn," 270. In SAA 10 no. 294, Urad-Gula claims to be old (ln. r. 30), and that his father had partitioned his land between Urad-Gula and his brother (ll. r. 21–22).

tions of their employment in the Neo-Assyrian period and that this was understandable to those reading the text in the Persian period.

As the story unfolds, a literary reversal inverts the professional expectation of nepotism, and instead of Nadin appealing to his adoptive father for professional recommendation, he accuses Ahiqar of treason. Nadin's actions are owed to the fact that he was appointed to replace (√חלף) Ahiqar who remained a threat to Nadin's job so long as Ahiqar was alive. This is significantly different than Urad-Gula's situation because he was an exorcist in a lower position than his father Adad-šuma-uṣur, the king's exorcist.[88] Thus, the root of the conflict in the tale lies in Ahiqar's decision to retire rather than to serve his term until he died. This decision results in two scribes holding the same position, and thus narrative conflict is seeded.

The manuscript's first column ends with Nadin's interview and appointment, and the next column begins with Ahiqar speaking to Esarhaddon. Ahiqar asks that Nadin take his position immediately, so that Ahiqar may retire.[89] When the king had previously expressed his concern about Ahiqar's age, he believed that Ahiqar was nearing death, at least in the parallel episode in a Syriac manuscript:

Camb. Cod. Add. 2020 1.13
He can depart (from) life.   ܡܚܘ ܢܥܢܐ ܠܢܦܫ

The text is broken in the Elephantine manuscript, but it is clear that after the king approves Nadin's appointment and while the king is in a good mood, Ahiqar requests his retirement in the Aramaic. Ahiqar says:

Ahiq. Plate A.14–B.2
When I s⌜aw⌝ (that) the face of ⌜ʾ⌝Esaraḥ⌜ʾ⌝iddin, king of ⌜ʾ⌝Atûr, was delighted, I responded and [said, "My lord, you know I have served]⌜you (and) I have⌝ [ser]v⌜ed⌝ [Šennaḥ]a⌜ʾ⌝rîb, the [ki]n[g], your father [w]ho reigned[before you.] (Now) I am old. I will be unable to work at the Gate of the P⌜a⌝lace.[. . . In]⌜deed⌝, the one named Nadin, my son is grown. He can replace me as [the] scribe."

... כזי ח⌜זי⌝ת אנפי אסרחאדן מלך אתור טבן ענית ו]אמרת מראי אנת ידע אנה פלחת ל[⌜י⌝כ אנה⌝ [פ]⌜ל⌝י⌝חת⌝ ל[⌜ש⌝נח[⌝אריב [מ]⌜ל⌝[כ]⌜א⌝ אבוכ [ז]⌜י⌝ מלך הו]ה קדמתכ[⁹⁰ שב אנה לא אכהל למפלח בבב ה⌜י⌝כלא[...] [⌜ה⌝]⌜א⌝ נדן שמה ברי רבא והו יחלף לי ספר[א ...]

---

88 Parpola, SAA 10, xxvi.
89 Here Grelot, *Documents*, 434–447 inserts the maxims between Ahiq. plates A and B.
90 *TAD* following *AP* restores an illegible sixteenth line on Ahiq. plate A, but this is impossible given the physical limits of the manuscript.

In this exchange, Ahiqar claims to have been too old to perform his scribal work at the Palace Gate. Many large city gates in Mesopotamian and Syrian settlements contained offices were scribal activity occurred, and the Palace Gate was one of the foremost bureaus of scribal influence due to its proximity to the king.[91] The discussion between the king and Ahiqar alludes to, firstly, the notion that age was a significant concern among ancient scholars. Ahiqar cites his future inability to perform his work (B.1) and makes no mention of his death. Thus he wishes to leave his post rather than work until he dies. Neo-Assyrian scholarly letters echo Ahiqar's worry, but portray scholars working through their old age. For instance, while having significant debt and no son, Urad-Gula pleads to the king to reinstate him because he is old and has no one to provide for him (SAA 10 no. 294 ln. r. 30).[92]

There is little to no evidence that scribes retired in Mesopotamia, and it appears that they never forsook their official title. The case of Urad-Gula illustrates how a king my decide to no longer utilize a scribe's services, but the writer still sees himself as an exorcist, who is unemployed.[93] The evidence suggests that Urad-Gula would hold his title for life. In the letter from the old astrologer Marduk-šapik-zeri (SAA 10 no. 160), he also explicitly states his intention to work in the king's service until he dies. This scholar is deeply concerned about his ability to continue his work as an employee, and from his perspective, retirement is not an option. He explicitly states that he would rather die than not fulfill his service to the king (SAA 10 no. 160 ll. 32–33). The notion that a royal scribe held his title for life and that there was an expectation that he works until he dies can also be found in the literary tale of the Underworld Vision of an Assyrian Prince (SAA 3 no. 32), in which the scribal protagonist learns by the end of that tale that a divine ritual had dictated his position. This scribe, who held his father's

---

91 In the Neo-Assyrian sources the elliptical expression *ēkallu* "Palace" (for *bāb ēkalli*) is used to refer to these bureaus and residences (e.g., SAA 10 no. 7) in the Palace Gate, but the tradition of Palace scribes is represented in the richest surviving archival data from even the second millennium BCE (e.g., Postgate, *Bronze*, 348–349). The Ahiqar narrative uses two Aramaic terms gate "gate": בב (A.9; B.1, 16) and תרע (C.13). For Kottsieper, "Aramaic," 122 this difference in word choice supports his attempt to rearrange the order of the manuscript, but conservatively interpreted, it is simply a sign of two Aramaic minds interacting in the manuscript history of the tale, one that prefers the word בב, which is a loanword from Akkadian *bābu*, versus one that prefers the native Northwest Semitic form תרע.
92 See Parpola's translation, "[Also], I am [50?] years (already) and they say: 'Once you have reached old age, who will support you?'" (SAA 10 no. 294 ln. r. 30).
93 This is implied in the letter on the basis that Urad-Gula still views himself as an exorcist capable of working for the king (see SAA 10 no. 294 ll. r. 16–17).

post (SAA 3 no. 32 ln. r. 33), comes to a revelation. The text states, "That scribe... spoke to himself: 'Let me always carry out my actions as [Nergal] has ordered!' He went and repeated it to the palace, saying: 'Let this be my expiation!'" (SAA 3 no. 32 ln. r. 35).[94] This scribe learned not to question the professional status that fate dictated to him.[95] The letters of Urad-Gula and Marduk-šapik-zeri as well as the Underworld Vision of an Assyrian Prince, demonstrate the social expectation that dynastic scribal positions in the royal court were titles held until death and that a scribe was expected to work until that time. Furthermore, when he did not have work due to the king's decision, as in the case of Urad-Gula, or because he left his post as depicted in the Underworld Vision of the Assyrian Prince, terrible circumstances would befall him. As the Story of Ahiqar unfolds, the same motif plays out because all of Ahiqar's problems begin with his decision to retire.

Ahiqar's request to retire and the king's approval of Nadin creates the circumstances in which the plot's conflict develops. Nadin is able to turn on his teacher in the next scene only because Ahiqar is absent from his post. Similar to Urad-Gula's disdain for the Ekallate exorcist who held his same position, so too Nadin seeks to eliminate his competitor. A motif of dynastic competition over the same position was foreshadowed in the plot when it placed dynastic succession adjacent to scribal succession early in the narrative (A.3–4). It created a clear duality: there can be only one king, so there can be only one scribe. Furthermore, like the scribe in the Underworld Vision of an Assyrian Prince, Ahiqar takes it upon himself to make a decision about his career. In so doing, he violates not only an expected social norm, but also his own teaching to Nadin in which he states "that it is not in a m[a]n's ability to lift his feet or to set them down with[out (the) gods (...). For it is not in your hands (to) lift your foot (or) to set it down."[96] The reader is left asking: who is more to blame for the conflict, Ahiqar or Nadin? This question will be addressed further in chapter four.

---

94 Translation by Livingstone, SAA 3 no. 32. In this literary context "my expiation" (*namburbîya*) means "to learn a moral from an ominous/numinous experience that causes one to change his ways." For the meaning of *namburbî* in general see Caplice, *Akkadian*, 7 and Veldhuis, "Interpreting," 145–154.
95 See discussion above and divinatory queries for professional courtier appointments in SAA 4 nos. 149–173.
96 From F.i.12–13: ‏[אלהין די]בלע מן ומנחתותהם רגלהם א[ש]מנ אנשא בידי לא כי‎. Scholars generally agree on the reconstruction of אלהין (see Weigl, *aramäischen*, 418 n. 117). Despite this, one must be careful not to over emphasize this as a theodicy, as Bledsoe has done ("Wisdom," 346). That said, he is correct that the duplication of the point and shift in person is striking (162 n. 188),

Now having discussed the major plot elements in this scene, final comments about the scene's scribal and courtly terminology can be made. First, while Ahiqar's official title is either "the wise scribe" (ספרא חכימא) or "the seal-bearer" (רב עזקה]). Esarhaddon calls Ahiqar "the wise scribe (who) counsels all of Assyria" [ס]פרא חכימא יעט אתור כלה (A.12), and later the king and Nabûsumiskun will claim that "upon his counsel (עטתה) and his words all of Assyria had relied" (B.12; C.12; D.i.7–8, 12–13). Nabûsumiskun also refers to him as "the master of good counsel" (בעל עטתא טבתא; C.11). Elsewhere, Ahiqar takes pride in his own counsel when he explains to Nabûsumiskun that the king will seek it in the future (D.i.5). As Ahiqar's literary foil, Nabûsumiskun is also seen as giving good counsel (D.i.9). It is clear that the concept of counseling plays a significant role in the plot and that the tale's two high-ranking royal personnel, Ahiqar and Nabûsumiskun, are capable of giving it.

The Story of Ahiqar is the oldest datable occurrence of the term יעט "counselor" in Aramaic, and it does not appear in other Elephantine manuscripts. Outside of Elephantine, it is found in Ezra 7:14 where it appears in the context of a letter, supposedly from Artaxerxes to Ezra, that explains that the king and "his seven counsellors" (שִׁבְעַת יָעֲטֹהִי; Ezra 7:14) have sent Ezra to inquire about the status of Judea. Clearly, in this context the counselors are courtiers, and the term could be construed as an official title. In the Story of Ahiqar, however, "counselor" is a qualitative attribution of high-ranking royal personnel. Furthermore, the pairing of the noun "counsel" with "words" in the Story of Ahiqar calls to mind Mesopotamian instructional texts, such as Šimâ Milka, for which counsel (*milku*) comes in the form of wise sayings.[97] As "the wise scribe," Ahiqar claims, in his own proud and hyperbolic autobiographical style, to supply the most consequential counsel for the kingdom.

Another courtly term appears in line 10, which begins with the legible word נגדוהי followed by the sentence, קרבתה קדם אסרחאדן "I presented him before ʾEsaraḥʾiddin." The end of the previous line is broken, so the context is difficult to explain. The term נגדוהי appears to be a nominal form, or at least a substantive, from a participle functioning as a noun.[98] The term is commonly interpreted as a

---

and so too is his more general observation that it is productive to study the narrative and the thematic content of the maxims together rather than in isolation.
97 E.g., Šimâ Milka ll. 1–7. See note above and Parpola, *LAS*, p. 474.
98 Late Biblical Hebrew uses the term נָגִיד to refer to a type of leader, the rank or status of which seems confused, at least in the books of Chronicles. This late Hebrew term matches the nominal form (*qatīl*) which may derive from an Aramaic passive participle (Joüon §88b and 96D.b). But in Aramaic and Syriac the cognate appears in the *nomina agentis* (Nöldeke, *Syriac*, §107), נָגוֹד and ܢܳܓܽܘܕܳܐ.

type of "officer," "overseer," or "commander."⁹⁹ It appears in at least one Old Aramaic text from Sefire (*KAI* 224) where its reading is contested—whether to read נגד or נגר,¹⁰⁰ but must mean some type of "officer." Among the Elephantine papyri published in *TAD*, it appears in this broken context in the Story of Ahiqar and in a broken context in the letter that Adon, king of Ekron, sent to Pharaoh (*TAD* A1 8).¹⁰¹ In the Story of Ahiqar, the term has a masculine singular suffix -והי attached to a masculine plural noun. Since only the king possesses "officials," one should consider restoring מלכא in the preceding lacuna (ll. 9–10).

There is no way to identify the term's exact social meaning in this broken context, but comparative evidence suggests that it is a reference to high-ranking scribal courtiers among whom works the "wise scribe" or seal-bearer. Evidence for this comes from its use in the Sefire inscription (*KAI* 224), part of which includes a threat by the king against a future attempted coup. The term appears in the apodosis of a conditional clause, which reads:

KAI 224 ll. 9–11

If one of my brothers, someone from the house of my father, one of my sons, one of my NGD, one of my officials, one of the people under my authority, or one of my enemies seeks my head.	הן מן חד אחי או מן בית אבי או מן חד בני או מן חד נגדי או מן [פ]קדי או מן חד עמיא זי בידי או מן חד שנאי ויבעה ראשי

Clearly this is a list of professional ranks and social classes. The first in the list who are not of royal lineage are the נגדין. If the term has the same meaning in the Story of Ahiqar, then it refers to a group of courtiers nearest to the king. Fitzmyer translates the term in *KAI* 224 as "officers" or "military commanders," and claims that it is a "position ... among the royal princes and the 'officials.'"¹⁰² Perhaps more accurately they are placed between the princes (בני) and the officials ([פ]קיד) in this list. Thus, the נגדין are best described as high ranking courti-

---

99 See *DNWSI*, 714.
100 The CAL is decisive, referring to נגד as a "minor ruler, leader" ("ngd, ngdʔ n.m. #2" with the added note "hardly carpenters!"), but compare the note on article "ngr, ngrʔ n.m. #3" (accessed 12FEB2021). The history of various readings is more complex. See the various citations in *DNWSI* 713–4 ("ngd3") and 715 ("ngr2"). By comparison see Younger, *Political*, 61, who prefers נגר "herald," but this is likely incorrect. As of now, it seems coincidence that the so-called title *nāgir ekalli* "palace herald" was used during the Neo-Assyrian period. This title is not attested syllabically, but based on the logogram NIGIR (Mattila, *King's Magnates*, 29–44 esp. 29 n. 1).
101 In addition to other references listed in Schwiderski, *Inschriften*, see Lozachmeur, *Collection*, nos. 94, X18, and esp. 195.
102 Fitzmyer, *Sefire*, 151–152.

ers, whether their role is military in nature is yet to be determined.¹⁰³ The Assyrian court was known to have a variety of positions as the surviving lists of royal courtiers demonstrate (SAA 7 nos. 1–7), but there is no agreed upon Akkadian cognate for the נגדין. So, the rank of נגדין appears to be a distinctly Aramaic category, and from the Story of Ahiqar it can be surmised that among them worked "the wise scribe," at least in this tale.

2.5 Scribal Conspiracy and Defamation (B.6–14)

At the end of the previous scene, Ahiqar leaves the royal court and goes to his home (B.6). He then recounts how Nadin libeled him. The text is broken at key points in the scene and is missing details, such as why Ahiqar believes Nadin acted treacherously (ln. 8) and the means by which Nadin defames his uncle (ln. 9). In the Syriac manuscripts, as well as in the Life of Aesop, the wicked student betrays his teacher by forging treasonous letters.¹⁰⁴ Forging documents was a cunning, yet criminal, scribal offense in antiquity, and since Ahiqar, and subsequently Nadin, were the king's seal-bearers, they were capable of causing severe damage to the kingdom, as Esarhaddon acknowledges in the next scene (C.5). Forgery was a realistic concern in the Neo-Assyrian period, and one letter alludes to the meticulous inspection of seal impressions in order to identify a forged document (SAA 15 no. 125). In view of the fact that Ahiqar is the king's seal-bearer, that all surviving manuscripts and related works of the tale refer to

---

103 Note the discussion in Hasel, *TDOT* 9:188–9. The semantic complexity of the similar Hebrew term נָגִיד, which appears frequently though not exclusively in later biblical Hebrew texts is not instructive for this early understanding of the term in the Sefire inscription or in the Story of Ahiqar. But the rejection of the meaning "prince" (*TDOT* 9:196) divorces the term from an appellative given to a person of royal lineage, and thereby agrees in a general sense with the Aramaic meaning found here.

104 The Ethiopic version differs from the Syriac in that it (1) only contains one letter to a foreign king, Pharaoh. The letter to "the king of Persia and Elam" had to be deleted since Ahiqar is re-contextualized in the Persian, rather than Assyrian, court. (2) The Ethiopic reverses the order of the letters. In Syriac, Nadin forges letters to (a) the king of Persia and Elam, (b) Pharaoh, and finally to Ahiqar (on behalf of Esarhaddon). Since the king of Persia originally appeared first and since the Ethiopic setting is the Persian court, the writer of the Ethiopic recension put the letter to Ahiqar on behalf of the Persian king first--in place of the letter to the Persian and Elamite king, who is construed as the foreigner in the Syriac recension. Even the deviant Armenian recension contains letters. And so too does the Life of Aesop, in which Aesop's son "forged a letter" (c. xxiv in Charles, *APOT*, 780).

forged letters, and that the forgery of seals was meticulously monitored in Mesopotamia. I tentatively reconstruct the section as:

Ahiq. Plate B.9–11
My [ne]ʳphʳew, whom I reared, contrived [evil] against [me in his heart. And he wrote a letter as though it were from my mouth and he said, "O my king,] ʾA[ḥîqar] has ʳinʳ[sulted us! He wrote that letter to your enemy in order to make war against you like that which was made] against Šennaḥe[rî]b the king, your [fa]ther."

[בר א]ʳחʳתי זי אנה רבית עשת על[י בישתא בלבה וכתב אגרת מן פומי ואמר מלכי] קרציא [ילי]ן [אכל א]חיקר כתב אגרתא זך לבעלדבבך למעבד קרב לך כזי עביד] לשנחא[רי]ב מלכא אבוך

All other surviving manuscripts that contain this scene claim that Nadin forged letters to trap Ahiqar. Even in the Life of Aesop a letter is the instrument that evokes the king's ire. The scribal context of the tale; the historical realities of treason in the Neo-Assyrian empire, which required a traitor to sign an oath (see *KAI* 233); and the scribal features of this narrative, impels one to restore a reference to written documentation that Nadin brought to the king as evidence of Ahiqar's alleged treason.

In this passage, the undisputable letters אכל have been a crux for interpreters. No such comparable word is found in the Syriac scenes, and so far, reconstructions and translations have been unsatisfactory.[105] I have adopted to restore the Aramaic idiom, אכל קרצ(י)א "to eat the morsel(s) (of another)" which means "to insult or denounce" (see MT Dan 3:8; 6:25),[106] and the cognate of which in Akkadian *karšī akālu* is well attested (CAD K 222–3). Furthermore, this reconstruction fits the break. As for the reconstruction of [עשת על[י בישתא בלבה, this is conceptually paralleled in the Syriac manuscripts.

The relevant passage in Camb. Cod. Add. 2020 is expansive, and includes two letters: one to the king of Persia and Elam, which appears to be the older scene in the tale, and another to Pharaoh, which is the plot element the story

---

105 Kottsieper, "Aramaic," 122–3, claims that this section does not tell of Nadin's plot against Ahiqar. Presumably, this decision is made to justify his idiosyncratic arrangement of the plates, but if Ahiq. plate C follows Ahiq. plate B, as most others hold, then the latter half of Ahiq. plate B must have contained Nadin's act of defamation against Ahiqar. Presumably, Kottsieper has the Syriac in mind when he notes, "[Ahiqar] allowed [Nadin] 'to eat' his teaching (II 10 [25])" (123). But the Syriac is significantly different, not referring to "eating" but to the satisfaction had from bread and water: ܐܬܦܢܝ̈ ܐܠܦܗ ܡܠܦܢܐ ܡܝ̈ܐ ܘܠܚܡܐ ܡܢ "I satisfied him (with) instruction as (with) bread and water" (Camb. Cod. Add. 2020 1.15 ≈ Graffin 2.7).
106 The abbreviated form without אכל is known from *TAD* D20 2.5.

will follow.¹⁰⁷ The context immediately before the insertion of the letters serves as grounds for reconstructing the Elephantine manuscript.¹⁰⁸ It reads:

Camb. Cod. Add. 2020 3.7
For then Nadan my son, when he heard, became angry and went to the Gate of the King. And he contrived evil in his heart. So he sat down (and) wrote two letters to two kings, enemies of Sanḥerîb my lord.

ܟܕ ܥܟܕ ܕܝܢ ܢܕܢ ܒܪܝ ܐܝܟ ܕܫܡܥ ܗܠܝܢ ܐܙܠ ܠܬܪܥܐ ܕܡܠܟܐ. ܘܒܐܫܬܐ ܐܬܡܠܟ ܒܠܒܗ. ܘܝܬܒ ܘܟܬܒ ܐܓܪ̈ܬܐ ܬܪ̈ܬܝܢ ܠܬܪܝܢ ܡܠܟܝܢ ܕܠܕܒܒܘܗܝ, ܕܣܢܚܪܝܒ ܡܪܝ,

The motive for Nadin's betrayal is described in a short scene in the Syriac manuscripts that characterizes Nadin as abusive, ungrateful, and jealous, so in turn Ahiqar complains to the king.¹⁰⁹ There is not enough room in the Elephantine manuscript to include these details, but since the event is told by the victim's—Ahiqar's—firsthand autobiographical account it is nonetheless scandalizing in the Elephantine manuscript.¹¹⁰ In the moment that Ahiqar remembers Nadin's "treachery" (√בדא, B.14), he emotionally responds by disowning the son that he had longed to have. He refers to Nadin at this point as "my son, who is not my son" (ברי זי לא ברי, B.14).

Ungrateful or errant sons who do not heed the wisdom of their fathers/teachers are well known in Mesopotamian literary sources, particularly wisdom literature. In the previously mentioned short folkloric tail preserved in a bilingual Sumerian-Akkadian tablet from the Neo-Assyrian period (K

---

107 Both letters ask the respective kings to come and take over Assyria (Camb. Cod. Add. 2020 3.7–9). The term "latter" in my statement does not necessarily mean the adaptation occurred in the Syriac; it may have occurred in an earlier Aramaic tradition.
108 The literary motivations for expanding narratives by inserting documents, particularly letters, is not yet well understood in the study of Semitic literatures, but for a similar phenomenon in Classical and Late Antique studies see Rosenmeyer, *Ancient*.
109 Immediately after the first lecture to Nadin in which Ahiqar dictates 75 instructional maxims for courtly service (Camb. Cod. Add. 2020), Nadin, in his new position, begins mistreating Ahiqar's property. In a short scene, Ahiqar turns to the king to secure his own command over his own property (i.e. to take back rights to his position), and at the same time Nadin witnesses Ahiqar speaking with Nadin's brother (perhaps a fellow student) Nabûzardan (Akk. *Nabû-zēru-iddina*; Camb. Cod. Add 2020 3.1–6). Nadin responds with envy over the idea that Ahiqar may try to bestow the office and its benefits on another.
110 Contra Bledsoe, "Wisdom," 116 which claims, "We (as processors of the narrative) can only know that Nadin fills the role of Opponent *after* having a basic understanding of the entire plot" (emphasis original).

4347+16161) is found a scholar who advises his king, becomes disgraced because the king ignores his advice, but is later rehabilitated.[111] The text reads:

(Lambert, *BWL*) K4347+16161 ii 50–63
Their gods have returned to the ruin. Clamor has entered the fallen house. (Where) the ingrate is tenant, the wise man does not reach old age, the wise scholar, whose wisdom his lord has not heeded. But any valuable (person) forgotten by his master, when a need arises for him (i.e. for his wisdom), he will be reinstated.[112]

ana <na>mê ilūšunu itūrū ana bīti nadî īterub ikkillum aššab raggu ul ulabbar ḫassu ummâna emqa ša nēmeqšu bēlšu la ḫassu u mamma aqra ša bēlšu imšûšu ibbašši ḫišiḫtašu-ma innaši rīssu[113]

In this folkloric tale the king is portrayed as the student, but the idea that a student does not heed his teacher's wisdom is felt in this scene in the Elephantine manuscript, and the Syriac tradition explicitly states that Nadin did not listen to Ahiqar's teachings; his own insolence becomes the motivation for his maltreatment of others, his jealousy, and his actions (Camb. Cod. Add. 2020 3.1, 6).

Again, it seems that scribal elements in the plot can be found in a variety of literary sources across the ages. The narrative motifs of students not listening to and betraying their teachers as well as situations in which a betrayer uses documentary evidence can be found as far back as the Old Babylonian period. There is now known the Old Babylonian bilingual composition that Andrew George calls The Scholars of Uruk in which a teacher reprimands a son for attempting to supplant him (CUSAS 10 no. 14). A contemporary text shows how family tensions between uncles and nephews was a literary trope. For instance, in the so-called Tribulations of Gimil-Marduk (CUSAS 10 no. 17) one finds a model court document in which a (great) nephew lays claim against his villainous (great) uncle and wins. The operative prop in the trail's verdict is the presence of a sealed tablet. This along with its focus on an uncle-nephew relationship calls to mind the letters of Nadin in the surviving Syriac manuscripts of the Story of Ahiqar. In the editio princeps George notes that "[t]he folklore motif of

---

111 The best surviving copy is from Ashurbanipal's library and was edited in Lambert, *BWL*, 239–250. A very damaged duplicate is known from the Nabû temple in Kalḫu ND 5497/23 published in CTN 4 202. A third tablet containing three similar proverbs is published in Frahm, "The Latest Sumerian Proverbs," 155–184. The text was consulted in the Late Babylonian period as is seen from commentaries that discuss some of the proverbs on the tablet (Frahm, " Latest," 168–181). Neither the duplicate nor the allusions to the tablet in other texts make reference to the section studied here.
112 This translation is loosely based on Reiner, "Etiological," 8.
113 The Sumerian version is partially broken.

the wicked uncle" was widespread and known in Egypt in the contemporary Middle Egyptian tale of Horus and Seth. George provides convincing comparisons between the narrative elements of Horus and Seth and the Tribulations of Gimil-Marduk (CUSAS 10, pp. 147–148). The Aramaic writer of Ahiqar draws on this timeless and international motif of a wicked uncle blended with that of an ungrateful son to produce the multiple meanings found in the Story of Ahiqar, meanings which rest on the use of scribal props, such as documentary evidence and letters.

On the surface, Ahiqar's emotional tone in the Elephantine manuscript paints Nadin as a villain and suggests that he did not use the wisdom that was taught to him (A.6) nor that which he had apparently proven himself capable of during his interview (A.10). The level of emotion in Ahiqar's response obscures the fact that Nadin is following his teacher's model and ethic in broad terms.[114] Because Ahiqar is still alive he has become a professional threat to Nadin, who replaced him. As the story unfolds (at least in the surviving editions and presumably in the lacuna of the Elephantine manuscript), the plot reveals that Nadin's failure was in his choice of victim, not in his actions; he chose a victim who had more resourcefulness and guile than he. Nadin had not anticipated that the old Ahiqar would survive political attack. Had Nadin learned from his teacher, however, he would have elevated his status at the expense of a lesser soul, in much the same way that Ahiqar conspires against an innocent eunuch later in the tale. For presumably a long time, Nadin's gambit paid off, and only an unforeseeable series of events would unravel his plans. So while the theme of rebellion is immediately felt in Nadin's actions—as Ahiqar describes them to us—Nadin may be seen as a tragic character trained and put in a position in which he must rebel. A cunning act was the only way in which Nadin could secure his position. Neo-Assyrian literary sources place great value in cunning trickery,[115] and had it not been for Ahiqar's derogatory tone, a learned ancient reader may have interpreted Nadin as the hero. To my knowledge, autobiographers do not fail in their own stories in antiquity, so although the end of the Elephantine manuscript's narrative is missing, Ahiqar is expected to prevail as he does in the surviving Syriac tradition.

---

114 In scenes such as this, the first-person narration functions as a type of propaganda. Compare the Darius Inscription, which is also composed in autobiographical narration. For a discussion of that text see Granerød, "Favour," 455–480, esp. 460.
115 See e.g., texts and discussions in George, "Ninurta-Pāqidāt's;" Gurney, "Tale;" Ellis, "New Fragment;" Foster, *Before*, 931–938.

2.6 The Consequences of a Scribe's Rebellion (C.1–8)

Nadin betrayed a relative and a professional colleague, but the details by which he betrayed Ahiqar are lost in the lacuna of Ahiq. plate B. Clues to his actions are found in the king's reaction to Nadin's words in Ahiq. plate C. In the first scene on Ahiq. plate C (ll. 1–8), the king indicates that Ahiqar "will damage the land" (יחבל מתא; ln. 5),[116] and the king takes offense. This suggests that Nadin betrayed Ahiqar by claiming that he committed some act of treason in Ahiq. plate B. One might surmise that, Nadin had turned Ahiqar into a rebel of the state. As with the variations on the theme of succession found in the first two scenes, the second two scenes depict variations on the theme of rebellion.

Treason was rampant in the Neo-Assyrian empire. Groups and regions that felt oppressed by the empire portrayed rebellion in a positive light, while kings admonished the practice.[117] Kings encouraged scribes to inform on other scribes who aligned themselves with known enemies of the state or engaged in sedition (e.g., SAA 16 no. 21). Sedition and threats of insurrection were so dire in the latter part of the Neo-Assyrian period that the queen grandmother, Zakutu, took up the cause and issued a treaty against rebels (SAA 2 no. 8).[118] The motifs of Ahiqar echo the stipulations of Zakutu's treaty,[119] and its final stipulation gave the right for associations of courtiers to turn on each other. It reads:

SAA 2 no. 8 ll. r. 18–27 (with Translation)[120]
And if you, hear and know that there are men instigating armed rebellion or foment-   *u šumma attunu tašammâni tuddâni mā ummānū* (ERIM.MEŠ) *mušamḫiṣṣūte mušad-*

---

116 As a rhetorical feature of the text, the writer uses a similar phrase when Nabûsumiskun explains how Nadin defamed Ahiqar, "He, whom you appointed at the Palace Gate, has damaged you" (זי הקימת בתרע היכלא הו חבלך, C.13). Furthermore, this may have been a literary trope in Egyptian Aramaic in this period. See the 4ᵗʰ century BCE text of the Shek Faḍl inscription אל חבל[י] מצרין "he mustn't damage Egypt" (*TAD* D23 9.6) and, although the date is not secure, MT Ezra 4:22 לְמָה יִשְׂגֵּא חֲבָלָא לְהַנְזָקַת מַלְכִין "why shall the damage increase, causing injury to kings?"
117 E.g., MT 2 Kgs 17 claims that the Israelite king Hoshea, whom Tiglath-Pileser III set on the throne of Samaria, revolted during the reign of Shalmaneser V. He sent envoys to King So of Egypt, which evoked the rage of Shalmaneser, who eventually exiled the land of Israel as a consequence for Hoshea's treason. For the Assyrian perspective on the event see RINAP 1 Tig-Pil III no. 42 ln. 17'.
118 After she lost her husband, Sennacherib, to assassination and saw threats plague her son Esarhaddon, she took a vocal and active stance against rebellion at the start of her grandson's, Ashurbanipal's, reign.
119 Parpola, "retroterra," 111 hypothesizes that Zakutu, an Aramean, inspired or sponsored the composition of the Story of Ahiqar.
120 Quarter brackets removed.

ing conspiracy in your midst, be they bearded (officials) or eunuchs or his brothers or of royal line of your brothers or friends or anyone in the entire nation—should you hear and [know] (this), you shall seize and [kill] them and bring them to Zakutu [his mother and to Assurbani]pal, [king of Assyria, your lord].

bibūte <ša> ina birtukkunu lū ina ša-ziqnī lū ina ša-rēsī (^{LÚ2}SAG.MEŠ) lū ina aḫḫīšu (PAB.MEŠ-ŠU₂) lū ina zēr šarri (NUMUN MAN) lū aḫḫīkunu (PAB.MEŠ-KU-NU) lū bēl (EN) ṭābtēkunu [lū] ina nīšī māti (UN.MEŠ KUR) gabbu tašammâni [tuddâni] lā taṣabbatāninni [lā tadukkāni ina] muḫḫi (UGU) ^{f}Zakūte [immīšu] ([AMA-ŠU₂]) [u ina muḫḫi (UGU) ^{m}Aššurban]ipal [šar māti Aššur] ([MAN KUR AŠ]) [bēlīkunu lā tubbal]ānin[ni]

It is noteworthy that "friends" (bēl ṭābtī) and "brothers" (aḫḫū) are emphasized in this edict. They call to mind Ahiqar's relationship with Nabûsumiskun, which was "like one with his brother" (כאיש עם אחוהי, D.i.1),[121] as well as the good things (טבתא) that Ahiqar was known for (C.11), which he gives to Nadin (A.9), and which he had hoped to receive in return (B.8).

Treason and rebellion were prominent themes in royal propaganda, such as in the Vassal Treaties of Esarhaddon (SAA 2 no. 6), and threats against the crown were an ongoing problem for the Neo-Babylonian and later Achaemenid rulers. Perhaps the most radical example of a state issued anti-treason publication is the Persian period autobiographical Darius Inscription from Behsitun, an Aramaic copy of which was discovered at Elephantine with the Story of Ahiqar. In it, Darius mentions king after king who revolted against him through various political schemes and collusion, including attempts at impersonation, which appears to have been a finely tuned act of conspiracy by the Persian period. Impersonation calls to mind both Nadin acting on behalf of Ahiqar and the eunuch standing in the place of Ahiqar. Other motifs from this inscription, such as political subversion and clandestine alliance with foreign states, can be found in the Story of Ahiqar. But in the Darius Inscription, unlike in Neo-Assyrian documents and unlike in the Story of Ahiqar, the king is portrayed as a prosecutor and pursuer of vigilantes, whereas in the earlier Neo-Assyrian period, the

---

121 The Syriac manuscripts refer to him as ܡܣܟܢܝ ܚܒܪܝ "the muškên, my colleague." Harris did not understand this title (Story, 112 n. 6, 114 n. 6). The term ܡܣܟܢ normally means "poor" in Syriac, but here it likely derives from its Akkadian cognate muškēnu which refers to a "commoner" in the king's service. The character's "poor" image serves a literary feature in the Syriac tradition as he becomes rich when Ahiqar bestows his reward on him (Camb. Cod. Add. 2020 7.23).

king's court were encouraged to pursue sedition on their own, just as Nadin does.¹²²

With the introduction of Nabûsumiskun in this scene, the text connects the motif of rebellion against the state to a well-known Neo-Assyrian insurrection. Nabu-šuma-iškun (Aram. Nabûsumiskun) was a historical figure whom the text uses as a literary foil for the dilemma that Ahiqar finds himself in. According to the highly publicized accounts of Sennacherib's eighth campaign, some¹²³ of the sons of Marduk-apla-iddina II (biblical Merodach-Baladan), the king of Babylon, joined forces with the Elamite king and rebelled against Assyria (RINAP 3/1 Senn no. 22 v 17–vi 35); Nabu-šuma-iškun was one of those rebellious sons. The text describes how all of the rebels were killed except for Nabu-šuma-iškun who was instead captured (RINAP 3/1 Senn no. 22 vi 24–35). His revolt may have been especially personal to Sennacherib because he may have been the chariot driver of the king and responsible for arresting criminals for high crimes (SAA 6 no. 57).¹²⁴ According to Parpola, Esarhaddon likely knew that Nabu-šuma-iškun even played a role in the assassination of Sennacherib.¹²⁵

Nabu-šuma-iškun also shared a name with a mid-eighth century king of Babylon who was a hero of the Arameans. At least two royal inscriptions of this Nabu-šuma-iškun survive (RIBo 6 Nabu-šuma-iškun nos. 1–2). The first of these texts is an account of his reign, which portrays him as a ruthless leader but also one who enriched the "Chaldeans and Arameans" and promoted their gods (iii 26', 42'). While he later becomes king (RIBo 6 Nabu-šuma-iškun no. 2 i 17), his successful exploits occurred while he was a "prince" (*rubû*; RIBo 6 Nabu-šuma-iškun no. 1 iii 32'–33').¹²⁶ Only a few decades after this first Nabu-šuma-iškun ruled Babylon, the second Nabu-šuma-iškun and son of Marduk-apla-iddina II

---

122 Even Esarhaddon claims to have sent men to kill rebels rather than portraying himself as the pursuer (RINAP 4 Esar no. 1 ii 40–64). Neo-Assyrian kings are typically only portrayed as pursuers when they are on a military campaign.

123 At least one son, Nabu-zer-kitti-lišir, appears to not have taken part in the rebellion. He is not mentioned in the texts of the eighth campaign and (later ?) gave an honorary gift to Sennacherib (RINAP 3/2 Senn no. 109).

124 Parpola, "retroterra," 106 has made this association. The text in reconstructed to read [*mukīl ap*]*pāti*.

125 Parpola, "retroterra," 106. Parpola cites SAA 18 no. 100 (ABL 1091) as evidence.

126 See also RINAP 3/2 Senn no. 213 ln. 33 which uses the term *rubûtu* "princely status" to refer to Maduk-alpa-idinna (the father of Nabu-šuma-iškun), whom Sennacherib established over Babylon but then vanquished.

becomes a well-publicized figure.¹²⁷ In this later era, Sennacherib identified Marduk-apla-iddina II the father of the latter Nabu-šuma-iškun as one of his rubûtu, that is "one holding princely status" (RINAP 3/2 Senn no. 213 ln. 33).¹²⁸ The evidence collected here suggests that the Aramaic text of the Story of Ahiqar may have merged the literary depictions of the two historical Nabu-šuma-iškun's, one who was known and admired by Arameans and the other who committed treason and lived.

The knowledge of literary and historical personas embedded in the name of Nabûsumiskun provides the groundwork for understanding the unique title, רביא, given to Nabûsumiskun in the Story of Ahiqar. The term רביא is curious because of its spelling with a yod; at first glance, one might expect it to be spelled רבא. Ungnad identified the term with Akkadian *rabû* "to be great."¹²⁹ Cowley followed this derivation without further explanation.¹³⁰ The first to reconsider this curious spelling in some detail was Kaufman, and his full discussion is worth repeating:

> *rabû*, "great"—The term GAL, usually in the plural GAL.MEŠ, is used in late Akkadian for "officers, officials" and is generally read *rabûti*, of which the singular would be *rabû*. This Akkadian term must be the origin of the strange form *rby*, "officer," in the Ahiqar narrative. On the other hand, the construct form *rab*, "chief," in Akkadian is almost certainly of Amorite origin. In OB it occurs only in the expression GAL.MAR.TU "chief of the Amorites." Later it is common in the western peripheral dialects and in Assyrian. Thus, the Heb. and Ar. term *raḇ* is a native West Semitic development.¹³¹

Kaufman appears to see רב as a bi-literal Amorite root, which is borrowed into Akkadian for specific job titles that indicate the "chief" of something. One might assume that it is either a homonym to the adjective רב, so distinguishing the noun from the substantive is difficult in earlier unvocalized texts. But the problem is even more complex than Kaufman presents because four different plural forms of words that refer to some type of "chief" or "official" are attested in Aramaic, and it is difficult to determine which derive from *raḇ*, which from *rabû*, and which may have undergone change within Aramaic regardless of

---

127 According to Ran Zadok, the insurrection lead by the eighth century Babylonian king, Nabu-šuma-iškun, "foreshadowed the approach of Marduk-apla-iddina II," whose son is the other Nabu-šuma-iškun discussed here ("Account," 265).
128 For a discussion of the titles of other members in this family see Beaulieu, "Ea-dayān," 109.
129 Ungnad, *Aramäische*, 65–66.
130 *AP*, 229 and Folmer, *Aramaic*, 223.
131 Kaufman, *Akkadian*, 87. Muraoka and Porten, *Grammar*, 377 follow this explanation.

whether an etymological loanword can be identified. The plural terms are attested as רבי (Ahiq. C.2), רבני (TAD B4 3.11), רברבנוהי (e.g., MT Dan 5:1), and רברבי (1Q20 ixx.24). All of these appear to refer to palace officials.[132] Suppletion must have occurred in the declension of this Aramaic noun (רב) in which the singular derives from Amorite *rab* while the plural רבני can be explained as either a loan from Akkadian *rabiānu* with a secondary plural by-form with the expected orthography רבי (< *rab*) or as an internal Aramaic development on the nominal pattern ending in -*ān*.[133] So the singular רב, plural רבניך* with a by-form רבי could have been used by analogy in a reduplicated pattern, thus producing the plural רברבנוהי and the by-form (a substantive from the adjective used in a technical nominal context) רברבי ($R_1aR_2R_1aR_2 < R_1aR_2$, here *rab*).

There are two peculiar things about רביא, which is Nabûsumiskun's title in the Story of Ahiqar, that do not match the spellings of רב "chief." First, the narrative attests to the use of the title רב "chief" without a final yod (D.i.12 and discussion above); this suggests that רבי(א) (see C.2) is a different title. Second, רביא is clearly a singular determined noun, but its yod makes it look as though it were plural. Hence Kaufman's attempt to derive it from Akkadian *rabû* (with a final long vowel) rather than Amorite *rab*. Historical and contextual evidence from the Story of Ahiqar suggests, however, that it may instead derive from Akkadian *rubû* (Assyrian *rubê*, logographically nun) "prince."

A vast bureaucratic network of provincial rulers and satellite states made up the Neo-Assyrian imperial union. At the top of this complex social hierarchy sat the "king of kings" (*šar šarri*) who was, at least in the time of Ashurbanipal, "the prince/ruler without rival" (*rubû lā šanān*; RIBo 6 Ash. no. 15 ln. 7). A "prince" (*rubû*) held a dynastic claim to a noble family. This included satellite states or vassals which the Neo-Assyrian empire managed. The lineage of these provincial leaders, who were called *rubû*, distinguished them in status from the (*bēl*) *pīḫāti* "provincial governors" who were not of noble birth.[134] The "princes"

---

132 The term רבני resembles Akkadian *rabiānu* "mayor," which in turn derives from *rabû*. It is unclear in context if the plural form רבי refers to "chiefs" (רב < *rab*) or "princes" (רבי < *rubê*).

133 While it is plausible that a nominal pattern may be applied to a third weak or biconsonantal root, one may expect a *yod* to appear as a third radical. See examples in Muraoka and Porten, *Grammar*, §19f, but if borrowed from Akk. *rabiānu* the third radical (Akk.) ʔ may have been construed as an ā and therefore not necessary in the Imperial Aramaic orthography. The issue remains undecided; see Kaufman, *Akkadian*, 128–9 and notes.

134 Imperial Aramaic uses *pīḫāti* "provincial governor" (פחה) as a loanword, even at Elephantine. See linguistic discussion in the literature noted by Kaufman, *Akkadian*, 82. For a text that is instructive in this regard because it contains many such Akkadian titles for Babylonian positions during Neo-Assyrian domination, see RIBo 6 Marduk-zakir-šumi no. 2. For a historical

of the Aramaic court were not the courtiers (נגדין), and the plural reference to רבי in C.2 makes this clear when Esarhaddon refers to Nabûsumiskun as ⁱחⁱד ⁱמנⁱ רבי אבי "one of the princes of my father" (C.2).[135] The evidence suggests that the Story of Ahiqar borrowed the term for "the prince" (רביא) from Assyrian *rubû/ê*.

There is no evidence that "a prince" was a scribal figure, and Nabûsumiskun serves no scribal function in the tale, even though he is the literary foil of Ahiqar. He was, however, a master of eunuchs, and eunuchs are frequently portrayed as scribal characters, as will be discussed in the next section.

2.7 The Collusion of Courtiers (C.8–D.i.15)

Up to this point, the tale has drawn on the motifs of dynastic royal succession, dynastic scribal succession, the rebellion of student and kin, and the rebellion of scholar and statesman. The final legible scene in the Elephantine manuscript is a long exchange between Ahiqar and Nabûsumiskun, the latter of whom is accompanied by two men whom the king appointed. Their objective is to find and kill Ahiqar. When Nabûsumiskun meets Ahiqar, he has an emotional reaction of grief. Ahiqar claims that Nabûsumiskun "tore ⁱhisⁱ cloⁱtheⁱs and lameⁱntⁱed" (הייללⁱ ⁱכⁱתⁱיⁱנⁱה בזע; C.10). Nabûsumiskun then explains that Nadin had acted treacherously (C.13). According to Ahiqar's first-person account, Nabûsumiskun knew that Ahiqar was innocent. Ahiqar responds with fear (C.14), and in order to preserve his life, Ahiqar conspires with Nabûsumiskun, who agrees to hide Ahiqar until the opportunity arises for him to reestablish his reputation (C.15–D.i.8). Nabûsumiskun then persuades the men with him to agree to the plan (D.i.8–13). He proposes that they kill a eunuch, who is Nabûsumiskun's servant, and present the body in Ahiqar's place (D.i.13–15).

Nabûsumiskun's initial emotional response suggests that his commitments were divided between loyalty to the king's orders and the social debt that he owed Ahiqar.[136] Ahiqar reminds Nabûsumiskun how he had previously spared his life and had saved him "ⁱfrⁱom an innoceⁱntⁱ muⁱrdⁱer" (ⁱזכיⁱ קיטל מנⁱⁱ; C.15). He states, "ⁱIⁱ brought ⁱyouⁱ to ⁱmyⁱ oⁱwⁱn house. There I ⁱhⁱad been your

---

discussion of the meaning of the term in the Persian period, see Moore, "Who Gave," 70 n. 3, 73–75.

135 This reference is also conceptually parallel to אבי בית חד מנ in *KAI* 224 ll. 9–10.

136 Bledsoe, "Wisdom," 224–225 describes the relationship between Ahiqar and Nabûsumiskun as a friendship. The surviving text does not use the term "friend." Ahiqar makes an emotional plea to a kinsman's responsibility in Ahiq. plate D.i.1. The immediate concern regards a social exchange, which Bledsoe astutely calls "reciprocity."

⸢supportˌer, like a man with his brother" ⸢יבלˌיתכˌ לביתאˌ ז⸢יˌיˌלˌיˌ תמה ⸢הˌוית מˌיסבלˌ⸢ לכ כˌאיש עמ אחוהי; C.17–D.i.1). Ahiqar is able to convince Nabûsumiskun to spare his life, and thus become disloyal to the king.[137]

As in the previous scenes, Ahiqar uses crafty rhetoric and presents himself as a victim. He convinces Nabûsumiskun that he was once also a victim. The informed reader could arguably have viewed Nabûsumiskun as a criminal. As discussed above, his literary persona connotes a sense of sedition against the present Assyrian dynasty. His past actions were corrupt not innocent. The use of the term innocent applies more to Ahiqar than to Nabûsumiskun, which works in this scene because Nabûsumiskun is Ahiqar's literary foil. Ahiqar spins the historical record and implies that his experience is similar to Nabûsumiskun's because they are both viewed unfavorably by the king. That is, both Ahiqar and Nabûsumiskun have shared the disgrace of being enemies of the crown. The acknowledgement that the king dictates the characters' identity supports the text's royal propagandistic message.

By equating himself with Nabûsumiskun, Ahiqar is able to call in on the social debt that his acquaintance owes and thereby engages in cronyism. Cronyism and nepotism are similar concepts. In an earlier scene, Ahiqar's nepotism gave his nephew an unearned advantage at a scribal appointment. Nepotism manifested itself as a generational bias for a family member. Cronyism, however, establishes an unfair advantage for one's associate. In this tale, both cronyism and nepotism operate within a semantic range of familial relations. For instance, Nadin was Ahiqar's nephew, but was conceived of as his "son" (A.2), and Nabûsumiskun was Ahiqar's acquaintance, but likened to his "brother" (C.1).

Although the Elephantine manuscript is normally concise, it elaborates on the context in which Ahiqar and Nabûsumiskun contrive a plan to save Ahiqar. They must resort to underhanded tactics to avoid Ahiqar's death. The scholar and prince decide to deceive the king by killing a eunuch in Ahiqar's place and by hiding Ahiqar until an opportunity arises for his vindication.[138] But

---

137 Bledsoe, "Wisdom," 226–227 connects this to a maxim later in the tale (G.i.1) in which the gods vindicate a righteous person.

138 This part of the scene is broken (D.ii). The plan to hide Ahiqar is a deduction drawn from Ahiqar's explanation as to how he saved Nabûsumiskun. Ahiqar tells Nabûsumiskun:

והצפנתכ מנה אמרת קטלתה עד זי לעד⸢יˌנˌ [א]חרנ וליומנ אחרנ שגיאנ קרבתכ קדמ סנחאריב מלכא

"And I hid you from him. I said, 'I had killed him.' Unt⸢ilˌ [an]other time, after many days, I presented you before Sennaḥ²erîb the king" (D.i.1–2).

Later manuscripts confirm that Ahiqar went into hiding, though he hid in his own home rather than in Nabûsumiskun's.

Nabûsumiskun is not alone and must bring the two men with him in on the plan. It is not explicitly stated that the two men have anything to gain by agreeing to murder, but implicitly they are trading in the commerce of social investment and debt. If the plan works and Ahiqar is rehabilitated, then the two men will find themselves in a powerful association of courtiers running the empire. Of course, if their plan is discovered, they will probably die. They, like Nabûsumiskun and Ahiqar, wager that one truly innocent eunuch life is worth the risk. Nabûsumiskun's suggestion to kill an innocent eunuch in place of Ahiqar demonstrates the lengths to which cronies went to secure advantages for their colleagues and for themselves.

In this scene, the Story of Ahiqar relies on the fact that cronyism was an essential part of the social reality of the scholarly profession, and it uses this idea to advance the plot. Scholars working in royal courts knew that the currency of their job was knowledge and discretion.[139] They relied on cronyism to maintain their positions and used discretion to insulate themselves from competing social attacks. Small associations of cronies engaged in a fierce competition for power, and this can be seen in the examples of Akkadian scholars who write to the king in hopes of providing advantages for their associates (e.g., SAA 10 nos. 307, 308). These appeals depict the attempts that were made to keep the network of royal influence within the control of a small group of self-appointed elites.

Each of these associations that formed in the royal court attempted to manipulate the king or crown prince. For example, in a letter from a scholar named Tabnî to the crown prince, he admits to having convinced the crown prince to do him favors (*ṭābtu*; SAA 10 no. 182). He uses those "favors" as grounds on which he could complain about competing scribal associates who had managed to acquire his position of social influence. Similarly, Urad-Gula uses the king's *ikkibu* "confidential information" (SAA 10 no. 294 ll. 21, 27) as leverage to get his job back when his father was no longer around to defend his job performance.[140] Likewise, Ahiqar claims to have given Nadin "good things" (טבתא; A.9) and had hoped that Nadin would seek "good things" (טבתא) for him in return (B.8).

Ahiqar engages in acts of cronyism because he believes that he is innocent of Nadin's charges, but in Ahiqar's acts of self-preservation, he agrees to a plan that will take the life of a truly innocent scribal character, a young eunuch. Ahiqar and the eunuch who takes his place are literarily opposite characters, even though one can stand in for the other. In the first and second scenes,

---

139 See Lenzi, *Secrecy*, esp. 147–149.
140 For the meaning of *ikkibu* see Lenzi, *Secrecy*, 156–160.

Ahiqar admits to being old (שׂב) and becoming professionally unfit (A.6; B.1). By contrast, the innocent eunuch, who will be killed in his place is young (עלים), and therefore, professionally viable.[141] Furthermore, עלים in the context of this tale also connotes the eunuch's social rank; he is a "young servant."[142] This rank stands in contrast to Ahiqar's rank as one of the courtiers (נגדין).[143] Lastly, eunuchs (סריסין) are often depicted as students and scribal figures in Neo-Assyrian texts, while Ahiqar is "the wise scribe" of the kingdom.[144] The professional and social distance between the two interchangeable characters could not be greater. The message forms a stark contrast between a young and innocent scribe without rights and an old, retired, and privileged scribe who murders the innocent. Later editors of the tale tried to mitigate this literary contrast. For instance, Camb. Cod. Add. 2020 4.10 changes the eunuch to a servant of Ahiqar who is in prison and whom Ahiqar claims deserves death.[145] The later manuscripts' attempt to justify Ahiqar's actions demonstrate that ancient readers sensed Ahiqar's negative portal in earlier sources. What survives in the Elephantine manuscript scandalizes the reader. Its relatable autobiographical style brings the reader in on the crime and justifies a reprehensible act.

---

141 E.g., in one letter, an astrologer suggests that the king should rely on a eunuch with sharp sight, which is presumably the trait of the young (SAA 10 no. 84 ln. r. 7–8). For a discussion of the social mobility of eunuchs in the Neo-Babylonian period see Jursa, "Families," 601–602 and Jursa, "Nabû-šarrūssu-ukin," article 5.
142 Greenfield, "Wisdom," 45 n. 12.
143 Nabûsumiskun implies that the eunuch is one of many disposable servants when he claims that the eunuch is "a eu[nu]ch of m[ine]" ס[ר]יס זילי (D.i.13). In the Elephantine papyri, the syntax for the independent possessive pronoun זיל is rigidly held to. Determined nouns use the article א-, e.g., ביתא זילי "*the* house of mine;" (*TAD* A6 15.7) or sometimes the article (א-) plus a demonstrative pronoun, e.g., ארקא זך זיליכי "*that* land of yours" (*TAD* B2 3.19). When the noun preceding זיל is indefinite, it is intentionally so, e.g., איש זילכי "*a* man of yours (who files a lawsuit)" (*TAD* B2 3.12).
144 Eunuchs were often trained by scribes or scholars; in many texts they are portrayed as students. For instance, SAA 10 no. 294 in which Urad-Gula compares himself, for rhetorical purposes, to eunuchs (ll. 21–22) and as the teacher of eunuchs (ln. 30), similarly, SAA 10 no. 222 ln. 11.
145 The text reads, הא אית לי גבא כאשיא דילה גבדא מנצפר שמה מתיהב גתחסא "Indeed, I (Ahiqar) have a servant of my own in prison, Manzîpar by name. It has been deemed that he should die" (Camb. Cod. Add. 2020 4.10). Similarly, Graffin 12.4. From an anthropological point of view, this act stands in direct contrast to one of the few positive portrayals of Persian culture made by Herodotus. He writes, "I admire also the custom which forbids even the king himself to put a man to death for a single offence, and any Persian under similar circumstances to punish a servant by an irreparable injury" (Herod I 137 [Sélincourt]).

The use of a eunuch as Ahiqar's body double explains why Ahiqar did not train his own biological children at the start of the tale.[146] Although there is some question as to whether a eunuch (סריס, Akk. *ša-rēši*) refers to a castrated male, the evidence currently suggests that it does.[147] The Elephantine manuscript claims that the eunuch's body (פגר, D.i.15) will appear as evidence of Ahiqar's death to the king; the executioners needed to only mutilate the face of the eunuch.[148] Presumably the corpse would pass as Ahiqar's, and therefore, Ahiqar must have anatomically resembled a eunuch. The text explicitly states that once the body is on display at a mountain pass, the king will send other men to see that the corpse of this eunuch is, in fact, the corpse of Ahiqar:

Ahiq. Plate D.i.13–15

⌜We⌝ mustn't kill him. [I have on]⌜e⌝[servant,] a eu[nu]ch of m⌜ine⌝ (whom) I will ⌜give⌝ ⌜y⌝ou. He may ⌜be killed⌝ betwe[en the]⌜se⌝ two mountains in pla⌜ce⌝ of thi[s] ʾAḥ⌜i⌝qa⌜r⌝, and⌝ w⌜h⌝[en it is heard (that he is dead),] ⌜the k⌜i⌝ng will send⌝ othe⌜r m⌝e⌜n⌝ [a]f⌜ter us⌝ to insp⌜ect⌝ the ⌜co⌝rp⌜se o⌝f this ʾAḥiqar. ⌜The⌝n ⌜they will⌝[see the corpse] o⌜f⌝ [this] eunuch, m⌜y⌝ ser⌜va⌝nt.

אל ⌜נ⌝קטלנהי [איתי עלימ ח]⌜ד⌝ ס[ר]⌜יס ז⌝יל⌜י
א⌝נת⌜נ ליכ⌝ם ⌜יתקטל⌝ בי[נ] ⌜טוריא⌝ [אל]⌜ה⌝ תרין
חל⌜י⌝פ⌝ אחי⌜קר⌝ זנה ו⌜כ⌝ז⌜י⌝ ישתמיע [ו]⌜נ⌝בר⌜נ⌝
אחר⌜ננ מ⌜ל⌝כא ישלח⌝ [א]⌜חרינ פ⌜ג⌝רה⌝ זי אחיקר
זנה למח⌜זה אח⌝ר ⌜י⌝[חזונ פגר]⌜ה⌝ ז⌜י⌝ סריסא
[זנה] עליו⌜מא ז⌝יל⌜י⌝

The inspection of the corpse implies that the two bodies must carry similar identifiers, and if eunuchs are castrated, then Ahiqar is expected to have been castrated as well. Hence, he could not have had progeny at the start of the narrative. Implicitly, then, in this scene, the tale compounds the faults of Ahiqar's nepotism with the crimes of his cronyism.

---

146 Contra Greenfield, "Wisdom," 45 n. 12. According to Radner, "Unlike the magnates, scholars were only very rarely eunuchs; among all known learned specialists, only two extispicy experts are thus designated" ("Royal," 363). This is because "for learned men, temple offices offered the main alternative to a career in the king's entourage, and as those required the holder to be physically intact (Löhnert 2007), castration would have made this career path impossible" (363). In view of Radner's discussion, it is notable that Ahiqar works as the king's seal-bearer (A.3) at the Gate of the Palace (B.1) among the נגדן "courtiers." This then is further evidence that Ahiqar characterized himself as an unrealistic figure, a renaissance man who is both like a magnate of the palace (who would have been castrated [Radner, "Decision-Making," 359–360]) and an *ummânu* who generally was not. The tale's emphasis on the inspection of Ahiqar's corpse (D.i.15) suggests that, at least in the world of the narrative, Ahiqar was a eunuch.
147 Radner, "Pen Pals," 62 and citation.
148 Note that in the Syriac manuscripts, the king demands Ahiqar's head, not his body (Camb. Cod. Add. 2020 4.4, 11).

Nepotism and cronyism are powerful forces because they silence opposition and maintain a status quo that favors politically savvy groups at the expense of qualified individuals. The status quo creates an environment in which competing groups vie for power, and among the courtiers there are very few opportunities for outsiders to be brought into a scribal association. The two unnamed men whom Esarhaddon appointed with Nabûsumiskun, found themselves at the right place and time to be brought into Ahiqar's alliance, and they are marked in the story as those "with" (עם; D.i.8) Nabûsumiskun as oppose to the "others" (אחרנן; D.i.14) who will later be sent to inspect their work.[149] This us-versus-them dynamic reflects the reality of competing courtly associations.

Lastly, Nabûsumiskun appeals to Ahiqar's professional titles as evidence to the men with him that they should spare Ahiqar. He claims,

Ahiq. Plate D.i.12
⌈This⌉ is [ʾAḥ]⌈î⌉qar, the chief [cupbearer and the seal(-bearer)] of ʾEsar⌈aḥ⌉ʾi⌈ddi⌉⌈n⌉[, king of ʾAtûr;](it is) ⌈h⌉e.

⌈זנה⌉ ⌈אח⌉⌈י⌉קר רב [שקה ועז]קה זי אסר⌈חא⌉[ד]⌈נ⌉[] מלך אתור [⌉ה⌈ו

The grammar clearly presents Ahiqar as presently holding a courtly position. Nabûsumiskun also describes Ahiqar as אבוה זי אתו⌈ר⌉ כ⌈לה "the father of ⌈a⌉ll ʾAtû⌈r⌉" on whom the nation relies (D.i.7). Again, Ahiqar is presently depicted as the nation's teacher, that is its father.[150] This evidence complements the data from the first two scenes which suggested that there was a social expectation that courtly scribal employees held their titles until they died in their post. Again, Ahiqar's retirement was unorthodox.

The remainder of the tale is too damaged to provide further literary analysis. Presumably, the tale continues with Ahiqar's rehabilitation as it does in later manuscripts.[151] After all, one does not expect the autobiographer to fail.

---

149 The גברין who accompany Nabûsumiskun seem to be court employees, perhaps reliable guards. They might be compared with the *ša-ziqni* of the Neo-Assyrian court, but they do not appear to be "scribal" figures.
150 Holm, "Memories," 300 claims that "Ahiqar, 'the father of all Assyria,'" is the object of highest reverence, but does not elaborate further. Compare, Lemaire, *Écoles*, 61–62 for a discussion of "father" meaning "teacher."
151 Greenfield, "Wisdom," 47–49.

2.8 Concluding Remarks

This chapter has shown that the autobiographical style of the tale plays a crucial role in how the tale is to be interpreted. The first-person narration established a discourse between the reader and the narrator that results in empathy for the narrator. Thus, on first read, the tale is a lamentable reflection of a pitiable old scholar who was unjustly defamed by his own ungrateful kin. In all likelihood, the narrator finds resolve when he overcomes the assault and reestablishes his credibility as a faithful servant of the king. It cannot be overstated, that it seems unlikely that the autobiographer would paint himself as a failure. In this reading, the moral of the story is that a good royal scribe is one who remains loyal to his king in the face of oppression. The tale's autobiographical style, however, can be viewed as a manipulative literary tactic that obscures the immoral allusions to the scribal profession in order to promote a pro-monarchic message.

The narrative structure and motifs are carefully organized around scribal concepts and experiences. The first scene in the Story of Ahiqar establishes the motif of dynastic succession by focusing on how Esarhaddon had taken the place of his father for whom Ahiqar had worked. It also introduces Ahiqar and his interest in securing an heir. The second scene extends the motif of dynastic succession to the domain of royal scribal employment, and this reflects the historical data in which dynastic succession was practiced by the highest ranking (Akkadian) scholars. Following the Akkadian precedent of nepotistic appointments, Ahiqar ensures that his nephew will replace him. While in the king's good graces, Ahiqar requests that the king grants him retirement. This decision proved to be detrimental to Ahiqar. The historical evidence demonstrates that high-ranking Akkadian scholars held their posts until they were either disgracefully removed (e.g., SAA 10 no. 294) or died in service (SAA 10 no. 160). Ahiqar's retirement starts the narrative's central conflict, and results in two scholars holding the same post, Ahiqar and Nadin. Nadin, who was well trained in scholarly etiquette, adheres to the philosophy that a scholar should hold his post until he dies, and so he concocts a plan to expedite Ahiqar's death. While Ahiqar overcomes the attack on his life and shows himself to have been innocent from the king's point of view (in the lacuna), his loyalty to the king comes at a great cost. Presumably, the broken sections of the tale unfolded in a way similar to the Syriac manuscripts, and Nadin was punished or killed for his libel. In this more careful reading, Ahiqar does not succeed in obtaining the heir which he had set out to secure. So while he may have been a good royal servant and advisor, he failed as a father and teacher. Furthermore, in his efforts to save his own reputation as a loyal official, Ahiqar coerced his acquaintance,

Nabûsumiskun, to engage in disloyalty and to not follow direct orders from the king. Ahiqar's path to loyalty was founded on an urge to save himself, even while manipulating the morals of others.

The motifs in the Story of Ahiqar reflect an intimate knowledge of Neo-Assyrian texts and social expectations of the scribal profession. The motifs of succession and rebellion are prominent in Neo-Assyrian treaties, such as the treaty of Zakutu or the Vassal Treaties of Esarhaddon (SAA 2 no. 6). The correspondences between the motifs of such treaties and the Story of Ahiqar are made all the more apparent because the Story of Ahiqar is set in Esarhaddon's royal court. In order to combat rebellion, Neo-Assyrian inscriptions, instruct citizens to turn on each other, and the king makes reprisals for sedition by sending men to assassinate rebels of the state. This is different than the depiction of the king pursuing rebels in Persian period texts, such as the Darius Inscription. When facing political turmoil, Ahiqar hides and relies on his crony to find a way to rehabilitate his political reputation, just as Ahiqar had done for his friend in a backstory. This very specific motif is known from the inscriptions of Esarhaddon who likewise went into hiding before his coronation (RINAP 4 Esar no. 1 i 14). In addition to these motifs that are prominent in sources from the reign of Esarhaddon, the text of the Story of Ahiqar also shares social allusions to the scribal profession that were of concern to royal scholars, such as Urad-Gula, in the court of Ashurbanipal.

The Story of Ahiqar also uses Akkadian loanwords and distinctly Aramaic terms to describe royal (scribal) personnel. The terms רביא "the prince" and סריסא "the eunuch" are Akkadian loanwords and appear to reflect their usage in Akkadian sources. The terms עזקה "seal/seal-bearer," נגדין "courtiers," and עלים "servant" are distinctly Aramaic social terms. The word מהיר "skilled one" is also distinctly Aramaic though it may be a latter Persian period explanation of Ahiqar's position. The participle יעט "counselor" is not a professional title but a qualification of Ahiqar's scribal character. It is a distinctly Aramaic term though it refers to a cross-cultural feature of scribal characters who are known for their "words" and their "counsel." Lastly, Ahiqar is called ספרא חכימא as a literary epithet that makes him appear as though he is a (or the) chief Akkadian scholar to Sennacherib and Esarhaddon; the title also entails many distinct scribal expectations performed by a variety of scribal professionals all of whom Ahiqar encompasses.

The conflict between the Aramaic and Akkadian scribal cultures embedded in the Story of Ahiqar may reflect the circumstances of language shift in Syria and Mesopotamian that was occurring in the 7th and 6th centuries BCE. In this period are found in the Akkadian scribal tradition critiques against those who do not learn to read Sumerian; these may be interpreted as a scribal tradition looking to the past in the face of a changing present and uncertain future. Texts such as In Praise of the Scribal Art or Ninurta-Pāqidāt's Dog Bite present an Akkadian scribal culture in flux;[152] one in which the ancient dead language of Sumerian is becoming obsolete. Learning it is deemed a cultural success in these tales, but the historical circumstances reveal that apart from a short-lived revival of Sumerian language and literature in the reign of Nebuchadnezzar, it was not a practical skill for a scribal professional to learn. The timing of these texts corresponds with an increase in bilingual Akkadian-Aramaic activity. It is quite probable that the more complex cultural message of the Story of Ahiqar, particularly its interest in a precarious professional experience of generation change in the scribal profession, is speaking to this same cultural concern, but from the Aramaic writer's perspective. The implications of these observations will be fleshed out in chapter four where these findings are brought into dialogue with the Tale of Jeremiah and Baruch's Scroll.

---

152 For In Praise of the Scribal Art see Sjöberg, "Praise," 126–131; Hurowitz, "Literary,'" 49–56; and Foster, *Before*, 1023–1024. For Ninurta-Pāqidāt's Dog Bite see George, "Ninurta-Pāqidāt's," 63–75 and Foster, *Before*, 937–938.

3 Allusions to the Hebrew Scribal Profession in the Tale of Jeremiah and Baruch's Scroll

Unlike my study on the Story of Ahiqar in the previous chapter, the present chapter will not draw as heavily on documentary sources to interpret the social historical circumstances of the ancient scribal experience in the Tale of Jeremiah and Baruch's Scroll because so few documentary data from the Judahite kingdom in which the tale is set survive. Much of the scantly data constitutes seals and bullae, which I frequently reference in footnotes. In lieu of the evidence, in this chapter I explore the social allusions to the scribal profession in the Tale of Jeremiah and Baruch's Scroll by identifying social and historical data points in the narrative then historically interpreting the nuance among the families of manuscripts (MT and LXX) concerning these data points.

Two ancient families of manuscripts, which I refer to as editions, of the text of the book of Jeremiah are known, LXX and MT, and they contain significant textual differences.[1] Text-critical studies have demonstrated that generally, but not in all cases, LXX contains older and shorter readings.[2] On text-critical grounds, then, LXX more than MT becomes a necessary starting place for a close reading of any passage in the book of Jeremiah, such as that conducted in this chapter on the Tale of Jeremiah and Baruch's Scroll in MT Jer 36 / LXX Jer 43. One should not assume, however, that LXX preserves a better reading at every point at which it varies from MT. Therefore, this chapter will reassess variants throughout MT Jer 36 and LXX Jer 43, paying close attention to those that are relevant for understanding the socio-historical allusions to the scribal profes-

---

[1] The MT manuscript used in this study is Leningrad Codex B19a as published in *BHS*. The LXX is an eclectic edition, which prioritizes the so-called B (Vaticanus) and S (Sinaiticus) textual traditions (LXX p. 125). Where applicable in this chapter further investigation into manuscript variants as noted in the LXX apparatus have been negotiated and interpreted. As noted in the introduction, this episode in the book of Jeremiah is not known from the surviving Dead Sea Scrolls. The Aramaic Targumim are recognized as secondary and interpretative translations of an early Hebrew manuscript that resembles MT. They are valuable for justifying the interpretation of passages, but not for reading the most ancient forms of the text. The Peshitta is also based on an early Hebrew manuscript tradition that resembles MT, but the Peshitta and MT are not identical (Greenberg, "Jeremiah," 340–1). Unlike the Targumim there is no evidence that the Peshitta translator sought to include ideological information, and therefore the Peshitta's attempt at producing a precise translation is more in line with modern scholarly sentiments; its variants are, therefore, of historical value.

[2] Janzen, *Studies*; Tov, *Septuagint*; Stipp, *masoretische*. The surviving Old Latin manuscripts may also confirm this; see Bogaert, "Vetus," 51–82.

sion in this tale. I will show that LXX Jer 43 contains older readings at a number of points of variance, and that its text presents a more dynamic depiction of scribal interactions in the royal court of Judah than does MT. MT's alterations and additions are nonetheless significant points of data, because they provide insights into how the editor of MT interpreted the professional experience of the tale's scribal characters.³

In addition to the empirical variants between LXX and MT, verses 3, 7, and 31 stand out from the points of sense, coherence, and comprehension. They provide information that shapes the explicit moral of the tale, and thus have been the focus of theological debates as well as redaction-critical and source-critical studies, particularly by biblical scholars interested in the shared ideology of the book of Jeremiah and the book of Deuteronomy. Such discussions focus on how the writers and editors are connecting themes and wording across literary works and the speculative world of scribal schools, rather than on the social realities that these actors embed in their works. For this reason, many mainstream approaches to MT Jer 36, and these three verses in particular, fall outside the scope of this study.

In both MT and LXX, the tale is episodic and each scene consists of scribal characters engaging with each other and using scribal props within a particular locus of professional scribal activity.⁴ The tale begins and ends in an undisclosed and private scribal workshop in which Jeremiah and Baruch compose a scroll of Jeremiah's teachings and concoct a plan to present the scroll's message to the people of Judah and its leaders. Once they have contrived their plan, the

---

3 A Deuteronomistic editor is thought to be responsible for verses 3, 7, and 31, which in their current form supply a theological motif of "eine verfehlte Möglichkeit der Rettung," according to Thiel, *deuteronomistiche*, 50. I agree that verses 3 and 31 are conceptually out of place in their current form. I agree that verse 7 reads as though it is an addition because it adds little to the narrative of the current episode but adds to a larger thematic issue of importance in the book. (On the book's themes, but with minimal engagement with the concept of Deuteronomistic redaction, see di Pede, *Au-delà*, 96 n. 118, 294–297.) Furthermore, in antiquity this verse was seen as a link for harmonizing other biblical passages, as seen in the PESHITTA's harmonization with PESHITTA Jer 26:3 and 13 (Greenberg, "Jeremiah," 343–4, 353).
4 Matthews, "Jeremiah's," 116–124 prompted me to consider more seriously the episode's various settings and is, to my knowledge, the only other study that does this, though it is limited to MT Jer 36. Matthews argues that "situated meanings. . . bring to mind [a] particular social understanding for the reader" (118). He maintains that the tale's first setting is the temple (118–120), its second is the palace's scribal chamber (120–121), and its final setting is the king's winter apartment (121–123). He overlooks the importance of the first and the last scenes. His focus is on *the scroll*, which he interprets as a "'chained-space artifact' that links the original setting to each subsequent site" (120).

scroll is read at three different loci of scribal presentation: the temple, the palace's scribal chambers, and the king's presence. As the story unfolds at these various settings of scribal activity, each scene contains allusions to the social interactions of professional scribal figures in the tale's constructed historical setting of 605–601 BCE.[5] While the text refers to scribal props, such as writing tools and media, these items will not be the focus of this study, since previous research on scribal culture has already advanced our understanding of these features (see chapter one). Instead, this close reading of the passage sets out to study how the tale portrays professional scribal interaction within loci of scribal activity. The tale depicts the late Judahite court as having a complex structure in which the high-ranking palace courtiers were scribal figures who operated out of public view, yet had significant power over the king and the social and cultic agenda of the nation. The royal court consisted of princes and higher and lower courtiers, and the text characterizes the chief courtiers (הַשָּׂרִים) as scribal figures. These courtiers differed in their motivations and strategies for political success; they formed small alliances to promote their ideas. Furthermore, the story illustrates how scribal characters developed their agendas and alliances based on an advanced practice of professional debate about, and intellectual reasoning through, written material.

The story's socio-historical allusions are evident within the tale's repetitive literary patterns, in which the characters interact with each other and with Baruch's scroll in loci of scribal activity. The story begins in an undisclosed scribal workshop in which two scribal characters, Jeremiah and Baruch, form a small scribal association that centers on the teachings of Jeremiah. In this workshop, they produce a document and contrive a plan to promote their message in public and political venues. The scene then moves to the temple, in which Baruch presents the document to the Judahite public gathered therein. Baruch delivers his message from the vantage point of a scribal chamber in the temple's public outer courtyard. Despite the public nature of his address, Baruch directs his message to a scribal associate of the palace's chief courtiers, Micaiah, who is the only one in the audience to understand (√שמע) Baruch's message. Micaiah, serving as an informant, orally reports to the chief courtiers in the palace's scribal chamber. They then summon Baruch, whereupon he reads the scroll as he did in the temple. At the center of the tale, the courtiers debate the scroll's content and question Baruch about his document. As in the previous scene, an

---

[5] This follows LXX's dating in verses 1 and 9, see discussion below. At times this study will refer to the "late Judahite period" or "late Judahite kingdom," which refers to the reign of Hezekiah to the fall of Jerusalem.

informant is sent to a new location of scribal activity, the king's presence, in order to orally report on the scroll's content to its next intended audience. As before, the scroll is then brought from its previous location to the king's winter quarters in the palace's private courtyard. This private setting stands in contrast to the public courtyard of the previous scene. Before the king, the scroll is once again read, but this time by Jehudi, an antagonistic character and representative of a competing scribal view. In a dramatic act, he burns the scroll as he reads it, despite protests from his colleagues. The scene then moves back to a scribal workshop in which Jeremiah and Baruch rewrite the first scroll.

The narrative contains five scenes set in four loci of scribal activity. The plot advances by means of scribal characters who orally report the contents of Baruch's scroll from the temple to the palace's scribal chamber, then again from the scribal chamber to the king's presence. In each scene, this is followed by the retrieval of the scroll from its previous location and its reading in the new location. Embedded in these literary patterns and narrative details are allusions to the professional scribal experience as it was conceived to have been during the late Judahite kingdom.

3.1 Training and Conspiring in the Scribal Workshop (MT 36:1–8 / LXX 43:1–8)

The opening scene of the Tale of Jeremiah and Baruch's Scroll begins with a regnal formula (v. 1) that situates the event in the fourth year of king Jehoiakim (605 BCE). As noted in the introductory chapter of this book, the fourth year of Jehoiakim was a significant year in ancient Near Eastern history and in the historiographic picture painted by various biblical writers. Historically, the fourth year of King Jehoiakim coincides with both the great Egyptian and Mesopotamian battle of Carchemish and the ascension of Nebuchadnezzar II. In this year, Judah found itself caught between these two warring powers, as it had been only four years earlier, when according to the biblical historiography, King Josiah lost his life in 609 BCE (MT 2 Kgs 23:29). The mention of Jehoiakim's fourth year sets a fateful tone for the story and alludes to political and national tumult, which drives the plot as the episode unfolds.[6]

---

6 Similarly, de Pede interprets the reference to the fourth year of Jehoiakim as a trigger that connects other passages set in this year with the notion of punishment; the point in this passage, as with MT Jer 26:3 (see MT Jer 36:3 אוּלַי), is that forgiveness may be possible (*Au-delà*, 185, 293–4). As noted in the introduction, the use of historical *realia* does not mean that the

The opening regnal formula introduces Jehoiakim as Josiah's successor, יְהוֹיָקִים בֶּן־יֹאשִׁיָּהוּ מֶלֶךְ יְהוּדָה / τῷ Ιωακιμ υἱῷ Ιωσία βασιλέως Ιουδα, "Jehoiakim son of Josiah king of Judah" (v. 1), and this reference to succession proves significant in verse 2. There, Yahweh commands Jeremiah to write down the prophecies that he spoke from the days of Josiah:

LXX Jer 43:2b[7]	MT Jer 36:2b
ἀφ' ἧς ἡμέρας λαλήσαντός μου[8] πρὸς σέ, ἀφ' ἡμερῶν Ιωσία βασιλέως Ιουδα καὶ ἕως τῆς ἡμέρας ταύτης	מִיּוֹם דִּבַּרְתִּי אֵלֶיךָ מִימֵי יֹאשִׁיָּהוּ וְעַד הַיּוֹם הַזֶּה
... from the day of my speaking to you, from the days of King Iosias of Iouda even until this day (NETS).	... from (the) day I spoke to you, from the days of Josiah until this day.

This passage draws a subtle contrast between Josiah and Jehoiakim and establishes a motif of succession that it will echo, albeit in the context of a different social relationship, when Baruch succeeds Jeremiah in the next scene.[9]

Following the regnal formula, an introductory statement presents Jeremiah. In MT, a narrator refers to Jeremiah in the third person. This stands in contrast to the narrative style of LXX, which uses a first-person reference that portrays Jeremiah as narrator of his own experience. The texts read:

LXX Jer 43:1	MT Jer 36:1
ἐγενήθη λόγος κυρίου πρός με λέγων	הָיָה הַדָּבָר הַזֶּה אֶל־יִרְמְיָהוּ מֵאֵת יְהוָה לֵאמֹר
And so it was, a word of the Lord to[10] me, saying	This word was[11] to Jeremiah from Yahweh, saying

LXX's reading here is the *lectio difficilior*, the shorter reading, and uses a more expected syntactical form than MT, but only a minority of scholars prefer this

---

events recorded in the tale are historical or realistic. It does, however, lend credence to the notion that the tale's scribal interactions may reflect interactions thought to have existed in the late Judahite kingdom.

7 I have opted to use conventional English spellings of names and locations for my translations of the Hebrew and Greek biblical texts. NETS and Brenton differ on these matters.
8 Lit. "from the days which I have spoken;" see McKane, *Jeremiah*, 900.
9 So too McKane, *Jeremiah*, 913.
10 The phrase ἐγενήθη λόγος κυρίου πρός με closely follows the Hebrew phrase that probably appeared in its *Vorlage*, אֵלִי יהוה דבר היה. For related constructions, see MT/LXX Jer 14:1; 18:5; et al. NETS translates ἐγενήθη... πρός more idiomatically: "a word of the Lord came to me saying."
11 The phrase (אֶל) הַדָּבָר הָיָה, "the word belonged to (PN)" is idiomatic and best translated into English with "the word *came* to (PN)."

reading.¹² Nearly all commentators regard LXX's autobiographical reference as an error because the tale continues with third-person narration.¹³ As is the case in the Story of Ahiqar, a first-person edition of this tale might add a unique narrative depth to its professional scribal allusions.¹⁴ But regardless of whether one favors LXX's or MT's reading, both versions depict Jeremiah's—and only Jeremiah's—ability to hear the words of Yahweh. Jeremiah's knowledge derives from a divine author known only in his own cognitive experience.¹⁵

The scene's introduction sets a dramatic political tone for the tale and demonstrates that Jeremiah's thoughts have a divine origin. Jeremiah's intention is to construct a collection of his sayings, which had been delivered throughout the reigns of two kings. In order to perform this task, he enlists the help of Baruch, and the two of them compose a scroll in an unidentified scribal workshop.

For the purpose of this study, I define a workshop within the framework of its commonly held definitions: as a designated location in which materials are kept and worked with to produce goods or as a setting for a meeting intended to produce a particular project. Both aspects of a workshop are found in the first scene of this tale. Yahweh commands Jeremiah, קַח־לְךָ מְגִלַּת־סֵפֶר וְכָתַבְתָּ אֵלֶיהָ / Λάβε σεαυτῷ χαρτίον βιβλίου καὶ γράψον ἐπ' αὐτοῦ, "take yourself a scroll document and write on it" (v. 2).¹⁶ Jeremiah executes this plan by summoning Baruch, who begins to write (v. 4). The text does not state that Baruch supplied the

---

12 E.g., Silver, "Prophet," 86, rejects the first-person form in LXX without analysis. Stipp, *masoretische*, 71 is the only study to my knowledge to layout the evidence and concludes that MT is a "secondary transposition" (*sekundäre Umstellung*). For the formula ἐγενήθη λόγος κυρίου πρός με/Ιερεμιαν λέγων, see LXX Jer 1:4, 11, 13; 13:3, 8; 14:1; 18:5; 24:4; 35:12; 36:30; 39:26; 40:1; 41:12; 42:12; 43:1, 27; 44:6; 49:7; 50:8. The construction מֵאֵת אֶל־יִרְמְיָהוּ הַזֶּה הַדָּבָר הָיָה יְהוָה appears only in MT Jer 27:1 and 36:1. A related version of it appears in 26:1 (see LXX. For PESHITTA see Greenberg, *Translation*, 38). For a study of these formulas in MT (but not LXX), see Lawlor, "Word," 231–243, esp. 232.
13 Holladay, *Jeremiah 2*, 251 and Rudolph, *Jeremia*, 228. Duhm, *Buch*, 289 suggests that אֵלַי (= LXX *Vorlage*) can be an abbreviation for אֶל־יִרְמְיָהוּ. So too Carroll, *Jeremiah*, 538 (for MT Jer 28:1). For a longer list of supposed abbreviations in Biblical Hebrew, see Driver, "Abbreviations," 121. I find the idea unconvincing.
14 See chapter two above.
15 Crenshaw, *Education*, 239–253 studies a variety of wisdom texts and comes to the conclusion that "a divine gift of understanding supplements human effort" (253). In studies on prophetic literature, Reventlow, *Liturgie*, 51 sees the divine "I" and prophetic "I" used interchangeably throughout Jeremiah. The text here presents Jeremiah, the prophet, as an instructor, because his thoughts were divinely inspired.
16 For the difference in the verbal forms וְכָתַבְתָּ (imperfect) and γράψον (imperative), see discussion below.

writing materials, and the reader is left to assume that Jeremiah acquired a scroll document, as was his stated idea in verse 2. Verse 4 simply introduces Baruch, who begins the task of writing. The relevant text reads, וַיִּקְרָא יִרְמְיָהוּ אֶת־ בָּרוּךְ בֶּן־נֵרִיָּה וַיִּכְתֹּב... מִפִּי יִרְמְיָהוּ / καὶ ἐκάλεσεν Ιερεμίας τὸν Βαρουχ υἱὸν Νηρίου, καὶ ἔγραψεν ἀπὸ στόματος Ιερεμίου, "Jeremiah summoned Baruch, the son of Neriah, and he wrote according to the mouth of Jeremiah" (v. 4). The reader is left to gap-fill, and the simplest interpretation is to understand Jeremiah in a location in which he had access to scribal materials; clearly this location served as a meeting place for him and Baruch to work on a writing project. He and Baruch were not in the palace or the Jerusalem temple, two known loci of scribal activity.[17] Thus, the setting of this first scene is best understood as a private and undisclosed scribal workshop,[18] and the setting of the final scene will occur in a similar (if not the same) locus of scribal activity (MT Jer 36:28, 32).

Furthermore, Jeremiah's access to scribal materials as well as Yahweh's command to Jeremiah to write (וְכָתַבְתָּ / γράψον; v. 2) is an indication that the scene depicts Jeremiah as a scribal character.[19] According to verse 2, Yahweh commands Jeremiah to take a "scroll-document" (מְגִלַּת־סֵפֶר) and to write on it all of the words (כָּל־הַדְּבָרִים) that Yahweh spoke to Jeremiah against Israel, Judah, and the nations (עַל־יִשְׂרָאֵל וְעַל־יְהוּדָה וְעַל־כָּל־הַגּוֹיִם) since the days of Josiah (v. 2). Readers of the received editions of Jeremiah can reasonably assume that the character Jeremiah was literate on two bases: First, Jeremiah was the son of a priest (1:1). The position of a priest, unlike many other occupations, was a hereditary post, and priests were highly educated.[20] As Carr notes, priests were "among the most literate members of the populace, and priests, particularly Levites, are often depicted in biblical narratives as keepers of the texts (e.g., [MT] Deut 31:9–11; see [MT] Num 5:23) and the teachers of Israel ([MT] Hos 4:6;

---

17 See Schniedewind, *How*, 111–114.
18 The term "workshop" is broad enough to even refer to the impromptu designation of a space, so long as the characters have access to and are qualified to use scribal materials. The location of this workshop is unknown, but the only other place that Baruch and Jeremiah are said to have met is in Anathoth, a small settlement on the outskirts of Jerusalem (MT Jer 32), where Jeremiah's uncle had property and where his father was said to have served as a priest (MT Jer 1:2).
19 Based solely on MT Jer 36, Römer, "Prophet," 89–90 states, "Jeremiah is neither a visionary (as in [MT] 1:4–9; 24) nor a messenger of divine oracles. He is a prototype of a 'senior scribe' who dictates to another scribe the words to be written on a scroll."
20 Jeremiah is not referred to as a prophet in LXX Jer 43, though MT's editor ascribes this title to him in MT Jer 36:8, 26. Thus, a number of professional attributes of Jeremiah coalesce in this passage in LXX: his priestliness, his prophetic character, and his scribal abilities.

[MT] Deut 17:9–12; 31:10–13; [MT] 2 Chr 19:8–11; [MT] Neh 8:8–9)."[21] Since it is not known whether the Tale of Jeremiah and Baruch's Scroll was accompanied by references to Jeremiah's priestly lineage, this point must not be over stressed, but the passage's similarities to the plot of MT Jer 26, suggest that his prophetic character at least stood in contrast to priests as opposing scribal professionals.

Second, the textual data contains prophecies of Jeremiah that refer to the act of writing (MT Jer 17:1 [- LXX], 13 [≈ LXX]; 31:33 [≈ LXX Jer 38:33]).[22] In other narrative portions of the book, Jeremiah claims to have been commanded by Yahweh to write down his own prophecies (e.g., MT Jer 30:1 ≈ LXX Jer 37:1), and in these references, there is no indication that Jeremiah required help in the writing process.[23] In addition, at the end of a major portion of the book, the text explicitly states that Jeremiah—not Baruch—wrote down his prophecies against Babylon:[24]

LXX Jer 28:60	MT Jer 51:50
καὶ ἔγραψεν Ιερεμίας πάντα τὰ κακά, ἃ ἥξει ἐπὶ Βαβυλῶνα, ἐν βιβλίῳ ἑνί, πάντας τοὺς λόγους τούτους τοὺς γεγραμμένους ἐπὶ Βαβυλῶνα.	וַיִּכְתֹּב יִרְמְיָהוּ אֵת כָּל־הָרָעָה אֲשֶׁר־תָּבוֹא אֶל־בָּבֶל אֶל־סֵפֶר אֶחָד אֵת כָּל־הַדְּבָרִים הָאֵלֶּה הַכְּתֻבִים אֶל־בָּבֶל
And Ieremias wrote in one book all the evils that would come on Babylon, all these words that have been written regarding Babylon (NETS).	And Jeremiah wrote down in a single document all of the evils which will come upon Babylon—all of these words written to Babylon.

The narrative of the book of Jeremiah portrays the character Jeremiah as one having intimate knowledge of the scribal craft, so Yahweh's command that he compose his own scroll in MT Jer 36:4 is not surprising.[25]

---

21 Carr, *Writing*, 152. See Widengren, *Literary*, 71–74; Leuchter, *Josiah's*, 13–15; Orton, *Understanding*, 44.

22 Carr, *Writing*, 146 states, "Jeremiah does not use teaching terminology for his prophecy, at least not to the same extent we saw in passages like [MT] Isaiah 8:16–18. Nevertheless, there are indications that Jeremiah, like Isaiah, drew on oral-written processes for transmission of his prophecies." I would add that Jeremiah's allusions to the scribal craft are not pedantic, as are Isaiah's, but rather Jeremiah expects his readership to have an intimate knowledge of advanced scribal perspectives and practices, that is, Jeremiah is speaking to his intellectual peers and educated colleagues.

23 Other prophets are also known to have been literate and to have composed complex literary works. See van der Toorn, *Scribal*, 178–182.

24 MT Jer 36:29 indicates that Baruch's scroll contained prophecies pertaining to Judah and Babylon. For the narrative complexity of MT Jer 36:29, see Venema, *Reading*, 134–137.

25 Contra Dearman, "Servants," 419, which claims that "there is no indication in *Jeremiah* that the prophet himself could either read or write competently enough to compile his own records." Leuchter, *Josiah's*, 13–15 identifies Jeremiah as a learned scribe, even one "reflecting a

When Jeremiah's scribal character is combined with a reference to a scroll MT Jer 36:2, 4, and 6 and the act of writing (MT Jer 36:4), a number of implied props beyond the explicit reference to the scroll can be reasonably assumed. The setting must have included at its most basic level ink, a thinning agent, a palette, and a pen. Scholarship has yet to determine the posture of a Northwest Semitic writer, so it is unclear if Jeremiah and Baruch's workshop could be read as including a writing board used across the writer's lap, as Egyptian scribes are typically depicted, or if some other surface (e.g., a bench of some kind) was intended. Presumably, the ancient reader would have conceptualized the writer, his surface, and his posture. The material which one envisions the scroll to have been would presuppose slightly different tools used by the writers,[26] but both papyrus and parchment would require a scribal knife and likely a straight edge for trimming. One writing on parchment, with the intention of forming a multicolumn roll as the story later describes (MT Jer 36:23), would have a needle and thread/cord on hand to compile or repair the leather sheets. If the text is written on papyrus, it is very probable that glue would be on hand in order to join sheets into a longer edited roll as needed.[27] Should one conceptualize the workshop as a more permanent location, rather than an impromptu site for the writing project, the space may include reference works and other written sources or drafting materials, such as writing boards,[28] particularly given Jeremiah's priestly and temple affiliation.[29]

---

deep understanding of Mesopotamian religious literature" (14). Carr holds that Jeremiah "probably received an earlier traditional education," (*Writing*, 146), but previously argued that Jeremiah had not been sufficiently literate to write his own prophecies (120). Young, "Israelite," 248 cites this passage along with MT Est 8:8–9 as evidence that the verb כתב can mean "to have someone write for one." The two contexts are not comparable as the Persian bureaucratic system had administrative practices in place to issue the types of local ordinances that the passage has in view (see Moore, "Persian"). Even the language of Esther, in which כתב is used as a noun, indicates a markedly different linguistic horizon than that of MT Jer 36.

26 For a recent discussion of the surviving references to scribal tools in biblical and related sources see Zhakevich, *Scribal*, who sees papyrus and ostraca as the most common writing mediums in Canaan and Israel and traces their use to an Egyptian scribal influence (esp. chap. 6).

27 Many longer, especially literary and collected works, were not initially planned around the constraints of the papyrus material. As a result, the writer would need to trim and glue sheets together as needed. See Krutzsch, "Blattklebungen," 93–98, taf. xxvi esp. the discussion of the *Schreiberklebung* throughout. For a discussion of the construction of the Ahiqar roll, see Yardeni, "Maritime," 67–68 and *TAD* C, p. 23.

28 See Haran, "Codex," 212–222; Zhakevich, *Scribal*, chap. 4 §2.B–D.

29 Van der Toorn, *Scribal*, 2 places significant weight on the idea that between 500–200 BCE, biblical works were generally produced in scribal workshops within temples.

Jeremiah's interactions with Baruch in the scribal workshop take on new meaning once Jeremiah is seen as a scribal character. Those with a critical eye for scribal training have noted that Baruch takes on the role of Jeremiah's student in this scene.[30] Römer sees Jeremiah as a "senior scribe" here,[31] and Carr sees Baruch as a student. Carr writes that Baruch "comes to Jeremiah already a 'scribe,' much as more advanced students would have come after receiving early education in their family or (more rarely) a school."[32] The textual data generally support these views, as the text depicts a hierarchical relationship between Jeremiah and Baruch. Jeremiah is the one who acquires the scribal materials (v. 2). Jeremiah directs Baruch's actions by "summoning" him (v. 4). Jeremiah instructs Baruch as to what he must do with the scroll once it is complete (v. 6), and Baruch says nothing as the scene unfolds. The power dynamic between Jeremiah and Baruch suggests a type of learning environment, and the scene's overt scribal context suggests that this may reflect a type of professional scribal training.[33] The scene, however, focuses on Jeremiah's preparation of Baruch as a replacement for Jeremiah. As such, the power dynamic in the scene illustrates a type of professional preparation, not an elementary education. Education consists of training a pupil in prerequisite skills and knowledge, whereas Baruch already knows how to read and write: he is trained in the art of stenography[34] and has the ability to compose "all of the words" (כָּל־הַדְּבָרִים) spoken to him "from the mouth of Jeremiah" (מִפִּי יִרְמְיָהוּ). In this sense, their relationship might best be described as an apprenticeship rather than a teacher-

---

30 Even in the Hellenistic period Josephus refers to "the student Baruch" (τὸν μαθητὴν Βαροῦχον, Jos Ant 10.9.1).
31 Römer, "Prophet," 89–90.
32 Carr, Writing, 147. Dearman, "Servants," 411 refers to Baruch, his brother Seraiah, his father Neriah, and his grandfather Mahseiah as a "scribal family." Neriah and Mehseiah are not characters in the Bible. They appear only in the patronymics of Baruch and Seraiah (MT Jer 32:12; 51:59).
33 The editor of MT does not supply a professional title to Baruch until Baruch has completed the task that Jeremiah told him to do. This can be interpreted as MT elevating Baruch's professional status as the story develops (see discussion below).
34 Janzen sees MT's addition of Baruch's title, "the scribe," later in the passage to be an interpretation of his "stenographic" function, but he also observes, "Baruch's activity and relationship to Jeremiah went beyond that of a scribe. . . and his literary activity probably is to be seen more in the context of the בני הנביאים" (Studies, 72). See discussion below. Carr, Writing, 147 sees Baruch's ability to compose at Jeremiah's dictation as a sign of "advanced" scribal training.

student relationship. This apprenticeship prepares Baruch to replace Jeremiah in the next scenes.³⁵

The text uses the idiom מִפִּי יִרְמְיָהוּ (lit. "from the mouth of Jeremiah") to indicate that the content of the scroll comprises Jeremiah's ideas and not Baruch's.³⁶ This idiom occurs four times in the passage (not counting two erroneous instances in MT³⁷). In other passages in the book of Jeremiah, it is used to identify the originator of an idea, as in the phrase "from the mouth of Yahweh" (מִפִּי יְהוָה / ἀπὸ στόματος κυρίου) in MT Jer 23:16 ≈ LXX Jer 39:16.³⁸ Comparative evidence supports this understanding and demonstrates that this is a widely distributed Semitic idiom. In Elephantine Aramaic, כפם, "according to" (lit. "as the mouth of"), is a legal term that indicates the speaker of a legally binding clause, that is, the one responsible for the claims.³⁹ Within a scribal context, the Akkadian phrase *ša pî*, "of/from the mouth," refers to the author, though not necessarily the editor, of a literary work.⁴⁰ This comparative evidence suggests that the phrase מִפִּי יִרְמְיָהוּ ascribes to Jeremiah the responsibility for the state-

---

35 Lemaire sees the philosophical training of the prophets as following an apprentice model rather than an institutionalized program like that found in the palace or temple (*Écoles*, 50–52, 61, 70–71).

36 Similarly, Matthews, "Jeremiah's," 120–121.

37 The erroneous additions are found in verses 6 and 17. In my view, the addition of the statement יְהוָה אֶת־דִּבְרֵי אֲשֶׁר־כָּתַבְתָּ מִפִּי, "on which you have written, at my dictation, the words of Yahweh" (MT v. 6), is a gloss added by the editor to provide a masculine plural antecedent (יְהוָה דִּבְרֵי, "the words [m.pl.] of Yahweh") for the suffix ם- "them" in תִּקְרָאֵם, "you shall read them." See LXX, which reads ἀναγινώσῃ αὐτοῖς, "you shall read to them [dative]." LXX uses the verb ἀναγινώσκω, "to read," intransitively in verses 15 and 21. Therefore, the dative pronoun αὐτοῖς must refer to the audience to whom the act of reading occurs and not the object read. The translator rightly interpreted תִּקְרָאֵם here with the meaning "to call out to (the people [הָעָם / λαοῦ] from the document);" when קרא√ is to be understood in the sense of "calling," its direct object is the person to whom the summons is made. See *TDNT* 1:344, n. 1.

Verse 17 ends with מִפִּיו in MT, which appears to be an error; see Rudolph, *Jeremia*, 232. It may be the result of paraplepsis from the next verse, where מִפִּי appears. Furthermore, בְּדִיוֹ at the end of verse 18 is very similar to מִפִּי in ancient scripts, and may have worked its way into MT from the errors forming around the word מִפִּיו in verse 17. For a different view see McKane, *Jeremiah*, 905.

38 See Yair Hoffman, "Aetiology," 184–5, which claims that "the only purpose of the author in introducing this dialogue was to impress upon the readers' mind that it was not Jeremiah who wrote the scroll [but Yahweh]." Matthews, "Jeremiah's," 120–121 follows Hoffman.

39 I am indebted to Bezalel Porten, who brought to my attention that כפם, "according to," in Elephantine legal material refers to a scribe who has paraphrased his source, but in MT Jer 36 Baruch is quoting his source verbatim (personal communication, August 2016, Jerusalem).

40 See Lambert, "Catalogue," 72 and van der Toorn, *Scribal*, 43. Van der Toorn does not connect *ša pî* with מִפִּי in his discussion of MT Jer 36 (186). See also Gevaryahu, "Baruch," 204.

ments that Baruch writes. The narrative of the first scene in MT Jer 36 depicts Jeremiah initiating the writing project with Baruch and states that Jeremiah is responsible for "all of the words" (כָּל־הַדְּבָרִים). In an abstract sense, then, Jeremiah is the author of this group-writing project,[41] but, as will be shown below, the characters hold Baruch equally responsible for its content.

Baruch writes Jeremiah's dictations on a מְגִלַּת־סֵפֶר, a scroll document. Van der Toorn has convincingly argued that the phrase מְגִלַּת־סֵפֶר (vv. 2 and 4) specifically refers to a collected composition, and as such, those responsible for producing it are thought to be compilers or editors.[42] When the passage describes Jehudi slicing the מְגִלַּת־סֵפֶר into pieces that are three to four columns long, the document is shown to have been of considerable length (v. 23). Such a long document, containing all of Jeremiah's professionally delivered prophetic messages, would have required editing.[43] Thus, Baruch's professional training under Jeremiah included an editorial task.

A final query about the production of the scroll remains: Where did "all of the words" (כָּל־הַדְּבָרִים, v. 2) from prophecies of past years come from? There are two possibilities. Either Jeremiah remembered, verbatim, all of his prophecies over the course of his career without textual aids, or he used textual aids as he dictated to Baruch. The passage does not supply data to directly answer this query,[44] but other passages in the book indicate that Jeremiah wrote his own

---

41 Baruch's statement to the chief courtiers in LXX verse 18 conveys this: ἀνήγγειλέ μοι Ιερεμίας πάντας τοὺς λόγους τούτους, καὶ ἔγραφον ἐν βιβλίῳ, "Jeremiah recounted to me all of these words, and I wrote (them) on a scroll." Compare SAA 8 no. 158, which is a text written by a "scribe of a temple" ([lu2]A.BA É DINGIR, SAA 8 no. 158 ln. r. 6), Nabû-mušeṣi. This writer composes 17 known astrological reports for the king (SAA 8 nos. 143–159), at least one letter (SAA 13 no. 145), and one co-authored letter (SAA 10 no. 205). In one of his reports he cites an omen from a scholar (ummânu) (SAA 8 no. 158 ln. r. 4): anniu ša pî umm[âni], "This (report) is from the mouth of the scho[lar]." In this text we have an educated scribe recording the words of a highly educated scholar as he receives divine information. In the same way, Baruch records the words of Jeremiah. For a similar conclusion using different evidence, see Gevaryahu, "Baruch," 204–205.
42 Van der Toorn, Scribal, 175. He bases this view on the use of the term in MT Ezek 2:9.
43 Here I refer to the conventions of physically preparing a long document: cutting, pasting (or sewing if on parchment), copying various accounts into a single text, etc.
44 Note that according to BHS, a few manuscripts (which are not identified) read יִרְמְיָהוּ אֶל־בָּרוּךְ וַיִּקְרָא rather than יִרְמְיָהוּ וַיִּקְרָא אֶת־בָּרוּךְ in verse 4. This might be construed as "Jeremiah *read to* Baruch." The PESHITTA, ܡܐ ܐܪܝܡܐ ܠܒܪܘܟ, can (but need not) be construed the same way. Here LXX (and Vul.) chose to translate קרא√ as "to summon." But note that in late antiquity, Jerome admits having struggled with the variety of ways that קרא√ is used in the book of Jeremiah: "proclaiming, crying out, and reading" (Graves, *Jerome's*, 166). Furthermore, Josephus may have also been confused on the matter, as his interpretation can be read as suggesting

prophecies (MT Jer 30:1; 51:60). Therefore, he might have used such writings to trigger his memory as he dictated to Baruch. Studies on scribal culture discuss the mnemonic character of instructional texts and the role of memory in the educational process,[45] but little is known about how memory functioned for the professional ancient Judahite orator, such as Jeremiah, particularly within a scribal context, such as this passage.[46] Heuristically, one may draw on the Greek and Roman rhetoricians, who were the first to reflect on the role of memory within the context of oral presentation and scribal habits.[47] Works designed to train rhetoricians within a scribal context, such as Cicero's *de Oratore* or Quintilian's *Oratoria*,[48] illustrate how memory and writing work together, and even how scribal training served as an analogy for the process of memorization.[49] The scribal setting of Jeremiah and Baruch's workshop, the evidence that Jeremiah wrote some of his own prophecies, and the ancient evidence that textual sources aided memory recall in scribal contexts lead to the conclusion that Jeremiah used textual aids to trigger his memory.[50] After all, Jeremiah is expected to have access to blank scrolls (v. 2), and it is, therefore, reasonable to assume that he also had access to scrolls with written content.[51] This interpretation confirms general observations made by both Carr and van der Toorn. Carr argues that an oral-written databank of knowledge was the source for later tradents who compiled much of the biblical corpus, and van der Toorn holds that indi-

---

that Jeremiah wrote the scroll (*Ant* 10.6.2). Alternatively, Josephus may be relying on a different version of the tale.

45 Crenshaw, *Education*, 230–233 discusses the mnemonic character of wisdom texts.
46 Van der Toorn, *Scribal*, 195–199 discusses the role of memory for the writer of the book of Jeremiah, but not for the character of the prophet. Regardless, van der Toorn sees the process of the composition of prophetic oracles and narrative as the result of the collective social memory of a tradition *and of the reliance on textual sources* (195, 198).
47 See Small, *Wax*, esp. 126–131, 181–188.
48 E.g., Quin *Inst Orat* 2.4.27–41, 10.1.19, 11.2–6; Cic *de Orat* 2.86.351–2.88.360.
49 Cicero writes, "I have myself met eminent people with almost superhuman powers of memory, Charmadas at Athens and Metrodorus of Scepsis in Asia, who is said to be still living, each of whom used to say that he wrote down things he wanted to remember in certain 'localities' in his possession by means of images, just as if he were inscribing letters on wax" (*de Orat* 2.88.360).
50 So too Widengren, *Literary*, 78–80 and Rudolph, *Jeremia*, 231 and n. 2.
51 The only surviving evidence of long literary documents written in Northwest Semitic, affiliated with ancient Judeans, and from the mid-first millennium BCE, are the papyri of the Ahiqar manuscript and the Darius Inscription (*TAD* C2) from Elephantine. Both are written over erased collections of earlier documents, the Darius Inscription, in particular includes a list of compiled memoranda, which may have not been erased when the Darius text was copied. Presumably Jeremiah and Baruch are using similar scribal mediums to compile their long scroll.

vidual prophecies may have been written and filed in administrative centers, such as temples.⁵² The evidence from Jeremiah agrees with both claims and also supports Sanders's view that writing occurred throughout Judah and was not limited to the activities in the Jerusalem palace or temple.⁵³

After Baruch composes the scroll, Jeremiah informs Baruch that he, Jeremiah, will not be able to enter the temple. Jeremiah states, אֲנִי עָצוּר לֹא אוּכַל לָבוֹא בֵּית יְהוָה, "I am inhibited, I will not be able to enter the House of Yahweh" (v. 5). Scholars have attempted to explain this statement by looking elsewhere in the book, but the reason for Jeremiah's inability to perform his task in the temple remains unknown.⁵⁴ According to Holladay, Jeremiah's restriction provides "the motive for writing the prophecies down."⁵⁵ One may assume that Jeremiah had intended to read the scroll himself in the temple (see MT Jer 26:1; 30:1), but realizing his future restriction, he decided to professionally train Baruch to be his successor (see evidence above), a motif already established in the narrative when it referenced Josiah in verses 1–2. With the motif of succession comes the notion of "legacy." In addition to serving the practical function of promoting Jeremiah's message in the temple, the recruitment of Baruch helps establish that Jeremiah's legacy will be carried into another generation. Baruch's loyalty and commitment to perpetuating Jeremiah's work provide proof of Jeremiah's success as an advanced scribal professional.⁵⁶ It can be concluded, then, that his inability to enter the temple thwarted his intention to deliver the scroll himself.

A survey of the use of the passive participle עָצוּר reveals that in other passages the term refers to a limitation on an individual imposed or managed by an

---

52 Van der Toorn, *Scribal*, 178–182. Van der Toorn believes that an oracle archive does not explain Baruch's source, but rather that the text's writer also relied on a surviving oral tradition about Jeremiah (186).
53 Sanders, *Invention*, 131.
54 Holladay, *Jeremiah 2*, 255. In light of the various scribal loci and scribal chambers that appear in this passage, I am inclined to speculate that Jeremiah once held a לִשְׁכָּה in the temple's outer court but was dismissed from it by the priest in charge of the rooms. He then had to use Baruch's scribal connections to Micaiah (see discussion below) in order to present the scroll. See MT Neh 13:4–5, which claims that the priest, Eliashib, was in charge of the Temple's לְשָׁכוֹת and was able to rearrange them to accommodate Tobiah by assigning him a לִשְׁכָּה that was previously used for storage. See also Muilenburg, "Baruch," 224–225, who muses (along with Galling, "Halle," 56) that the לִשְׁכָּה from which Baruch reads in the temple could have been the very chamber from which Jeremiah gave his sermon in MT Jer 26:2.
55 Holladay, *Jeremiah 2*, 255.
56 So too Widengren, *Literary*, 94–97, referring in this case to the success of Jeremiah's prophetic legacy.

outside agent.⁵⁷ Previous scholars have suggested that עָצוּר refers to a "vorübergehende Behinderung kultischer Art" but, as Rudolph notes, Jeremiah had experienced a "polizeiliches Tempelverbot," according to MT Jer 20:1–4.⁵⁸ While I find it difficult to use the narrative circumstances of MT Jer 20 to justify the narrative circumstances of MT Jer 36 as Rudolph does, he may be correct to see עָצוּר as a reference to a political limitation since the context reveals that a temple presentation is the only opportunity for his message to be considered by the chief courtiers (compare MT Jer 26). Similarly, Wright and Milgrom claim that the term in MT Jer 36:5 can be interpreted in view of the meaning of עָצוּר in MT 1 Chr 12:1, which reads, וְאֵלֶּה הַבָּאִים אֶל־דָּוִיד לְצִיקְלַג עוֹד עָצוּר מִפְּנֵי שָׁאוּל "The following are those who came to David at Ziklag, while he could not move about freely because of Saul" (NRSV).⁵⁹ Ziklag was a strategic military vantage point for David, but it was also the boundary of his political and military power (cf. MT 1 Sam 30; 2 Sam 1:1; 2 Sam 4:10). So too, within the context of MT Jer 36:5, Jeremiah was sanctioned from entering the temple by the politically minded courtly scribal class.⁶⁰

Lastly, in Jeremiah's scribal workshop, he contrives a plan for Baruch to read the scroll in the temple (v. 6). Jeremiah's plan and the scenes that follow demonstrate that Baruch has advanced beyond the status of an apprentice and is in the process of becoming a junior colleague of Jeremiah. As colleagues, the two engage in a treasonous conspiracy that damages the king's reputation (v.

---

57 This is generally true for the full verbal range of the root with the exception of two not well attested semantic categories (Wright and Milgrom, *TDOT*, 11:311 meanings "d" and "e"), but due to the technical meaning ascribed to the Gp-stem, a study of the passive forms are most pertinent. The term appears in the dyad עָצוּר וְעָזוּב "bond or free (men)" MT Deut 32:36; 1 Kgs 14:10; 21:21, 2 Kgs 9:8; 14:26 (as וְאֶפֶס עָצוּר וְאֶפֶס עָזוּב), and a number of proposals have been made about this phrase's meaning, see Wright and Milgrom, *TDOT*, 11:312–313. The term appears three times in the book of Jeremiah as a passive participle standing alone. In MT Jer 33:1 (LXX Jer 40:1 δεδεμένος "bound") the word refers to the state of Jeremiah, while under house arrest. Lundbom equates the term here to כָּלוּא "chained," but notes that it means something different in MT Jer 36:5, where "the term simply means 'under restraint,' i.e. under surveillance" (*Jeremiah 21–36*, 528). The occurrence of the term in MT Jer 39:15 is problematic. According to Holladay, *Jeremiah 2*, 269 MT Jer 39:15–18 is out of place, and he moves the verses after MT Jer 38:27, following the LXX Jer 45:27 correlate. Furthermore, an equivalent to עָצוּר is not found in LXX Jer 46:15. Lundom, *Jeremiah 37–52*, 98 argues there that MT is original and LXX is in error due to haplography. The wording of the line in MT matches that found in MT Jer 33:1, and so too does its meaning; Jeremiah was imprisoned. But this is not the case in MT Jer 36:5, where it appears to have the meaning of "sanctioned" or "deterred."
58 Rudolph, *Jeremia*, 233.
59 See Wright and Milgrom, *TDOT*, 6:336.
60 For a possible reason see discussion in chapter four.

29). It is unclear whether their scheme was intended to unfold as it does in the following scenes, but Baruch's seemingly intentional choice to read the scroll from Gemariah's temple chamber (v. 10; see below) suggests that Baruch and Jeremiah had hoped that their scroll would be recognized by the scribal figures in the palace, and perhaps even by the king (v. 23).

The first scene of the Tale of Jeremiah and Baruch's Scroll describes the divine origin of Jeremiah's sayings, alludes to his scribal abilities, and takes place in his undisclosed scribal workshop. The scene depicts the training of an apprentice who is preparing to succeed his teacher and to become a junior colleague. This small alliance of scribal characters then contrives an elaborate plan to promote sayings produced by Jeremiah throughout his career. This scene illustrates the type of alliance and political aspirations that scribal characters, even those outside the king's circle of influence, were capable of. In the next scene, scribal alliances and associations will prove to be the avenue by which Baruch gains access to the most elite and influential scribal figures in the nation, those who have the potential to persuade the king and shape the national discourse.

3.2 Professional Scribal Characters in the Temple Complex (MT 36:9–11 / LXX 43:9–11)

In verse 9, Baruch initiates the plan that he and Jeremiah concocted in the scribal workshop. Jeremiah had instructed Baruch to read the scroll in earshot of the people gathered in the temple (בְּאָזְנֵי הָעָם בֵּית יְהוָה; v. 6).[61] Verse 9 begins a scene in which Jeremiah's plan will come to fruition. According to the scene's new regnal formula, a national day of fasting was held in the temple, either in the fifth year of Jehoiakim (MT) or in his eighth year (LXX).[62] Here, LXX produces a conceptually more difficult narrative. The two editions read:

---

[61] Although the English idiom "in earshot" is colloquial, it serves an analytical purpose below.

[62] The historical circumstances of the fast are unknown, but see Freedy and Redford, "Dates," 465–466 for an attempt at discussing it within the political history of the region. Whether or not the fast was a historical event, it functions as a literary device that allows for Baruch's public address.

LXX Jer 43:9
Καὶ ἐγενήθη ἐν τῷ ἔτει τῷ ὀγδόῳ τῷ βασιλεῖ Ιωακιμ ἐν τῷ μηνὶ τῷ ἐνάτῳ ἐξεκλησίασαν νηστείαν κατὰ πρόσωπον κυρίου πᾶς ὁ λαὸς ἐν Ιερουσαλημ καὶ οἶκος Ιουδα.

And it happened in the eighth year of King Ioakim, in the ninth month, all the people in Ierousalem and the house of Iouda proclaimed in assembly a fast before the Lord (NETS).

MT Jer 36:9
וַיְהִי בַשָּׁנָה הַחֲמִשִׁית לִיהוֹיָקִים בֶּן־יֹאשִׁיָּהוּ מֶלֶךְ־יְהוּדָה בַּחֹדֶשׁ הַתְּשִׁעִי קָרְאוּ צוֹם לִפְנֵי יְהוָה כָּל־הָעָם בִּירוּשָׁלָ͏ִם וְכָל־הָעָם הַבָּאִים מֵעָרֵי יְהוּדָה בִּירוּשָׁלָ͏ִם:

And so it was in the fifth year of Jehoiakim, son of Josiah, king of Judah, in the ninth month, all of the people in Jerusalem and all of the people coming from the cities of Judah into Jerusalem congregated for a fast before the Lord.[63]

It is difficult to explain LXX's reference to the eighth (τῷ ἔτει) year of Jehoiakim, and here a methodological observation can be made. Whether a scholar chooses reading the "fifth"[64] or the "eighth"[65] year, she will justify her claims by finding historical evidence for a significant event to have occurred in the history of Judah during that year. This suggests that a scholar either reads the text to be historically accurate or assumes the ancient reader would have connected the fifth or the eighth year of Jehoiakim to a significant event that would color the

---

63 Alternatively translate, "A fast was convened before the Lord (with) all of the people in Jerusalem." See the PESHITTA:

ܘܗܘܐ ܒܫܢܬܐ ܚܡܝܫܝܬܐ ܕܝܘܝܩܝܡ ܒܪ ܝܘܫܝܐ ܡܠܟܐ ܕܝܗܘܕܐ ܒܝܪܚܐ ܬܫܝܥܝܐ. ܓܙܪܘ ܨܘܡܐ ܩܕܡ ܡܪܝܐ ܠܟܠܗ ܥܡܐ ܕܒܐܘܪܫܠܡ. ܘܩܪܐ ܒܪܘܟ ܩܕܡ ܟܠܗ ܥܡܐ ܕܐܬܐ ܡܢ ܩܘܪܝܐ ܕܝܗܘܕܐ ܠܐܘܪܫܠܡ.

"And so it was, on the fifth year of Jehoiakim, son of Josiah, king of Judah, on the ninth month, a fast was decreed (lit. they [impersonal] decreed a fast) before the Lord (with) all of the people in Jerusalem. And Baruch read before all of the people who came from the towns of Judah into Jerusalem."

The PESHITTA is aiming for a more precise meaning here (Greenberg, "Jeremiah," 343). While at first glance "all of the people" can be understood as the subject of the verb in PESHITTA, the syntax argues against it. Furthermore, the events of this passage are conspicuously similar to those in MT 1 Kgs 21:9, in which Jezebel writes, under the name of Ahaz, to the elders (הַזְּקֵנִים) and to the leaders (הַחֹרִים) urging them to convene a fast (קִרְאוּ־צוֹם). It is difficult to determine whether MT lost the phrase ܩܕܡ ܟܠܗ ܥܡܐ present in the PESHITTA or whether (the *Vorlage* of) the PESHITTA added it for clarity. Verse 10a in PESHITTA contains a variant that resulted in an expansion, so perhaps a similar issue occurred in verse 9. Lastly, note that the use of the patronymic for Josiah follows MT's tendency to expand names and titles, which suggests that MT's reading is secondary (Stipp, "Prophetic," 67–68). LXX has no problem with all of the people convening a fast and reads πᾶς ὁ λαὸς ἐν Ιερουσαλημ καὶ οἶκος Ιουδα as the subject of the verb. I believe the participial phrase הַבָּאִים . . . בִּירוּשָׁלָ͏ִם, "the ones coming... into Jerusalem," to be a late and problematic reading, since normally travelers "go up to" (√עלה) Jerusalem.
64 Rudolph, *Jeremias*, 230.
65 Holladay, *Jeremiah 2*, 251, 255–256.

way in which the text is to be understood. I wish to put historical questions aside and to ask: what does the duration of time tell us about the scribal profession in each edition?

Baruch began his training and the construction of the מְגִלַּת־סֵפֶר in the fourth year of Jehoiakim (605 BCE); the month and day are unknown.[66] If one accepts MT's reading of the fifth year and ninth month in v. 9, then Jeremiah and Baruch had roughly 10–21 months in the scribal workshop to compose the scroll and to plan Baruch's actions. However, if one accepts LXX's reading of the eighth year and ninth month, then Jeremiah and Baruch had three to four years to prepare for Baruch's presentation in the temple. These variants produce different perspectives on the commitment required by scribal associations to compile a document of significant length[67] and to train professionals.

From a literary point of view, LXX's reading is preferable, because it produces a literary parallelism between the first and the last scenes of the passage. In the last scene, Jeremiah's prophecy against Jehoiakim (vv. 30–31) foresees his imminent death, which occurred c. 598 BCE (LXX 2 Kgs 23:36–37). Thus, the time that Jeremiah and Baruch spend in the first and the last scenes preparing the scroll is nearly equal in LXX. In the first scene Jeremiah and Baruch take approximately three to four years (c. 604/5–601 BCE) to prepare a scroll (vv. 1–8). The scroll is then destroyed on a single day in 601 BCE. Following this, Jeremiah and Baruch spend another three years preparing the second scroll, which was composed just like the first (LXX Jer 43:32). This second scroll (LXX Jer 43:28) is made on the horizon of Jehoiakim's death (c. 598 BCE), as shown by the additional prophecy to be included in it that predicts his death (LXX Jer 43:29–31). In LXX, the time and care that Jeremiah and Baruch invest in their document and their plan stand in stark contrast to the single day in which their scribal critics, the chief courtiers, destroy their work.

In verses 9–11, the temple serves as a second locus of scribal activity. There Baruch enters a chamber in the (outer) courtyard of the temple, from which he is able to read his scroll within earshot of the people (v. 10), just as he and Jeremiah planned. The image of Baruch reading a text within the temple precinct calls to mind priestly figures such as Moses[68] or Ezra,[69] but for the reader of Jer-

---

[66] This is perhaps a sign that the story is evoking historical events for literary rather than historical purposes. See discussion in the introduction.
[67] The document must have been long enough to contain at least a few multicolumn sheets (v. 23), yet short enough to have been read three times in its entirety on the same day (vv. 10–11, 15, 23).
[68] See Römer, "Prophet," 87–90 and Davis, *Cave 4*, 245.
[69] See Grätz, "Wisdom," 195–197.

emiah the scene also evokes the images of Jeremiah himself in MT Jer 26.⁷⁰ So in the temple, Baruch takes on the role of a religious functionary before the people, and the location from which he performs his reading (i.e., the temple's scribal chamber) is perhaps the key to understanding his characterization.

In the temple, Baruch gains access to the "chamber" (לִשְׁכָּה, v. 10)⁷¹ belonging to the scribal character Gemariah. This appears to be one of many rooms in the temple's public outer courtyard that held personnel who had scribal responsibilities (MT Jer 35:2, 4; 2 Kgs 23:11).⁷² According to MT Jer 35:4, there was a chamber in the temple called the לִשְׁכַּת הַשָּׂרִים, which was occupied by the high-ranking palace officials.⁷³ Such references allude to the palace's oversight of the temple precinct. In addition, in some respects, Gemariah's temple chamber resembles the unidentified workshop in which Jeremiah and Baruch wrote. But the function of Gemariah's scribal space in the temple is different from that of the space in which Jeremiah and Baruch prepared the scroll; Gemariah's לִשְׁכָּה is not a location of scribal production, but rather a locus of scribal presentation, a place from which one can read to the public and be heard by a scribal colleague.⁷⁴

---

70 Here I make a literary, and not a historical, observation about the relationship between MT Jer 26 and MT Jer 36. See similarly Muilenburg, "Baruch," 224–225. The book of Jeremiah frequently pairs prophets and priests (MT Jer 2:8, 26; 4:9; 5:31; 6:13; 8:1, 10; 13:13; 14:18; 18:18; 23:11, 33; 26:7, 11, 16; 27:16; 28:1, 5; 29:1, 29; 32:32; 37:3). Even Jeremiah's own characterization blends the two roles, e.g., MT Jer 1:1–4.
71 The meaning of לִשְׁכָּה remains difficult. Assuming the same word lay behind LXX's *Vorlagen*, it translates it as οἶκος, "house," but elsewhere one finds οἱ περίπατοι, "the walkways" (LXX Ezek 42:5), and ἐξέδρα, "hall" (LXX Ezek 42:9, 13; 44:19; 46:19). In LXX Jer 42:4 (MT Jer 35:4), one finds παστοφόριον and οἶκος used for two separate occurrences of לִשְׁכָּה in MT. Most scholars cite Galling, "Halle," 51–57 as the authority on the matter.
72 These appear to be rooms on the upper terrace of the temple's courtyard (MT Ezek 40:17; 42:3). Chambers for the priests and singers appear in a different location than those for the scribal characters (MT Ezek 40:44). In the second temple, these may have been where the aristocratic families resided (MT Ezra 8:29). Some of these rooms may have contained commodities for the temple, which would have required accountants (i.e., scribal characters) to maintain them (MT Neh 10:37–39). Although the historical accuracy of these verses remains suspect, they nonetheless demonstrate that the reader of the book of Jeremiah could reasonably assume how the events in MT Jer 36 unfolded. For this reason, the text does not supply the reader with superfluous detail. See also Muilenburg, "Baruch," 228–231.
73 See discussion in Galling, "Halle," 53–55.
74 Lemaire, "Sage," 177–178 holds that the chamber in the temple "could well have indicated a room open on one side with benches along the other three walls (Koehler-Baumgarner 2:309), this was clearly a place convenient for public reading within the temple enclosure."

Significant to the social interactions in the tale is the fact that Baruch appears to enter this chamber in Gemariah's absence (v. 10), since the next scene depicts Gemariah in the palace (v. 12, 14). This datum makes one wonder how Baruch gained access to the room. It can be inferred that Baruch had previously fostered a close relationship with Gemariah or with those who had access to Gemariah's chambers,[75] like Micaiah, who was Gemariah's son (v. 11). Since Micaiah is present, it seems that Baruch is utilizing a scribal alliance with him to gain access to a particular locus of scribal power. How he gained this connection remains unknown, though it seems to relate to the shared scribal culture of Baruch and Micaiah, Gemariah's son. In this scene, one finds the next generation of scribal characters, Baruch and Micaiah, collaborating even though they each maintain their own allegiance to their scribal affiliations. Furthermore, it is notable that the father-son relationship between Gemariah and his son Micaiah calls to mind the master-apprentice relationship between Jeremiah and Baruch.[76]

The text identifies Micaiah as a member of a scribal family, and therefore depicts him as a scribal character.[77] It reads:[78]

LXX Jer 43:11	MT Jer 36:11
καὶ ἤκουσεν Μιχαιας υἱὸς Γαμαριου υἱοῦ Σαφαν ἅπαντας τοὺς λόγους κυρίου ἐκ τοῦ βιβλίου·	וַיִּשְׁמַע מִכָיְהוּ בֶן־גְּמַרְיָהוּ בֶן־שָׁפָן אֶת־כָּל־דִּבְרֵי יְהוָה מֵעַל הַסֵּפֶר
And Michaias son of Gamarias son of Saphan heard all the words of the Lord from the book.	And Micaiah, son of Gemariah, son of Shaphan, heard all of the words of Yahweh from the document

---

75 Holladay speculates that this was due to their shared training in a "scribal school" (*Jeremiah 2*, 257).
76 Although Jeremiah and Baruch are not biologically related, the term "son" is used to designate a "student" throughout most cultures and periods of the ancient Near East, including ancient Judah. See Carr, *Writing*, 21, 65, and, in the context of a discussion of ancient Israel, 129–130.
77 Dearman, "Servants," 411 identifies all the members of Shaphan's and Baruch's families as having scribal training.
78 Note that Micaiah hears the words of Yahweh, דִּבְרֵי יְהוָה / τοὺς λόγους κυρίου (v. 11), and not "the words of Jeremiah" (דִּבְרֵי יִרְמְיָהוּ), which is how the content of the scroll is referred to in the presence of the שָׂרִים (v. 10). Micaiah did not yet know that Jeremiah was the author of Baruch's scroll. This is a sign that Micaiah interpreted Baruch to be a priest or a prophet whose own words were divinely inspired. The שָׂרִים will wonder the same until Baruch tells them in verse 18 that Jeremiah is the scroll's "author."

Micaiah's patronymic extends to his grandfather, and one understands from his name that Micaiah has the right to be in his father's chamber and that he is acquainted with the customs of its scholarly milieu.[79] As the grandson of the great scholar Shaphan, Micaiah was part of a scholarly family,[80] and, as will be seen below, this legacy affords him credibility among the other professional characters whom he will meet in the next locus of scribal activity, the palace's scribal chamber. The present scene embeds in the narrative many allusions to the scribal profession. Most notably, it identifies the temple as a locus of scribal activity, in which Baruch and Micaiah interact regarding the content of Baruch's document. When Baruch reads all of the words of Yahweh (כָּל־דִּבְרֵי יְהוָה; v. 11), Micaiah "understands" (√שׁמע) them, because Micaiah is a scribal character, unlike the laity, who are merely within earshot of the reading (בְּאָזְנֵי כָּל־הָעָם; v. 10). Micaiah reports Baruch's activity to the palace scribal characters, the שָׂרִים, and in doing so transitions the tale to the next scene. Micaiah's access to his father's chamber and the fact that the שָׂרִים in the next scene respect his report demonstrate that he is a junior associate of the שָׂרִים, who relied on him for intelligence on the activities in the temple.[81]

3.3 Courtly Scribal Interactions in the Palace (MT 36:12–19 / LXX 43:12–19)

Thus far, the story has presented two scribal loci: (1) an unknown scribal workshop where scribal training and the preparation of a scroll took place, and (2) a scribal chamber in the temple where a public lecture and an interaction with a scribal colleague occurred. In the transition from the first to the second scene, Baruch bore his scroll from one location to another. Similarly, as the text transitions from the second to the third scene, Micaiah will bear news of Baruch's scroll to a new locus of scribal activity, the palace's scribal chamber. After this, Baruch and his scroll will enter the scene to repeat in the palace the reading that he staged earlier in the temple.

---

79 Alternatively, one could understand Micaiah as positioned in the audience, as one of the Judahites listening to Baruch. I believe, however, that the writer's use of Micaiah's patronymic suggests that he is entitled to be *in* the chamber of his father. For further discussion of Baruch's audience, see Matthews, "Jeremiah's," esp. 120.
80 Lundbom, *Jeremiah*, 598 identifies Gemariah as a "professionally trained scribe."
81 Note that Demsky, *Literacy*, 148–152, 154–157 deduced a similar phenomenon by studying surviving seals and references to the "king's scribe" in biblical literature.

According to verse 12, Micaiah left the temple and entered the "palace" (‏בֵּית־‎ ‏הַמֶּלֶךְ‎), and more specifically, the scribal chamber (‏לִשְׁכַּת הַסֹּפֵר‎ / τὸν οἶκον τοῦ γραμματέως, "the residence of the scribe"), but there is some debate as to whether the events in this scene all occur in the same chamber. As the scene unfolds, one of the chief courtiers will escort Baruch and the scroll "to them" (‏אֲלֵיהֶם‎), that is, presumably to those in the ‏לִשְׁכַּת הַסֹּפֵר‎ (v. 14), and in the next scene the scroll will be said to reside in ‏לִשְׁכַּת אֱלִישָׁמָע הַסֹּפֵר‎, "the chamber of Elishama, the scribe" (vv. 20, 21). But LXX refers to this second location as only οἴκῳ/οἴκου Ελισαμα "the residence of Elishama."[82] Because ‏לִשְׁכַּת הַסֹּפֵר‎ and οἴκῳ/οἴκου Ελισαμα are not the same phrases, Holladay is reluctant to identify "the chamber of Elishama" with "the scribal chamber."[83] From a stylistic and narrative point of view, however, the two readings are best understood as references to the same location.[84] The passage pays close attention to the locations to which Baruch and the scroll travel, and there is no indication that the scroll moved from "the chamber of the scribe" to "Elishama's chamber." Furthermore, as will be shown below, only one individual in the palace holds the position ‏הַסֹּפֵר‎ at a given time, and thus ‏לִשְׁכַּת הַסֹּפֵר‎ likely refers to the office assigned to ‏הַסֹּפֵר‎, which in the narrative is "Elishama the scribe" (‏אֱלִישָׁמָע הַסֹּפֵר‎ / Ελισαμα ὁ γραμματεύς; v. 12). Thus, the third locus of scribal activity in the tale is the palace chamber of Elishama, the scribe, which is also known as the chamber of the scribe.

When Micaiah comes down from the temple in scene two and arrives at Elishama's scribal chamber in scene three, the chamber contains ‏כָּל־הַשָּׂרִים‎, "all of the chief courtiers" (πάντες οἱ ἄρχοντες; v. 12). Contextualizing the meaning and function of ‏שָׂרִים‎ in this passage is central to understanding the allusions to the scribal profession and the complexity of the sociology of the scribal courtiers for the whole pericope. This scene depicts the ‏שָׂרִים‎ as intellectually and socially divided over Baruch's scroll; it portrays an individual who actively opposes the scroll (Jehudi), individuals who appear unaffiliated in the debate over the scroll (Elishama and Zedekiah), and an alliance of those who are open to the scroll's ideas (Delaiah, Elnathan, and Gemariah). The remainder of this section discusses the meaning of ‏שָׂרִים‎, the characters who represent these three views, and the process by which the ‏שָׂרִים‎ intellectually engage with Baruch and his document in the scribal chamber.

---

82 Again MT is marked by its interest in expanding names and titles. See Stipp, "Prophetic," 67–68.
83 Holladay, *Jeremiah 2*, 257.
84 McKane, *Jeremiah*, 906.

On multiple occasions in the book of Jeremiah, either Jeremiah or Baruch comes into contact with the שָׂרִים. This term is generally translated as "officials" or "princes," but the exact capacity in which these characters served remains unknown; it may in fact have had an ambiguous or polyvalent meaning which allows it to be (re)contextualized in various biblical narratives.[85] It is clear that those called שָׂרִים in MT Jer 36 are subordinate to the king, yet they appear to be a powerful and leading subgroup of עַבְדֵי הַמֶּלֶךְ, "the royal servants" or "courtiers" (v. 24).[86] Unlike a "prince" (בֶּן־הַמֶּלֶךְ / υἱῷ τοῦ βασιλέως; v. 26), however, they are employees of the king and not his relatives, at least in MT Jer 36.[87] As such, the שָׂרִים are best referred to as "high-ranking courtiers"[88] or "chief courtiers" and seen as holding the status of עַבְדֵי הַמֶּלֶךְ "royal servants."[89]

In the oracles and the narrative passages of the book of Jeremiah, these chief courtiers appear in lists with other known professional titles or ranks. There are also references that pair kings with הַשָּׂרִים (MT Jer 17:25; 24:1, 8; 25:18; 29:2; 34:21; 49:3). They are paired with priests in MT Jer 1:18; 2:26; 4:9; 8:1; 32:33. Within the narrative context of MT Jer 26, which is literarily similar to MT Jer 36, one finds references to the king (הַמֶּלֶךְ), the chief courtiers (הַשָּׂרִים), the priests

---

[85] The word שַׂר, in the singular, was used in occupational titles, which were usually military in nature, to indicate a superior rank, e.g., שַׂר הַצָּבָא "commander of the army" (2 Kgs 4:13). But the palace שָׂרִים appear to have carried titles that did not include שַׂר in the singular, e.g., in 2 Kgs 18:18, אֲשֶׁר עַל־הַבַּיִת, "the palace overseer," הַסֹּפֵר, "the scribe," and הַמַּזְכִּיר, "the recorder." In short, to refer to הַשָּׂרִים in MT Jer 36 as "officials" or "princes" is misleading. "Official" connotes specific qualities and not a specific professional rank, while "prince" is a dynastic rank that operates separately from the royal court's system of professional appointments and titles. While elite individuals may have fostered nepotism by modeling dynastic rights, the appointments of the chief courtiers were ultimately contingent on factors other than bloodline. Fox, *Service*, 158–163 provides an etymological overview of the word but concludes its etymology remains elusive and unfortunately settles on the meaning "official" for its Hebrew usage (163).

[86] McKane, *Jeremiah*, 907. Fox, *Service*, distinguishes הַמֶּלֶךְ עַבְדֵי as a title of status (53–63) from שָׂרִים a functional title (158–163).

[87] For discussion of the meaning of בֶּן־הַמֶּלֶךְ, see below.

[88] MT Jer 38 and 39 refer frequently to the שָׂרֵי הַמֶּלֶךְ, "*chief courtiers* of the king (of Babylon)." Terms and phrases such as those in these chapters demonstrate that the term שָׂרִים refers to a rank or status in a royal court; positions that refer to Babylonian or Elamite (MT Jer 49:38) שָׂרִים were Hebrew translations of the Akkadian/Aramaic word *rab*/רב (Fox, *Service*, 163). The titles of such foreign characters ultimately became part of their names in Hebrew; see the list of specific Babylonian שָׂרִים in MT Jer 39:3 and LXX Jer 46:3.

[89] Niehr, *TDOT*, 14:196–197. Note that he finds etymological connections between שַׂר and either Egyptian *śr* or Akkadian *šarru* to be dubious. Within the Judahite kingdom this term refers to slightly different sociological positions than it does in neighboring (and earlier) cultures.

(הַכֹּהֲנִים), and the prophets (הַנְּבִיאִים), in that order. The king and chief courtiers are associated with the palace, while the priests and prophets are religious functionaries who work in the temple. Immediately, one notices that this list of titles includes determined nouns, which suggests that they can be read as occupations or statuses.[90] It is reasonable to deduce from MT Jer 26, that the reader may have assumed that the priests (הַכֹּהֲנִים) and the prophets (הַנְּבִיאִים) were unmentioned attendees in scene two, and this is triggered by titles and status that appear in scenes three and four.

MT Jer 36:12 identifies five of the שָׂרִים by name:

LXX Jer 43:12b[91]
Ελισαμα ὁ γραμματεὺς καὶ Δαλαιας υἱὸς Σελεμιου καὶ Ελναθαν υἱὸς Ακχοβωρ καὶ Γαμαριας υἱὸς Σαφαν καὶ Σεδεκιας υἱὸς Ανανιου καὶ πάντες οἱ ἄρχοντες
Elisama the secretary and Dalaias son of Selemias and Ionathan son of Akchobor and Gamarias son of Saphan and Sedekias son of Hananias and all the rulers.

MT Jer 36:12b
אֱלִישָׁמָע הַסֹּפֵר וּדְלָיָהוּ בֶן־שְׁמַעְיָהוּ וְאֶלְנָתָן בֶּן־עַכְבּוֹר וּגְמַרְיָהוּ בֶן־שָׁפָן וְצִדְקִיָּהוּ בֶן־חֲנַנְיָהוּ וְכָל־הַשָּׂרִים
Elishama, the scribe; Delaiah, son of Shemaiah;[92] Elnathan, son of Achbor; Gemariah, son of Shaphan; Zedekiah, son of Hananiah; and all the chief courtiers

At least two of these five characters have been identified as historical figures.[93] Late Judahite epigraphic evidence suggests that a class of royal שָׂרִים existed and

---

90 GKC §126m.
91 LXX Ιωναθαν and MT אֶלְנָתָן refer to the same person (McKane, *Jeremiah*, 904). In LXX one finds Δαλαιας υἱὸς Σελεμιου (v. 12), but in verse 25 where one expects Δαλαιας, there is Γοδολίας (≈גדליהו). For a possible explanation, see Holladay, *Jeremiah 2*, 253 and Stipp, *masoretische*, 124. LXX verse 25 is in error.
92 LXX reads Σελεμίου (≈ שלמיהו), and may be a corruption from verse 14 (Holladay, *Jeremiah 2*, 251).
93 The name Delaiah is known from a late 7th cent. BCE bulla from the City of David excavations, ו[ה]ושעיה בן / לדליהו[1] (Ariel, *Excavations*, 32, 43). This name is also sometimes restored on Lach 22.4; see Dobbs-Allsopp et al., *Hebrew*, 339. HaE, II/2 reads the name on five bullae and seals: nos. 2.7 (from the "House of the Bullae," city of David), 4.3 (unprovenanced), 4.4 (the aforementioned City of David bulla), 5.21 (unprovenanced), 15.24 (unprovenanced). The name Gemariah is also known from the City of David excavations (Avigad and Sass, *Corpus*, 191–192). The name Zedekiah has been proposed as a restoration for a questionable line on Lach 11 obv. 6. Lemaire published an unprovenanced bulla from the E. Borowski Collection in "Nouveaux," 113*–114*, no. 22 which reads לצדקי[ה]ו / נ[ב]ני חנני, "Belonging to Zediqiah son of Hanani." If this is an authentic bulla, and if it and MT Jer 36 refer to the same person, one may understand חנני as a hypocoristicon for חנניהו. Elishama is a common West Semitic name that describes at least six distinct characters in the Bible and appears on a number of Hebrew seals; the name is also found on a Moabite altar (see *HALOT*; Avigad and Sass, *Corpus*, index; and Ahituv, *Echoes*,

imbues the narrative with sense of realia. That said, even the most conservative scholarly views date the Tale of Jeremiah and Baruch's Scroll to the early exilic period, that is, to a time in which the Judahite שָׂרִים no longer existed.[94] So the depictions of the שָׂרִים in this passage must have been built on recollections (or perhaps based on other written sources) about the שָׂרִים, rather than on contemporary observations. This historical distance between the writing of the narrative and attempts at characterization allow for later social allusions to be mapped on a tale set in an earlier time, and disambiguating the historical from the literary may be impossible. Nonetheless, there is much to be learned about the scribal characterization of the שָׂרִים in MT Jer 36.

Elishama is the first in the list of שָׂרִים, and is the only one of the five named שָׂרִים who bears a specific professional title, "the scribe" (הַסֹּפֵר), rather than a patronymic. As the first in this list of שָׂרִים, he might be seen as their leader; certainly, they are gathered in his chamber.[95] Kegler observes that as the story unfolds Elishama shows neither support nor disdain for Baruch and his scroll.[96] Elishama is a significant figure in the scene,[97] and his ambivalence in the debate among the שָׂרִים about Baruch's scroll demonstrates the complexity of the political environment in the palace's scribal chamber: the שָׂרִים are not servants or a unified guild, but a group of politicians with competing, and sometimes ambiguous, views on social and intellectual matters.

Along with Elishama, the text introduces a small group of three individuals who play no role in this scene but will be important in the next scene, in which they argue for the survival of Baruch's scroll (v. 25): Delaiah, son of Shemaiah (דְּלָיָהוּ בֶן־שְׁמַעְיָהוּ); Elnathan, son of Achbor (אֶלְנָתָן בֶּן־עַכְבּוֹר);[98] and Gemariah, son of Shaphan (גְמַרְיָהוּ בֶן־שָׁפָן). Achbor and Shaphan, the fathers of Elnathan and Gemariah, appear in other narrative contexts, most notably MT 2 Kgs 22–23, in

---

423–426). Although the name is well attested in the NWS onomasticon, in the context of this story, it serves a literary function, since the text uses שמע as a literary device (see below). The character of אלישמע "(the one whom) my god heard" is placed in a position "to hear" or "to comprehend" Baruch's scroll.

94 E.g., Holladay, *Jeremiah 2*, 16.
95 McKane, *Jeremiah*, 907.
96 Kegler, "Prophetic," 52–53.
97 Kegler, "Prophetic," 52–53.
98 Elnathan's father was Achbor (עַכְבּוֹר), who, according to MT 2 Kgs 22:12–14, accompanied Shaphan and Ahiqam during political negotiations, which eventually engendered Josiah's reform. If this is the same Elnathan mentioned in MT 2 Kgs 24:8, then he is the progenitor of the final royal line of Judah. According to MT 2 Kgs 24:8, Elnathan is the father of Nehushta, the mother of Jehoiakin.

which they are courtly figures who instigate a political reform by means of a document.⁹⁹ There was a scribal and courtly tradition associated with these names that MT Jer 36 evokes. Behind this allusion is a notion of nepotism that can be associated with scribal characters in the Judahite court. On the one hand, nepotism may have fostered exclusion and the consolidation of power for scribal groups, but on the other, it may also have fostered resentment that forced small scribal associations to make and to shift alliances.¹⁰⁰ In addition, these three characters are grouped together because they represent an alliance that supports serious engagement with Baruch's scroll, though they do not explicitly support its content. Dynamics such as this among scribal associations in the palace mark Baruch as an outsider among the שָׂרִים. Baruch is, nonetheless, respected by a few of them.

The mention of Zedekiah, son of Hananiah (צִדְקִיָּהוּ בֶן־חֲנַנְיָהוּ, LXX Σεδεκίας υἱὸς Ανανίου; v. 12), among these five named שָׂרִים is puzzling. Every named individual in this story plays a major or supporting role in the plot of this tale, except for Zedekiah, about whom nothing definitive can be said.¹⁰¹ Without further evidence, Zedekiah may be supposed to have taken an unaffiliated and ambiguous stance on Baruch and his document, like Elishama. If this is the case, then he contributes to the size of the ambivalent scribal association.

The text introduces a sixth member of the שָׂרִים in verse 14, יְהוּדִי בֶּן־נְתַנְיָהוּ בֶּן־שֶׁלֶמְיָהוּ בֶן־כּוּשִׁי, "Jehudi, son of Nethaniah, son of Shelemiah, son of Cushi."¹⁰²

---

99 I mean this solely as a cultural and literary-comparative statement, though many see MT 2 Kgs 22–23 as a textual source for MT Jer 36 (propagated by Isbell, "Stylistic," 35). At least one scholar maintains that sections of the book of Jeremiah was the source for sections of the books of Kings (Hardmeier, *Prophetie*, and Seizt, "Review," 511–513). Blenkinsopp, "Deuteronomistic" 356 implies that 2 Kgs 22–23 is reacting to tales about Jeremiah, and thus such tales predate MT 2 Kgs 22–23 in some form (oral or written).
100 Works such as Dearman, "Servants," and Kegler, "Prophetic," also study the subtle social allusions in this list of names, and they come to the conclusion that these three figures are Baruch's supporters.
101 Kegler, "Prophetic," 53; Holladay, *Jeremiah 2*, 257; Lundbom, *Jeremiah*, 600. Perhaps it is worth noting that a very late Jeremiah Apocryphon recasts this story in the reign of king Zedekiah (Mingana with Harris, "Jeremiah," 154).
102 The name יְהוּדִי is not attested in the Bible outside of this passage, nor is it attested in the Judahite onomasticon. In MT Gen 26:34, and especially in the Persian and Hellenistic periods, one finds the name יהודית (Judith), and it should be noted that LXX ms. A reads Ιουδιν in LXX Gen 26:34 as it does in MT Jer 36:14 for יְהוּדִי. (According to Wills, this spelling in LXX Gen 26:34 may be because the word is in the accusative case. I thank Wills for sharing this thought with me [personal communication, September 2016].) Scholars have long noted that a name expounded to the fourth generation is unusual, even more so since this is not "a character of distinction" (Peake, *Jeremiah Vol II*, 156). Lundbom believes the name is authentic, because

This character plays an antagonistic role in the next scene, in which he reads and destroys Baruch's scroll (v. 23). The present scene portrays him as the one whom the chief courtiers selected to escort Baruch to the chamber of Elishama (v. 14). This act reveals two important clues about the שָׂרִים and their associates. First, Micaiah, as their informant, did not have the authority to bring Baruch to the palace's scribal chamber; only a higher-ranking official could do that. This leads to the second observation, that the שָׂרִים were responsible for policing and for making judgments on activities that occurred in the temple[103] in a way that the religious personnel, the priests and prophets, could not.[104] Jehudi's authoritative, and later antagonistic, characterization takes on a new dimension when one sees him as a representation of the Judahite stance against Baruch and his scroll. It appears to be more than a coincidence that a scribal character by the name of Jehudi (i.e., "the Judahite") appears as a villain in a tale in which the Judahites do not understand Baruch (vv. 9–11), and in which Baruch insults the

---

"'Nethaniah' and 'Shelemiah' have turned up on various extrabiblical ostraca, seals, and inscriptions" (Lundbom, *Jeremiah*, 601). Others have argued that one should amend the text to "Jehudi son of Nethaniah <and> Shelemiah son of Cushi" (See Hyatt, "Book," 1066). Names derived from gentilic adjectives have received little attention other than Noth's short remark about their existence (*israelitischen*). Jehudi's name contains two gentilic adjectives: יְהוּדִי and כּוּשִׁי.

103 See MT Jer 26, in which Jeremiah causes a disturbance among the priests and prophets in the temple, but they have no authority over his actions. Only the שָׂרִים, who had to come from the palace to the temple, could judge Jeremiah's civil-religious predicament and could punish him (MT Jer 26:10). Only God is called a "judge," שפט, in the book of Jeremiah (MT Jer 11:20). The term "judge," however, is not used as a professional rank or title in book (also see MT Isa 1:26). In the Hellenistic period, communities revived the position of "the judge," if only ideologically. CD-A x 4–6 refers to a "rule for the judges of the congregation" (העדה לשפטי סרך). This and similar late revivalists' efforts tend to be attributed to Hezekiah, and thus came to be known by Ibn Ezra, who anachronistically wrote of MT Isa 1:26, "When the kingdom of Israel, the ten tribes, with their judges, shall cease here, and the judges of Ahaz shall likewise have gone, Hezekiah will appoint upright judges; and this is in fact recorded of him" (Friedländer, *Commentary*, 12).

104 See Hardmeier, "Schriftgestützten," 107–8 and Niehr, *TDOT* 14:195 for an analysis of the term שר in the Lachish ostraca, in which it refers to both a military and a civil functionary. MT Jer 20:1–2 makes reference to "the priest" (הַכֹּהֵן) Pashhur (a name of Egyptian origin) who was the יְהוָה בְּבֵית נָגִיד פָּקִיד "chief officer in the house of the LORD" (NRSV), and who had detained Jeremiah in הַמַּהְפֶּכֶת "stocks ?" (LXX καταρράκτην "dungeon;" PESHITTA ܐܘܢܐ "the room") in the שַׁעַר בִּנְיָמִן הָעֶלְיוֹן אֲשֶׁר בְּבֵית יְהוָה "upper gate of Benjamin which was in the temple of Yahweh" (vv. 1–2). But he releases Jeremiah the next day (v. 3), and makes no legal claim against him.

Judahite king (publicly and privately) with a pro-Babylonian document (v. 29).[105]

Jehudi escorts Baruch to the palace's scribal chamber, where he waits for them to request that he read the scroll again (שֵׁב),[106] but now within earshot[107] of all of the שָׂרִים (v. 15). The way in which the שָׂרִים react to the scroll and to Baruch's reading illustrates one way in which scribal professionals dealt with intellectual ideas conveyed in textual form. Verse 16 reads:

LXX Jer 43:16	MT Jer 36:16
καὶ ἐγενήθη ὡς ἤκουσαν πάντας τοὺς λόγους, συνεβουλεύσαντο ἕκαστος πρὸς τὸν πλησίον αὐτοῦ καὶ εἶπαν Ἀναγγέλλοντες ἀναγγείλωμεν τῷ βασιλεῖ πάντας τοὺς λόγους τούτους.	וַיְהִי כְּשָׁמְעָם אֶת־כָּל־הַדְּבָרִים פָּחֲדוּ אִישׁ אֶל־רֵעֵהוּ וַיֹּאמְרוּ אֶל־בָּרוּךְ הַגֵּיד נַגִּיד לַמֶּלֶךְ אֵת כָּל־הַדְּבָרִים הָאֵלֶּה
And it happened, when they heard all the words, they took counsel, each with his fellow, and they said, "In reporting let us report all these words to the king" (NETS)	And so it was, when they heard all of the words, they became afraid, each to his friend. And they said to Baruch, "We must report all of these words to the king!"

In this passage the שָׂרִים are said to have "heard," that is, "comprehended" (√שׁמע), the words of the scroll, and then they "debated with each other" (συνεβουλεύσαντο ἕκαστος πρὸς τὸν πλησίον αὐτοῦ). McKane describes the textual problems in this passage and why LXX's reading is to be preferred. He writes,

> The difficulty of the expression פחדו איש אל רעהו (v. 16) has been overcome by the transposition of ויאמר to precede איש (Volz, Rudolph, Bright; Wanke, 1971, p. 661). That this device was thought necessary makes it all the more significant that Sept. has συνεβουλεύσαντο ἕκαστος. There is no reason to doubt that this rests on a Hebrew Vorlage which had ויעצו [sic] or the like instead of פחדו. נועץ is rendered as συνεβουλεύσαντο at [MT] Isa 40.14; נועצו יחדו as

---

105 From this perspective, even כּוּשִׁי (lit. "Nubian") may allude to Jehoiakim's alliance with Egypt/Nubia rather than Babylon.

106 MT here punctuates the word as שֵׁב, "sit," but LXX reads Πάλιν, "again" (≈ שָׁב); see Holladay, *Jeremiah 2*, 252. The problem is compounded by the נָא in MT. Had נָא been in LXX's *Vorlage*, the reading would have been unambiguously an imperative. Peshitta (ܒ݁ܐ) and Vul. (*sede*) both read "sit," and thus attest to the antiquity of MT's reading. It seems that early in MT's manuscript history, an editor added נָא (and a conjunction ו on קראנה) as a way of punctuating, and therefore interpreting, the text.

107 MT contains בְּאָזְנֵינוּ (x2) in verse 15, whereas LXX only has an equivalent reading for MT's first occurrence (εἰς τὰ ὦτα ἡμῶν). Peshitta reads ܡܕܢܐ and ܡܕܢܝܗܘܢ, suggesting that it saw לפנינו and לפניהם in its *Vorlage*; see verse 13, where it reads ܟܐܢܘ, ܡܕܢܝܗܘܢ ܕ. (≈ MT הָעָם בְּאָזְנֵי). LXX should be preferred, so too Janzen, *Studies*, 52.

ἐβουλεύσαντο at [MT] Ps. 71.10; נועצו לב יחדו as ἐβουλεύσαντο at [MT] Ps 83.6; אתם נועצים as συμβουλεύετε at [MT] 1 Kgs 12.9; ויעצו as ἐβουλεύσατο at [MT] 2 Chr 30.23. The sense of Sept. at 36.16 is that there was a meeting of the minds, a consideration or deliberation of what response should be made to the situation created by the events of which the שׂרים had been informed by Micaiah. Sept. should be preferred to MT which has arisen as a consequence of the alteration of נועצו or the like to פחדו under the influence of ולא פחדו (v. [MT] 24).[108]

McKane is correct that LXX presents this scene as "a meeting of the minds" and that this is best seen in LXX's depiction of the שָׂרִים debating a document's content. The scribal characters did not debate after hearing the oral report (√נגד) of Baruch's scroll (v. 13), but only after having heard it read (√קרא; v. 15) and when the document was in their presence. This provides evidence that the שָׂרִים are "scribal," even though only one of them carries the title "the scribe."[109]

Furthermore, the שָׂרִים not only debate with each other, but interrogate Baruch on the nature of his writing process and thereby reveal their knowledge of professional scribal activities. At the start of the scene, Micaiah assumes that Baruch's source was Yahweh (v. 11), but the שָׂרִים do not jump to such a conclusion. Instead, they ask Baruch, אֵיךְ כָּתַבְתָּ אֶת־כָּל־הַדְּבָרִים הָאֵלֶּה, "how did you compose all of these words" (Πόθεν ἔγραψας πάντας τοὺς λόγους τούτους; v. 17)?[110] He responds by stating that Jeremiah was his source:

LXX Jer 43:18	MT Jer 36:18
καὶ εἶπε Βαρουχ Ἀπὸ στόματος αὐτοῦ ἀνήγγειλέ μοι Ιερεμίας πάντας τοὺς λόγους τούτους, καὶ ἔγραφον ἐν βιβλίῳ.	וַיֹּאמֶר לָהֶם בָּרוּךְ מִפִּיו יִקְרָא אֵלַי אֵת כָּל־הַדְּבָרִים הָאֵלֶּה וַאֲנִי כֹּתֵב עַל־הַסֵּפֶר בַּדְּיוֹ
And Barouch said, "From his mouth Ieremias proclaimed to me all these words, and I would write them in a book" (NETS).	And Baruch said to them, "From his mouth he would proclaim to me all of these words while I wrote on a document with ink.

The antecedent to "his" in MT must be Jeremiah (see v. 4), but this scene has yet to mention Jeremiah in MT. Therefore, in MT the שָׂרִים could see the antecedent to "his" as Yahweh, since Micaiah had primed them to do so (v. 11). The editor of

---

108 McKane, *Jeremiah*, 904–905. I would clarify that אֶל־רֵעֵהוּ אִישׁ פָּחֲדוּ poses a semantic/syntactical problem. A person cannot be "afraid *to his friend*" in Classical Hebrew though attempts have been made to idiomatically justify this unique statement (Stipp, *Jeremia*, 76). But see Fischer, who sees the group afraid "miteinander" (*Jeremia 26–52*, 295).
109 See Lachish Letter 6, which refers to the ספרי השר[ים], "the documents of the chief courtier[s]."
110 MT הַגֶּד־נָא לָנוּ is not represented in LXX (Stipp, *masoretische*, 104), and מִפִּיו is an addition (Janzen, *Studies*, 52 and discussion above).

MT attempts to elevate the role of Yahweh throughout this passage,[111] and here the same objective is achieved by removing Jeremiah from verse 18. But clearly the שָׂרִים hold Jeremiah responsible, along with Baruch, in verse 19, when they encourage Baruch and Jeremiah to go into hiding. Hence, LXX's reference to Jeremiah in verse 18 should be preferred.[112]

After hearing that Jeremiah was responsible for the scroll's content, the שָׂרִים advise Baruch to hide along with Jeremiah (v. 19). Their advice reveals two things. First, they hold Baruch as responsible as Jeremiah for the scroll's content. This indicates that even though Jeremiah was the scroll's source, the שָׂרִים viewed Baruch as more than a mere stenographer or amanuensis. He, as writer and presenter of the scroll, was equally responsible for its content.[113] Second, the advice of the שָׂרִים demonstrates that they were attempting to distance themselves from the scroll's content. The שָׂרִים are not among Jeremiah and Baruch's supporters, though some of them[114] are willing to entertain Baruch's message a bit longer.

This scene (vv. 12–18), which takes place in the palace's scribal chamber, has revealed a number of features of the professional experience of scribal characters. It has shown that the palace's scribal characters, the שָׂרִים, possess significant social power. They are portrayed as a group separate from the regular Judahite populace. Yet while they remain cloistered in their palace chamber, they have associates and liaisons keeping watch over the population's activities. They debate over the content of written material, which can result in the emergence of competing factions. This scene depicts at least three factions among the שָׂרִים, namely, those willing to consider Baruch's message (Delaiah, Elnathan, and Gemariah), those antagonistic towards Baruch (Jehudi), and those who remain unaffiliated (Elishama and perhaps Zedekiah).

---

111 MT's editor has added Yahweh in verses 6 and 26.
112 So too Carroll, *Jeremiah*, 660.
113 MT Jer 8:8 alludes to a similar view on scribal activity. In this verse, Jeremiah censures the "sages" (חֲכָמִים) and "scribes" (סֹפְרִים) for editing a document (תּוֹרַת יְהוָה).
114 In verse 19, LXX reads καὶ εἶπαν τῷ Βαρουχ Βάδισον κατακρύβηθι, while MT has וַיֹּאמְרוּ הַשָּׂרִים אֶל־בָּרוּךְ לֵךְ הִסָּתֵר. MT here follows its expected editorial pattern of adding character names and titles (Stipp, "Prophetic," 67–68). Only here in MT Jer 36 one finds הַשָּׂרִים rather than כָּל־הַשָּׂרִים. It seems that MT's editor realized that not all of the שָׂרִים were interested in Baruch's scroll or his life. Perhaps הַשָּׂרִים here refers to Delaiah, Elnathan, and Gemariah (vv. 12 and 25)?

3.4 Courtly Scribes in the Royal Chamber (MT 36:20–26a / LXX 43:20–26a)

As the scene in the palace's scribal chamber comes to an end, Baruch and Jeremiah presumably have gone into hiding (v. 19), and the next scene will reveal that the king's presence is another locus of scribal activity. All of the שָׂרִים move from the scribe's chamber to the king's courtyard, where they orally report (וַיַּגִּידוּ) to him what they witnessed (v. 20). The text is careful to note that Baruch's scroll was not with the שָׂרִים when they brought word to the king. Instead, they left it in the chamber of Elishama. The wording at this point is curious and deserves attention, because it reveals a subtle feature of the scribal profession. The editions and translations each present a slightly different reading of verse 20, which describes the scroll's whereabouts:

LXX Jer 43:20		MT Jer 36:20	
καὶ εἰσῆλθον πρὸς τὸν βασιλέα εἰς τὴν αὐλήν, καὶ τὸ χαρτίον ἔδωκαν φυλάσσειν ἐν οἴκῳ Ελισαμα, καὶ ἀνήγγειλαν τῷ βασιλεῖ πάντας τοὺς λόγους.		וַיָּבֹאוּ אֶל־הַמֶּלֶךְ חָצֵרָה וְאֶת־הַמְּגִלָּה הִפְקִדוּ בְּלִשְׁכַּת אֱלִישָׁמָע הַסֹּפֵר וַיַּגִּידוּ בְּאָזְנֵי הַמֶּלֶךְ אֵת כָּל־הַדְּבָרִים	
And they entered to the king in the court, and the small roll they gave to be watched in the house of Elisama, and they reported all the words to the king (NETS).	And they went into the king into the court, and gave the roll to one to keep in the house of Elisama; and they told the king all these words (Brenton).	And they went to the king in the court, after leaving the scroll in the chamber of the scribe Elishama. And they reported all these matters to the king (NJPS).	And they went in to the king, to the courtyard, but the scroll they had stored in the chamber of Elishama [the scribe:] they told in the ears of the king all the words (Holladay, Jeremiah 2, 252).

Where MT reads הִפְקִדוּ, the Vulgate has *commendaverunt*, "they deposited," and the Syriac ܣܡܘܗܝ ܒ, "they put it in." The Vulgate, the Syriac, and the NJPS translation of MT suggest that the scroll was not in Elishama's chamber but rather put into it before the שָׂרִים went to the king. This interpretation overlooks the fact that Elishama is the palace's scribe, and therefore his chamber is the scribal chamber (see argument above). LXX implies that the chambers were the same and that verse 20 is a reference to the treatment, not the placement, of the scroll. LXX probably saw the same consonantal text as that in MT, את מגלה הפקדו ב,[115] and interpreted it to mean ἔδωκαν φυλάσσειν, "they gave (it) to be watched,"

---

115 So too McKane, *Jeremiah*, 906.

that is, they kept it safe, in Elishama's chamber.[116] Or perhaps LXX's reading means that the scroll was catalogued (פקד√) in the scribal chamber as part of a royal archive.[117] Regardless LXX's interpretation, which seems to better grasp the context, reveals the concern that the שָׂרִים had for the scroll, and that they suspected that the king (and Jehudi) would have wanted it destroyed. As Fischer notes, "Das zurücklassen der Rolle am früheren Versammlungsort manifestiert einen Wunsch, sie zu schützen, und zugleich einen richtig vorausahnende Einschätzung des Königs."[118]

The act of securing the scroll in a scribal chamber also allows for literary parallelism between this and the previous two scenes. Earlier in the narrative, Micaiah left Baruch and the scroll in the temple courtyard (חָצֵר; v. 10) and orally reported (נגד√) the scroll's contents in earshot of (בְּאָזְנֵי) the שָׂרִים at the next locus of scribal activity, the palace's scribal chamber. Likewise, the שָׂרִים leave the scroll in Elishama's scribal chamber, go to the palace courtyard, and orally report (נגד√) the scroll's content in earshot (בְּאָזְנֵי) of the king (v. 20). As before (v. 14), Jehudi is then sent to ensure that the scroll reaches its next audience (v. 21). The narrator then explains that the king sat in his winter quarters (בֵּית הַחֹרֶף / ἐν οἴκῳ χειμερινῷ; v. 22), which must have been connected to the palace's courtyard.[119] This location resembles לִשְׁכַּת גְּמַרְיָהוּ in the courtyard's upper terrace (הָעֶלְיוֹן) in the temple, where Baruch first read the scroll to the people (v. 10). It is unlikely, however, that a winter chamber, which contains a hearth or brazier (אָח; v. 23), would have been located on the upper floors of a structure.[120] As a result, the literary contrast is stark: Baruch's scroll will end in a location similar to where it began, but instead of having been read from a high courtyard

---

116 So too Fischer, *Jeremias*, 297 "-פקד ב Hi, in Verbindung mit einem nicht-menschlichen Objekt 'etwas anvertrauen, in Verwahrung geben in. . .', hat als einzige Parallele [MT] Ps 31,6." See McKane, *Jeremiah*, 906.

117 Note that Schniedewind, *How*, 149–157 argues that palace archiving increased during the end of the monarchy, and that Judean royal families may have persevered and edited texts to support their dynastic claims (157). And it should be noted that even Elishama's grandson fought for a stake in the crumbling Judahite kingdom. Ishmael son of Nethaniah son of Elishama (MT 2 Kgs 25:25; Jer 41:1) is said to have assassinated Gedaliah, the appointee of Judah's Babylonian puppet regime (MT 2 Kgs 25:23), and to have assembled the שָׂרִים in favor of an Egyptian coalition. Elishama may have had ulterior motives when Baruch's treasonous and pro-Babylonian scroll was stored/catalogued in his scribal chamber, but this idea cannot be verified.

118 Fischer, *Jeremias*, 297.

119 See Holladay, *Jeremiah 2*, 259.

120 Some have argued that it is too cold to have been outside (Carroll, *Jeremiah*, 660), but this overlooks the fact that the whole population met outside in verse 10.

chamber in public view, it will find its demise in a low and private courtyard chamber.

A curious social allusion to competing scribal alliances occurs in the king's winter quarters, when Jehudi reads the scroll. One might have expected Elishama, the scribe, to read the scroll to the king, but this is not the case.[121]

LXX Jer 43:23	MT Jer 36:23
καὶ ἐγενήθη ἀναγινώσκοντος Ιουδιν τρεῖς σελίδας καὶ τέσσαρας, ἀπέτεμνεν αὐτὰς τῷ ξυρῷ τοῦ γραμματέως καὶ ἔρριπτεν εἰς τὸ πῦρ τὸ ἐπὶ τῆς ἐσχάρας, ἕως ἐξέλιπε πᾶς ὁ χάρτης εἰς τὸ πῦρ τὸ ἐπὶ τῆς ἐσχάρας.	וַיְהִי כִּקְרוֹא יְהוּדִי שָׁלֹשׁ דְּלָתוֹת וְאַרְבָּעָה יִקְרָעֶהָ בְּתַעַר הַסֹּפֵר וְהַשְׁלֵךְ אֶל־הָאֵשׁ אֲשֶׁר אֶל־הָאָח עַד־תֹּם כָּל־הַמְּגִלָּה עַל־הָאֵשׁ אֲשֶׁר עַל־הָאָח
And it happened when Ioudin would read three or four columns, he[122] would cut them off with the secretary's penknife and would throw them into the fire that was in the hearth, until the entire roll had vanished into the fire that was in the hearth (NETS).	And so it was, as Jehudi read three or four columns, he would cut it with a penknife and cast (it) into the fire which (burned) on the brazier, until the whole scroll was destroyed in the fire that was on the brazier.

Jehudi appears to be the most influential among the שָׂרִים, and certainly the most aggressive among them in the tale. It is on his watch that the scroll moves from location to location (vv. 14 and 23), and he appears to have begun destroying the scroll in verse 23 of his own volition, without instructions from the king. In fact, verse 24 claims that there was no fear or sign of distress as this event unfolded, apart from a small faction of שָׂרִים who protested the burning of the scroll (v. 25), to no avail. As a result, the text presents the king's presence as a final locus of scribal activity in which a text will meet its fate: it will either be acknowledged or disregarded, and its fate ultimately rests on the scribal alliances and the degree of influence that scribal characters have on the king.

---

121 See a similar narrative episode in MT 2 Kgs 22:10, in which Shaphan, the scribe, reads Hilkiah's scroll to the king.

122 NETS contains a footnote that reads, "i.e. the king," and many modern scholars have long seen the king as the subject of יִקְרָעֶהָ / ἀπέτεμνεν, because verses 25 and 29 give the king credit for destroying the scroll. But Holladay rightly remarks that "as the text stands, 'Jehudi' is the subject of the verbs. Of course it is the king who is responsible for destroying the scroll (vv. 25 and 29); but the king would hardly have wielded the scribe's knife himself—that is the task of an underling" (*Jeremiah 2*, 259). As for the knife, its blade must be about the size of a razor, and extremely sharp in order to trim papyri, score parchment, and sharpen styli. But of the few identifiable accoutrements of the scribal trade that survive from this period, it is unclear whether or why Jehudi would be in possession of a penknife. An Aramaic scribe's palette survives from Elephantine in the Brooklyn Museum (16.99a-d), and it does not contain a knife or blade—only reeds and ink.

The above interpretation of the scribal activities in the king's winter quarters suggests that the king is a puppet of the most influential שָׂרִים and that although it is in his presence that an issue of concern to a scribal character meets its final judgement, the king is not a scribal figure and is incapable of engaging intellectually at the level of the scribal characters.

As was shown in the previous scene, the scribal characters debated over Baruch's scroll (v. 16). Debate appears to be a hallmark of the scribal profession in this passage, but it is in the king's winter quarters that the text's allusions to the process of intellectual reasoning become apparent. Throughout the tale, the text contrasts the idea of being "within earshot of" (בְּאָזְנֵי) "all of the words" (כֹּל הַדְּבָרִים), with "hearing" or "comprehending" (√שמע) all of the words. The phrase כֹּל הַדְּבָרִים, "all of the words," occurs twelve times in this short passage.[123] All of the words of the scroll are written down, then read (√קרא) three times (vv. 10, 15, and 23), in three different loci of scribal activity. First, all of the words move from one locus to another by means of oral report (√נגד, vv. 12 and 21). This is followed by confirmation that all of the words should be read directly from their source text.[124] On two of the scroll's three recitations, it is read "in earshot" (בְּאֹזֶן) of an audience (v. 13 the people; v. 20 the king) that is not said to have comprehended it. In the first locus, the temple, Baruch reads in earshot of the people, but only Micaiah, a scribal character, understands all of the words of the scroll (v. 11).[125] In the second locus, the palace's scribal chamber, Baruch reads all of the words within earshot of the שָׂרִים, and all of these scribal characters "comprehend" and debate them (v. 15–16). In the third locus, the king's presence, Jehudi reads the scroll, but as he reads, he destroys the scroll in sections. This inhibits the king from understanding all of the words, and the king shows no interest in the appeals of Delaiah, Elnathan, and Gemariah to save the

---

123 Verses 2, 13, 16 (x2), 17, 18, 20, 24, 28. On three occasions the phrase appears as כָּל־דִּבְרֵי, "all of the words of (Yahweh/Jeremiah)" (vv. 4, 11, and 32). Some see the use of דְּבָרִים, "words," in this passage as a literary device that emphasizes their divine origin (Keown, Scalise, and Smothers, *Jeremiah*, 207–208; Carroll, *Jeremiah*, 666). A careful reading of the data suggests that the emphasis should rest on hearing (√שמע) *all* (כֹּל) the words rather than part of them. Whether the words belong to Yahweh, Jeremiah, Baruch, or the scroll, the process of scholarly reasoning should be the same; intellectuals debate *all* of the data before making a decision.

124 Note that this may be an allusion to the types of oral-written activity that Carr, *Writing*, discusses (e.g., 168).

125 I take the statement by Matthews, "Jeremiah's," 119 to be a similar observation: "It is possible that Baruch's words did not carry or were muffled by the crowd noises. More likely, however, his efforts were directed primarily at the higher echelon audience of the priestly community and royal advisers."

scroll, presumably so that all of its words might be understood (v. 25). Verse 24, which describes the response to the third reading, is ambiguous:

LXX Jer 43:24		MT Jer 36:24	
καὶ οὐκ ἐξέστησαν καὶ οὐ διέρρηξαν τὰ ἱμάτια αὐτῶν ὁ βασιλεὺς καὶ οἱ παῖδες αὐτοῦ οἱ ἀκούοντες[126] πάντας τοὺς λόγους τούτους·		וְלֹא פָחֲדוּ וְלֹא קָרְעוּ אֶת־בִּגְדֵיהֶם הַמֶּלֶךְ וְכָל־עֲבָדָיו הַשֹּׁמְעִים אֵת כָּל־הַדְּבָרִים הָאֵלֶּה	
And they were not alarmed nor did they rend their garments, (neither) the king nor his servants hearing all of these words (literal translation).	And the king and his servants, who were hearing all these words, were not alarmed, and they did not tear their garments (NETS).	And they were not afraid nor did they rend their garments, (neither) the king nor all of his servants who heard all of these words. (literal translation).	Yet neither the king, nor any of his servants who heard all these words, was alarmed, nor did they tear their garments (NRSV).

The ambiguity here is whether הַשֹּׁמְעִים "the ones who hear/heard" in the participial phrase הַשֹּׁמְעִים אֵת כָּל־הַדְּבָרִים הָאֵלֶּה refers to עֲבָדָיו, or to both הַמֶּלֶךְ and עֲבָדָיו,[127] and whether the participial action is contemporaneous or antecedent to the action of the main verbs לֹא פָחֲדוּ וְלֹא קָרְעוּ. If the participial phrase refers to the servants and the king, then the king is shown as having understood the scroll. The key to knowing if the phrase refers to the servants and the king is to determine if the term הַשֹּׁמְעִים refers to hearing the words as the scroll is read or prior to the reading in the king's chamber. In antiquity, versions read the text both ways. For example, the Syriac reads the king and his servants (הַמֶּלֶךְ וְכָל־עֲבָדָיו) as a compound subject, both of whom heard the words.[128] LXX manuscripts are grammatically ambiguous as to the subject of the participial phrase—as is the Hebrew—but LXX manuscripts attest both to a contemporaneous participial phrase (mss. reading ἀκούοντες, B, S, 239, 311) and to an antecedent

---

126 For the variant ακουσαντες, see discussion below.
127 Note that McKane, *Jeremiah*, 908 has proposed that the LXX translator was keen to the social dynamics of the scene and may have omitted כל from his *Vorlage* because it is at odds with the evidence that the three "servants" in verse 25 seek to preserve the scroll. The manuscripts, however, suggest that LXX's *Vorlage* never contained כל and that MT may have added it due to its later, inaccurate views of the sociology of the Judahite court (see discussion below).
128 PESHITTA uses ܟܕ, "when," plus a perfect verb, making it difficult to read "the king and all of his servants" as anything other than a compound subject of the verb ܫܡܥܘ, "they heard": ܡܠܟܐ ܘܟܠܗܘܢ ܥܒܕܘܗܝ, ܟܕ ܫܡܥܘ ܟܠܗܘܢ ܦܬܓܡܐ ܗܠܝܢ, "the king and all of his servants, when they had heard all of these words."

phrase (mss. reading ακουσαντες, all others). In Hebrew, participles are typically described as "atemporal" and determined by context.[129] At present, the issue cannot be definitively resolved, but within the greater literary construction of the passage, I argue that the participial phrase הַשֹּׁמְעִים אֵת כָּל־הַדְּבָרִים הָאֵלֶּה refers only to the king's servants and not to the king (following the majority of LXX manuscripts, esp. ms. A). After all, the text claims in verse 31 that the king did not comprehend (√שמע) the words. As a result, the king remains ignorant of the scroll's contents, which only the scribal characters (i.e., the king's servants) have intellectually reasoned through.

Scholars have debated who exactly the king's servants in verse 24 are. The text has focused predominantly on the שָׂרִים, the high-ranking courtiers, who in the scene are "standing over the king."[130] But in verse 26, the narrator reveals that a prince and two other courtiers without titles were present as well. Scholars have argued that (כָּל־)עֲבָדָיו may refer to the שָׂרִים, to the בֶּן הַמֶּלֶךְ and his companions (v. 26), or to a combination of שָׂרִים and other courtly figures.[131] It is best to see "the servants of the king" as a general reference to a variety of palace employees. This would include the highest-ranking courtiers, the שָׂרִים, as well as attendants to other royal personnel, such as the two companions of Jerahmeel (v. 26). But it would not include Jerahmeel himself,[132] because he was of royal blood, a בֶּן הַמֶּלֶךְ,[133] and, as the next scene demonstrates, the servants of the king (עֲבָדָיו / τοὺς παῖδας αὐτοῦ) and his offspring (זַרְעוֹ / τὸ γένος αὐτοῦ; v.

---

129 Joüon §121. The specific participle הַשֹּׁמֵעַ is used to refer to an action before the context of the main clause (antecedent, MT Lev 24:14; Zech 8:9) or in a hypothetical or durative sense, MT 2 Sam 17:9; 1 Kgs 10:8. In these four cases the participle operates outside of the time of the main clause.
130 The text reads, וַיִּקְרָאֶהָ יְהוּדִי בְּאָזְנֵי הַמֶּלֶךְ וּבְאָזְנֵי כָּל־הַשָּׂרִים הָעֹמְדִים מֵעַל הַמֶּלֶךְ, "And Jehudi read it in earshot of the king, and in earshot of all of the chief courtiers who were standing over the king" (v. 21). Note that here one finds a similar construction to the participial phrase discussed in verse 24, and here the participial phrase clearly refers only to the second noun in the compound direct object.
131 For a thorough discussion of the various views, see McKane, *Jeremiah*, 660–681, 907–908.
132 Contra Holladay, *Jeremiah 2*, 261.
133 Scholars debate whether בֶּן הַמֶּלֶךְ should be taken literally. McKane, *Jeremiah*, 909 surveys the evidence and concludes, along with Hyatt, that it is a reference to a blood relative, because Jehoiakim may not have been old enough to have a son who could serve as a policeman. Lemaire, "Note," 59–65 has shown that בֶּן הַמֶּלֶךְ here may be taken literally, particularly if the LXX's date in verse 9 is accurate. Holladay, *Jeremiah 2*, 261, however, favors seeing בֶּן הַמֶּלֶךְ as an official job title. Fox, *Service*, 44–46, provides a less than convincing argument when she begs the question: "why are these particular functionaries distinguished from the שָׂרִים. More simply as I have shown above, in MT Jer 36 the שָׂרִים are equated to "his [the king's] servants" עֲבָדָיו, and therefore, his זַרְעוֹ must be a reference to בֶּן הַמֶּלֶךְ in this passage.

31) are two separate ranks of courtiers. Besides, to return to the point made above, the servants in verse 24 have comprehended all of the words of the scroll, which identifies them as scribal characters apart from the king. The king does not intellectually reason through the scroll's content because it is destroyed while it is read. Once it is destroyed it can no longer be debated or explained to him. The tale, then, portrays the king as one ignorant of the ways of scribal reasoning.[134]

This scene illustrates that the king's presence is a locus of scribal activity. Before the king, a social exchange occurs among the scribal characters, who hold competing views about Baruch's document (v. 25). Unlike in the scribal chamber, in which scribal characters can debate and disagree, in the king's presence, only one view can prevail. In this case, the alliance between Delaiah, Elnathan, and Gemariah fails against Jehudi, who has the power of persuasion over the king. This scene makes subtle reference to other social groups, as well. Other employees, that is, servants of the crown, are present, in addition to the high-ranking שָׂרִים who are involved in the scribal presentation of Baruch's scroll. Also in the scene is a member of the royal family, Jerahmeel, who is called בֶּן־הַמֶּלֶךְ and whom the king trusts to apprehend Baruch and Jeremiah.

The rancor and disruption that Baruch's scroll causes among the שָׂרִים and the king illustrates the power that scribal activity had over the clandestine decisions of the Judahite nation. It also portrays the political tumult that scribal professionals serving at the highest offices in the king's court had to endure. It is noteworthy that this political disruption is caused by Baruch and Jeremiah, two scribal characters not counted among the high-ranking שָׂרִים. It is by means of their scribal abilities that they are capable of inciting a reaction from the powerful שָׂרִים, as well as from the king, who makes national decisions while cloistered away from public view. As such, the power of scribal professionalism appears to go beyond the social barriers that constrain scribal characters themselves.[135] As did the שָׂרִים in the previous scene (v. 19), the king ultimately holds both source and editor—Jeremiah and Baruch—responsible for the scroll, and sends Jerahmeel and his two cronies to apprehend them. Jeremiah and Baruch take the sagacious advice that Baruch received earlier in the scribal chamber (v.

---

134 The editor of MT appears to realize this. In verse 25 he adds, וְלֹא שָׁמַע אֲלֵיהֶם, "but (the king) did not listen to them (i.e., Delaiah, Elnathan, and Gemariah, who wished to preserve the scroll)." See Stipp, *Masoretische*, 100 n. 1.
135 Compare MT Jer 26, in which Jeremiah made a similar speech (rather than reading a lecture). In this passage, the שָׂרִים came to him to judge his fate rather than to bring him into the palace and ultimately before the king.

19) and hide (v. 26).¹³⁶ In the final scene, they appear to have hidden in a scribal workshop that resembles the one in the first scene.

3.5 Regrouping in the Scribal Workshop (MT 36:26b–32 / LXX 43:26b–32)

The final scene opens with Yahweh once again speaking to Jeremiah, who has been absent for much of the tale.¹³⁷ Presumably, in this scene, Jeremiah and Baruch are in hiding in a location similar to, if not the same as, the undisclosed scribal workshop in which they began. There they will engage in the scribal activities with the same resources as they had in the first scene. In this last scene, Jeremiah receives instructions from Yahweh to recompose the scroll, which Jehudi destroyed. The literary parallelism between the opening and closing scenes is clear. Both open with an introduction to Yahweh's words:¹³⁸

LXX Jer 43:1	MT Jer 36:1	LXX Jer 43:27a	MT Jer 36:27a
ἐγενήθη λόγος κυρίου πρός με λέγων	הָיָה הַדָּבָר הַזֶּה אֶל־יִרְמְיָהוּ מֵאֵת יְהוָה לֵאמֹר:	Καὶ ἐγένετο λόγος κυρίου πρὸς Ιερεμίαν... λέγων	וַיְהִי דְבַר־יְהוָה אֶל־יִרְמְיָהוּ... לֵאמֹר:
So it was, the word of the Lord (came) to me, saying:	So it was (that) this word came to Jeremiah from Yahweh, saying:	And so it was, the word of the Lord (came) to Jeremiah... saying	And so it was, the word of Yahweh (came) to Jeremiah... saying:

A command to write on a scroll follows the introductory statement in both scenes:

LXX Jer 43:2aα	MT Jer 36:2aα	LXX Jer 43:28a, bα	MT Jer 36:28a, bα
Λάβε σεαυτῷ χαρτίον βιβλίου καὶ γράψον ἐπ' αὐτοῦ πάντας τοὺς λόγους,	קַח־לְךָ מְגִלַּת־סֵפֶר וְכָתַבְתָּ אֵלֶיהָ אֶת כָּל־הַדְּבָרִים	Πάλιν λάβε χαρτίον ἕτερον καὶ γράψον πάντας τοὺς λόγους	28שׁוּב קַח־לְךָ מְגִלָּה אַחֶרֶת וּכְתֹב עָלֶיהָ אֵת כָּל־הַדְּבָרִים

---

136 For verse 26, most scholars follow LXX καὶ ατεκρύβησαν, "and they hid," rather than MT וַיַּסְתִּרֵם יְהוָה, "and Yahweh hid them." This is an example of the theological interests of MT's editor, who attempts to introduce Yahweh's providence into the tale. See Carroll, *Jeremiah*, 661 and the discussion of verses 6 and 18 above.
137 Di Pede, *Au-delà*, part. III, chap. 3 interprets Jeremiah's absence here (and in MT Jer 40:–41) as a significant datum that illustrates Jeremiah taking on the role of God (307–8) in order to highlight the characterization of the others in the episode (323).
138 Double underlines represent correspondences.

| Take for yourself a scroll document and write on it all of the words | Take for yourself a scroll document and you shall write on it all of the words | Again, take another scroll and write all of the words | Again, take for yourself another scroll and write on it all of the words |

In both scenes, Baruch takes on the task of writing:

LXX Jer 43:4	MT Jer 36:4	LXX Jer 43:32	MT Jer 36:32
καὶ ἐκάλεσεν Ιερεμίας τὸν Βαρουχ υἱὸν Νηρίου, καὶ ἔγραψεν ἀπὸ στόματος Ιερεμίου πάντας τοὺς λόγους κυρίου, οὓς ἐχρημάτισε πρὸς αὐτόν, εἰς χαρτίον βιβλίου.	וַיִּקְרָא יִרְמְיָהוּ אֶת־בָּרוּךְ בֶּן־נֵרִיָּה וַיִּכְתֹּב בָּרוּךְ מִפִּי יִרְמְיָהוּ אֵת כָּל־דִּבְרֵי יְהוָה אֲשֶׁר־דִּבֶּר אֵלָיו עַל־מְגִלַּת־סֵפֶר	καὶ ἔλαβε Βαρουχ χαρτίον ἕτερον καὶ ἔγραψεν ἐπ' αὐτῷ ἀπὸ στόματος Ιερεμίου πάντας τοὺς λόγους τοῦ βιβλίου, οὓς κατέκαυσεν Ιωακιμ· καὶ ἔτι προσετέθησαν αὐτῷ λόγοι πλείονες ὡς οὗτοι.	וְיִרְמְיָהוּ לָקַח מְגִלָּה אַחֶרֶת וַיִּתְּנָהּ אֶל־בָּרוּךְ בֶּן־נֵרִיָּהוּ הַסֹּפֵר וַיִּכְתֹּב עָלֶיהָ מִפִּי יִרְמְיָהוּ אֵת כָּל־דִּבְרֵי הַסֵּפֶר אֲשֶׁר שָׂרַף יְהוֹיָקִים מֶלֶךְ־יְהוּדָה בָּאֵשׁ וְעוֹד נוֹסַף עֲלֵיהֶם דְּבָרִים רַבִּים כָּהֵמָּה
And Jeremiah summoned Baruch, the son of Neriah, and according to Jeremiah, he wrote all of the words of the Lord, which he had declared to him, on a scroll document.	And Jeremiah summoned Baruch, the son of Neriah, and according to Jeremiah, Baruch wrote all of the words of Yahweh, which he had spoken to him, on a scroll document.	And Baruch took another scroll, and he wrote on it, according to Jeremiah, all of the words of the document which Jehoiakim had burned. Moreover, many words like these were added to it.	And Jeremiah took another scroll and gave it to Baruch, son of Neriah, the scribe. And he wrote on it, according to Jeremiah, all of the words of the document, which Jehoiakim, the king of Judah, had burned in the fire. Moreover many words like these were added unto them.

The final scene also implicitly connects the two scrolls by referring to the second scroll as "another scroll" (מְגִלָּה אַחֶרֶת / χαρτίον ἕτερον; v. 28). MT clarifies the connection by also adding a reference to the "first scroll" (הַמְּגִלָּה הָרִאשֹׁנָה; v. 28).[139]

In both the first and the last scenes, intervening material of a moralistic tone appears between Yahweh's command to Jeremiah and the start of Baruch's writing process. In verse 3 one finds the hand of the so-called Deuteronomistic Historian at work in the first scene, and perhaps the same hand in vv. 27–31 in the second scene also.[140] Both moralistic sections contain references to the ability of their audience to comprehend Jeremiah's words. Verse 3 begins אוּלַי יִשְׁמְעוּ, "perhaps they will hear/comprehend," and in verse 31 Jeremiah's statement ends with וְלֹא שָׁמֵעוּ, "but they did not hear/comprehend."[141] In view of the passage's emphasis on scribal reasoning, shown by a scribal character's ability to "comprehend" (√שׁמע) the written word, these two moralistic sections (v. 3 and vv. 27–31, esp. 31) provide a clue to the scribal critique that the passage is making in its present form:[142] only truly scribal characters are able to comprehend written documentation. In the last scene in particular, Jeremiah critiques the ignorance of Jehoiakim, the royals (זַרְעוֹ), and the palace's employees (עֲבָדָיו; v. 31) in the same spirit.

Finally, the first and final scenes contain a notable difference. In the first scene, Jeremiah summons Baruch and he begins to write (v. 4), but in the corresponding statement in the final scene, LXX verse 32 portrays Baruch as taking the initiative. It reads:

LXX Jer 43:32a	MT Jer 36:32a
ἔλαβε Βαρουχ χαρτίον ἕτερον καὶ ἔγραψεν	וְיִרְמְיָהוּ לָקַח מְגִלָּה אַחֶרֶת וַיִּתְּנָהּ אֶל־בָּרוּךְ בֶּן־נֵרִיָּהוּ הַסֹּפֵר וַיִּכְתֹּב
Baruch took another scroll and wrote	And Jeremiah took another scroll and gave it to Baruch, son of Neriah, the scribe, and he wrote

---

139 So too Stipp, *Jeremia*, 95. In so doing, MT may also be drawing a connection between this passage and the delivery of the decalogue in Exodus. See MT Exod 34:1 and discussion in Holladay, *Jeremiah 2*, 261–262.
140 Thiel, *deuteronomistiche*, 50 refers to these "insertions" as a missed opportunity of salvation. Compare Kessler's view that the motif of repentance "crept . . . into this dramatic narrative" ("Form-Critical," 392). More recently, see Maier, *Jeremia*, 147.
141 Hartenstein, "Prophets," 90 rightly observes, "To characterize [MT Jer 36:3 and 7] only as Deuteronomistic could be misleading since their horizon of literary allusions goes beyond Deuteronomy and what usually is labeled Deuteronomistic literature."
142 In view of this study, it seems difficult to simply delete verse 3 as a so-called Deuteronomistic Historian's addition without replacing it with something similar. After all, why would Jeremiah and Baruch go to the trouble to promote their agenda if they did not believe that it could be effective?

MT's longer reading is secondary, due to a harmonization with verse 28.¹⁴³ In LXX's reading, one may conclude that Baruch is no longer in need of Jeremiah's guidance. He has moved from an apprentice to a professional because he has lived through a scribal mission. Despite Baruch's change in status, he will rewrite the scroll in generally the same way that he wrote the first. Jeremiah will once again serve as his source, as shown by the references to מִפִּי יִרְמְיָהוּ (lit. "from the mouth of Jeremiah;" vv. 27 and 32), and Baruch will once again serve as the writer/editor of the scroll (v. 32).

The discussion of Baruch's role in the story brings this study to the meaning of the title הַסֹּפֵר, "the scribe," which is given to Baruch in MT verses 32 and 26. Baruch is commonly referred to as "the scribe" or "the secretary" in scholarship, but, in fact, of the 21 times that Baruch appears in MT Jer, he is only referred to as "the scribe" (הַסֹּפֵר) in MT's edition of Jer 36:26 and 32. In the corresponding passages in LXX, he is simply referred to as Baruch (Βαρουχ), without his patronymic and without a professional title,¹⁴⁴ and LXX never identifies Baruch as a scribe. This is surprising because, by contrast, LXX identifies both Gemariah (v. 10)¹⁴⁵ and Elishama (v. 12) as "the scribe" (ὁ γραμματεὺς ≈ הַסֹּפֵר) in this chapter. The textual evidence leaves one wondering whether Baruch is actually a scribe and what it means for MT to call him "the scribe."¹⁴⁶

As Janzen notes, the editor of MT glossed the text with the term הַסֹּפֵר.¹⁴⁷ He further believes that this was an interpretive move on the part of MT's editor, and that Baruch's stenographic function inspired the gloss. Perhaps Baruch's stenographic function played a role in MT's reasoning, but why would MT add

---

143 Stipp, *Jeremia*, 79–81 and Janzen, *Studies*, 72, 107. Hill, "Book," 159 holds the aberrant view that this is part of MT's effort at "downgrading" Baruch.
144 Baruch is mentioned 22 times in LXX Jer–Bar (39:12–13, 16; 43:4–5, 8, 10, 13–15, 17–19, 26, 27, 32; 50:3, 6; 51:31; Bar 1:1, 3), and 8 of those times he is called "Baruch son Neriah," Βαρουχ υἱὸς Νηρίου (39:12, 16, 43:4, 14; 50:3, 6; 51:31; Bar 1:1).
145 Lundbom, *Jeremiah*, 597–598 argues that the term "'the scribe' identified Shaphan, not Gemariah, although the latter is also trained in the profession," but I have been unable to find another instance where a title at the end of a patronymic refers to a name in the patronymic rather than the forename of the character. It is argued below that Gemariah was "the scribe." Similarly, see Wahl, "Entstehungder," 379.
146 Jeremiah is referred to as "the prophet" (הַנָּבִיא) in MT verses 8 and 26, but not in LXX. These additions are typical of MT (McKane, *Jeremiah*, 903). Jeremiah was a known prophet, so his title is not surprising. Baruch, however, is not known to have been a scribe. Therefore, the insertion of הַסֹּפֵר in verses 26 and 32 may be interpretive, as Janzen suspects (*Studies*, 72).
147 Janzen, *Studies*, 72. Generally, LXX includes a title only during the first mention of a character, e.g., Ελισαμα ὁ γραμματεὺς (v. 12), but only Ελισαμα in verses 20 and 21. See Stipp, *masoretische*, 87–89.

the title הַסֹּפֵר here and not in MT Jer 32:12–14, where Baruch is working in an official secretarial capacity as the writer of a land deed?[148] What does the term הַסֹּפֵר in MT Jer 36 accomplish?

The term הַסֹּפֵר, which is often translated "the scribe" (Gk. ὁ γραμματεύς), has been the subject of scholarly interest, but often rarely is the term discussed within its socio-linguistic, historical, and contextual environments.[149] Most often it has been discussed as a title within the context of the Judahite king's court.[150] The following paragraphs demonstrate that in depictions of the late Judahite kingdom, only one individual in a social group or institution was identified as "the scribe" (הַסֹּפֵר). Furthermore, the position of the palace scribe expanded in the late Judahite kingdom from a secretarial position to a position of political power, and perhaps even to a position of leadership over the high-ranking courtiers, the שָׂרִים.

It is often stated that the term הַסֹּפֵר refers to a specific position in the state hierarchy or royal court in the late Judahite kingdom,[151] but this is complicated by evidence suggesting that multiple figures carried the title. (1) Jer 8:8 refers to סֹפְרִים, "scribes" (indefinite plural),[152] which suggests that there was more than one scribe.[153] (2) In the present tale, LXX contains two characters identified as "the scribe": Γαμαριου υἱοῦ Σαφαν τοῦ γραμματέως, "Gemariah, son of Shaphan, the scribe" (v. 10), and Ελισαμα ὁ γραμματεὺς, "Elishama the scribe" (v. 12). MT identifies three scribes in the same story: גְּמַרְיָהוּ בֶן־שָׁפָן הַסֹּפֵר, "Gema-

---

148 Lundbom, *Jeremiah Among the Prophets*, 120 speculates that Jeremiah may have written the deed. It was not commonplace for scribes to write their own legal documents; rather, they would have a third party, who was not the proprietor or buyer, compose a legal document. Jeremiah, however, could have written the deed and Baruch the legal copies. See Ishodad of Merv's commentary on Jeremiah, which states, "For the ancients made two deeds for their purchases: one that was wrapped and sealed, and another that was a copy which served as the receipt of the purchase" (CSCO 328, 29).
149 For more general socio-historical studies, see Conrad, *TDOT* 10:318–326 and Perdue, "Baruch among the Sages," 260–265. Conrad, in particular, divides his study into the early monarchy, the late monarchy, the exile, and the postexilic period. He holds that the scribe was an official position as "the head of the royal chancellery" (323). He sees the term undergoing semantic change only in the postexilic period (324).
150 Fox, *Service*, 96–110.
151 See Fox, *Service*, 98–9; McKane, *Jeremiah*, 903–904; Conrad, *TDOT* 10:324; Jeremias, *TDNT* 1:740–1.
152 See Joüon §137f.3.1 as well as Barr's reservations about the article in poetry in "'Determination,'" 310–312.
153 This is the only instance in the book of Jeremiah in which סֹפְרִים are referred to in the plural. All other references are to הַסֹּפֵר: MT Jer 36:10, 12, 20, 21, 23, 26, 32; 37:15, 20; 52:25. The Greek ὁ γραμματεύς is found in LXX Jer 8:8; 43:10, 12, 23; 44:15, 20; 52:25.

riah, son of Shaphan, the scribe" (v. 10); אֱלִישָׁמָע הַסֹּפֵר, "Elishama the scribe" (v. 12); and בָּרוּךְ הַסֹּפֵר, "Baruch the scribe" (v. 26). (3) A small number of unprovenanced seals dating to the mid-first millennium BCE uses the term הספר, "the scribe," for more than one individual.[154]

On the other hand, evidence establishing the singularity of the position also exists. (1) Outside of MT Jer 36, narratives only identify one character as הַסֹּפֵר in a given story (e.g., Shebnah in MT 2 Kgs 18–19 or Shaphan in MT 2 Kgs 22). (2) MT Jer 36 claims that the שָׂרִים gather in the chamber of the scribe (לִשְׁכַּת הַסֹּפֵר, MT 36:12; τὸν οἶκον τοῦ γραμματέως, LXX 43:12), in which the term הַסֹּפֵר "the scribe" (τοῦ γραμματέως) is singular rather than plural. This datum suggests that there was only one scribal character who occupied that office.

In order to reconcile the little, yet contradictory, evidence, one can see the term הַסֹּפֵר as referring to a single professional title given to an individual in a particular institution. Such an approach makes sense of the narrative material referring to the Israelite or Judahite kingdom.[155] In this way, Elishama can be seen as הַסֹּפֵר of the palace, while Gemariah held the title הַסֹּפֵר in the temple, where his chamber resided.[156]

A complication to this deduction comes from the epigraphic material. As noted above, Gemariah appears to have been a historical figure, as evidenced by a bulla with his name on it found in situ in the City of David.[157] However, the bulla does not carry the title הספר, which one might expect if Gemariah occu-

---

154 E.g., Avigad and Sass, *Corpus*, no. 21 עדיהו בן/ הספר; no. 22 הספר / לגאליהו בן; no. למאש/ בן מנח; 23 הספר / בן אדניהו / לשלם (all unprovenanced). I also mention here the unprovenanced "Assessment Ostracon," purportedly from the Shephelah, that refers to הספר. דעויהו "Daʿuyahu, the scribe." This character appears to play the role of an accountant who either receives or, more likely, oversees a transaction of silver. For the most recent edition of the text, see Ahituv, *Echoes*, 190–193.

155 This is not to say that it reflects historical reality. Furthermore, MT Esther 3:12 and 8:9 refer to a plurality of courtly scribes, סֹפְרֵי־הַמֶּלֶךְ. That these are references to those responsible for royal edicts as Fox, *Service*, 102 correctly notes, is likely a historically accurate allusion to the fact that standardized Achaemenid decrees require "the scribe" to ensure their enactment (Moore, "Persian," 1–14 and Moore, "Who Gave," 76–78). One wonders if the accounting function of ס(וֹ)פֵר הַמֶּלֶךְ (MT 2 Kgs 12:11 ‖ 2 Chr 24:11) is a reference to a Persian period title rather than an allusion to a Judahite courtly figure. Surprisingly, this possibility is not considered by Fox, *Service*, 102–103 who holds a positivistic view on the reliability of the data found in Chronicles (14–23), which is known to be late. She finds the phrase's parallel, instead, in the much earlier Amarna Letters (106 n. 104). But certainly, the Achaemenid imperial administration oversaw temple accounting in the provinces (e.g., Pap. Ber. P. 13540).

156 See Wahl, "Entstehung," 379 who interprets Gemariah as a "Tempelschreiber."

157 Shiloh, "Group," 33. For a more recent study, see Mykytiuk, *Identifying*, 139–147.

pied this professional position at the time the seal was crafted.¹⁵⁸ Furthermore, the position הַסֹּפֵר tends to replace the patronymic of the one who bears the title when it is found in the Hebrew Bible. For example, Shaphan is called הַסֹּפֵר frequently in the tale of Josiah's reform (MT 2 Kgs 22:8–10, 12; 2 Chr 34:15, 18, 20), and his patronymic rarely occurs (only in MT 2 Kgs 22:3 ≈ 2 Chr 34:8).¹⁵⁹ Likewise, Shebnah, who was הַסֹּפֵר during the reign of Hezekiah, is only known by his position and never his patronymic (MT 2 Kgs 18:18, 26, 37; 19:2; Isa 22:15 36:3, 11, 22; 37:2). It seems that the term replaces a character's patronymic when he is הַסֹּפֵר in the royal court of Jerusalem in the late Judahite kingdom.¹⁶⁰

In fact, the term הַסֹּפֵר, with the definite article, first appears in reference to Shebnah in MT 2 Kgs 18:18.¹⁶¹ Shebnah is a transitional figure with whom the position gained prestige in the Hebrew Bible. In the days of Shebnah and prior to him, the highest-ranking position in the palace was called אֲשֶׁר עַל־הַבַּיִת, "the palace overseer;"¹⁶² this is an official title and not a descriptive clause.¹⁶³ Shebnah is the only character to hold both roles: he is the first character called the scribe (הַסֹּפֵר; MT 2 Kgs 18:18) and one of the last called the palace overseer (אֲשֶׁר עַל־הַבַּיִת; MT Isa 22:15).¹⁶⁴ In a rare example of a prophecy against a specific royal employee, the prophet Isaiah condemns Shebnah for building a tomb that honors his position as the palace overseer and states that Shebnah will be demoted

---

158 For a detailed discussion of professional titles on Judahite bullae, see Avigad and Sass, *Corpus*, 466–468. Among the 51 bullae found in Area G, only one bears a professional title, הרפא, "the healer" (no. 4). See Shiloh, "Group," 16–38, esp. 32.

159 Note that MT 2 Chr 34:8 only refers to him as שָׁפָן בֶּן־אֲצַלְיָהוּ, whereas MT 2 Kgs 22:3 contains an extensive patronymic that scholars tend to trust as historically accurate, שָׁפָן בֶּן־אֲצַלְיָהוּ בֶן־מְשֻׁלָּם הַסֹּפֵר. Apart from this reference, the name Meshullam is only otherwise known in post-exilic texts, see Bloch, "Judeans," 133 n. 34.

160 This practice is known from Persian administration (Moore, "Persian," n. 12), but the practice is also found in sources dating to the late Judahite kingdom. Patronymics are left out in letters in which the person or people in power would be known to the reader (e.g., השרים in Lach 6) or when the addressee is a ranking officer (e.g., השר in *KAI* 200 ln. 1). On the other hand, when an author writes to an addressee about a specific third-party ranking officer, the name of the third party may be used (e.g., שר הצבא כניהו בן אלנתן in Lach 3).

161 As opposed to ס(וֹ)פֵר (note the *mater lectionis*!) in MT 2 Sam 8:17; 20:25; 1 Kgs 4:3 (plural סֹפְרִים); 1 Chr 18:16; or סֹ(וֹ)פֵר הַמֶּלֶךְ in 2 Kgs 12:11; 2 Chr 24:11. Carr, *Writing*, 116–118 discusses the different titles in general terms.

162 MT 1 Kgs 16:9; 18:3; 2 Kgs 10:5; 18:18, 37; 19:2; Isa 22:15; 36:3, 22; 37:2. See Fox, *Service*, 81–96.

163 Using relative pronouns in professional titles is common in Akkadian, esp. Neo-Assyrian; see *ša-rēši*, "the eunuch," or *ša-ziqni*, "the bearded (official)."

164 Eliqam, who was Shebnah's contemporary and who may have taken his place, is the last mentioned אֲשֶׁר עַל־הַבַּיִת.

(MT Isa 22:15–25).[165] In the book of Kings, Shebnah appears only as the scribe (הַסֹּפֵר).[166] Given the existing data, it can be argued that the political conflict in the royal court between Isaiah and Shebnah forced the king to give Shebnah a new position, that of "the scribe," and that his political acumen allowed him to quickly turn it from the rather insignificant role that "a (royal) scribe" once had into a position of power. This analysis explains why the position of הַסֹּפֵר carried significant social capital among the palace's chief courtiers (הַשָּׂרִים) by the time of the constructed setting of MT Jer 36. Indeed, MT Jer 36 depicts the chief courtiers congregating around Elishama, the scribe, when Baruch encounters them. But as with the position of the palace overseer, only one bearing the title הַסֹּפֵר appears in the palace at a time.[167]

The degree to which this explanation reflects the historical circumstances is unclear; the documentary data is missing. Nonetheless, my explanation provides a view into the conception of late Judahite scribal culture in biblical narrative and provides a window into the how scribal allusions operate. This provides a basis for explaining why an editor of MT Jer 36 describes Baruch as "the scribe."

The editor of MT Jer 36:26 and 32 deduced that Baruch was "the scribe" of some social institution other than the palace or Jerusalem temple, neither of which are Baruch and Jeremiah associated with. The text makes it clear that the palace and the temple are two distinct loci of scribal activity, and that Baruch and Jeremiah work in an undisclosed scribal workshop apart from these two institutional centers. By adding הַסֹּפֵר to verses 26 and 32, MT's editor reveals his understanding of the scribal profession and of the professional standing of Baruch. Baruch returns to Jeremiah, not as his apprentice, but as his colleague. Only after Baruch has undergone his training and accomplished his first professional task of presenting his scroll does MT identify him with the professional

---

165 In Siloam, on the outskirts of Jerusalem, Clermont-Ganneau discovered a tomb inscription written in the ancient Hebrew script, which contains the phrase אשר על הבית (*KAI* 191). Avigad has argued that the text should be restored to read the patron's name as [שבנ]יהו and claims that שבנא is a hypocoristicon of it ("Epitaph," 150).

166 See discussion in Cogan and Tadmor, *II Kings*, 230.

167 Contra Fox, *Service*, 105–6 who argues it is difficult to ascertain the number of individuals who held the office at one time; she sees various ranks within the class of scribe, rather than a single scribe in each institution. Presumably, this is a result of the comparative data (107). A single palace overseer also existed in *each* palace of the kingdom. See MT 1 Kgs 16:9, אַרְצָא אֲשֶׁר עַל־הַבַּיִת בְּתִרְצָה, "Artza, the overseer of the palace in Tirzah" and given Shebnah's transformation of the titles, it seems best to see them each as a singular office.

title of הַסֹּפֵר.[168] Now as a professional, Baruch begins the task of recomposing the scroll that was burned (v. 32).[169]

3.6 Concluding Remarks

The five scenes of the Tale of Jeremiah and Baruch's Scroll take place in four loci of scribal activity. The first is an undisclosed scribal workshop, in which Baruch and Jeremiah prepare their scroll and plan to publicize it. The scribal workshop is a place that gives them immediate access to the tools of the scribal craft, such as papyrus, ink, styli, and perhaps archival texts containing notes of Jeremiah's previous prophetic sayings. The passage also contains three other loci of scribal presentation: the temple, the palace's scribal chamber, and the king's presence. Each of these latter three loci are places in which a scroll can be presented and debated for its social significance. In these loci of scribal presentation are characters of social importance, and as the plot moves from scene to scene, the audience increases in social importance. Baruch and his scroll move from a public presentation in the temple to a private scribal audience in the palace's scribal chamber, and finally, the scroll alone moves to the king's seat of national power to be read and decided on.

Literary patterns appear as the plot develops from one scene to another, and these patterns can be charted as follows:

---

[168] Note that PESHITTA may have a similar socio-historical interpretation, but instead places Baruch's promotion to scribe at the point that he leaves the scribal workshop. It refers to Baruch as ܣܦܪܐ, "the scribe," from verse 10 onward, but not while he is under Jeremiah's tutelage, in vv. 1–8. Fox, *Service*, 103–4 discusses how the duty of the royal scribe "was to read documents in the presence of the king or other ministers," and this I would argue extends to the scribe of any institution in biblical narratives.

[169] The final clause is enigmatic. It can be viewed as a self-reflective statement regarding the process of textual growth (Hartenstein, "Prophets," 90–91 following Konrad Schmid). It appears to be a secondary addition to the tale.

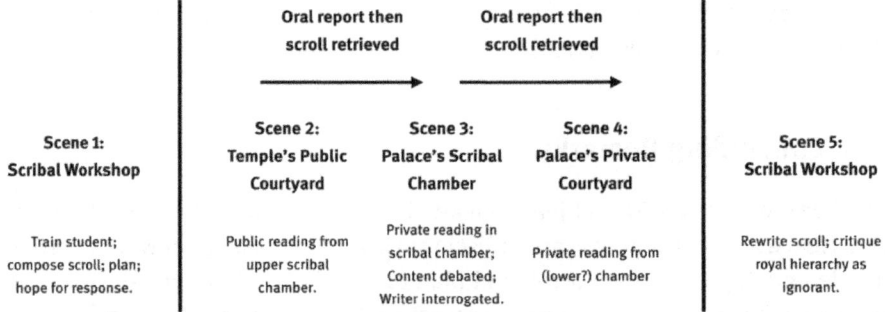

Fig. 1: Literary Patterns in the Scenes of Jeremiah 36

The scenes that take place in the scribal workshop, scenes 1 and 5, serve as an introduction and epilogue to the plot; they bookend it. The settings in 2 and 4 mirror each other. Both occur in rooms connected to courtyards, but in scene 2 Baruch's reading takes place from an upper room of a public courtyard, while in scene 4, Jehudi reads Baruch's scroll from a (possibly) lower room in a private courtyard. The focus of the story's narrative arc is scene 3, which is set in the palace's scribal chamber and which depicts the scribal interactions and processes of scribal reasoning that occur over Baruch's scroll.

Harald Knobloch maps the three middle scenes in a similar way, but does not recognize their placement between the workshop scenes in which the scrolls are written. For him, "Sie finden ihren Höhepunkt in der dritten [my 4th] Szene, die von einem paronomastischen Phänomen dominiert wird: Der dreifachen Verlesung durch Baruch (קרא) wird kontrastierend das Zerschneiden der Schriftrolle (קרע) entgegen gehalten."[170] Knobloch's argument is based on MT (and perhaps a forced Aristotelian narrative arc) and on what he sees as the high point of social dynamics in the episode's development. Knobloch recognizes that Stipp had seen, as I do, the scribal debate in verse 16 as an integral literary critical point, but argues that when compared with MT Jer 26, this is not the case.[171] But when all five scenes of the episode are considered along with their parallelistic structure, the climax of the episode becomes the scholarly debate over the scroll in the palace's scribal chamber in LXX or courtiers' revelation of

---

170 Knobloch, *nachexilische*, 105–108, esp. 106.
171 Knobloch, *nachexilische*, 106–107, which refers to Stipp, *Jeremiah*, 74–77, 129. Stipp, *Jeremia*, 126 recognizes this, but does not elaborate on it, when he notes, "Im Sinne des Redaktors muß man die Verse 22-26 großzügig zugunsten seiner Helden lesen - was die Exegeten erfahrungsgemäß nicht ungern tun."

the fear of Yahweh in MT (v. 16). In either case the, focal point of the story rests on the chief courtiers' scribal actions and decisions.

The MT editors appear to have recognized the scribal dynamic at the story's climax. The fear of Yahweh is certainly a learned, and some would say scribal, concept in the Hebrew Bible's wisdom traditions. It is not, however, a practical response in the context of the current narrative, and for this reason MT had to make substantial changes to the episode. Many of the observations made in this chapter rest on a text-critical analysis and show a general trend of MT to interpret its Vorlage by adding to the text. On two occasions, in verses 6 and 26, MT expanded the role that Yahweh plays in the narrative, and in verse 18 it deleted the name of Jeremiah in order to achieve the same effect. In LXX's edition, Yahweh exists solely in the cognitive experience of Jeremiah—the two function as the same character. In verse 6, however, the editor of MT ascribes responsibility for the ideas in the scroll to Yahweh, thereby separating him from Jeremiah. Moreover, MT's editor made Yahweh into Jeremiah and Baruch's independent savior in verse 26, in which Yahweh hides the two troubled characters, as opposed to LXX's edition, in which they hide themselves.

Other textual differences show MT's attempt to understand the social dynamics of the scribal characters in this passage. For instance, in verse 19, MT supplies הַשָּׂרִים as the subject of the verb, but it does not include all (כָּל) of the שָׂרִים in its addition, because at this point in the narrative, the שָׂרִים split into competing groups that have different views about Baruch's scroll. The most profound social observation that MT made was to identify Baruch as הַסֹּפֵר, "the scribe," of his and Jeremiah's scribal group. MT's addition of הַסֹּפֵר in verses 26 and 32 has made an indelible mark on the history of modern scholarship, which has come to refer to "Baruch the scribe." Important in this study is the observation that Baruch is seen in MT's text as the scribe of a localized scribal group that existed outside of the palace's and the temple's operations.

A wider study on the term הַסֹּפֵר in this chapter has shown that different groups or institutions had a position designated "the scribe" (הַסֹּפֵר), and that the one who held this position was more than a mere scrivener.[172] The scribe was a powerful political figure. In the case of the palace's chief courtiers (the שָׂרִים),

---

172 Schniedewind, *How*, 7 distinguishes between "palace scribes" as administrators and a סֹפֵר as a "transmitter of tradition and text rather than an author." But he still runs into semantic limitations, as is the case in his discussion of a Moabite scribe who produces a highly literary royal inscription despite his occupation as a "royal scribe," i.e. an administrator (41). Demsky, *Literacy*, 148 sees the birth of a scribal class owed to administrative needs of a growing empire with Jerusalem as its capital.

"the scribe" appears to have been their operational leader, because they congregated in his chamber (v. 12). Although the palace scribe was socially powerful, other שָׂרִים may have wielded more political influence over the king. All שָׂרִים appear to have been "scribal" characters, though only one was called "the scribe."

The passage attributes scribal traits to various שָׂרִים, who are depicted as either explicitly (as in the case of Jehudi or Gemariah) or implicitly literate. All of the chief courtiers (כָּל־הַשָּׂרִים) exhibit an ability to intellectually reason through and debate a document of national concern. For this reason, they may all be seen as "scribal." Although the palace's שָׂרִים debate and adjudicate on activities of national interest that occurred in the temple, there is no direct evidence in this passage that such scribal characters were responsible for explicitly drafting or managing cultic agendas or cultural affairs. But it seems reasonable that men with such far-reaching power proposed legislation for both the civil and cultic life of the kingdom.[173] The שָׂרִים in this passage act as educated intellectuals and as politicians, but also as ones deputized to police the public affairs of the kingdom, even within the cultic sphere. Within their control was the consolidation of a number of social and legal powers. The text implies that they maintained control by using a network of associates, such as Micaiah, to monitor public and cultic activity.

Little in this passage has to do with cultic or religious life, though there are some allusions to it. Because Jeremiah is a known prophetic figure—though LXX does not refer to him as such in this passage—and because Baruch's reading in the temple resembles the actions of a priest, the text alludes to a simplistic sociology of the temple's professional ranks of prophets and priests. This, combined with its explicit depiction of palace courtiers and even one royal, allow for a basic social assessment of the text's stated and implied terms for scribal and courtly characters.

The following figure organizes the terms that are actually used in the Tale of Jeremiah and Baruch's Scroll (those in bold) and the professional terms implied in the text (those in italics). The only identifiably specific professional title is הַסֹּפֵר, which is double underlined. The other terms identify ranks of professionals in the palace and temple. The terms appear in order of their social hierarchy. They reveal a simple two-tiered hierarchy under the king: two upper classes, the high-ranking courtiers, הַשָּׂרִים, and the royals, בֶּן הַמֶּלֶךְ; and a lower class, the

---

[173] Outside the scope of this study is MT Jer 8:8, in which Jeremiah accuses חֲכָמִים, "sages," whom he calls "scribes" סֹפְרִים (indefinite), of manipulating culturally significant documents (תּוֹרַת יְהוָה). See Whybray, *Intellectual*, 15.

lower-ranking royal servants, עֲבָדִים. The distinction between the royals and the upper-class servants may simply be that the latter were hired employees. There is no evidence in the passage that בֶּן הַמֶּלֶךְ was a scribal character, but rather a trusted member of the royal court. The tale is not concerned with the lower-class servants.[174] The two classes of religious ranks in the temple are only implied in the tale and may be derived from MT Jer 26, which shares a similar plot structure to MT Jer 36 and is frequently studied with it.[175]

Institution of בֵּית הַמֶּלֶךְ		Institution of בֵּית יְהוָה
הַמֶּלֶךְ		
עַבְדֵי הַמֶּלֶךְ (עֲבָדָיו)	בֶּן הַמֶּלֶךְ	הַכֹּהֲנִים
הַשָּׂרִים		
הַסֹּפֵר		הַנְּבִיאִים
Lower-Ranking עֲבָדִים		

Fig. 2: Ranks of Scribal and Related Positions in Jeremiah 36

To be sure, the concept of Judahite "scribal" professionals must have been more elaborate than this, but the findings in this chapter have at least nuanced previ-

---

174 MT Jer 36:24 adds כָּל־עֲבָדָיו, "all of (the king's) servants," to the scene in the king's winter quarters, but they are not present in LXX. In the final prophecy against Jehoiakim, his servants are called out: וּפָקַדְתִּי עָלָיו וְעַל־זַרְעוֹ וְעַל־עֲבָדָיו, "And I will punish him, his lineage and his servants" (καὶ ἐπισκέψομαι ἐπ' αὐτὸν καὶ ἐπὶ τὸ γένος αὐτοῦ καὶ ἐπὶ τοὺς παῖδας αὐτοῦ). These should be taken as עַבְדֵי הַמֶּלֶךְ, "servants of the king," and as a poetic and metonymical reference to הַשָּׂרִים in particular (see McKane, *Jeremiah*, 907). Note how בֶּן הַמֶּלֶךְ parallels זַרְעוֹ and עֲבָדָיו parallels הַשָּׂרִים.

175 A detailed discussion of MT Jer 26 is beyond the scope of this study, but it is notable that Jeremiah is portrayed in the received editions (MT and LXX) as both a priest and a prophet. Leuchter has argued that the received text presents Jeremiah as a Levite and scribe (*Levites*, chap. 6), and his argument is convincing. By extension the characterization of the priests and prophets in the book of Jeremiah may fairly be studied through the lens of scribal professions. The difficulty with the book of Jeremiah and the larger Jeremiah-traditions, however, is that the *narrative* texts of Jeremiah provide the context by which the few poetic references to scribal characters or activity may be interpreted as a "repeated emphasis" on literacy (note the citations in Leuchter, *Levites*, 194 and similarly the study of the document's self-reference by Eggleston, *See*, chap. 3). We simply need more Jeremiah manuscripts or comparative studies on large scale compositions based on similar traditions, such as the diverse manuscript history of the Story of Ahiqar, to determine if the composers of particular narrative pericopes in Jeremiah had his priestly heritage in mind, or if this is a late development that editors of the surviving Jeremiah-tradition invented.

ous views about the professional experience of late Judahite "scribes."[176] According to Schniedewind, it was in the late Judahite period, as illustrated by Hilkiah's discovery of the Torah scroll, that the epicenter of writing shifted from the palace to the temple. But this study has shown that the temple was only one of three significant scribal centers operating in the late Judahite kingdom: the Jerusalem palace, the Jerusalem temple, and the private scribal workshops outside of these two institutions. That this text depicts scribal activity happening independent of an institution provides further support for Schniedewind's ideas about the authorial community of biblical works. That is, MT Jer 36 may not merely be an etiology for the formation of the book of Jeremiah, as many understand it,[177] but foremost a subversive appeal for the decentralization of an intellectual and religious tradition maintained by a select group of cloistered scribal professionals.[178] Although Jeremiah and Baruch's attempt at a scribal uprising failed during Jehoiakim's reign, it would take hold as a grassroots movement in the exilic period, during which neither a Judahite palace nor a temple institution existed. In this way, this passage is not only the explanation for the survival of an authoritative Jeremiah-book,[179] but also the validation of the unaffiliated scribal professionals who were rejected during the monarchy. In this sense, Jeremiah and Baruch were community-grown scholars and byproducts of the "democratization of writing" in the late Judahite period.[180]

---

[176] For instance, van der Toorn sees royal scribes (as opposed to temple scribes) "that are mentioned in connection with the court as secretaries of state rather than professionals of writing" (*Scribal*, 85). This study has shown palace scribes to be adroit at intellectual reasoning and to have a stake in cultural affairs.

[177] E.g., Holladay, *Jeremiah 2*, 10–24.

[178] Sanders, *Invention*, 140 makes a similar deduction regarding the Siloam and Deir Alla inscriptions. He writes, "And these accounts no longer assign primary responsibility to the king: their protagonists are craftsmen and prophets. This trend finds its most extensive expression in biblical narrative, which is never authored by the king and where people and prophets assume new prominence as agents."

[179] Per van der Toorn, *Scribal*, 173–204.

[180] See Schniedewind, *Social*, 99–126, esp. 104, 120–122.

4 The Story of Ahiqar and the Tale of Jeremiah and Baruch's Scroll in Comparative Perspective

This study on the allusions to the professional scribal experience in the Story of Ahiqar and the Tale of Jeremiah and Baruch's Scroll has yielded new insights into the meaning of each text. I have argued that according to the Elephantine Ahiqar manuscript, royal scribes maneuvered through intricate state and professional politics and this reflects the realistic experiences of Neo-Assyrian scholars, even though the known Aramaic manuscript comes from the Persian period and shows signs of having been updated. The Aramaic text of the Story of Ahiqar engages in implicit attacks against Akkadian scribal culture, while explicitly producing a work of royal propaganda. The Tale of Jeremiah and Baruch's Scroll, unlike the Story of Ahiqar, is a subversive work that uses the social world of Hebrew scribal interactions within loci of scribal activity to convey an anti-monarchic message. Although both tales center on the scribal profession, the two works contain different objectives. The Story of Ahiqar, as found in the Elephantine manuscript, is a political tale about the value of loyalty to the crown that circulated around Persian period Egypt, a provincial region prone to rebellion against its Persian overlords. The Tale of Jeremiah and Baruch's Scroll mocks the failed state of Judah for not considering the advice of a scribal outsider when the king and his court had the chance.

Each of these tales sets part of its narrative in a royal court, and each plot develops around the courtly scribal experience. The similar settings for both tales and the similar positions of the characters produce comparable scenarios and conflicts. This chapter will begin its comparative discussion of these two tales by discussing them in connection with the court tale genre. It will then discuss eight specific literary motifs shared between the Story of Ahiqar and the Tale of Jeremiah and Baruch's Scroll. These motifs are (1) a focus on introductory words of the senior scribal protagonist, (2) a historical reference to the succession of kings, (3) the imparting of knowledge on a scribal student/apprentice, (4) the senior scribal protagonist's self-acknowledged inability to perform his scribal duty, (5) professional conflict brought about by the scribal student's/apprentice's actions, (6) an angry king who commands a prince to capture/kill the protagonist, (7) courtly characters who intervene in the protagonists' conflict, and (8) courtly colleagues who save the protagonists' lives by hiding them away or encouraging them to hide. As the similarities in each motif are discussed so too are the different ways in which each motif is expressed in the two tales.

This chapter will then turn to the issue of narrative voice and discuss the evolution of autobiographies to biographies based on examples from the manuscript histories of each work. The extensive manuscript history of the Story of Ahiqar which shows an evolution from first- to third-person narration is used as a heuristic model to contribute to the debate over a difficult autobiographical variant in LXX Jer 43:1 (≈ MT Jer 36:1). The implications of this comparison are far reaching for other narrative portions of the book of Jeremiah and provide an alternative perspective in the deadlocked debate about the book's manuscript history.

The chapter will end with a sociolinguistic and etymological discussion of how the comparative framework of this study has led to a nuanced understanding of the term scribe.

4.1 The Story of Ahiqar, the Tale of Jeremiah and Baruch's Scroll, and the Court Tale Genre

The Story of Ahiqar has long been studied as an exemplar of the court tale genre, which was used cross-culturally throughout the ancient Near East.[1] Some have also studied it as a wisdom narrative,[2] a satire on wisdom,[3] or as belonging to a genre of fictional autobiographies,[4] all of which can be seen in some way connected to royal courts. The present study has shown that by focusing on how Ahiqar characterizes himself as a scribe in a royal courtly setting in autobiographical style, the tale explicitly conveys a propagandistic royal message that favors allegiance to the monarch though the scribe faces unfair oppression. However, it implicitly presents a critique on Akkadian scribal culture from an Aramaic scribe's point of view. In this way, the subtextual messages of the Elephantine manuscript align, to some degree, with Wills' satirical reading of the Syriac version of Ahiqar known from Cod. Camb. Add. 2020. According to Wills,

---

1 Burt, *Courtier*; Dalley, "Assyrian," 149–161; and Niditch and Doran, "Success," 179–193. Holm, *Courtiers* studies the Story of Ahiqar within the context of the "story collection" genre. Holm claims, "Ahiqar does not represent a story-collection *per se*, but its court conflict or tale of rivalry between ministers at a Mesopotamian court and the wise sayings attributed to the superior Ahiqar provide a tantalizing view of, once again, the proclivity of court settings and courtiers to attract collected narrative materials" (77).
2 Müller, "weisheitliche," 77–98; Kottsieper, "Aramaic," 120; Kratz, *Historical*, 144–145; Kratz, *Historisches*, 98–99; Kratz, "Mille," 45; and Weigl, *aramäischen*, 1–12.
3 Wills, *Jew*, 44–49 and Wills, "Observations," 57–66.
4 Longman, *Fictional*, 43–48, 103–119.

"The satire in Ahikar seems to be aimed at demolishing one ideal of wisdom, the pompous court sage, and replacing it with another, the cunning hero."[5] For Wills, this satirical reading only applies to the Syriac manuscript in which the wise sayings are presented in two different narrative contexts, once in the event of professional instruction and again in the event of professional admonition. Wills is correct that the Elephantine manuscript does not satirize the notion of wisdom, but it does satirize the unfair advantages of an old guard of scribal professionals while craftily presenting a court tale of royal propaganda.

Despite the literary motifs that it shares with the Story of Ahiqar, the Tale of Jeremiah and Baruch's Scroll is not a court tale. According to Niditch and Doran, a court tale contains four narrative features: (1) a person of lower status is called before a person of higher status, (2) the person of higher status poses an unsolvable problem, (3) the person of lower status solves the problem, thereby (4) receiving a reward.[6] These narrative features function around the central theme of clever acts or words.[7] In the Tale of Jeremiah and Baruch's Scroll, Baruch and the clever words of Jeremiah found on his scroll match three of these four elements: (1) Baruch, as a private scribal apprentice, is called before the chief royal courtiers in the palace. (2) The courtiers interrogate Baruch, and (3) he answers well enough for them to spare his life. While sparing one's life is a type of reward, it does not match the expected reward of prestige or possessions that are found in court tales. In fact, Jeremiah is so embittered that Baruch's scroll was not accepted in the royal court that Jeremiah speaks a life threatening and treasonous reprisal against the king and his courtiers (MT Jer 36:31). The Tale of Jeremiah and Baruch's Scroll contains three of the four court tale themes, but ends as a subversive reprisal against the Judahite monarchy. This is due to the fact that unlike court tales and unlike the Story of Ahiqar, the Tale of Jeremiah and Baruch's Scroll does not begin within the context of a royal court.

Unlike the doublespeak that can be found in the crafty and propagandistic rhetoric of the Story of Ahiqar, the Tale of Jeremiah and Baruch's Scroll presents a message of rebellion and sedition, rather than of unjust accusations and rehabilitation. The opposite messages of the two works are owed to the fact that the

---

5 Wills, *Jew*, 48. Similarly, about the Elephantine text Vayntrub writes, "[The Story of Ahiqar] is a story of the failure of wisdom's transmission" ("Book," 108.)
6 Niditch and Doran, "Success," 180. This remains the only study to clearly map a possible structure of the court tale genre. Holm, *Courtiers*, focuses on the larger generic category of the story-collection, and sees the court tale as a sub-genre (64).
7 Niditch and Doran, "Success," 180.

central characters of each exist in different sectors of society. Ahiqar and Nadin are royal scribes serving in the highest scribal office in the capital of the world's most powerful empire. Jeremiah and Baruch, however, belong to neither of the two major scribal institutions of their land, the palace or (main) temple. The protagonists in the Tale of Jeremiah and Baruch's Scroll are a small association of private scribal figures from a suburban, or more likely rural, setting. They interact with royal scribes, some of whom show a respect for their message, but their status as outsiders is felt throughout the tale. In fact, neither of them is deemed worthy enough to appear before the king as anything other than criminals. Unlike, the Story of Ahiqar, the Tale of Jeremiah and Baruch's Scroll does not critique the sociological structure in which scribal figures operate. The senior scribe's inability to perform his job motivates the conflict in both stories, but in the case of the Tale of Jeremiah and Baruch's Scroll this merely means that the old scribe will prepare an apprentice to perform a similar job but in a different way and with more scribal acumen. Rather than using prophetic performance, Jeremiah prepares Baruch to give a scribal lecture. Although the lecture does not achieve its intended purpose, in the end Baruch evolves into Jeremiah's colleague, and the two continue their work with separate functions and positions in their small scribal association.

These two tales are united by their focus on scribal protagonists and their use of royal courts as settings of professional scribal conflict. In terms of their messages, however, they are significantly different, and each illustrates the flexibility of a royal court as a literary topos through which ideological messages can be presented in an entertaining and believable way. In fact, the two tales are effective, due in part to the believability and relatability of the conflict and scenarios in which their scribal protagonists find themselves. Both tales are framed in their present form within real historical circumstances. The flexibility of those circumstances does not detract from their messages. For instance, the Ethiopic manuscripts of the Story of Ahiqar reframe the tale within the world of an unnamed Persian king and Syriac-Karshuni manuscripts of a Jeremiah apocryphon, which likely derive from a very old source, recasts the Tale of Jeremiah and Baruch's Scroll in the reign of king Zedekiah.[8] So while an aura of historicity remains in the tales as they evolve, their scribal conflicts and court settings anchor them within the court tale genre, which makes them recognizable regardless of their many literary idiosyncrasies. In view of these stories, it might

---

8 Harris believes that this apocryphon derives from an early Greek original, and Mingana agrees only to postulate a possible Coptic intermediary (Mingana with Harris, "Jeremiah," 127, 149).

now be possible to speak of a scribal conflict narrative as a sub-genre of the court tale, which includes a number of literary motifs.⁹

4.2 Shared Motifs between the Story of Ahiqar and the Tale of Jeremiah and Baruch's Scroll

Beyond sharing part of the structure of the court tale genre, the Story of Ahiqar and the Tale of Jeremiah and Baruch's Scroll also share specific motifs with each other. The following list includes motifs shared between MT Jer 36 (along with LXX Jer 43) and the Elephantine Ahiqar manuscript.

4.2.1 Introductory Focus on the "Word(s)" of the Scribal Protagonist

Ahiq. A.1	Ahiq. Gv^{upside down}	LXX Jer 43:1b	MT Jer 36:1b
[ספר] ˹מלי˺ אחיקר שמה ספר חכים ומהיר	למ ב ש ו שנג למרא מלכן סנח[אריב מ]˹לכא˺ בכלח ˹יעטת מלוכת˺ אתור	ἐγενήθη λόγος κυρίου πρός με λέγων	הָיָה הַדָּבָר הַזֶּה אֶל־יִרְמְיָהוּ מֵאֵת יְהוָה לֵאמֹר
[The account of] ˹the maxims˺ of the one named ˀAḥiqar, a wise and expert scribe ...	Saying: 24 years belong(ed) to (the) Lord of Kings, Senn[aḥˀerîb]˹the˺[k]ing. In Kalaḥ I advised the kingdom/ kingship of ˀAtûr.	So it was, a word of the Lord came to me, saying ...	So it was, this word came to Jeremiah from Yahweh, saying ...

The statement "the words of the Lord came to a prophet" in MT Jer 36 is a stock phrase used throughout prophetic literature, especially the book of Jeremiah, so at first glance it does not stand out as a unique motif.¹⁰ However, as the story unfolds, written words, particularly "all of the words" of the scroll are significant props with which the scribal characters interact. Similarly, in the Story of Ahiqar, "words" (מלין), which are used interchangeably with counsel (עטה),

---

9 The degree to which two independent sources constitute a "sub-genre" may be questioned, but it should be borne in mind that the surviving mid-first millennium Northwest Semitic dataset is extremely limited. I hold that given this limit, it is astonishing that two narratives share so many motifs and structural features.
10 The clause is also found in MT Jer 36:27.

function as a prop that demands respect from the other characters and creates a dramatic tension between them. The words of Jeremiah and Baruch's scroll do the same in that tale. Furthermore, both stories include wise maxims or sayings that admonish the story's villain with "words" (MT Jer 36:27–31; Ahiq. E–H, J–L) at the end of the story.[11] In the Story of Ahiqar the prologue states that the narrative is an account of the "words," which suggests that the narrative was written to facilitate a reading of the maxims. Comparatively, this supports claims that the Tale of Jeremiah and Baruch's Scroll is written to authenticate Jeremiah's broader collection of prophecies, though within the narrow context of the chapter, it is an admonition against Jehoiakim, his offspring, and his courtiers that is in view. It is Ahiqar's sayings that show him as a teacher and his narrative to be didactic. By comparison, the Tale of Jeremiah and Baruch's Scroll might also be seen as a didactic narrative.

4.2.2 The Succession of Kings

Ahiq. A.4–5

הוה שנחאריב מלכ אתור א[חר מית ש[נחאריב
מל[כ אתור אנה פלחת] אסרחאדן שמה ברה והוה
מלכ באתור חל[פ שנחאריב [א¹בוהי

(Now) Śennaḥʾerîb was king of ʾAtûr. A[fter Śenna]ḥʾerîb, the k[ing of ʾAtûr, had died, I served] the one named ʾEsaraḥʾiddin, his son. And he was king in ʾAtûr; he repla[ced Śennaḥʾerîb,] his ⸢fa⸣ther.

MT Jer 36:1a ≈ LXX Jer 43:1a

וַיְהִי בַּשָּׁנָה הָרְבִיעִת לִיהוֹיָקִים בֶּן־יֹאשִׁיָּהוּ מֶלֶךְ יְהוּדָה

And so it was, in the fourth year of Jehoiakim, son of Josiah, king of Judah.

The succession of kings is an important plot element in both narratives, but a regnal (or a regnal-like) formula is also used in a variety of historiographic works. In the court tale genre, the historical circumstances of a particular king may increase the believability of the tale or enrich the complexity of its possible interpretations, but it is not necessary for the reader to know such details. All that is necessary is that the story introduces a king in some way. The incipit on the verso of the Ahiqar manuscript, Ahiq. Gv[upside down] (see above), and the opening lines of some of the Syriac manuscripts of the Story of Ahiqar begin the tale with a historiographic reference to Sennacherib's last year and/or the accession year of Esarhaddon.[12] The Elephantine manuscript, however, contains an unu-

---

11 See Jong, "Rewriting," 139 for a discussion of how "oracles were an indispensable part of the political decision making" in neighboring kingdoms and Judah.
12 For example, Camb. Cod. Add. 2020 1.1

sual emphasis on the replacement of Sennacherib with Esarhaddon, rather than on the year in which the tale takes place. This statement of replacement, והוה מלכ באתור חל]פ שנחאריב [א]בוהי "And he was king in ʾAtûr; he repla[ced Šennaḥʾerîb,] his ʿfaʾther" (A.5), is a specific claim that may have been adapted from the Akkadian inscriptions of Esarhaddon, which were well published throughout Mesopotamia but not known in Egypt.[13] According to those texts, Sennacherib confirmed his choice of heir by divine decision, in which Šamaš and Adad are claimed to have said, *šū tēnûka* "he (Esarhaddon) is your (Sennacherib's) replacement" (RINAP 4 Esar no. 1 i 14). The emphasis on replacement serves a literary purpose in the Story of Ahiqar; the succession of Esarhaddon mirrors the succession of Nadin. Like Nadin, Esarhaddon was not the expected heir of his father (RINAP 4 Esar no. 1 i 8–16).

The Tale of Jeremiah and Baruch's Scroll uses an imprecise regnal formula that sets the narrative at some point in the fourth year of Jehoiakim. Jehoiakim's fourth year is a literary topos in the book of Jeremiah that marks the beginning of institutional collapse in the kingdom of Judah. This allusion injects a sense of anticipation into the tale. Although it is not as clear as in the Story of Ahiqar, a notion of regnal succession occurs in MT Jer 36:2b, in which Yahweh commands Jeremiah to write down his prophecies מִיּוֹם דִּבַּרְתִּי אֵלֶיךָ מִימֵי יֹאשִׁיָּהוּ וְעַד הַיּוֹם הַזֶּה "from the day that I spoke to you, from the days of Josiah until now." This line suggests a continuity in the words of Jeremiah, despite monarchic succession, and implies that the change in the monarch prompts the need for subversive scribal activity to escalate. That is, as in the case of the Story of Ahiqar, a change in the monarch puts a social demand on the scribal protagonist, and in both stories each protagonist responds by training a student or apprentice to replace him.

4.2.3 Imparting Knowledge to a Student or Apprentice

Ahiq. A.1, 8–9	MT Jer 36:4
אחיקר... זי חכם לברה ... וחכמתה וטבתא [י]הבת לה]	וַיִּקְרָא יִרְמְיָהוּ אֶת־בָּרוּךְ בֶּן־נֵרִיָּה וַיִּכְתֹּב בָּרוּךְ מִפִּי יִרְמְיָהוּ אֵת כָּל־דִּבְרֵי יְהוָה
Ahiqar... who taught his son ... I have taught wisdom to him, and [I] ʿgʾ[ave] good (things) [to him]	Jeremiah summoned Baruch, son of Neriah, and Baruch wrote all of the words of Yahweh (verbatim) from the mouth of Jeremiah.

In the twentieth year of Sanḥerîb, son of Sarḥaddôm, king of Assyria and Nineveh.
[13] See RINAP 4 Esar no. 1 i 9–10.

Both stories depict the transfer of knowledge from one scribal student to another, who will eventually take the senior scribe's place in the plot. It is noteworthy that the success of the senior scribe is not important here, but rather his motivations for choosing a pupil. In the Tale of Jeremiah and Baruch's Scroll, Jeremiah successfully prepares Baruch to present a prophetic document, and despite Baruch's failure to influence the courtiers, the two remain partners at the end of the tale. In the Story of Ahiqar, however, Ahiqar fails Nadin as a teacher. The reasons for Ahiqar's failure are owed to his adherence to a number of self-destructive norms practiced by elite Akkadian writers that encourage Ahiqar to select a relative, rather than find a qualified student as does Jeremiah. Ahiqar attempts to train his student in the ways of a wise scribe, not realizing that Nadin contains a character flaw that contradicts Ahiqar's instructions. This means that the tale does not critique Ahiqar for his efforts as a teacher, but for his social motivations and his choice of a student—that is, for his attempted nepotism. For this reason, the text propagates the content of his teachings though his legacy is lost. In the Tale of Jeremiah and Baruch's Scroll, however, both Jeremiah's teachings and legacy are maintained by Baruch. Jeremiah did not suffer Ahiqar's fate since Jeremiah chose an advanced scribal apprentice who had already shown himself professionally capable (MT Jer 32:16–25).

Although the two tales share this literary motif, each points to a different social reality of the scribal profession. The Tale of Jeremiah and Baruch's Scroll refers to a practical strategy undertaken by advanced students working with a scholar; the curriculum includes copying the teacher's instructions. While this phenomenon is well known in cultures for which an extensive textual record survives, this is the only evidence in an early Hebrew source for this type of professional scribal transference. Baruch is learning the value of precisely crafted documents and the political value of using writing mediums, an investment which will later yield social returns when his scroll grants him access to the royal court. The word choice in the Story of Ahiqar, however, is curiously different. Unlike in the Tale of Jeremiah and Baruch's Scroll, no practical strategies are referred to. Instead, Ahiqar claims to have made Nadin wise (√חכם D-stem) and given him good things, which as discussed in chapter two, refers to social favors or privileges, which Ahiqar expects Nadin to reciprocate. In the tale, the social realities of imparting scribal knowledge allude to propriety, mannerism, and expectations of the advanced student who is an employee in the royal court. Ahiqar imparts to Nadin how the scribal profession must include, foremost, social strategies for a student's self-preservation, and most importantly from Ahiqar's perspective, for the self-preservation of the teacher.

4.2.4 Protagonist's Confessed Inability to Perform his Scribal Duty

Ahiq. B.1	MT Jer 36:5 ≈ LXX Jer 43:5
שב אנה לא אכהל למפלח בבב היכלא	אֲנִי עָצוּר לֹא אוּכַל לָבוֹא בֵּית יְהוָה
1(Now) I am old. I will be unable to work at the Gate of the Palace.	I am inhibited, I will not be able to enter the House of Yahweh.

Central to the plot of both tales is the senior scribe's self-acknowledgment that he is unable to perform the duties of his position. These statements provide the practical reason why the protagonists take on a scribal student or apprentice during a period of monarchic succession, and thus, these statements initiate the stories' conflicts. Both stories contain a strikingly similarly worded statement.

Turning first to the Tale of Jeremiah and Baruch's Scroll one finds that MT Jer 36:5 appears to be similar to LXX's Vorlage, but LXX may have misinterpreted the meaning of the line. LXX reads, Ἐγὼ φυλάσσομαι, οὐ μὴ δύνωμαι εἰσελθεῖν εἰς οἶκον κυρίου "I am detained; I am unable to enter the house of the Lord." The verbal forms are clearly in the present tense (and so too in Peshitta, V, and Targ.—all witnesses otherwise similar to MT). But MT uses an imprecise modal construction which may be understood as "I am inhibited; I cannot enter the house of Yahweh."[14] The text immediately continues with verbs in the future-perfect tense, which convey mandatory instructions and which are a logical consequence of Jeremiah's present inhibition: "I am inhibited... You shall go." The point is that the context presents Jeremiah as anticipating his inability to perform his function as a prophet. This anticipation suggests that his desire to bring Baruch under his tutelage is an ongoing and long-term plan, not an impromptu response to his current predicament.

In some respects, the Story of Ahiqar presents the motif of confessed inability in a more advanced literary context. Like the Hebrew of MT Jer 36:5, the Aramaic of Ahiq. B.1 uses an imprecise modal construction, which is followed by verbs in the future tense (יחלף, B.2). Furthermore, Ahiqar had already referred to himself as "old" in the broken line of Ahiq. A.6 prior to admitting his imminent inability to perform his scribal duty. In his earlier statement, his old age serves as the impetus for his adoption of Nadin (A.6–7). Then the scene changes, and the king inquires of Ahiqar as to who will replace him at his death (A.7–8), which again parallels the language used to explain the succession of kings (A.4–5). Ahiqar brings his scribal student to the king's attention (A.8–10), and presents him to the king for an interview (A.10). The king is happy with the student (A.10–12), and Ahiqar continues his sycophantic praise of the king in

---

14 For the modal meaning "can" see Joüon §75i and 112a.

order to ultimately make a statement about his impending inability to perform his job at the Palace Gate (B.1). When Ahiqar tells the king (not his successor as does Jeremiah) that he will not be able to do his job, Ahiqar attempts to manipulate the king, so that the king might allow Ahiqar to retire before he dies (A.14–B.1). Despite its more advanced literary build up, Ahiqar's statement about his inability to perform his job serves the same narratological function as that of the similar statement in MT Jer 36.[15] It provides the motivation for the tale's central conflict.

These similar statements in both tales also contain grammatical, lexical, and syntactical corollaries. Both characters begin these statements with a verbless clause and use passive or stative participles: אֲנִי עָצוּר "I am inhibited" and שב אנה "I am old." Next, both characters use the same phrase to express their future inability: לֹא אוּכַל "I (cannot and) will be unable" and לא אכהל "I (cannot and) will be unable." Lastly, they both use an infinitive construction that mentions a locus of scribal activity that they cannot work in or enter: לָבוֹא בֵּית יְהוָה "to enter the House of Yahweh" and למפלח בבב היכלא "to work at the Gate of the Palace." These corollaries along with the same function of the line in the respective tales leave one wondering if these similarities are more than coincidence.

While the central motivations for each plot (MT Jer 36:5 and Ahiq. B.1) are similar in syntax and content as discussed earlier in this chapter, these confessions by the protagonists regarding their inability to perform their duties contain a fundamental difference: Jeremiah's inability derives from social or political circumstances, while Ahiqar's is a self-identified character flaw. As discussed in chapter three, the reason for Jeremiah's inhibition remains unknown, but it is clear that Jeremiah's status was imposed on him by outside political forces. Jeremiah's inhibition is not owed to an inherent character flaw. This interpretation agrees with the view argued in chapter three that the passage makes a subversive political statement with overtones of social suppression of an outsider's message.

Unlike in the book of Jeremiah, Ahiqar's inhibition is the result of a personal character flaw rather than outside political forces. Ahiqar claims that he will

---

15 Like any plot element, later editors can adapt this statement for their own artistic purposes. This is clearly seen in Camb. Cod. Add. 2020 and related manuscripts as well as in Graffin and related manuscripts. In both manuscript groups editors put the statement of Ahiqar's inability in the mouth of Nadin, the tale's villain, for example,
Camb. Cod. Add. 2020 3.1

ܘܐܡܪ ܕܐܚܝܩܪ ܐܒܝ ܣܐܒ ܠܗ. ܘܥܠ ܐܦܝ ܩܒܪܗ ܩܐܡ
And (Nādān) said that ʾAḥîqar, my father, is growing old and at the entrance of his grave he stands.

not be able to perform the functions of his office because he is "old" שב (B.1). The Mesopotamian texts discussed in chapter two portray scribal characters who were unable to do their jobs because of similar personal character flaws: old age played a role in Urad-Gula's complaint (SAA 10 no. 294), old age was a concern in the folkloric tale on K4347+16161 ii 50–63, and the old scholar of SAA 10 no. 160 was concerned about his illness impeding his work, and in a similar vein the scribe of the Underworld Vision of the Assyrian Prince (SAA 3 no. 32) chose his own professional path. Certainly, limitations imposed by others played a role in the political maneuvering of many Assyrian scholars, but the tale of the Story of Ahiqar depicts such professional problems as a consequence brought on by Ahiqar's stated character flaw. He complained that he was too old to fulfill his duties. This turns out not to be the case, and clues from the narrative suggest that Ahiqar knew this all along. For instance, when Ahiqar learns from Nabûsumiskun of Nadin's betrayal he immediately devises a plan with Nabûsumiskun, in which he claims that Esarhaddon יזכרני ועטתי יבעה "will remember me, and [he will] seek my counsel" (D.i.5). Clearly, Ahiqar still feels equipped to complete his duties as the king's counselor. Just as he deceives the king with the help of Nabûsumiskun, so too he deceived the king when he complained that he could no longer perform the professional scribal duties expected of him.

4.2.5 Professional Conflict Brought on by the Scribal Student's Actions

Ahiq. B.9; C.5	MT Jer 36:10 ≈ LXX Jer 43:10
{Broken, but alluded to} [בר א]ֹ[ח]ֹתי זי אנה רבית עשת על[י בישתא ... {missing actions of Nadin} [... למה הו יחבל מתא עלין {Broken, but alluded to} [My ne]ʿphʾew, whom I reared, contrived [evil] against [me in his heart {missing actions of Nadin}]... Why does he damage the land against us?	וַיִּקְרָא בָרוּךְ בַּסֵּפֶר אֶת־דִּבְרֵי יִרְמְיָהוּ בֵּית יְהוָה בְּלִשְׁכַּת גְּמַרְיָהוּ בֶן־שָׁפָן הַסֹּפֵר בֶּחָצֵר הָעֶלְיוֹן פֶּתַח שַׁעַר בֵּית־יְהוָה הֶחָדָשׁ בְּאָזְנֵי כָּל־הָעָם In the hearing of all of the people, Baruch read the document of the words of Jeremiah in the House of Yahweh, from the chamber of Gemariah, son of Shaphan, the scribe (located) in the upper (outer) courtyard at the entrance of the New Gate of the House of Yahweh.

In both the Tale of Jeremiah and Baruch's Scroll and the Story of Ahiqar, junior scribes use their scribal skills to incite the king's or the court's wrath. In the case of the tale of Jeremiah and Baruch's Scroll, Baruch reads his scroll in the temple precinct, which has no noticeable effect on the people or religious functionaries, but sends the palace courtiers into a frenzy and eventually incites the king's anger. In the Story of Ahiqar, Nadin accuses his teacher of treason before the king. Here too the scribal student provokes the king's anger against the senior scribe, and Ahiqar's fellow courtier laments the situation (C.10). Although the Elephantine text is broken, it is likely that Nadin's accusations are successful because he uses forged documents.¹⁶

4.2.6 An Angry King Who Commands a Prince to Capture/Kill the Protagonist

Ahiq. C.1–4	LXX Jer 43:26	MT Jer 36:26
[אס]רחאדנ מלכ אתור ואמר [לנבוסמסכנ שמה רביא ... למ ... אנת] חד מנ רבי אבי זי לחמ אבי [אכלת ... אחיקר (זכ)] [תבעה אתר זי אנת תהשכח [אחיקר תקטלה ות(הי)תה לי פגרה]	καὶ ἐνετείλατο ὁ βασιλεὺς τῷ Ιερεμεηλ υἱῷ τοῦ βασιλέως καὶ τῷ Σαραια υἱῷ Εσριηλ συλλαβεῖν τὸν Βαρουχ καὶ τὸν Ιερεμίαν.	יְצַוֶּה הַמֶּלֶךְ אֶת־יְרַחְמְאֵל בֶּן־הַמֶּלֶךְ וְאֶת־שְׂרָיָהוּ בֶן־עַזְרִיאֵל וְאֶת־שֶׁלֶמְיָהוּ בֶּן־עַבְדְּאֵל לָקַחַת אֶת־בָּרוּךְ הַסֹּפֵר וְאֵת יִרְמְיָהוּ הַנָּבִיא
[ʾEs]araḥʾiddin, the king of Assyria [responded] and said [to the one named Nabûsumiskun, the prince, ... you are] one of the my father's princes/chiefs, who [ate] my father's bread [...] You must look for [(this) ʾAḥîqar]. Wherever you find [ʾAḥîqar, you must kill him and bring me his body].	And the king commanded Jeremeel, the king's son, and Saraia son of Esriel to seize Baruch and Jeremiah.	And the king commanded Jerahmeel the prince and Seraiah son of Azriel and Shelemiah son of Abdeel to seize Baruch, the scribe, and Jeremiah, the prophet.

In both stories, once the king is informed of the protagonist's insults, he sends a prince after the scribal protagonist(s). Esarhaddon sends Nabûsumiskun "the prince" (רביא) and two unnamed men after Ahiqar (C.6). Similarly, Jehoiakim sends "the prince" (בֶּן־הַמֶּלֶךְ) Jerahmeel along with and another man (in LXX, two men in MT) to capture Jeremiah and Baruch (Jer 36:26). This motif depicts how kings relied on royals along with courtly employees when pursuing those accused of treason. In both cases, courtiers accompany the prince. It is explicitly stated in the Story of Ahiqar that the men are to confirm that the prince fulfills his mission, and in order to curb conspiracy a second team will be sent to confirm their work (D.i.14–15). By comparison, this can be assumed to be the reason that Jehoiakim assigned a man to accompany Jerahmeel in the Tale of Jeremiah and Baruch's Scroll.

---

16 See chapter two for discussion and a possible reconstruction.

Both Neo-Assyrian and Hebrew sources recount the risk of usurpation by royal court officials who were not blood relatives. MT 2 Kgs 21:23 recounts how the courtiers of king Amon of Judah (great grandfather of Jehoiakim) assassinated him in an attempted coup. Furthermore, the Story of Ahiqar is set in the period of Esarhaddon's succession, which was the result of a conspiracy planned by courtiers in conjunction with one of Sennacherib's sons (SAA 18 no. 100; MT 2 Kgs 19:36–17). Echoes of Sennacherib's assassination may lay behind Nadin's betrayal; Ahiqar rejects Nadin by calling him "my son who is not my son" (Ahiq. B.14) only after the betrayal. So while dynastic characters are generally more reliable because they had a vested interest in maintaining political control, their power was checked by the courtiers assigned to confirm their work. These courtly dynamics played out in both tales and were realistic hazards of the scribal profession; scribes were at risk of quickly becoming the enemy of the king. The anger of the king is a fundamental component of the court tale; it is a reflection of the real-life circumstances that becomes a literary topos. The prince and scribe's relationship, whether written in a complementary tone (The Story of Ahiqar) or antagonistically (the Tale of Jeremiah and Baruch's Scroll), exhibits the power of their political alliance.

4.2.7 Courtly Characters Intervene in the Protagonist's Fate

Ahiq. C.10	LXX Jer 43:16	MT Jer 36:16
[נ]ב׳וסמסכן רביא ׳זכ׳ ק׳רב׳תא בזע כתונה הילל	καὶ ἐγενήθη ὡς ἤκουσαν πάντας τοὺς λόγους, συνεβουλεύσαντο ἕκαστος πρὸς τὸν πλησίον αὐτοῦ	וַיְהִי כְּשָׁמְעָם אֶת־כָּל־הַדְּבָרִים פָּחֲדוּ אִישׁ אֶל־רֵעֵהוּ
[(When) Naʳbʰûsumiskun, ʳthatʳ prince, [(saw me)] he began to tear his tunic. He lamented.	And so it was, when they heard all of the words, they debated each with his peer.	And so it was, when they heard all of the words, they became afraid, each before his neighbor.

In each tale, courtly characters react to the actions of the scribal protagonists and decide to intervene and to aid them. The impetus for the courtiers to intervene derives from their emotional or intellectual relationship with the accused scribal character and his works. Nabûsumiskun decides to aid Ahiqar because he carried a social debt to Ahiqar for having saved him from a similar situation in a backstory; this triggered for Nabûsumiskun an emotional reaction to the mission that the king ordered him to complete. How could he kill a man who saved his life? Likewise, in MT Jer 36, the courtiers respond emotionally to Baruch and his scroll, and this provokes (some of) them to advise Baruch (MT Jer

36:17). In LXX Jer 43:16, however, the scribal courtiers respond intellectually to Baruch and his scroll. This implies that their motivation to spare Baruch, but not his scroll, derives from a feeling of professional respect. Scribal interactions and allusions to the process of forming scribal and courtly alliances are at the core of these interventions.

In the Elephantine manuscript, when the prince Nabûsumiskun spots Ahiqar from a distance, he laments (C.10). Lamenting is not a scribal reaction,[17] but nonetheless implies that Nabûsumiskun was considering the circumstances of the situation carefully. While he is not a scribal character in a strict sense, Ahiqar equates himself with Nabûsumiskun, and therefore, functionally turns him into a scribal character for this scene. Furthermore, as part of the plan to save Ahiqar, it is Nabûsumiskun—not Ahiqar—who contrives the idea to replace Ahiqar's body with a eunuch's, who is a scribal figure.

When viewed in comparative perspective, this motif produces a new insight into the episode in the Tale of Jeremiah and Baruch's Scroll. In the Story of Ahiqar, Nabûsumiskun and the two men with him endanger their own lives to help spare Ahiqar's. The scribal characters in the Tale of Jeremiah and Baruch's Scroll tell Baruch that he should not reveal to them where he hides, so that they are not culpable for his escape. Nonetheless, they advised him to escape. Their actions, like Nabûsumiskun's, demonstrate the value of scribal lives, even at the expense of their work. No character in the Tale of Jeremiah and Baruch's Scroll thought that the scroll was important enough to endanger their own lives nor to allow Baruch and Jeremiah to die for its message. Baruch and Jeremiah agree that their lives are not worth their message, as their act of hiding demonstrates. In a way, then, the motif of the intervention of scribal characters brings to the fore a theme of scribal self-preservation in both tales.

4.2.8 Scribal Colleagues Encourage the Protagonist(s) to Hide

Ahiq. C.17–D.i.1	LXX Jer 43:19, 26	MT Jer 36:19, 26
{Broken, but alluded to in Nabûsumiskun's backstory, which serves as a literary foil for Ahiqar's predicament} תמה הוית מסבל לב כאיש עמ אחוהי והצפנתכ מנה אמרת קטלתה	καὶ εἶπαν τῷ Βαρουχ Βάδισον κατακρύβηθι, σὺ καὶ Ιερεμίας· ἄνθρωπος μὴ γνώτω ποῦ ὑμεῖς... καὶ ἀτεκρύβησαν	וַיֹּאמְרוּ הַשָּׂרִים אֶל־בָּרוּךְ לֵךְ הִסָּתֵר אַתָּה וְיִרְמְיָהוּ וְאִישׁ אַל־יֵדַע אֵיפֹה אַתֶּם... וַיַּסְתִּרֵם יְהוָה

---

17 In Akkadian, one of the *ummânu* was known as the *kalû* the lamentation priest who served as the courtly poet, but there is no indication that this is alluded to here.

There I (Ahiqar) had been your benefactor, like a man with his brother. And I hid you from him. I said, "I had killed him."	And they said to Baruch, "Go! Hide—you and Jeremiah. No one must know where you are"… And they hid.	And the chief courtiers said to Baruch, "Go! Hide—you and Jeremiah. No one must know where you are"… And Yahweh hid them.

One might assume that hiding would be a common feature of conflict narratives set in a royal court, but among the most popular ancient court tales, the theme of hiding is only found, to my knowledge, in the Story of Ahiqar, in the Tale of Jeremiah and Baruch's Scroll,[18] in the book of Tobit (Tob 1:18–2:1) which may have adapted it from the Story of Ahiqar, and in the Egyptian tale of Sinuhe. In a typical court tale, as the conflict develops the courtier faces the problem directly,[19] but as the conflict develops in the Story of Ahiqar and the Tale of Jeremiah and Baruch's Scroll, the narrative moves the protagonists into hiding. The plot then focuses on the court in the protagonist's absence, at least in the Tale of Jeremiah and Baruch's Scroll and some Syriac manuscripts of the Story of Ahiqar; the Elephantine text is broken here. To be sure, scribal characters are associated with secrecy, hidden knowledge, and hidden items (e.g., MT Dan 2:22),[20] but this is so they can reveal these things to the other characters. For these two narratives to send their scribal protagonists into hiding, however, is a

---

[18] For an example of an Egyptian story that shares loose literary motifs with the Tale of Jeremiah and Baruch's Scroll but not the hiding scene see the Middle Egyptian tale, The Eloquent Peasant (COS, 1.43), in which a peasant petitions a nobleman many times about the same matter, each time writing the petition on a scroll. At the end, the nobleman constructs a new scroll of the compiled petitions and presents it to the king who is pleased. For the discussion of this text and its self-reference to its own composition, see Hagen, "Constructing," 186–188. Hagen notes that the court setting of The Eloquent Peasant (and Neferti) "is presented as a direct result of the desire of the king to be entertained—itself a well-known topos in the Egyptian literary tradition" (187). MT Jer 36 differs in three significant ways: (1) its content focuses on the professional acts and lives of scribal characters, (2) it does not include the sayings of Jeremiah, and (3) the king is not pleased with Baruch's actions or the scroll. The Story of Ahiqar has also been studied in comparison with Egyptian works. For example, Lichtheim, *Late*, 13–21 claims, "The author of the Demotic Instructions of Ankhsheshonqy was familiar with the Aramaic Wisdom of Ahiqar in a version (or versions) which stood much closer to the Syriac and other translations than to the fifth century BCE text from Elephantine" (21).

[19] The tale of Sinuhe is different than the other two tales. In the Story of Ahiqar and the book of Tobit, characters advise or hide the protagonist, and it is well known that Tobit relies on the Story of Ahiqar (see introduction). The character of Sinuhe, however, hides himself (COS 1.38.b.1–15). Thus, only the Story of Ahiqar and the Tale of Jeremiah and Baruch's Scroll are independently similar.

[20] See Lenzi, *Secrecy*.

unique nuance, and perhaps even a reflection that the scribes embody their own hidden knowledge. As noted in chapter two, the Story of Ahiqar borrowed the motif of hiding a political outsider from the well-publicized inscriptions of Esarhaddon, who was known to have gone into hiding after the assassination of his father and before his coronation. The origin of this motif in the Tale of Jeremiah and Baruch's Scroll may be a result of a lost historical circumstance, or it may derive from literary expectations current at the time.[21]

4.2.9 Discussion of the Shared Motifs

This list of eight shared literary motifs reveals what one could expect in a mid-first millennium tale about a scribe facing conflict in a royal court. Scribal protagonists are characterized by their words and their interest in developing an intellectual legacy. New generations of scribal figures are empowered to act when senior scribal characters are unable, or claim to be unable, to perform their professional duties for a new king. The narrative backdrop of generational scribal transition allows for a setting in which a conflict may develop between an old guard and an avant-garde scribal perspective. Both motifs of succession and professional inability may be played out in different ways depending on the structure of the narrative settings. In the case of the Tale of Jeremiah and Baruch's Scroll, the scribal succession allowed for competing scribal associations positioned in different loci of scribal power to clash. In the case of the Story of Ahiqar, the conflict takes place in the same scribal locus and the generational conflict occurs between an older and younger character of the same scribal association. The generational tension is exaggerated by the younger's avant-garde approach or message, which clashes with the old guard who runs or had previously run the royal court.[22] Ultimately, the generational conflict among the courtiers threatens the king, who is also a product of a parallel generational shift; the inexperienced king does not know who to trust and, therefore, retaliates in anger.

---

21 The act of hiding under the guidance of an advisor is found in MT Jos 2:1–8, but this is in an attempt to infiltrate an enemy, not to flee from one. Hiding one's self from political conflict can be found in a number of biblical tales (e.g., MT Jos 10; 1 Kgs 18). In 1 Kgs 17, Elijah hides from political conflict at Yahweh's counsel, but this can be interpreted as Elijah's own decision not as done under guidance. The only reference, known to me, of a political dissident hiding at the advice of a courtly figure is David hiding at the advice of Jonathan (MT 1 Sam 19–20).
22 See the various schemata in Wills, *Jew*, 199–204.

The generational conflict among scribal characters is linked to the tensions between the king and his courtiers. Literacy is powerful social capital in such a conflict and has the potential to subjugate the opposition.[23] Just as in today's society, in which political scandal often rests on the documentation of an act, so too in antiquity were documents used as evidence of power over political opponents. Documents were required for the conviction of scribal crimes, as in the case of Jehoiakim's conviction of Baruch and Jeremiah after having seen the scroll (MT Jer 36:26). In the Story of Ahiqar the manuscript evidence suggests that Ahiqar in the Elephantine manuscript was also condemned based on— albeit forged—documentary evidence.

Both tales also demonstrate that the consolidation of power leaves few scribal positions to be filled by many who desire them. By depicting a single scribal replacement in both tales—and building its narrative conflict around this motif in the case of the Story of Ahiqar—one might deduce that the apprentice model of education, whereby a single teacher takes on a single student, was an attempt at maintaining the consolidation of power in the hands of a few scribes and their limited circles of influence. Despite such attempts, competing groups emerged, and so the conflict between scribal protagonists and scribal antagonists, both of whom claim a divine right to social power, clash in a contest.

The strategy in a scribal contest is to succeed through connivance and intellectual debate.[24] The struggle is not acted out with tools of warfare, but with instruments of the scribal craft, such as styli, writing mediums, and seals.[25]

---

[23] See Levi-Strauss' view that "The only phenomenon with which writing has always been concomitant is the creation of cities and empires, that is the integration of large numbers of individuals into a political system and their grading into castes or classes... My hypothesis, if correct, would oblige us to recognize the fact that the primary function of written communication is to facilitate slavery. The use of writing for disinterested purposes, and as a source of intellectual and aesthetic pleasure, is a secondary result, and more often than not it may even be turned into a means of strengthening, justifying or concealing the other" (*Tristes*, 299). Similarly, Sharp, "Aporia," 45 writes about MT Jer 36: "Reading and writing and rewriting are acts of power." This is in the context of understanding Jeremiah as literature of the diaspora.

[24] Bledsoe "Wisdom," 251 states, "Perhaps the most prominent ethic which underlies nearly all of Ahiqar's teachings is the ethic of caution." This important observation may be perceived as a component of the stratagem of connivance. But I would go further and argue that connivance includes secrecy (see Lenzi, *Secrecy*), which is a deliberate and offensive strategy unlike caution, which I understand to be defensive.

[25] As Sharp observes, tremendous professional "risk" is taken in MT Jer 36 ("Aporia," 40). Matthews, "Jeremiah's," 117 refers to the scroll as a "prop" in a passing way. By comparison, for an insightful study of the use of letters in Greek works see Rosenmeyer, *Ancient*, esp. 5–7, and for the function of documents in Egyptian tales see Hagen, "Constructing," 185–209. For a

Those in power ensured that only a few could wield these tools effectively in a court setting. If these strategies are passed along successfully, as in the case of Jeremiah passing on his strategies to Baruch, then the new apprentice proves to be a formidable challenge for alliances of old guard courtly scribal figures.

The two tales also show how scribal conflict rests on the competition for power in which one side promotes an old guard ideology and the other an avant-garde philosophy. Theoretically, depending on the objectives of a text's composer, either the old guard's or the avant-garde's ideology might be promoted in the narrative, and in both of the scribal tales studied here, the old guard succeeds against the new guard. But in both tales, the success of the old guard becomes the critique that the moral of the stories tries to highlight.

Among the many interpretations that one may find for the Story of Ahiqar and the Tale of Jeremiah and Baruch's Scroll is an overarching moral that unless the younger scribal generation and their messages succeed, scribal culture will suffer. In the Story of Ahiqar, an Aramaic writer portrays the previous culture of chief scribal characters, which is embodied in the persona of Ahiqar, as old and dying. While this old guard will be remembered in literature, it will no longer acquire students to promote it. The Tale of Jeremiah and Baruch's Scroll, however, explicitly critiques the Judahite political philosophy as a failure and favors an implied message of radical reform. In this text, the senior scribe's views, which are preserved by his apprentice Baruch, were avant-garde because they represent the views of an outsider from the perspective of the palace's and temple's political philosophies. Both texts are literary retrospections of cultural change that have history on their side.

To summarize, this section has shown that the similar motifs in these scribal conflict narratives are a framework for viewing the ethos of the scribal experience as understood by mid-first millennium BCE Northwest Semitic readers. The professional lives of courtly scribal characters and those who interacted with them were a matrix of complex social exchanges. These eight motifs and the central message to accept the new generation or the outsider's scribal perspective at the expense of the old guard of scribal courtiers may be said to represent the features of a scribal conflict narrative, which is derivative of the court tale.

---

discussion of the "performative" act of writing in MT Jer 36 see Gosse, "écrits," 53–72 and Levtow, "Text," 111–140.

4.3 A Possible Explanation for the Evolution from First- to Third-Person Narration in Jeremiah Manuscripts in view of the Transmission History of the Story of Ahiqar

These two scribal conflict narratives not only share similar motifs and language, but they also share a complicated relationship with narrative voice. As discussed in both chapters two and three, the manuscript histories of the Story of Ahiqar and the Tale of Jeremiah and Baruch's Scroll exhibit complicated variants that present parts of the narrative in first-person and other parts in third-person. This is not a unique feature of a scribal conflict narrative, per se, but one wonders what affects narrative voice has on the respective tales in view of these variants. This section will explore the evolving narrative voice of the two tales and argue that the first-person scribal narration is more original, but due to conceptual difficulties it evolved overtime to third-person narration.

The book of Jeremiah opens with a third-person prologue followed by an autobiographical reference, which is maintained in MT Jer 1:4 and most, though not all, LXX manuscripts.[26] The variant LXX readings resembled the expected type of mixed data known from Ahiqar manuscripts, which also attests to a third-person prologue followed by an autobiographical narrative.[27] The extensive manuscript histories of each work attest to an evolution in narrative person. No surviving manuscript of either tale is solely autobiographical, but some manuscripts of the Story of Ahiqar (e.g., Ethiopic and many Arabic manuscripts) are only biographical and large portions of, especially MT Jeremiah are, likewise, biographical. The surviving manuscripts of the book of Jeremiah exhibit an intermediary stage of development between first-person and third-person narration.[28] Some of the Ahiqar manuscripts exhibit the whole evolution, while by comparison, the Jeremiah manuscripts exhibit a mixed narrative voice that appears to be evolving into third-person.

---

[26] Manuscripts B, S, and 239–410 read "to him;" the rest read "to me" (LXX Jer 1:4).
[27] For a critical discussion of Ahiqar prologues see Moore, "'Ahikariana,'" *forthcoming*.
[28] See Sharp's discussion of Emanuel Tov's work in "Take," 489–490, in which she rejects the notion of an *Urtext* and favors an approach to textual criticism that logically negotiates "the pressure to correct one text to another" versus the "precision and fidelity that have characterized the transmission of Jeremiah" (490). In an additional study Sharp argues that ancient readers coped with and interpreted manuscripts with contradictory information, "Aporia," 35–46. One may conclude then that motivations for changing confusing Jeremiah manuscripts must have been completely unintentional or pointedly motivated.

The Aramaic and Syriac manuscripts of the Story of Ahiqar are structured in an autobiographical style resembling those found in wisdom texts[29] and memorial inscriptions[30] written in both Akkadian and Aramaic sources from the Neo-Assyrian and later periods.[31] Comparative study of Ahiqar manuscripts reveals a gradual shift from first-person narration to third-person narration. The Elephantine manuscript and most Syriac (and Karshuni)[32] manuscripts retain first-person narration. The Demotic Egyptian manuscript, which pre-dates the Syriac manuscripts, attests to a third-person version of the story by the first century CE and the third-person version in the Life of Aesop is known from at least a third century CE

---

29 The narrative frame of Akkadian wisdom compositions is frequently autobiographical, for example, Šima Milka, which has a distinctly peripheral (western) Akkadian purview. The text survives from Hattuša (KUB 4.3 and KBo 12.70), Emar (Arnaud *Emar VI tome 2*, no. 778–780), and Ugarit (RS 22.439, RS94.2544+, and RS 94.5028). Its narrative frame includes a debate between a student and a teacher, much like that embodied in the courtier debate of LXX's version of the story of Jeremiah and Baruch. The end of the narrative frame resembles a statement of an unresolved plot found at the end of some Syriac Ahiqar manuscripts, for example, Camb. Cod. Add. 2020 8.39

ܐܠܐ ܐܠܗܐ ܗܘ ܕܐܚܝܢܝ ܘܗܘ ܢܕܘܢ ܒܝܢܬܢ

But God is who has kept me alive; he will judge between us.
Compare:
Šima Milka ln. 146' (following Cohen's edition in *Wisdom*)
annâ dabāba abu mārušu mitḫāriš idīnū
This argument, the father (and) his son disputed together.
Note also the wordplay in that ܗܘ sounds like ܢܝ. For another reference to a dispute poem and their history in the proverbial section of the Elephantine Ahiqar manuscript, see Brock, "Dispute," 3.
30 The collection of Akkadian autobiographical memorial (normally royal) inscriptions is vast, see Longman, *Fictional*; Longman, "Israelite," 177–195; and Westenholz, *Legends*. The genre is known in Aramaic in the same period and locations (e.g., KAI 202 A 2; 216 ln. 1; 217 1.1). Other NWS languages attest to this style, such as Phoenician (KAI 24 ln. 1, KAI 26 A.i.1) and Moabite (KAI 181 ln. 1). Scholars frequently note that the Greek writer Democritus (c. 5th cent. BCE), purportedly encountered and translated a stele (στηλην) of Ahiqar (την Ακικαρου) (Harris, *Story*, xli; Nöldeke, *Untersuchungen*, 21–23).
31 Egyptian literary sources also frequently employ autobiographical literary style and provide an interesting avenue for future comparative research. Although significantly earlier than the Story of Ahiqar, the Report of Wenamun and the Tale of Sinuhe stand out as compelling autobiographical legendary narratives in which the protagonist travels to a Semitic land. So, although this study is limited to the purview of historically close and linguistically similar sources, it should not be assumed *a priori* that Egyptian literary techniques are not associated with the larger literary trends in the ancient Near East. But a careful study with a clearly defined method is needed for such research.
32 The unpublished Karshuni manuscripts that I have viewed are in first-person (Sachau 339 and Mingana 258).

manuscript.[33] The Ethiopic and published Arabic manuscripts are also in third-person.[34] The motivations behind the evolution from first- to third-person narration in the Demotic, Ethiopic, and Arabic manuscripts as well as in the Life of Aesop are either impossible to determine due to a lack of manuscript evidence or are beyond my expertise to deduce. One wonders if the act of translating from one language to another has something to do with the change in person or if it is due, in part, to a mixed first- and third-person Vorlage, which was changed by the translators to a third-person biographical account. The fact that completely third-person versions of the tale are only found in derivative languages suggests that translation technique may play a role. Regardless, the manuscript history of the Aramaic and Syriac manuscripts reveals that the change from first- to third-person narration is owed in large part to either (1) difficult to understand narrative contexts in which a copyist unintentionally changed the narrative voice or (2) intentionally inserted third-person section dividers.

The autobiographical style of the Elephantine manuscript can be cumbersome at times to follow because, throughout, the narrator refers to himself in both the first- and third-persons. He begins with the expected marker of autobiographical narration, [אנ]ה אחיקר] "I am Ahiqar" (A.2). He also must refer to himself as a character in past episodes. This produces language which is difficult to follow and at one point even the copyist of the Elephantine manuscript leaves out an integral first-person pronoun, thereby effectively changing a section to a third-person biographical account:

Ahiq. C.14–15

[קר]בתא דחלת לם <אנה> אחיקר ענית ואמרת לנבוסמ[סכנ ...]אנה הו אחיקר זי קדמן שזבכ מנ קטל זכי
[Imme]diately I became afraid. <I> ʾAḥîqar responded and said to Nabûsum[iskun ...]I am he ʾAḥîqar who previously saved you from innocent murder.[35]

---

33 The fragments of the Life of Aesop are also in third-person. Its earliest manuscripts date to 200–299 CE (*Oxyrh. Pap* 47 #3331 and *Oxyrh. Pap.* 53 #3720).
34 The supposed Arabic *Vorlage* to the Ethiopic was, in my view, a uniquely western edition that came from a lost Greek or Coptic version in Egypt.
35 Compare Camb. Cod. Add 2020 4:9

ܗܝܕܝܢ ܐܢܐ ܐܚܝܩܪ ܥܠܬ ܘܐܡܪܬ ܠܝܒܘܣܡܟ

Then I, ʾAḥîqar, entered and said to Yābûsmāk
And
Graffin 12:1

ܗܝܕܝܢ ܐܢܐ ܐܚܝܩܪ ܐܡܪܬ ܠܩܛܘܠܐ

Then I, ʾAḥîqar, said to the executioner
The Graffin manuscript streamlines the episode:
Graffin 12:3

The confusing context of these lines caused the copyist to conceptualize the narrator as "he" rather than "I" despite the first-person verbs.[36]

Similar types of first- to third-person errors can be found in the Syriac manuscripts. For example,

> Camb. Cod. Add. 2020 1.15
>
> ܗܝܕܝܢ ܟܕ ܫܡܥ ܡܠܟܐ ܗܕܐ܂ ܝܡܝܢܐ ܝܗܒܠܝ܂
>
> Then when the king had heard this, he gave to me (his) right hand.

But a similar manuscript belonging to the same recension reads,

> Houghton 80 fol. 3
>
> ܗܝܕܝܢ ܟܕ ܫܡܥ ܡܠܟܐ ܗܕܐ܂ ܝܡܝܢܐ ܝܗܒ ܠܗ
>
> Then when the king had heard this, he gave to him (his) right hand.

Here, as in the Elephantine text, a copyist was thinking in third-person at a difficult moment in the narration and unintentionally changed a first-person pronoun to a third-person form.

Syriac manuscripts also attest to a first- to third-person narrative evolution based on the insertion of section titles. For example, in BM 7200 when Ahiqar explains to the reader that he had taught Nadin maxims, he says:

> BM 7200 fol. 144 r. 16–17
>
> ܘܗܟܢܐ ܐܡܪ ܗܘܝܬ ܠܗ
>
> And thus I was saying to him.

The maxims then follow. In Camb. Cod. Add. 2020 a longer descriptive first-person line is found.

> Camb. Cod. Add. 2020 1.15
>
> ܘܠܐ ܫܠܝܬ ܗܘܝܬ ܡܢ ܡܠܦܘܬܗ ܕܒܪܝ܂ ܥܕܡܐ ܕܐܣܒܥܬܗ ܡܠܦܢܘܬܐ ܐܝܟ ܠܚܡܐ ܘܡܝܐ܂ ܗܟܢ ܐܡܪ ܗܘܝܬ ܠܝ܂
>
> So I did not cease from my son's instruction until I had satisfied him (with) instruction as (with) bread and water. Thus, I was saying to myself.[37]

ܘܟܕ ܝܕܥܬ ܕܠܝܬ ܠܟ ܣܘܪܚܢ܂ ܛܫܝܬܟ ܘܠܐ ܩܛܠܬܟ ܥܕܡܐ ܕܢܚ ܪܘܓܙܗ ܕܡܠܟܐ

But when I knew that you had no fault, I hid you—I did not kill you—until the anger of the king subsided.

36 Another difficult and curious instance of Ahiqar referring to himself in the third-person is found in Ahiq. A.13–14, which reads:

[א]⸢ח⸣ר גהנת וסגד⸢ת⸣ למ אחיקר קדמ אסרח[אד]נ[מלכ]אתור[... א]חיקר

[Th]⸢e⸣n I bowed and prostrated [myself], saying, "ʾAḥîqar is before ʾEsaraḥ[ʾiddi]n[, king of]ʾAtûr[... ʾA]ḥîqar.

But at the end of the first collection of maxims in Camb. Cod. Add. 2020 is found this short third-person line that serves as a section divider between the maxims and the continuation of the narrative:

Camb. Cod. Add. 2020 2.75

ܗܕܐ ܡܠܦܢܐ ܕܐܠܦܗ ܐܚܝܩܪ ܠܢܕܢ ܒܪ ܚܬܗ܀

This is the instruction that ʾAḥîqar taught Nādān (his) nephew ().

In the Graffin manuscript an editor had inserted a third-person section divider at both the start and the end of the first instructional maxims:[38]

Graffin 3.1, 73

ܠܐ ܓܝܪ ܫܠܝܬ ܡܢ ܡܠܦܢܘܬܐ ܕܡܠܦ ܗܘܝܬ ܠܒܪܝ ܥܕܡܐ ܕܣܒܥܬܗ ܠܢܕܢ ܡܠܦܢܘܬܐ ܐܝܟ ܠܚܡܐ ܘܡܝܐ. ܘܗܟܢܐ ܐܡܪ ܗܘܝܬ ܠܗ ܡ̈ܠܐ ܕܚܟܡܬܐ. ܡ̈ܠܐ ܕܐܠܦ ܐܚܝܩܪ ... ܗܟܢܐ ܩܛܥ ܐܚܝܩܪ ܡ̈ܠܐ ܕܚܟܡܬܗ ܕܡܠܦ ܗܘܐ ܠܢܕܢ܀

So I did not rest from the instruction which I was teaching to my son until I had satisfied Nadan with teaching as if with bread and water. And thus I was saying to him words of wisdom. The words that ʾAḥîqar taught ... Thus, ʾAḥîqar cut short his words of wisdom that he was teaching to Nadan.

Scene changes in the Syriac manuscripts often reflect the older autobiographical narrative frame by reaffirming ܐܢܐ ܐܚܝܩܪ "I, ʾAhîqar" (e.g., Camb. Cod. Add. 2020 1.14–15; 3.1, 6; 4.1, 6, 9; 5.1; 7.7), and it is at these places that competing third-person section titles may appear. Over time third-person section dividers worked themselves into the body of the manuscripts producing competing narrative voices, and since much of the tale is told as a retrospective and sometimes with language in which Ahiqar refers to himself in the third-person, many manuscripts exhibit a mixture of first-person and third-person narration.

This evolution may help to explain the variation from first- to third-person narration in the Tale of Jeremiah and Baruch's Scroll. Autobiographical references appear sporadically throughout the book of Jeremiah, depending on the manuscript. Reconciling the manuscript differences has proved to be an insurmountable challenge. The following proposal will not solve the problem completely, but rather aims to provide fresh light on a stagnant debate.

The problems in the narrative style of the book of Jeremiah are complex, and simply dismissing the autobiographical references in the book as errors is an irresponsible approach to the book's manuscript history because there ap-

---

37 Harris corrects the text to ܠܗ "(saying) to him."
38 The Graffin and related manuscripts contain many section titles throughout the tale.

pear to be authentic instances of autobiography in the book.³⁹ Furthermore, a so-called apocryphal fragment of a Jeremiah narrative from Qumran contains the hallmark autobiographical narrative device found in the Story of Ahiqar and other ancient autobiographies, ואני ירמיה "and I, Jeremiah" (4Q383 frag. 1.1), and thus shows that other autobiographical Jeremiah narrative sections circulated in antiquity. MT Jer 36 presents only one autobiographical variant, LXX Jer 43:1, but much of the tale recounts Baruch's experiences in the royal court, and so, much like how Ahiqar recounts activity in the royal court in the third-person, the Tale of Jeremiah and Baruch's Scroll requires mostly third-person references.⁴⁰ The narrative would only have needed slight updates where Jeremiah is referred to in the narrative frame (vv. 4, 5, 8, and 27) to change the whole episode into a biographical account. Not surprisingly, these occur at scene changes, so it is reasonable to see narrative interference at these points as the manuscripts of the Story of Ahiqar demonstrates.

The autobiographical reference in LXX Jer 43:1 occurs in an introductory formula that appears infrequently throughout the prophetic and narrative sections of the book of Jeremiah.⁴¹ The infrequent formula focuses on "the word," which is qualified by a dependent clause using the verb "to be,"... הַדָּבָר אֲשֶׁר הָיָה "The word which was..."⁴² Of the fourteen occurrences of this infrequent formu-

---

39 Carroll, *Jeremiah*, 93. Some of the most influential commentators see such instances as errors, Rudolph, *Jeremia*, 154, 210; Holladay, *Jeremiah 2*, 251; Lundbom, *Jeremiah*, 585.

40 Leuchter, "Personal," 275 notes how "Jeremiah fades into the background while the scribes of Jerusalem become the principal actors in the drama." He cites numerous sources, but neither he nor his sources consider Jeremiah's "fading" with regard to narrative role of autobiographical voice.

41 Driver, *Introduction*, 268.

42 MT Jer 7:1 (3.per) / LXX unattested; MT 11:1 (3.per followed by 1.per, v. 6) / LXX 11:1; MT 18:1 (3.per followed by 1.per, v. 3) / LXX 18:1; MT 21:1 (3.per followed by 3.per, v. 3) / LXX 21:1; MT 26:1 (no referent followed by 3.per, v. 7) / LXX 33:1; MT 27:1 (3.per followed by 1.per, v. 2) / LXX unattested (LXX 34:2 lacks referent; previous chap. 3.per); MT 30:1 (3.per) / LXX 37:1; MT 32:1 (usual form 6) (3.per followed by 1.per, v. 6) / LXX 39:1, 6 (see below); MT 34:1, 8 (note freq. form 12) (3.per followed by 3.per, v. 6) / LXX 41:1, 8, (note freq. form v. 12); MT 36:1 (3.per followed by 3.per, v. 4) / LXX 43:1 (1.per followed by 3.per, v. 4); MT 37:17 (3.per, in voice of king) / LXX 44:17; MT 40:1 (3.per followed by 3.per, v. 2) / LXX 47:1; MT 44:1 (3.per followed by 3.per, v. 15) / LXX 51:1. A hybrid form of the infrequent and frequent formulas can be found in the section headings of MT 1:2 (3.per followed by 1.per, v. 4) / LXX 1:2; MT 14:1 (3.per followed by 1.per, v. 11) / LXX 14:1; MT 46:1 (3.per followed by 3.per, v. 13) / LXX unattested; MT 47:1 (3.per) = LXX unattested; MT 49:34 (3.per) / LXX unattested. In a number of places, something similar to the infrequent formula occurs as a section heading but uses a verb of speech rather than the verb to be: MT 45:1 (Jeremiah to Baruch) / LXX 51:31; MT 46:13 (3.per) / LXX 26:13; MT 50:1 (no referent) / LXX 27:1; MT 51:59 (Jeremiah to Seriah) / LXX 28:59.

la, only one uses a first-person reference, MT Jer 36:1 / LXX 43:1, but before rushing to the conclusion that the first-person reference is an error, four points should be borne in mind. First, the more frequent formula, which is וַיְהִי דְבַר־ יְהוָה אֶל "And the word of the Lord was to...," demonstrates a mixed dataset in which the referent is first- or third-person depending on the manuscript and its location in the book. In some cases, the infrequent formula (third-person) interacts with the frequent formula (first-person) within the same narrative episode (MT Jer 32:1, 6 / LXX Jer 39:1, 6). Second, although there is only one first-person occurrence of the infrequent formula, in at least four places the infrequent formula introduces a section which is continued in first-person narration (MT Jer 11:1; 18:1; 27:1 32:1).[43] Third, in two places (MT Jer 7:1; 27:1) the infrequent formula appears in MT but is unattested in LXX,[44] and fourth, in one place (MT Jer 26:1) the infrequent formula completely lacks a referent (though the Syriac supplies one; see below). These observations demonstrate that the infrequent formula was conceived of as a modifiable major section heading, especially by the MT editors.

Of the occurrences of the infrequent formula, MT Jer 26:1 is most often discussed in conjunction with MT Jer 36:1 because of the narrative similarities shared between the two chapters.[45] Curiously, the occurrence in MT Jer 26:1 / LXX Jer 33:1, is the only one that lacks a referent and simply reads "the word that was from the Lord." Notably, the PESHITTA, which relies on some MT-like Vorlage adds "to Jeremiah" thus showing the preference in this manuscript tradition for a third-person reference and an interest in harmonizing two similar passages (PESHITTA Jer 26:1 and 36:1).[46] Undoubtedly, the history of MT Jer 26 and 36 is interrelated,[47] and it is noteworthy that of the fourteen occurrences of the infrequent formula, only these two similar narrative passages exhibit strange variants, MT Jer 26:1 lacks a referent and MT Jer 36:1 is first-person in LXX. But no autobiographical reference is found in surviving manuscripts of MT Jer 26, so discussion of the narrative relationship between the two passages need not be pursued further here.

---

[43] This is also true of two of the five occurrences of a hybrid form in MT, see previous note.
[44] This is also true of three of the five occurrences of a hybrid form in MT, see above notes.
[45] Scholarship on this comparison is vast. See recently Leuchter, "Personal," 275–294 and citations throughout.
[46] Note that MT Jer 45, which references the events of MT Jer 36, also harmonizes the introductory line, whereas the LXX counterpart, verse 51:31, does not.
[47] Rudolph believed that chapter 26 originally came before chapter 36 (*Jeremia*, 169). Holladay, *Jeremiah 2*, 22 sees the two chapters as bookends of a literary unit. Römer, "Prophet," 91 implies that 36 is a rewriting of 26.

Another important observation worth exploring in more detail is the fact that in some cases the infrequent formula introduces a passage that is otherwise autobiographical. Of these instances, MT Jer 32 / LXX Jer 39 is of importance because it is a narrative portion that includes Baruch, and structurally exhibits the inverse situation of that found in MT Jer 36 / LXX Jer 43. The most extensive section of first-person narrative in the book is in MT Jer 32:6–25 (LXX Jer 39:6–25), which begins with the infrequent formula with a third-person referent. In this regard, the infrequent formula resembles a third-person major section heading (v. 1). The following charts the references to the narrative voice(s) in this passage.

Verse	LXX Jer 39	MT Jer 32
1	Ὁ λόγος ὁ γενόμενος παρὰ κυρίου πρὸς Ιερεμίαν	הַדָּבָר אֲשֶׁר־הָיָה אֶל־יִרְמְיָהוּ מֵאֵת יְהוָה
6	καὶ λόγος κυρίου ἐγενήθη πρὸς Ιερεμίαν[48] λέγων	וַיֹּאמֶר יִרְמְיָהוּ הָיָה דְבַר־יְהוָה אֵלַי לֵאמֹר
8	καὶ ἦλθε πρός με... καὶ εἶπέ μοι... καὶ ἔγνων	וַיָּבֹא אֵלַי... וַיֹּאמֶר אֵלַי... וָאֵדַע
9	καὶ ἐκτησάμην... καὶ ἔστησα	וָאֶקְנֶה... וָאֶשְׁקֲלָה
10	καὶ ἔγραψα... ἐσφραγισάμην καὶ διεμαρτυράμην... καὶ ἔστησα	וָאֶכְתֹּב... וָאֶחְתֹּם וָאָעֵד... וָאֶשְׁקֹל
11	καὶ ἔλαβον	וָאֶקַּח
12	καὶ ἔδωκα... πατρός μου	וָאֶתֵּן... דֹּדִי
13	καὶ συνέταξα	וָאֲצַוֶּה
16	Καὶ προσευξάμην	וָאֶתְפַּלֵּל
25	καὶ σὺ λέγεις πρός με... καὶ ἔγραψα... καὶ ἐσφραγισάμην καὶ ἐπεμαρτυράμην	וְאַתָּה אָמַרְתָּ אֵלַי {Rest changed to 2.per. command of Yahweh to Jeremiah.}
27	Καὶ ἐγένετο λόγος κυρίου πρός με λέγων[49]	{Changes to third-person.}

Note that this passage is about Jeremiah's purchase of his cousin's field in Anathoth, and it explicitly portrays a literate Jeremiah who wrote down the purchase in a document and gave the document to Baruch (MT Jer 32:10–12);[50]

---

[48] A number of manuscripts, beyond The Three (Aquila, Symmachus, and Theodotion) and the Syro-Hexapla, which normally agree with MT, are a number of Greek manuscripts that read πρός με "to me" instead of πρός Ιερεμίαν "to Jeremiah," (mss V–26–46–534–544 O–Qmg–86mg–233 L´–538).

[49] The rest of the chapter is a long prophecy in the first-person voice of Yahweh. LXX Jer 40:1 (as continues MT Jer 33:1) changes to third-person narration.

[50] It is rare that a writer would compose his own deed. I know of only one Northwest Semitic example from Persian period Aramaic contracts (*TAD* B4.3).

the scribal themes in this passage are overt, but this is not a scribal conflict narrative on its own (as described in the previous section), though one could imagine it was an episode in a scribal conflict narrative with multiple episodes (see below). The first clause of verse 25, near the end of the section, is not necessarily an autobiographical reference. Instead, in MT Jeremiah speaks in the first-person voice of Yahweh, who in turn uses first-person pronouns. In LXX, the remaining clauses in verse 25 are Jeremiah's first-person narrative reflection, in which he describes how he fulfilled Yahweh's instructions. Here it can be reasoned that MT changes the autobiographical reference to imperatives and recasts them as instructions of Yahweh to Jeremiah.[51] MT then continues with the more simplistic third-person narration in verse 26, while LXX retains the more complex autobiographical style. The passage appears to have been changed in MT from first- to third-person.

Such complex narrative stylistic issues likely motivated the change from first- to third-person in other sections of the book where the manuscript history is not clear, such as in MT Jer 36 / LXX Jer 43. For this reason, any clue to a first-person reference should be considered carefully and studied for possible effects it may have on the whole of the narrative episode in which it appears. MT Jer 32 / LXX Jer 39 provides evidence that an original autobiographical narrative in an episode that includes Baruch and overtly scribal themes was given a section title like that in MT Jer 36 / LXX Jer 43, but while MT Jer 36 / LXX Jer 43 may only provide a clue to an older autobiographical narrative, MT Jer 32 / LXX Jer 39 demonstrates a measurable change in narrative voice. This measurable change is similar to data known from the manuscript history of the Story of Ahiqar, and provides strong circumstantial evidence that the narrative voice in MT Jer 36 / LXX Jer 43 may have also evolved from first- to third-person.

It was discussed in chapter two how the autobiographical voice of a scribal narrative can produce a special type of empathetic relationship between the narrator and reader that helps convince a reader of the narrator's perspective. Ahiqar's own narration presented Nadin as an evil student and helped to convince the reader that Ahiqar was a victim, but when his emotive autobiographical presentation is critically viewed and the behavior of the characters laid bare, it becomes apparent that Ahiqar's self-victimization is a ruse to cover up, among other things, his objectively failed attempt as a teacher and his atrocious act of murder of an innocent eunuch in an effort of self-preservation. By com-

---

[51] The remaining verbs are imperatives. One may hypothesize that the unvocalized first-person *waw*-consecutive verbs were construed as second-person singular verbs and updated to imperatives for clarity.

parison, what does the autobiographical narration of LXX Jer 43:1 offer to the reading?

Much of Jeremiah's prophetic sayings are presented in autobiographical form and in the voice of Yahweh, which effectively mutes, according to Martin J. Buss, the self-identity of the prophet and conflates the two characters.[52] This imbues a greater power on the character of Jeremiah and increases the believability of his words. Like Ahiqar, Jeremiah and Baruch fail at their intended mission, and this along with other readings in LXX provide a more realistic story than that found in MT. LXX's version of the story presents Jeremiah and Baruch as humans engaging in scribal institutions and with characters. In the end, Jeremiah and Baruch are failures, though they make a meager attempt to carry on (v. 32). The narrative conflict is personal and more strongly felt in LXX. So why would MT do away with this narrative dynamism? It may have just continued the intermediary transition from first- to third-person that the LXX Vorlage attests to, but when considered with the other changes made in MT Jer 36, removing the autobiographical reference may be owed to a different motivation. The answer may simply go back to the editor's desire to elevate the role of the deity and to separate the character of Yahweh from the character of Jeremiah.

As can be seen in the edits made in the transmission history of the Story of Ahiqar, such as changing the innocent eunuch whom Ahiqar kills into an evil character deserving death or editing the whole story to include only his acts as a successful teacher (e.g., Sachau 162), MT sought to disambiguate Yahweh from Jeremiah, so as to not portray Yahweh as a failure along with Jeremiah. LXX appears to represent a version of the tale in which the autobiographical references had already begun to change, and in LXX Jer 43:1 the sole surviving autobiographical reference, which is well attested in a variety of LXX manuscripts, is at least a clue to a narrative voice that once was. As Carolyn Sharp describes when dealing with equally difficult and peculiar variants between LXX and MT in Jeremiah's Oracles against the Nations, "The lack of harmonization of some discrepant details in the *Vorlagen* of the LXX and MT of Jeremiah is in its very rarity more telling than suspect."[53] This one variant can be explained as part of MT's larger program to extract Yahweh from Jeremiah's persona and make

---

52 Buss, "Social," 1–11.
53 Sharp, "Take," 507.

Yahweh a separate and heroic character in the tale, with independent volition and the ability to save Baruch and Jeremiah.[54]

The Tale the Jeremiah and Baruch's Scroll is a single episode compiled with many, and has provoked scholars to find literary boundaries that mark a section of the book's narrative as coherent (see introduction). In reality it may simply contain a story collection, a la Holm,[55] of small once more coherent episodic narratives. The implications of the discovery of first- to third-person development in the book's manuscript history combined with the interest in scribal characters and themes could be productive criteria for discussing the connections between different sections of the book. It seems quite plausible in view of the model provided by the Story of Ahiqar and the evidence from the Jeremiah manuscripts, that a core episodic autobiographical narrative once existed that was diffused into the mixed text we now read. This seems to me to be a productive avenue for future research, and such episodes as the letter of Jeremiah in MT Jer 29, the command to Jeremiah to write his own prophecies followed by a discussion of covenant writing in MT Jer 31, and the aforementioned autobiographical section of deed writing and prophesying in MT Jer 32 share scribal and autobiographical points of convergence with the Tale of Jeremiah and Baruch's Scroll. In fact, Leuchter has already discussed some productive correspondences between MT Jer 29 and MT Jer 36,[56] but there is more to be done, particularly when considering the various types of change, expansion, and contraction found in the extensive Ahiqar manuscript tradition. For now, however, it can be said that the autobiographical narration of the Story of Ahiqar evolved into a third-person narrative style which is traceable to editorial changes at narrative turns. By comparison with the Tale of Jeremiah and Baruch's Scroll similar phenomena may be witnessed that nuance the depth of the various editions of that scribal narrative. It is now to the topic of scribal features in these scribal narratives that this study will return.

---

54 It seems unlikely to me that the transitional text of LXX Jer 43 represents the product of compiling and supplementing disparate first- and third-person narrations rather than simply having been written in the first-person.
55 See previous section and Holm, *Courtiers*.
56 Leuchter, "Personal."

4.4 Differences between the Allusions to the Scribal Experience

The Tale of Jeremiah and Baruch's Scroll and the Story of Ahiqar each portrays the role and value of scribal professionalism in a different way. According to the opening verses of the Tale of Jeremiah and Baruch's Scroll, Jeremiah's scribal activity, and subsequently Baruch's, is the result of Jeremiah's own conviction that having Baruch write and present his words would fulfill divine will. This is different than Ahiqar's reasons for adopting Nadin. Ahiqar is interested in self-preservation within a greater matrix of social and professional expectations. Ahiqar may have viewed his role as a divine appointment, but his personal convictions would not have validated that appointment. In the Neo-Assyrian court, fellow scholarly experts and the king validated a professional appointment, normally via reference to the approval of deities who "spoke" to scholarly colleagues. Ahiqar's, and later Nadin's, position rested on their abilities to acquire and trade in social capital, which in turn secured their divine appointment. In a different narrative context Jeremiah and Baruch operated in their private scribal setting under the conviction that they knew their own divine calling, themselves. When the two stories are read alongside each other, one wonders: does Jeremiah desperately seek the approval of courtiers to justify to himself his divine appointment in a way that is similar to Ahiqar's attempt to consolidate courtly power?

This line of inquiry may help to explain why both tales allude to realistic professional ranks in their respective court settings, the courtiers (נגדין) and princes (רבין) in the Story of Ahiqar and the chief courtiers (הַשָּׂרִים) and a prince (בֶּן הַמֶּלֶךְ) in the Tale of Jeremiah and Baruch's Scroll. Both stories only focus, however, on one professional position among these ranks, "the scribe." Ahiqar refers to himself as "the wise scribe" (ספרא חכימא) as though it were a professional title. But his role appears to have been to oversee the בית עזקה "the house of the seal," which was located in or associated with the בב היכלא "The Gate of the Palace," where he and the other courtiers worked. His title "the wise scribe" is best explained as a literary invention that emphasizes his sagacious character and portrays him as an Akkadian, rather than Aramean scribal character. This wise scribe is also qualified as a "counselor" (יעט) another term that calls to mind Mesopotamian wise men, but not a professional title. In reality, Ahiqar, as the leader of the house of the seal, would have been the royal seal-bearer (רב עזקה/ן cf. Akk. *rab unqāti*), but the text does not develop this title the way that it develops his literary title "the wise scribe" (ספרא חכימא). So, despite the story's realistic portrayal of social conditions and expectations of the courtly scribal profession, it does not contain clear allusions to the roles and functions of a historical scribal office.

The Aramaic term for scribe ספר became a loanword in Akkadian *sēpiru* during the Neo-Assyrian period. It refers to an alphabetic scribe. Recent studies have shown that those bearing this title in Akkadian texts were partially or fully bilingual administrators.[57] The term appears as early as the Neo-Assyrian period. It is attested in various titles, often in the construction *sēpiru ša* + [institutional term/phrase]. Those titles ascribed to Ahiqar in the book of Tobit may reflect Akkadian titles from a Persian period version of the tale (see discussion in chapter two) without the phrase *sēpiru ša*. For instance, Ahiqar's title רב עזקה/ז may simply be an Aramaic version of *sēpiru ša bīt rab unqāti*. So, while Ahiqar's title ספרא is a professional title in the Elephantine manuscript, there is no historical evidence for a professional equivalent to ספרא חכימא "the wise scribe." As discussed in chapter two, the phrase ספרא חכימא appears to be a calque and wordplay on *ummânu emqu* "wise scholar." The current evidence suggests that Ahiqar's Aramaic title is a creative literary invention designed to hyperbolize Ahiqar's persona. His Akkadian scholarly quality combined with his obvious Northwest Semitic name allow the reader to see him as either an Aramaic or Akkadian scribe in Esarhaddon's court. This is valuable since the implicit message of the tale critiques the Akkadian scribal tradition, yet his Northwest Semitic name, his title ספרא which means "alphabetic scribe" in Akkadian (*sēpiru*), and the fact that the story is composed in Aramaic introduce some cognitive interference to this critique.

Aramaic ספרא, like its Hebrew counterpart in MT Jer 36 is a determined noun. As was discussed in chapter three, the relatively scant evidence of the term ספר in dateable Hebrew texts suggests that any given institution may have one scribe in the late Judahite period. Although Akkadian has no functional way of expressing definiteness in professional titles, the *sēpiru* evidence currently supports this view since the titles of Aramaic scribes are often accompanied by the institution which employs them. One must not, however, simplistically overlay the Hebrew or Aramaic evidence with the Akkadian. In both Aramaic and Hebrew, √ספר derives from the semantic relationship between the function of a document and its reader and in no way is related to the production of the document. Documents themselves (ספר) are described for what they do (recount) rather than what they are (written). Never does √ספר mean "to write" but only "to account/recount." As the √ספר was brought into Akkadian, however, it was

---

57 Pearce, "*sēpiru*," 364–366; Stolper, "Governor," 298–299; Bloch, *Alphabet*, chap. 1; Gzella, *Cultural*, 138.

reinterpreted, in at least one (early) Late-Babylonian text, to mean "to write in Aramaic" (CAD S 225 and SAA 17 no. 2).[58] So unlike in the Mesopotamian imperial courts of the first millennium BCE, in the small mostly monolingual Judahite court neither the verb ספר "to account/recount" nor the nouns "document" or "scribe" meant what the verb *sepēru* or the noun *sēpiru* meant in Akkadian sources.

Although it runs the risk of introducing more cultural variables into the problem, the way the term is used in Aramaic sources from Egypt is of significant value for understanding the meaning of ספר in its literary contexts in both Aramaic and Hebrew.[59] First, the mention of scribes is infrequent in the Aramaic sources from Egypt and surprisingly, those writing contracts are never identified as "scribes," as is common in Akkadian. Writers of contracts were most frequently identified in a descriptive phrase with the verb כתב "to write" as in: כתב מכבנת בר נרגי [ספ]רא זנה "Mkbnt son of Nrgy wrote this [docu]ment" (TAD B1 1.17) and this mirrors evidence from Demotic sources in which writers of various genres are identified with the phrase *šḥ* PN "wrote PN."

Second, the term ספרא accompanies the chancellor of provincial decrees in Persian period Aramaic sources, or in some cases the two are identified as the same person (Pap. Ber. P. 13540 [Dem. trans. of Aram.]; TAD A6 2; A6 8–13). This was part of Persian imperial protocol, and not localized to an Egyptian context as attested by copies of Late Persian decrees in Bactria (*ADAB* nos. A1–8).[60] Here too scribes are solely learned men with professional status and power.

Third, the phrases ספרי מדינתא "scribes of the provinces" (TAD A6 1), ספרי אוצרא "scribes of the treasury" (TAD B4 4), and ספריא "the scribes" (TAD A3 3) all appear as types of juridical/administrative bodies in Persian period Aramaic documentary sources from Egypt—the latter of which may be an elliptical form of one of the others. While scribes of the treasury probably have their counterpart in Akkadian administrative terminology (see chapter two), scribes of the provinces may refer to local Egyptian administrative titles grandfathered into

---

58 The relevant lines read: *ina libbi siprī* ᵏᵘʳ*Armaya lušpir-ma* "I shall write on Aramaic documents" (obv. 15–16).

59 Later Aramaic literature, which may have its origins in Persian period Aramaic sources, attests to a strong overlap between the Akkadian astrological scholarly and scribal terms and positions and Aramaic ספר (see Henryk, "Akkadian," esp. 395).

60 For discussion see Moore, "Persian," 51–52. Many of the Elamite sources excavated from the Persepolis fortification also resemble Aramaic decrees, yet with some differences. See Tavernier, "Multilingualism," 65–70 and Kottsieper, "Briefe," 153–154.

the Persian administration of Egypt.⁶¹ So while the Aramaic evidence has its difficulties due to its mostly Egyptian context, it nonetheless shows that the term scribe (ספר) was reserved for few high administrative officials.

At present the limited Hebrew evidence (see chapter three) presents a scribe as a high-ranking role in a particular institution in the late Judahite period.

Comparatively then, what we find in the Story of Ahiqar and the Tale of Jeremiah and Baruch's Scroll are references to the rarely held positions of "scribe" alongside other literate figures, mostly of royal or religious status. By this is meant that components in the modern study of scribal culture, such as a focus on textual production, literacy, and the like are large phenomena attested well beyond the position of "the scribe," and in fact the scribe in Northwest Semitic sources was literate and engaged in textual production, but these things are not the defining factors of their professional title, ספרא or הַסֹּפֵר.

Those in other positions may have been literate, and all of the royal court's chief courters in Jeremiah (הַשָּׂרִים) are portrayed as having the ability to intellectually engage with Baruch's written document. The scribe, as a politically powerful position in an institution, appears to be embellished in MT's edition, which identifies Baruch as "the scribe" only after he had completed his apprenticeship with Jeremiah in the scribal workshop and had survived a scribal mission. In some sense this is the opposite of Nadin's experience, who was given a position through nepotistic channels, and presumably was stripped of his title by the end (according to the Syriac manuscripts). In view of this comparative study, the notion that the private workshop of Jeremiah would contain a position for "the scribe" in the late Judahite Kingdom seems to be an interpretive embellishment, or at least an anachronistic gloss, supplied by MT's editor. The fact that Baruch's title does not appear in LXX supports this claim. The evidence discussed in chapter three further suggests that, in the late Judahite Kingdom, the temple had a politically appointed scribe (Gemariah, v. 10), and so too did the palace (Elishama, vv. 11–12). Thus, much like Ahiqar the wise scribe, "Baruch the scribe" is a literary and (anachronistic) invention.

The Story of Ahiqar and the Tale of Jeremiah and Baruch's Scroll are foremost, literary works, and teasing out reliable historical allusions to the scribal profession proved to be difficult in this study. The writer and editors of these two narratives drew inspiration from their own social and historical realities, which differ from the purported historical settings in each story. Writers and editors also used literary license and embellishment or aggrandizement. Despite

---

61 Schütze, "Local," 496–497 and Schütze, "Schreiberämter." The best source for this is P.Rylands 9 (written in 513 BCE).

this, new notions about the mid first millennium BCE professional scribal experience have come into view.

The conclusions drawn here do not advocate that there was only one ancient scribal professional experience. Instead, I have argued that the terms that define the scribal profession can, for now, only apply to the most elite scribal figures who were part of, or interacted with, courtiers. This circle of influence was small. Many other literate professionals existed in various sectors of society and their experiences are not directly represented in the scribal conflict narratives of the Story of Ahiqar and the Tale of Jeremiah and Baruch's Scroll. The popularity of the scribal professionals in royal courts was, however, a significant (and likely entertaining) draw in antiquity, as they are also today.

5 Conclusion

This study began with the presumption that the Story of Ahiqar and the Tale of Jeremiah and Baruch's Scroll are fundamentally different; they each have their own literary features, manuscript histories, and cultural contexts. Only the vaguest criteria united them: they share a date of composition within roughly a three century time span in the mid first millennium BCE, and they are examples of Northwest Semitic literature that focus on a scribe in the case of the Story of Ahiqar and on scribal activity in the case of the Tale of Jeremiah and Baruch's Scroll. The rarity of surviving Northwest Semitic evidence on scribal culture prompted them to be studied in dialogue here, but only after having considered the scribal allusions found in each tale separately.

This study has shown that a comparison between the two tales produces a deeper understanding of each text on a literary level and paints a more complex picture of the life of ancient scribal professionals in Northwest Semitic traditions. Both the Story of Ahiqar and the Tale of Jeremiah and Baruch's Scroll provide insights into Aramaic and Hebrew scribal culture by emphasizing different components of it: the Story of Ahiqar focuses on the political and social maneuverings of scribal figures and less so on the offices and locations in which these figures engaged each other. The Tale of Jeremiah and Baruch's Scroll, however, uses loci of scribal activity to construct four clearly defined narrative settings and depicts the politics of scribal professionals within those settings. Both tales, then, use realistic scenarios, but in different ways.

When considered in comparative perspective, it has been shown that the texts' realism places believable—though exaggerated—scribal personas within the settings of royal courts, thereby evoking a connection between the well-known court tale genre and the ancient scribal craft. They share motifs that produce similar scribal conflicts in each narrative. Both of them contain social critiques, but these critiques are directed at different groups. The Story of Ahiqar critiques an old guard of scribal professionals while promoting loyalty to the crown. The Tale of Jeremiah and Baruch's Scroll uses scribal professionalism and spaces in which scribes interact in order to libel the crown.

The dynamic narrative circumstances of both tales evolved as manuscripts were edited over time. Both tales demonstrate that in an earlier form, their narratives used autobiographical narrative style. This was essential in each narrative because these older versions of the tales portrayed their protagonists as more human than legendary. They underwent significant professional trials as scribal characters and the autobiographical narration helped obfuscate the distasteful character traits of Ahiqar in his story and cover up the ineffectiveness of Jeremiah's prophecies in his tale. This study has attempted to interpret the manuscript variation in each story as a type of reception history, and in so doing has been able to tease out from minute variants evidence that careful ancient editors witnessed these unsavory character traits and introduced changes that reframe the characters in a new light. Over time Ahiqar became more of a scholarly hero rather than an Aramaic critique on ancient Akkadian scribal culture. Likewise, in MT's attempt to separate the character of Yahweh from the mind of Jeremiah and to justify Jeremiah's attempt to find courtly scribal approval, it elevates the sovereignty of Yahweh, thereby portraying Jeremiah and Baruch's actions as the activities of faithful servants who tested the courtiers and king. Only within the context of the comparison of the two tales and their similarities in genre, motifs, narratological style, and trajectory of manuscript histories has it been possible to classify them both as related to the court tale, whereby the Story of Ahiqar is modeled on this age old genre while the Tale of Jeremiah and Baruch's Scroll drew on (or responded to) elements of it. In both cases they may be identified as a sub-genre of the court tale which I have called the scribal conflict narrative.

The implications of this study on autobiographical style may be far reaching in future studies in ancient (partially) autobiographical texts. For instance, beyond Ahiqar and the book of Jeremiah (esp. MT 1:1–4 and 36), the books of Tobit and Qohelet, for example, also contain the same third-person prologue structure followed by the formulaic autobiographical narrative indicator "I, PN" (Tob 1:1 "The book(roll) of the words of Tobit;" 1:3 "I (am) Tobit;" MT Qoh 1:1 "the words of Qohelet;" MT 2:1 "I (am) Qohelet"). The didactic function of this narrative style and its use and reuse in various genres is a promising avenue of future research.

Additionally, this study set out to discuss ancient scribal culture as it is portrayed in the narratives of the Story of Ahiqar and the Tale of Jeremiah and Baruch's Scroll. Unlike previous studies on scribal culture, which predominantly focus on the mechanics of textual production, on the general concept of literacy in antiquity, or on the preparatory education of scribal students, I have attempted to discuss how these two narratives allude to the professional experience of scribal figures who interact in royal courts. I have shown that a central concern for these scribal protagonists is to preserve their professional legacy. It has long been known that ancient scholars believed that writing and esoteric knowledge had a divine origin, but this study has shown that scribal figures saw their professional positions as divine appointments. The pragmatic consequences of such a belief resulted in competitive encounters among scribal figures, which in turn forced them to collude in competing groups. These groups were dynamic, and these shifting relationships resulted in a culture of distrust and rebellion among scribal figures and alliances working in royal courts. As each generation of new scribal characters would take their offices, they were forced to vie with each other, and especially with the old guard, to establish their legitimacy. The old generation fought to maintain a status quo with acts of self-preservation. In both tales (and historically) the old guard loses, despite their fight: Aramaic scribal culture eventually supplants Akkadian scribal culture, and the entire Judahite scribal court is lost to history. This image of the ancient scribal profession challenges the popular notion that scribes, even royal scribes, were merely copyists and mechanical producers of texts. To be sure, writing was their craft, but for those who felt called to their position and had the means to keep it, especially within a royal court, their calling had to be proved in a volatile social forum, in which they exchanged intellectual prowess and artful political maneuvering as a form of social currency.

The popularity of these two narratives in antiquity was owed, in part, to their relatable scribal content and cyclical narrative structure that brings each tale back to the conditions in which the protagonists began. This study has argued that the longevity of these two tales is owed, in part, to the entertaining narrative setting of the first millennium BCE royal court. The focus on scribal tools and materials, as well as on scribal interactions, took precedent in these tales, as is especially seen in the Tale of Jeremiah and Baruch's Scroll, in which the composition of a scroll in a scribal workshop bookends the account of its scribal presentation.

The plot of the Tale of Jeremiah and Baruch's Scroll begins with outsiders composing a scroll, which Baruch presents to high-ranking royal scribal characters before returning, once again, to his status as an outsider in a private scribal location. In the Story of Ahiqar, Nadin, like Baruch, used the advantages of his uniquely scribal abilities to defame his uncle in an attempt to destroy him, but his craft was merely a tool in that process, rather than a focal point in the plot. Ahiqar's defamation lowered him from a highly revered figure to a fugitive, yet his shrewd wisdom and drive for self-preservation allowed him to regain his status, and thus, these tales have mirrored plot structures.

This study's attempt to extract social and historical observations from ancient literature has further confirmed that texts are the product of complex social interactions that color the ways in which writers approached and edited manuscripts. The Story of Ahiqar and the Tale of Jeremiah and Baruch's Scroll are, foremost, works of ancient literature, but they are composed and edited by writers in real social contexts. As these writers composed, edited, or adapted the narratives, the narrative structures and many of the allusions to the scribal profession remained the same. Ultimately, Jeremiah, Baruch, Ahiqar, and Nadin, all succeed and fail in their scribal positions in similar ways across the manuscripts of their respective stories. What unites them, and the writers who persevered and altered their manuscripts, was a shared experience about a fickle profession and a looming worry that, either due to a self-assigned character flaw or an uncontrollable social force, they would be unable to do their jobs.

Appendix: Syriac Ahiqar Manuscripts Cited

Collection Number	Published Edition and/or Photographs
BM 7200, fol. 114	Harris, (1913), pp. 100–101 plus appendix. Photographs: author's copies.
BM Or. 2313, fol. 172a–180b	Unpublished. Photographs: unavailable (text collated by author).
BnF 422 = M.H. Pognon, fol. 96 and 111–136	Edition: Nau (1918–9), pp. 380–400 = Nau (1920), 72–92. Photographs: unavailable.
Camb. Cod. Add. 2020, fol. 66a–78a	Edition: Harris 1913, pp. 101–127, plus appendix. Photographs: author's copies.
Dayro d-Mor Gabriel 192, pp. 3–42	Unpublished. Photographs: HMML no. MGMT 00192.
Dom. Fr. Mosel 430	Unpublished. Photographs: HMML no. DMF 00430.
Graffin (transcription of a ms from Mar Elias ?; lost ?)	Edition: Nau (1918–9), pp. 274–307, 356–380 = Nau (1920), 14–71. Photographs: unavailable.
Houghton 80	Unpublished. Photographs: author's copies.
JerMkl no. 162	Unpublished. Photographs: HMML no. SMMJ 00162.
Mingana 433, fol. 1b–25a	Unpublished. Photographs: Mingana (1933).
Sachau 162, fol. 86a–92b	Edition: Nau (1918–1919), pp. 148–160 = Nau (1920), pp. 1–13. Photographs: StaBi.
Sachau 336, fol. 17b–57b	Edition: Maxims: Grünberg (1917); Narrative: Guzik (1936). Photographs: StaBi.

Bibliography

Ahituv, Shmuel. *Echoes from the Past: Hebrew and Cognate Inscriptions from the Biblical Period*. A Carta Handbook. Jerusalem: Carta, 2008.
Anderson, G.W. "Some Aspects of the Uppsala School of Old Testament Study," The Harvard Theological Review 43 (1950): 239–256.
Ariel, Donald T., ed. *Excavations at the City of David 1978–1985, Directed by Yigal Shiloh. Vol. VI, Inscriptions*. Qedem 41. Jerusalem: The Institute of Archaeology, The Hebrew University of Jerusalem, 2000.
Avigad, Nahman. "The Epitaph of a Royal Steward from Siloam Village." *Israel Exploration Journal* 3 (1953): 137–52.
Avigad, Nahman and Benjamin Sass. Corpus of West Semitic Stamp Seals. Publications of the Israel Academy of Sciences and Humanities. Jerusalem: The Israel Academy of Sciences and Humanities, The Israel Exploration Society, The Institute of Archaeology, the Hebrew University of Jerusalem, 1997.
Baker, David W. "Scribes as Transmitters of Tradition." In *Faith, Tradition, and History: Old Testament Historiography in Its Near Eastern Context*, edited by A.R. Millard, J.K. Hoffmeier, and D.W. Baker, 65–77. Winona Lake: Eisenbrauns, 1994.
Barr, James. "'Determination' and the Definite Article in Biblical Hebrew." *Journal of Semitic Studies* 34 (1989): 307–335.
Beaulieu, Paul-Alain. "Official and Vernacular Languages: The Shifting Sands of Imperial and Cultural Identities in First-Millennium B.C. Mesopotamia." In *Margins of Writing, Origins of Cultures*, edited by Seth Sanders, 191–120. Oriental Institute Seminars 2. Chicago: The Oriental Institute, 2006.
Beaulieu, Paul-Alain. "Ea-dayān, Governor of the Sealand, and Other Dignitaries of the Neo-Babylonian Empire." *Journal of Cuneiform Studies* 54 (2002): 99–123.
Bledsoe, Seth A. "Wisdom in Distress: A Literary and Socio-Historical Approach to the Aramaic Book of Ahiqar." Ph.D. dissertation. Tallahassee: Florida State University, 2015.
Bledsoe, Seth A. "Conflicting Loyalties: King and Context in the Aramaic Book of Ahiqar." In *Political Memory in and after the Persian Empire*, edited by Jason M. Silverman and Caroline Waerzeggers, 239–68. Atlanta: Society of Biblical Literature Press, 2015.
Blenkinsopp, Joseph. *Ezra-Nehemiah: A Commentary*. The Old Testament Library. Philadelphia: Westminster Press, 1988.
Blenkinsopp, Joseph. "Why does the Deuteronomistic History Make no Mention of the Prophets to Whom Books are Attributed?" In *On Stone and Scroll: Essays in Honour of Graham Ivor Davies*, edited by James K. Aitken, Katharine J. Dell, and Brian A. Mastin, 343–356. Beihefte zur Zeitschrift für die alttestamentliche Wissenschaft 420. Berlin: Walter de Gruyter, 2011.
Bloch, Yigal. "Judeans in Sippar and Susa during the First Century of the Babylonian Exile: Assimilation and Perseverance under Neo-Babylonian and Achaemenid Rule." *Journal of Ancient Near Eastern History* 1 (2014): 119–172.
Bloch, Yigal. *Alphabet Scribes in the Land of Cuneiform: Sepīru Professionals in Mesopotamia in the Neo-Babylonian and Achaemenid Periods*. Gorgias Studies in the Ancient Near East 11. Piscataway: Gorgias Press, 2018.
Bogaert, Pierre-Maurice. "La vetus latina de Jérémie: texte très court, témoin de la plus ancienne Septante et d'une forme plus ancienne de l'hébreu (Jer 39 et 52)." In *The*

Earliest Text of the Hebrew Bible: The Relationship Between the Masoretic Text and the Hebrew Bible Base of the Septuagint, edited by Adrian Schenker, 51–82. SBL Septuagint and Cognate Studies 52. Atlanta: Society of Biblical Literature, 2003.

Bojowald, Stefan. "Das Bespucken des Gesichtes als Zeichen der Verachtung. Zu einem literarischen Motiv in den aramäischen Achikar-Sprüchen und seinen ägyptischen Parallelen." Ugarit-Forschungen 44 (2013): 17–21.

Brettler, Marc Zvi. "Judaism in the Hebrew Bible? An Exploration of the Transition from Ancient Israelite Religion to Judaism." Catholic Biblical Quarterly 61 (1999): 429–47.

Briant, Pierre and Raymond Descat. "Un registre douanier de la satrapie d'Ëgypte à l'époque achéménide." In *Le commerce en Egypte ancienne*, edited by Nicolas-Christophe Grimal et al, 59–104. Bibliothéque d'étude 121. Le Caire: Institut français d'archéologie orientale, 1998.

Briquel-Chatonnet, Françoise. "L'histoire et la sagesse d'Ahiqar: fortune littéraire de l'histoire d'un dignitaire araméen à la cour assyrienne" In *D'un Orient l'autre. Actes des 3e Journées de l' Orient, Bordeaux, 2–4octobre 2002*, edited by J.-L. Bacqué-Grammont, A. Pino and S. Khoury, 17–40. Cahiers de la société asiatique, nouvelle série IV. Paris-Louvain: Peeters, 2005.

Brock, Sebastian P. "Ahiqar." In *Gorgias Encyclopedic Dictionary of the Syriac Heritage: With Contributions by Seventy-Six Scholars*, edited by Sebastian P. Brock et al, 11–12. Piscataway: Gorgias Press, 2011.

Brock, Sebastian P. "The Dispute Poem: From Sumer to Syriac." *Journal of Canadian Society for Syriac Studies* 1 (2001): 3–10.

Brock, Sebastian P. "Notes on Some Texts in the Mingana Collection." *Journal of Semitic Studies* 14 (1969): 205–226.

Broida, Marian W. *Forestalling Doom: "Apotropaic Intercession" in the Hebrew Bible and the Ancient Near East*. Alter Orient und Altes Testament 417. Münster: Ugarit-Verlag, 2014.

Brueggemann, Walter. *A Commentary on Jeremiah: Exile and Homecoming*. Grand Rapids: Eerdmans, 1998.

Bruner, Edward. "Introduction: The Ethnographic Self and The Personal Self." In *Anthropology and Literature*, edited by Paul Benson, 1–26. Chicago: University of Illinois Press, 1993.

Burke, Peter O. *What is Cultural History?* Second edition. Cambridge: Polity Press, 2013.

Burt, Sean. *Courtier and the Governor: Transformations of Genre in the Nehemiah Memoir*. Journal of Ancient Judaism Sup. 17. Göttingen: Vandenhoeck & Ruprecht, 2014.

Buss, Martin J. "The Social Psychology of Prophecy." In *Prophecy: Essays Presented to Georg Fohrer on His Sixty-Fifth Birthday, 6 September 1980*, edited by Georg Fohrer and J. A. Emerton, 1–11. Beihefte zur Zeitschrift für die alttestamentliche Wissenschaft 150. Berlin: de Gruyter, 1980.

Caplice, Richard I. *The Akkadian Namburbu Texts: An Introduction*. Sources from the Ancient Near East 1/1. Malibu: Undena Publications, 1974.

Carr, David M. *The Formation of the Hebrew Bible: A New Reconstruction*. Oxford: Oxford University Press, 2011.

Carr, David M. *Writing on the Tablet of the Heart: Origins of Scripture and Literature*. Oxford: Oxford Press, 2005.

Carr, David M. "Method in Determination of Direction of Dependence: An Empirical Test of Criteria Applied to Exodus 34, 11–26 and Its Parallels." In *Gottes Volk am Sinai: Untersuchungen zu Ex 32–34 und Dtn 9–10*, edited by Matthias Köckert and Erhard Blum,

107–140. Veröffentlichungen der Wissenschaftlichen Gesellschaft für Theologie 18. Gütersloh: Chr. Kaiser Gutersloher Verlagshaus, 2001.

Carroll, Robert P. *Jeremiah: A Commentary*. OTL. Philadelphia: The Westminster Press, 1986.

Cazelles, Henri. "Ahiqar, *Ummân* and *Amun*, and Biblical Wisdom Texts." In *Solving Riddles and Untying Knots: Biblical, Epigraphic, and Semitic Studies in Honor of Jonas C. Greenfield*, edited by Ziony Zevit, Seymour Gitin, and Michael Sokoloff, 45–55. Winona Lake: Eisenbrauns, 1995.

Charles, Robert Henry, ed. *The Apocrypha and Pseudepigrapha of the Old Testament in English with Introductions and Critical and Explanatory Notes to Several Books. Volume II Pseudepigrapha* [APOT]. Oxford: The Clarendon Press, 1913 [reprint 1964].

Charpin, Dominique. *Reading and Writing in Babylon*. Translated by Jane Marie Todd. Cambridge: Harvard University Press, 2010.

Chyutin, Michael. *Tendentious Hagiographies: Jewish Propagandist Fiction BCE*. Library of Second Temple Studies 77. London: T & T Clark, 2011.

Cicero, Marcus Tullius. *De Oratore*. Translated by E.W. Sutton. Cambridge: Harvard University Press, 1948.

Coakley, J.F. "Manuscripts for Sale: Urmia, 1890–2." *Journal of Assyrian Academic Studies* 20 (2006): 3–17.

Cogan, Mordechai and Hayim Tadmor. *II Kings*. Anchor Bible Commentary 11. New York: Doubleday, 1988.

Cohen, Marilyn. "Introduction: Anthropological Aspects of the Novel." In *Novel Approaches to Anthropology: Contributions to Literary Anthropology*, edited by Marilyn Cohen, 1–25. New York: Lexington Books, 2013.

Cohen, Yoram. *Wisdom from the Late Bronze Age*. Writings from the Ancient World 34. Atlanta: Society of Biblical Literature, 2013.

Conybeare, F.C., Rendel Harris and Agnes Smith Lewis. The Story of Aḥikar from the Aramaic, Syriac, Arabic, Armenian, Ethiopic, Old Turkish, Greek, and Slavic Versions. Second edition, enlarged and corrected. Cambridge: University Press, 1913; reprint London: Forgotten Books, 2012.

Conybeare, F.C., J. Rendel Harris, and Agnes Smith Lewis. *The Story of Aḥikar from Syriac, Arabic, Armenian, Ethiopic, Greek, and Slavonic Versions*. London: Clay, 1898.

Crenshaw, James L. *Education in Ancient Israel: Across the Deadening Silence*. The Anchor Bible Reference Library. New York: Doubleday, 1998.

Dalley, Stephanie. "Assyrian Court Narratives in Aramaic and Egyptian Historical Fiction." In *Historiography in the Cuneiform Worlds. Proceedings of the XLVe Rencontre Assyriologique Internationale. Part 1*, edited by T. Abusch, 149–161. Bethesda: CDL Press, 2001.

Davies, Philip R. *Scribes and Schools: The Canonization of the Hebrew Scriptures*. Library of Ancient Israel. Louisville: Westminster John Knox Press, 1998.

Davis, Kipp. *The Cave 4 Apocryphon of Jeremiah and the Qumran Jeremianic Traditions: Prophetic Persona and the Construction of Community Identity*. Studies on the Texts of the Desert of Judah 111. Leiden: Brill, 2014.

Dearman, J. Andrew. "My Servants the Scribes: Composition and Context in Jeremiah 36." *Journal of Biblical Literature* 109 (1990): 403–421.

Dell, Katherine. "Scribes, Sages and Seers in the First Temple." In *Scribes, Sages and Seers: The Sage in the Mediterranean World*, edited by L.G. Perdue, 125–144. Göttingen: Vandenhoeck & Ruprecht, 2008.

Demsky, Aaron. *Literacy in Ancient Israel*. The Biblical Encyclopedia Library 28. Jerusalem: The Bialik Institute, 2012. [Hebrew]
Demsky, Aaron. "ידיעת קרוא וכתוב בישראל ובשכנותיה בתקופת המקרא," Ph.D. dissertation. Jerusalem: The Hebrew University, 1976.
Denis, Albert-Marie et al. *Introduction à la littérature religieuse judéo-hellénistique. Tome 2 (pseudépigraphes de l'Ancien Testament)*. Turnhout: Brepols, 2000.
Di Pede, Elena. *Au-delà du refus: l'espoir: Recherches sur la cohérence narrative de Jr 32-45 (TM)*. Beihefte zur Zeitschrift für die alttestamentliche Wissenschaft 357. Berlin: de Gruyter, 2012.
Dobbs-Allsopp, F.W., J.J.M Roberts, C.L. Seow, and R.E. Whitaker. *Hebrew Inscriptions: Texts from the Biblical Period of the Monarchy*. New Haven: Yale University Press, 2005.
Doloughan, Fiona J. *Contemporary Narrative: Textual Production, Multimodality, and Multiliteracies*. London: Continuum, 2011.
Domínguez, César, Haun Saussy, and Darío Villaneuva. *Introducing Comparative Literature: New Trends and Applications*. London: Routledge, 2015.
Donbaz, Veysel, and Matthew W Stolper. "Gleanings from Murašû Texts in the Collections of the Istanbul Archaeological Museums." *Nouvelles Assyriologiques Brèves et Utilitaires* (1993): 85–86/article 102.
Driver, Godfrey R. "Abbreviations in the Masoretic Text." *Textus* 1 (1960): 121–131.
Driver, S. R. *An Introduction to the Literature of the Old Testament [ILOT]*. Cleveland: World Pub. Co., 1956.
Duhm, Bernhard. *Das Buch Jeremia*. Kruzer Hand-Commentar zum Alten Testament 11. Tübingen: Mohr Siebeck, 1901.
Eilers, Wilhelm. *Iranische Beamtennamen in der keilschriftlichen Überlieferung*. Abhandlungen für die Kunde des Morgenlandes 5. Leipzig: Deutsche Morgenländische Gesellschaft; Kraus Reprint Ltd., 1940.
Ellis, Maria deJ. "A New Fragment of the Tale of the Poor Man of Nippur." *Journal of Cuneiform Studies* 26 (1974): 88–89.
Fales, Frederick Mario. "Multilingualism on Multiple Media in the Neo-Assyrian Period: A Review of the Evidence." *State Archives of Assyria Bulletin* 16 (2007): 95–122.
Fales, Frederick Mario. "Aramaic Letters and Neo-Assyrian Letters: Philological and Methodological Notes." *Journal of the American Oriental Society* 107 (3): 451–69.
Fales, Frederick Mario. *Aramaic epigraphs on clay tablets of the Neo-Assyrian period*. Studi semitici. Rome: Università degli studi La Sapienza, 1986.
Ferrer, Joan, and Juan Pedro Monferrer. *Historia y enseñanzas de Ahíqar o la antigua sabiduría oriental*. Studia Semitica, series minor 2. Córdoba: La Universidad de Córdoba, 2006.
Fischer, Georg. "A New Understanding of the Book of Jeremiah. A Response to Robert R. Willson," In *Jeremiah's Scriptures Production, Reception, Interaction, and Transformation*, edited by H. Najman and K Schmid, 22–43. Journal for the Study of Judaism in the Persian, Hellenistic, and Roman Periods Sup. 173. Leiden: Brill, 2016.
Fischer, Georg. *Jeremia*. Two volumes. Herders Theologischer Kommentar zum Alten Testament. Freiburg: Herder, 2005.
Fishbane, Michael. *Biblical Interpretation in Ancient Israel*. Oxford: Clarendon Press, 1985.
Fitzmyer, Joseph A. *The Aramaic Inscriptions of Sefire*, revised edition. Biblica et orientalia 19/A. Rome: Pontificio Istituto Biblico, 1995.

Fitzmyer, Joseph A., S. J. "Review of *Textbook of Aramaic Documents from Ancient Egypt, 3: Literature, Accounts, Lists*, von Bezalel Porten und Ada Yardeni." *Journal of the American Oriental Society* 115 (1995): 710–11.

Folmer, M.L. *The Aramaic Language in the Achaemenid Period: A Study in Linguistic Variation*. Orientalia Lovaniensia Analecta 68. Leuven: Peeters, 1995.

Foster, Benjamin R. *Before the Muses: An Anthology of Akkadian Literature*, third edition. Bethesda: CDL Press, 2005.

Foucault, Michel. *Language, Counter-Memory, Practice: Selected Essays and Interviews*. Edited and translated by Donald F. Bouchard. Ithaca: Cornell University Press, 1980.

Fox, Nili Sacher. *In the Service of the King: Officialdom in Ancient Israel and Judah*. Monographs of the Hebrew Union College 23. Cincinnati: Hebrew Union College Press, 2000.

Frahm, Eckart. "The Latest Sumerian Proverbs." In *Opening the Tablet Box: Near Eastern Studies in Honor of Benjamin R. Foster*, edited by Sarah C. Melville and Alice L. Slotsky, 155–184. Culture and History of the Ancient Near East 42. Leiden: Brill, 2010.

Freedy, K.S. and Donald Redford. "The Dates in Ezekiel in Relation to Biblical, Babylonian and Egyptian Sources." *Journal of the American Oriental Society* 90 (1970): 462–485.

Friedländer, Michael. *The Commentary of Ibn Ezra on Isaiah: Edited from MSS and Translations with Notes, Introductions, and Indexes*. Society of Hebrew Literature. New York: P. Feldheim, 1964.

Frood, Elizabeth. *Biographical Texts from Ramessid Egypt*. Writings from the Ancient World 26. Atlanta: Society of Biblical Literature, 2007.

Gadd, C.J. *Teachers and Students in the Oldest Schools: An Inaugural Lecture Delivered on 6 March 1956*. London: School of Oriental and African Studies, 1956.

Gadotti, Alhena and Alexandra Kleinerman. "Unfulfilled Destinies. Yet again on the Old Babylonian Sumerian Scribal Curriculum." In *The Ancient Near East, A Life! Festschrift Karel Van Lerberghe*, edited by Tom Boiy et al, 209–214. Orientalia Lovaniensia Analecta 220. Leuven: Peeters, 2012.

Galling, Kurt. "Die Halle des Schreibers." *Palästina-Jahrbuch* 27 (1931): 51–57.

Geertz, Clifford. *Works and Lives: The Anthropologist as Author*. Stanford: Stanford University Press, 1988.

George, Andrew R. "Ninurta-Pāqidāt's Dog Bite, and Noted on Other Comic Tales." *Iraq* 55 (1993): 63–75.

Gevaryahu, H.M.I. "Baruch son of Neriah, the Scribe." In *Zalman Shazar Volume*, edited by N. Avigad, 191–243. Jerusalem: Israel Exploration Society, 1971. [Hebrew]

Gilbert, Maurice. "Jérémie en conflict avec les sages?" In *Le livre de Jérémie: le prophète et son milieu les oracles et leur transmission*, edited by P.-M. Bogaert, 105–118. Bibliotheca Ephemeridum Theologicarum Lovaniensium 54. Leuven: Leuven University Press, 1981.

Glassner, Jean-Jacques. *Mesopotamian Chronicles*. Writings from the Ancient World 19. Atlanta: Society of Biblical Literature, 2004.

Goren, Yuval and Eran Arie. "The Authenticity of the Bullae of Berekhyahu Son of Neriyahu the Scribe." *Bulletin of the American Schools of Oriental Research* 372 (2014): 147–158.

Grabbe, Lester L. *Ancient Israel*. Revised edition. London: Bloomsbury, 2017.

Grabbe, Lester L. "Biblical Historiography in the Persian Period: or How the Jews Took Over the Empire," In *Orientalism, Assyriology and the Bible*, edited by Steven W. Holloway, 400–414. Hebrew Bible Monographs 10. Sheffield: Sheffield Phoenix Press, 2006.

Grabbe, Lester L. "Prophets, Priests, Diviners and Sages in Ancient Israel." In *Of Prophets' Visions and the Wisdom of Sages: Essays in Honour of R. Norman Whybray on his*

Seventieth Birthday, edited by Heather A. McKay and David J.A. Clines, 43–62. Journal for the Study of the Old Testament Sup. 162. Sheffield: Sheffield Academic Press, 1993.

Granerød, Gard. "'By the Favour of Ahuramazda I am King': On the Promulgation of a Persian Propaganda Text Among Babylonians and Judaeans." *Journal for the Study of Judaism in the Persian, Hellenistic, and Roman Periods* 44 (2013): 455–480.

Grätz, Sebastian. "'Wisdom' and 'Torah' in the Book of Baruch." In *Wisdom and Torah: The Reception of 'Torah' in the Wisdom Literature of the Second Temple Period*, edited by B.U. Schipper and D.A. Teeter, 187–202. JSJ Supp. 163. Leiden: Brill, 2013.

Graves, Michael. *Jerome's Hebrew Philology: A Study Based on His Commentary on Jeremiah*. Supplements to Vigiliae Christianae 90. Leiden: Brill, 2007.

Green, Douglas. *"I Undertook Great Works": The Ideology of Domestic Achievements in West Semitic Royal Inscriptions*. Forschungen zum Alten Testament, 2. Reihe 41. Tübingen: Mohr Siebeck, 2010.

Greenberg, Gillian. "Jeremiah in the Peshitta." In *The Book of Jeremiah: Composition, Reception, and Interpretation*, edited by Jack R. Lundbom, Craig A. Evans, and Bradford A. Anderson, 340–58. Supplements to Vetus Testamentum 178. Leiden; Boston: Brill, 2018.

Greenberg, Gillian. *Translation Technique in the Peshiṭta to Jeremiah*. Monographs of the Peshiṭta Institute 13. Leiden: Brill, 2002.

Greenfield, Jonas C. "The Wisdom of Aḥiqar." In *Wisdom in Ancient Israel*, edited by J. Day et al, 43–54. Cambridge: Cambridge University Press, 1995.

Greenfield, Jonas C. "Ahiqar in the Book of Tobit." In *De la Tôrah au Messie. Mélanges Henri Cazelles*, edited by M. Carrez, J. Doré, and P. Grelot, 329–333. Paris: Desclée, 1981.

Greenfield, Jonas C. "Studies in Aramaic Lexicography I." *Journal of the American Oriental Society* 82 (1962): 290–99.

Grelot, P. *Documents araméens d'Égypte. Introduction, traduction, présentation*. Littératures Anciennes du Proche-Orient 5. Paris: Ed. du Cerf, 1972.

Grünberg, Smil. *Die weisen Sprüche des Achikar nach der syrischen Hs Cod. Sachau Nr. 336 der Kgl. Bibliothek in Berlin*. Berlin: Giessen, 1917.

Gurney, O. R. "The Tale of the Poor Man of Nippur and Its Folktale Parallels." *Anatolian Studies* 22 (1972): 149–58.

Guzik, Markus Hirsch. *Die Achikar-erzählung nach der syrischen handschrift Cod. Sachau Nr 336 der preussischen Staatsbibliothek in Berlin*. Krakau: Renaissance, 1936.

Gzella, Holger. *A Cultural History of Aramaic: From the Beginnings to the Advent of Islam*. Handbook of Oriental Studies 111. Leiden: Brill, 2015.

Gzella, Holger. "The Heritage of Imperial Aramaic in Eastern Aramaic." *Aramaic Studies* 6 (2008): 85–109.

Hagen, Fredrik. "Constructing Textual Identity: Framing and Self-Reference in Egyptian Texts." In *Ancient Egyptian Literature: Theory and Practice*, edited by Roland Enmarch and Verena M. Lepper with Eleanor Robson, 185–209. Oxford: Oxford University Press, 2013.

Halévy, J. "Les Nouveaux Papyrus d'Éléphantine." *Revue Sémitique* 20 (1912): 31–78.

Hallo, William W. "Compare and Contrast: The Contextual Approach to Biblical Literature." In *The Bible in Light of Cuneiform Literature: Scripture in Context III*, edited by William W Hallo et al, 1–30. Ancient Near Eastern Texts and Studies 8. Lewiston: The Edwin Mellon Press, 1990.

Haran, Menahem. "Codex, Pinax and Writing Slat." *Scripta Classica Israelica* 15 (1996): 212–222.

Hardmeier, Christof. "Zur schriftgestützten Expertentätigkeit Jeremias im Milieu der Jerusalemer Führungseliten (Jeremia 36): prophetische Literaturbildung und die Neuinterpretation älter Expertisen in Jeremia 21–23." In *Die Textualisierung der Religion*, edited by Joachim Schaper, 105–149. Tübingen: Mohr Siebeck, 2009.

Hardmeier, Christof. *Prophetie in Streit vor dem Untergang Judas: Erzählkommunikative Studien zur Entstehungssituation der Jesaya- und Jeremiaerzählungen in II Reg 18–20 und Jer 37–40*. Beihefte zur Zeitschrift für die alttestamentliche Wissenschaft 187. Berlin: Walter de Gruyter, 1990.

Harris, *Story*. See Conybeare, F.C et al.

Hartenstein, Friedhelm. "Prophets, Princes, and Kings: Prophecy and Prophetic Books according to Jeremiah 36." In *Jeremiah's Scriptures Production, Reception, Interaction, and Transformation*, edited by H. Najman and K Schmid, 70–91. Journal for the Study of Judaism in the Persian, Hellenistic, and Roman Periods Sup. 173. Leiden: Brill, 2016.

Heaton, E.W. *The School Tradition of the Old Testament: The Bampton Lectures for 1994*. Oxford: Oxford University Press, 1994.

Henryk, Drawnel. "Between Akkadian *Ṭupšarrūtu* and Aramaic ספר. Some Notes on the Social Context of Early Enochic Literature," *Revue de Qumran* 24 (2010): 373–404.

Hill, John. "The Book of Jeremiah (MT) and its Early Second Temple Background." In *Uprooting and Planting: Essays on Jeremiah for Leslie Allen*, edited by John Goldingay, 151–171. Library of Hebrew Bible; Old Testament Studies 459. New York: T & T Clark, 2007.

Hoffman, Yair. "Aetiology, Redaction and Historicity in Jeremiah XXXVI." *Vetus Testamentum* 46 (1996): 179–189.

Holladay, William L. *Jeremiah 2: A Commentary on the Book of the Prophet Jeremiah Chapters 26–52*. Hermeneia 7/1. Philadelphia: Fortress Press, 1989.

Holm, Tawny L. "Memories of Sennacherib in Aramaic Tradition." In *Sennacherib at the Gates of Jerusalem: Story, History and Historiography*, edited by Isaac Kalimi and Seth Richardson, 297–323. Leiden: Brill, 2014.

Holm, Tawny L. *Of Courtiers and Kings: The Biblical Daniel Narratives and Ancient Story-Collections*. Explorations in Ancient Near Eastern Civilizations 1. Winona Lake: Eisenbrauns, 2013.

Honroth, Wilhelm, Otto Rubensohn, and Friedrich Zucker. "Bericht über die Ausgrabungen auf Elephantine in den Jahren 1906-1908." *Zeitschrift für ägyptische Sprache* 45 (1910): 162–209.

Hurowitz, Victor Avigdor. "Tales of Two Sages—Towards an Image of the 'Wise Man' in Akkadian Writings." In *Scribes, Sages and Seers: The Sage in the Mediterranean World*, edited by L.G. Perdue, 64–94. Göttingen: Vandenhoeck & Ruprecht, 2008.

Hurowitz, Victor Avigdor. "Literary Observations on 'In Praise of the Scribal Art.'" *Journal of the Ancient Near Eastern Society* 27 (2000): 49–56.

Hyatt, James Philip. "The Book of Jeremiah." In *The Interpreter's Bible*, vol. v, edited by George Arthur Buttrick et al, 775–1142. New York: Abingdon Press, 1956.

Isbell, Charles D. "II Kings 22:3–23:24 and Jeremiah 36: A Stylistic Comparison," *Journal for the Study of the Old Testament* 8 (1978): 33–45.

Janzen, J. Gerald. *Studies in the Text of Jeremiah*. Harvard Semitic Monographs 6. Cambridge: Harvard University Press, 1973.

Jong, Matthijs J. de. "Rewriting the Past in Light of the Present: The Stories of the Prophet Jeremiah." In *Prophecy and Prophets in Stories: Papers Read at the Fifth Meeting of the*

Edinburgh Prophecy Network, Utrecht, October 2013, edited by Bob Becking and Hans M. Barstad, 124–140. *Oudtestamentische Studiën* 65. Leiden: Brill, 2015.

Jursa, Michael. "Nabû-šarrūssu-ukin, rab ša-rēši, und 'Nebusarsekim' (Jer 39:3)." *Nouvelles Assyriologiques Brèves et Utilitaires* (March 2008): 9–10/article 5.

Jursa, Michael and Caroline Waerzeggers. "Families, Officialdom, and Families of Royal Officials in Chaldean and Achaemenid Babylonia." In *Tradition and Innovation in the Ancient Near East: Proceedings of the 57th Rencontre Assyiologique Internationale at Rome 4–8 July 2011*, edited by Alfonso Archi and Armando Bramanti, 597–606. Winona Lake: Eisenbrauns, 2015.

Jursa, Michael with Caroline Waerzeggers. "On Aspects of Taxation in Achaemenid Babylonia: New Evidence from Borsippa." In *Organisation des pouvoirs et contacts culturels dans les pays de l'empire achéménide: actes du colloque organisé au Collège de France par la "Chaire d'Histoire et Civilisation du Monde Achéménide et de l'Empire d'Alexandre" et le "Réseau International d'Études et de Recherches Achéménides" (GDR 2538 CNRS), 9–10 novembre 2007*, edited by Pierre Briant and Collège de France, 237–269. Persika 14. Paris: De Boccard, 2009.

Kaufman, Stephen A. *The Akkadian Influences on Aramaic*. Assyriological Studies 19. Chicago: The University of Chicago Press, 1974.

Kegler, Jürgen. "The Prophetic Discourse and Political Praxis of Jeremiah: Observations on Jeremiah 26 and 36." In *God of the Lowly: Socio-Historical Interpretations of the Bible*, edited by Willy Schottroff and Wolfgang Stegemann, translated by Matthew J. O'Connell, 47–56. Maryknoll, NY: Orbis Books, 1984.

Keown, Gerald L., Pamela J. Scalise, and Thomas G. Smothers. *Jeremiah 26–52*. Word Biblical Commentary 27. Dallas, TX: Word Books, 1995.

Kessler, Marin. "Form-Critical Suggestions on Jer 36." *Catholic Biblical Quarterly* 28 (1966): 389–401.

Kley, Nicholas van. "American Fiction, Bodies, and Social Knowledge during the Era of Sociology." Ph.D. dissertation. Waltham, MA: Brandeis University, 2013.

Knobloch, Harald. *Die nachexilische Prophetentheorie des Jeremiabuches*. Beihefte zur Zeitschrift für altorientalische und biblische Rechtsgeschichte 12. Wiesbaden, Harrassowitz, 2009.

Kottsieper, Ingo. "The Aramaic Tradition: Ahikar." In *Scribes, Sages and Seers: The Sage in the Mediterranean World*, edited by L.G. Perdue, 109–124. Göttingen: Vandenhoeck & Ruprecht, 2008.

Kottsieper, Ingo. "Die Geschichte und die Sprüche des weisen Achiqar." *Texte aus der Umwelt des Alten Testaments (TUAT). III/2: Weischeitstexte II* (1982): 320–347.

Kottsieper, Ingo. "Briefe Als Rechtsurkunden: Zu einigen aramäischen Briefen des Aršames." In *The Letter: Law, State, Society and the Epistolary Format in the Ancient World: Legal Documents in Ancient Societies (LDAS) 1; Proceedings of a Colloquium Held at the American Academy in Rome, 28–30.9.2008*, edited by Uri Yiftaḥ-Firanḳo, 141–154. Legal Documents in Ancient Societies 1 = Philippika 55,1. Wiesbaden: Harrassowitz, 2013.

Kramer, Samuel. *From the Tablets of Sumer: Twenty-five Firsts in Man's Recorded History*. Indian Hills: The Falcon's Wing Press, 1956.

Kramer, Samuel. "Schooldays: A Sumerian Composition Relating to the Education of a Scribe." *Journal of the American Oriental Society* 69 (1949): 199–215.

Krappe, Alexander H. "Is the Story of Aḥikar the Wise of Indian Origin?" *Journal of the American Oriental Society* 61 (1941): 280–284.

Kratz, Reinhard Gregor. *Historical and Biblical Israel: The History, Tradition, and Archives of Israel and Judah*. Oxford: Oxford University Press, 2015.

Kratz, Reinhard Gregor. *Historisches und biblisches Israel: Drei Überblicke zum Alten Testament*. Tübingen: Mohr Siebeck, 2013.

Kratz, Reinhard Gregor. "Mille Ahiqar. 'The Words of Ahiqar' and the Literature of the Jewish Diaspora in Ancient Egypt," *Al-Abhath* 60–61 (2012–2013): 40–58.

Krutzsch, Myriam. "Blattklebungen Erkennen und Documentieren," *Archiv für Papyrusforschung* 24 (2008): 93–98, taf. xxvi.

Kvanvig, Helge S. "Who were the Advisors of the King? A Comparative Study of Royal Consultants in Mesopotamia and in Israel." In *Sibyls, Scripture, and Scrolls: John Collins at Seventy*, edited by Joel Baden, Hindy Najman, and Eibert Tigchelaar, 688–713. Journal for the Study of Judaism in the Persian, Hellenistic, and Roman Periods Sup. 175. Leiden: Brill, 2017.

Lambert, W.G. "A Catalogue of Texts and Authors." *Journal of Cuneiform Studies* 16 (1962): 59–77.

Lambert, W.G. *Babylonian Wisdom Literature [BWL]*. Oxford: Clarendon Press, 1960.

Laurenson, Diana T. and Alan Swingewood. *The Sociology of Literature*. New York: Schocken Books, 1972.

Lawlor, John I. "Word Event in Jeremiah: A Look at the Composition's 'Introductory Formulas.'" In *Inspired Speech: Prophecy in the Ancient Near East in Honour of Herbert B. Huffmon*, edited by John Kaltner, 231–243. Journal for the Study of the Old Testament Sup. 378. London: T & T Clark, 2004.

Lemaire, André. "Aramaic Literacy and School in Elephantine." *Maarav* 21 (2017): 295–307.

Lemaire, André. "Nouveaux sceaux et bulles paléo-hébraïques." *Eretz-Israel* 26 (1999): 106*–115*.

Lemaire, André. "The Sage in School and Temple." In *The Sage in Israel and the Ancient Near East*, edited by J. Gammie and L. Perdue, 165–181. Winona Lake: Eisenbrauns, 1990.

Lemaire, André. *Écoles et formation de la Bible*. Orbis Biblicus et Orientalis 39. Fribourg: Éditions universitaires, 1981.

Lemaire, André. "Note sur le titre *bn hmlk* dans l'ancien Israël." *Semitica* 29 (1979): 59–65.

Leichty, Erle. "The Colophon." In *Studies Presented to A. Leo Oppenhiem, June 7, 1964*, edited by Robert M. Adams, 147–154. Chicago: The Oriental Institute of the University of Chicago, 1964.

Lenzi, Alan. *Secrecy and the Gods: Secret Knowledge in Ancient Mesopotamia and Biblical Israel*. State Archives of Assyria 19. Helsinki: Neo-Assyrian Text Corpus Project of the University of Helsiki, 2008.

Lenzi, Alan. "The Uruk List of Kings and Sages and Late Mesopotamian Scholarship." *Journal of Ancient Near Eastern Religions* 8 (2008): 137–169.

Leuchter, Mark. "Personal Missives and National History: The Relationship between Jeremiah 29 and 36." In *Prophets, Prophecy, and Ancient Israelite Historiography*, edited by M. J. Bode et al, 275–294. Winona Lake: Eisenbrauns, 2013.

Leuchter, Mark. *Josiah's Reform and Jeremiah's Scroll: Historical Calamity and Prophetic Response*. Hebrew Bible Monographs 6. Sheffield: Sheffield Phoenix Press, 2006.

Leuchter, Mark. *The Polemics of Exile in Jeremiah 26–45*. Cambridge: Cambridge University Press, 2008.

Levi-Strauss, Claude. *Tristes Tropiques*. Translated by J. and D. Weightman. New York: Antheneum, 1975.

Levtow, Nathaniel B. "Text Production and Destruction in Ancient Israel: Ritual and Political Dimensions." In *Social Theory and the Study of Israelite Religion: Essays in Retrospect and Prospect*, edited by Saul M. Olyan, 111–140. Resources for Biblical Study 71. Atlanta: Society of Biblical Literature, 2012.

Lichtheim, Miriam. *Ancient Egyptian Literature: Volume III: The Late Period*. Berkeley: University of California Press, 2006.

Lindenberger, James M. "Ahiqar." In *The Old Testament Pseudepigrapha*, two volumes, edited by James H. Charlesworth, 2:479–508. New York: Doubleday, 1985.

Lindenberger, James M. *The Aramaic Proverbs of Aḥiqar*. Baltimore: Johns Hopkins University Press, 1983.

Lipiński, Edward. "New Aramaic Clay Tablets." *Biblica et Orientalia* 3 (2002): 245–259.

Longman, Tremper, III. "Israelite Genres in Their Ancient Near Eastern Context." In *The Changing Face of Form Criticism for the Twenty-first Century*, edited by Marvin A. Sweeney and Ehud Ben Zvi, 177–195. Grand Rapids: Eerdmans, 2003.

Longman, Tremper, III. *Fictional Akkadian Autobiography: A Generic and Comparative Study*. Winona Lake: Eisenbrauns, 1990.

Löschnigg, Martin. "Postclassical Narratology and theory of Autobiography." In *Postclassical Narratology: Approaches and Analyses*, edited by Jan Alber and Monika Fludernik, 255–274. Columbus: Ohio State University Press, 2010.

Lozachmeur, Hélène, with Pascale Ballet, Jean Menier, Anne Schmitt, Léonidas Tsacas, and Christian de Vartavan. *La Collection Clermont-Ganneau: Ostraca, Épigraphes sur jarre étiquettes de bois*. Two volumes. Mémoires AIBL 35. Paris: Diffusion de Boccard, 2006.

Lusini, Gianfrancesco. "The Ethiopic version of the 'Story of Ahiqar' ("Mäṣḥafä Ḥiqar")." *Rassegna di Studi Etiopici,* nuova serie 3 (2011): 219–248.

Lundbom, Jack R. *Writing up Jeremiah: The Prophet and the Book*. Eugene: Cascade Books, 2013.

Lundbom, Jack R. *Jeremiah Among the Prophets*. Cambridge: James Clarke & Co., 2012.

Lundbom, Jack R. *Jeremiah: A New Translation with Introduction and Commentary*. Anchor Bible 21a–c. New Haven: Yale University Press, 1999–2004.

Lundbom, Jack R. "Baruch, Seraiah, and Expanded Colophons in the Book of Jeremiah." *Journal for the Study of the Old Testament* 36 (1986): 89–114.

Maier, Christl. *Jeremia als Lehrer der Tora: soziale Gebote des Deuteronomiums in Fortschreibungen des Jeremiabuches*. Forschungen zur Religion und Literatur des Alten und Neuen Testaments 196. Göttingen: Vandenhoeck & Ruprecht, 2002.

Matthews, Victor H. "Jeremiah's Scroll and Linked Zones of Communication." *Biblical Theology Bulletin* 39 (2009): 116–124.

Mattila, Raija. *King's Magnates: A Study of the Highest Officials of the Neo-Assyrian Empire*. State Archives of Assyria Studies 11. Helsinki: Neo-Assyrian Text Corpus Project of the University of Helsiki, 2014.

McKane, William. "Jeremiah and the Wise." *Wisdom in Ancient Israel*, edited by J. Day et al, 142–151. Cambridge: Cambridge University Press, 1995.

McKane, William. *A Critical and Exegetical Commentary on Jeremiah*. Two volumes. ICC. Edinburgh: T. & T. Clark Limited, 1986.

McKane, William. *Prophets and Wise Men*. Studies in Biblical Theology. Naperville: Alec R. Allenson, Inc., 1965.

Michalowski, Piotr. "Biography of a Sentence: Assurbanipal, Nabonidus, and Cyrus." In *Extraction & Control: Studies in Honor of Matthew W. Stolper*, edited by Michael Kozuh et al,

203–210. Studies in Ancient Oriental Civilizations 68. Chicago: The Oriental Institute of the University of Chicago, 2014.

Milik, J.T. "Les modèles araméens du livre d'Esther dans la grotte 4 de Qumrân," Revue de Qumran 15 (1991): 321–399.

Milner, Andrew. *Literature, Culture, and Society.* Second edition. London: Routledge, 2005.

Mingana, A. with introduction by J. Rendel Harris. "A Jeremiah Apocryphon." *Woodbrooke Studies* 1 (1927): 125–233.

Moore, James D. *New Aramaic Papyri from Elephantine in Berlin.* Studies on Elephantine 1. Leiden: Brill, forthcoming.

Moore, James D. "'Ahikariana': New Readings of Berlin P. 13446 and Developments in Ahiqar Research." In *Elephantine in Context*, edited by Bernd Schipper und Reinhard Kratz, *forthcoming*. Forschungen zum Alten Testament. Tübingen: Mohr Siebeck, 2021.

Moore, James D. "Who Gave You a Decree? Anonymity as a Narrative Technique in Ezra 5:3, 9 in Light of Persian Period Decrees and Administrative Sources." *Journal of Biblical Literature* 140 (2021): 69–89.

Moore, James D. "The Persian Administrative Process in View of an Elephantine 'Aršāma Decree (TAD A6.2)." *Semitica et Classica* 13 (2020): 49–62.

Moore, James D. "Review of Laura Quick, Deuteronomy 28 and the Aramaic Curse Tradition." Review of Biblical Literature 2 (2019): 1–6.

Moore, James D. with Syriac text prepared by George A. Kiraz and Joseph Bali. *Leviticus.* Antioch Bible. Piscataway: Gorgias Press, 2015.

Mowinckel, Sigmund. *Zur Komposition des Buches Jeremia.* Kristiania: J. Dybwad, 1914.

Muffs, Yochanan. *Studies in Aramaic Legal Papyri from Elephantine.* Handbuch der Orientalistik 66. Leiden: Brill, 2003.

Muilenburg, James. "Baruch the Scribe." In *Proclamation and Presence: Old Testament Essays in Honour of Gwynne Henton Davies*, edited by John I. Durham and J.R. Porter, 215–238. Richmond: John Knox Press, 1970.

Müller, Hans-Peter. "Die weisheitliche Lehrerzählung im Alten Testament und seiner Umwelt." *Die Welt des Orients* 9 (1977): 77–98.

Müller, Wolfgang and Otto Rubensohn, "Die Papyrusgrabung auf Elephantine 1906-1908. Das Grabungstagebuch der 1. und 2. Kampagne," *Forschungen und Berichte* 20 (1980): 75–88.

Muraoka, Takamitsu and Bezalel Porten. *A Grammar of Egyptian Aramaic.* Handbuch der Orientalistik 66. Leiden: Brill, 1998.

Mykytiuk, Lawrence J. *Identifying Biblical Persons in Northwest Semitic Inscriptions of 1200–539 B.C.E.* Leiden: Brill, 2004.

Nau, François. *Histoire et sagesse d'Aḥikar l'assyrien.* Paris: Letouzey et Ané, Éditeurs, 1909.

Niditch, Susan and Robert Doran. "The Success Story of the Wise Courtier: A Formal Approach," *Journal of Biblical Literature* 96 (1977): 179–193.

Niehr, Herbert. *Aramäischer Ahiqar.* Jüdische Schriften aus hellenistisch-römischer Zeit, neue Folge II/2. Gütersloh: Gütersloher Verlag, 2007.

Nöldeke, Theodor. *Untersuchungen zum Achiqar-Roman.* Abhandlugen der Königlichen Gesellschaft der Wissenschaften zu Göttingen philologisch-historische Klasse, neue Folge 14/4. Berlin: Weidmannsche Buchhandlung, 1913.

Nöldeke, Theodor. *Compendious Syriac Grammar.* London: Williams and Norgate, 1904.

Noth, Martin. *Die israelitischen Personennamen im Rahmen der gemeinsemitischen Namensgebung.* Beiträge zur Wissenschaft vom Alten und Neuen Testament, 3. Folge, Heft 10. Hildesheim: Gg Olms, 1966.

Oppenheim, A. Leo. "Akk. *arad ekalli* = "Builder."" Archív orientální 17 (1949): 227–235.
Orton, David E. *The Understanding Scribe: Matthew and the Apocalyptic Ideal*. Sheffield: T & T Clark, 1989.
Oshima, "How 'Mesopotamian' was Ahiqar the Wise? A Search for Ahiqar in Cuneiform Texts". In *Wandering Arameans: Aramaeans Outside Syria: Textual and Archaeological Perspectives*, edited by A. Berlejung et al, 141–168. Leipziger altorientalistische Studien 5. Wiesbaden: Harrasowitz, 2017.
Panov, Lida. "King Jehoiakim's Attempt to Destroy the Written Word of God (Jeremiah 36). A Response to Friedhelm Hartenstein." In *Jeremiah's Scriptures Production, Reception, Interaction, and Transformation*, edited by H. Najman and K. Schmid, 92–97. Journal for the Study of Judaism in the Persian, Hellenistic, and Roman Periods Sup. 173. Leiden: Brill, 2016.
Parpola, Simo. "Il retroterra assiro di Ahiqar." In *Il saggio Ahiqar: Fortuna e trasformazioni di uno scritto sapienziale: Il testo più antico e le sue versioni*, edited by R. Contini and C. Grottanelli, 91–112. Studies in Biblical Literature 148. Brescia: Paideia, 2005.
Parpola, Simo. "The Assyrian Tree of Life: Tracing the Origins of Jewish Monotheism and Greek Philosophy." *Journal of Near Eastern Studies* 52 (1993): 161–208.
Parpola, Simo. "The Forlorn Scholar." In *Language, Literature, and History: Philological and Historical Studies Presented to Erica Reiner*, edited by F. Rochberg-Halton, 257–278. American Oriental Series 67. New Haven: Yale University Press, 1987.
Parpola, Simo. *Letters from the Assyrian Scholars to the Kings Esarhaddon and Assurbanipal: Part II Commentary and Appendices [LAS]*. Alter Orient und Altes Testament 5. Kevelaer: Verlag Butzon & Bercker, 1983.
Parpola, Simo. SAA 10. See Abbreviations.
Peake, A.S., ed. *Jeremiah and Lamentations, Vol. II, Jeremiah XXV to LII, Lamentations: Introduction Revised Version with Notes, Map and Index*. The Century Bible 17. Edinburgh: T.C. & E.C. Jack, 1911.
Pearce, Laurie E. "*sepīru* and ^{lú}A.BA: Scribes of the Late First Millennium." In *Languages and Cultures in Contact: At the Crossroads of Civilizations in the Syro-Mesopotamian Realm; Proceedings of the 42th RAI*, edited by Karel van Lerberghe and Gabriela Voet, 355–68. Orientalia Lovaniensia Analecta 96. Leuven: Peeters, 1999.
Pearce, Laurie E. and Cornelia Wunsch. CUSAS 28. See Abbreviations.
Peck, Jeffrey M. "From a Literary Critic/Germanist's Point of View: Anthropology." In *Culture/Contexture: Explorations in Anthropology and Literary Studies*, edited by E. Valentine Daniel and Jeffrey M. Peck, 13–20. Berkeley: University of California Press, 1996.
Perdue, Leo G., ed. *Scribes, Sages and Seers: The Sage in the Mediterranean World*. Göttingen: Vandenhoeck & Ruprecht, 2008.
Postgate, Nicholas. *Bronze Age Bureaucracy: Writing and the Practice of Government in Assyria*. Cambridge: Cambridge University Press, 2013.
Quack, Joachim Friedrich. "The Interaction of Egyptian and Aramaic Literature." In *Judah and the Judeans in the Achaemenid Period: Negotiating Identity in an International Context*, edited by Oded Lipschits, Gary N. Knoppers, and Manfred Oeming, 375–401. Winona Lake: Eisenbrauns, 2011.
Quack, Joachim Friedrich. "Die demotischen Fragmente der Erzählung und der Sprüche des Achiqar." In *Elephantine in Context*, edited by Bernd Schipper und Reinhard Kratz, *forthcoming*. Forschungen zum Alten Testament. Tübingen: Mohr Siebeck, 2021.

Quick, Laura E. *Deuteronomy 28 and the Aramaic Curse Tradition*. Old Testament Message. Oxford: Oxford University Press. 2018.

Radner, Karen. "Royal Pen Pals: The kings of Assyria in Correspondence with Officials, Clients, and Total Strangers (8th and 7th Centuries BC)." In *Official Epistolography and the Language(s) of Power: Proceedings of the First International Conference of the Research Network Imerium & Officium: Comparative Studies in Ancient Bureaucracy and Officialdom University of Vienna, 10–12 November 2010*, edited by Stephan Prochàzka et al, 61–71. Papyrologica Vindobonensia 8. Vienna: Österreichischen Akademie der Wissenschaften, 2015.

Radner, Karen. "Royal Decision-Making: Kings, Magnates, and Scholars." In *The Oxford Handbook of Cuneiform Culture*, edited by K. Radner and E. Robson, 358–379. Oxford: Oxford University Press, 2011.

Reiner, Erica. "The Etiological Myth of the Seven Sages." *Orientalia* 30 (1961): 1–11.

Reventlow, Henning Graf. Liturgie und prophetisches Ich bei Jeremia. Tübingen: Gütersloher Verlagshaus, 1963.

Reyna, S.P. "Literary Anthropology and the Case Against Science." *Man*, new series 29 (1994): 555–581.

Rietzschel, Claus. *Das Problem der Urrolle: Ein Beitrag zur Redaktionsgeschichte des Jeremiabuches*. Berlin: Gütersloher Verlagshaus/Gerd Mohn, 1966.

Roberts, Jonathan. "Introduction." In *The Oxford Handbook of the Reception History of the Bible*, edited by Michael Lieb, Emma Mason, and Jonathan Roberts. Oxford: Oxford University Press, 2013.

Rogers, Mary F. *Novels, Novelists, and Readers: Toward a Phenomenological Sociology of Literature*. SUNY Series in the Sociology of Culture. Albany: State University of New York Press, 1991.

Röllig, Wolfgang. "Aramäer und assyrer die Schriftzeugnisse bis zum ende es Assyrerreiches." In *Essays on Syria in the Iron Age*, edited by G. Bunnens, 177–186. ANES Sup. 7. Louvain: Peeters, 2000. Reprint 2008.

Rollston, Christopher A. *Writing and Literacy in the World of Ancient Israel: Epigraphic Evidence from the Iron Age*. Archaeology and Biblical Studies 11. Atlanta: Society of Biblical Literature, 2010.

Römer, Thomas. "From Prophet to Scribe; Jeremiah, Huldah and the Invention of the Book." In *Writing the Bible: Scribes, Scribalism, and Script*, edited by Philip R. Davies and Thomas Römer, 86–96. Biblical World. Durham: Acumen, 2013.

Rosenmeyer, Patricia A. *Ancient Greek Literary Letters: Selections in Translation*. Routledge Classical Translations. New York: Routledge, 2006.

Rudolph, Wilhelm. *Jeremia*. Second edition. Handbuch zum Alten Testament 1/12 Tübingen: Mohr Siebeck, 1968.

Sachau, Eduard. *Aramäische Papyrus und Ostraka aus einer jüdischen Militär-Kolonie zu Elephantine*. Altorientalische Sprachdenkmäler 5. Leipzig: Hinrichs, 1911.

Sachau, Eduard. *Verzeichniss der syrischen Handschriften*. Die Handschriften-Verzeichnisse der Koniglichen Bibliothek zur Berlin 23. Berlin: A. Asher & Co., 1899.

Sanders, Seth. *From Adapa to Enoch: Scribal Culture and Religious Vision in Judea and Babylon*. Texts and Studies in Ancient Judaism. Tübingen: Mohr Siebeck, 2017.

Sanders, Seth. *The Invention of Hebrew*. Urbana: University of Illinois Press, 2009.

Scafa, Paola Negri. "Continuity and Discontinuity in a Nuzi Scribal Family." In *Tradition and Innovation in the Ancient Near East: Proceedings of the 57th Rencontre Assyriologique*

Internationale at Rome 4–8 July 2011, edited by Alfonso Archi with Armando Bramanti, 345–353. Winona Lake: Eisenbrauns, 2015.

Schmitt, Armin. "Die Achikar-Notiz bei Tobit I,21b-22 in aramäischer (pap4QTob'ar–4Q196) und griechischer Fassung." In *Text and Transmission: An Empirical Model for the Literary Development of Old Testament Narratives*, edited by Christian Wagner, 103–123. Beihefte zur Zeitschrift für die alttestamentliche Wissenschaft 221. Berlin: De Gruyter, 1994.

Schneider, Roger. "L'histoire d'Ahiqar en éthiopien." *Annales d'ethiopie* 11 (1978): 141–152.

Schniedewind, William M. *The Finger of the Scribe: How Scribes Learned to Write the Bible*. New York: Oxford University Press, 2019.

Schniedewind, William M. *A Social History of Hebrew: Its Origins Through the Rabbinic Period*. Anchor Bible Reference Library. New Haven: Yale University Press, 2013.

Schniedewind, William M. *How the Bible Became a Book: The Textualization of Ancient Israel*. Cambridge: Cambridge University Press, 2004.

Schütze, Alexander. "Local Administration in Persian Period Egypt According to Aramaic and Demotic Sources." In *Die Verwaltung im Achämenidenreich: imperiale Muster und Strukturen: Akten des 6. Internationalen Kolloquiums zum Thema "Vorderasien im Spannungsfeld Klassischer und Altorientalischer Überlieferungen" aus Anlass der 80-Jahr-Feier der Entdeckung des Festungsarchivs von Persepolis, Landgut Castelen bei Basel, 14.-17. Mai 2013 = Administration in the Achaemenid empire*, edited by Bruno Jacobs, Wouter F. M. Henkelman, and Matthew W. Stolper, 489–515. Classica et Orientalia 17. Wiesbaden: Harrassowitz, 2017.

Schütze, Alexander. "Schreiberämter in den aramäischen Urkunden aus dem Ägypten des fünften Jarhhunderts v. Chr." In *Texte—Theben—Tonfragmente: Festschrift für Günter Burkard*, edited by Dieter Kessler et al, 377–384. ÄAT 76. Wiesbaden: Harrassowitz, 2009.

Schwiderski, Dirk, ed. *Die alt- und reichsaramäischen Inschriften The Old and Imperial Aramaic Inscriptions*. Two volumes. Fontes et Subsidia ad Biblian pertinentes 4. New York: Walter de Gruyter, 2008.

Seizt, Christopher R. "A Review of *Prophetie in Streit vor dem Untergang Judas: Erzählkommunikative Studien zur Entstehungssituation der Jesaya- und Jeremiaerzählungen in II Reg 18–20 und Jer 37–40*, by Christof Hardmeier." *Journal of Biblical Literature* 110 (1991): 511–513.

Sharp, Carolyn J. "Jeremiah in the Land of Aporia: Reconfiguring Redaction Criticism as Witness to Foreignness." In *Jeremiah (Dis)placed: New Directions in Writing/Reading Jeremiah*, edited by A.R. Pete Diamond and Louis Stulman, 35–46. The Library of Hebrew Bible/Old Testament Studies 529. New York: T & T Clark, 2011.

Sharp, Carolyn J. "'Take Another Scroll and Write:' A Study of the LXX and the MT of Jeremiah's Oracles against Egypt and Babylon," *Vetus Testamentum* 47 (1997): 487–516.

Shiloh, Yigal. "A Group of Hebrew Bullae from the City of David." *Israel Exploration Journal* 36 (1986): 16–38.

Silver, Edward. "The Prophet and the Lying Pen: Jeremiah's Poetic Challenge to the Deuteronomic School." Ph.D. Dissertation. Chicago: University of Chicago Divinity School, 2009.

Sims-Williams, Nicholas. *Biblical and Other Christian Sogdian Texts from the Turfan Collection*. Berliner Turfantexte 32. Turnhout: Brepols, 2014.

Sjöberg, Åke W. "In Praise of the Scribal Art." *Journal of Cuneiform Studies* 24 (1972): 126–131.

Small, Jocelyn Penny. *Wax Tablet of the Mind: Cognitive Studies of Memory and Literacy in Classical Antiquity*. London: Routledge, 1997.

Smith, Morton. "Pseudepigraphy in the Israelite Literary Tradition." In P*seudepigrapha I: pseudopythogorica—lettres de Platon littérature pseudépigraphique juive*, edited by Ronald Syme et al, 190–227. Entretiens sur l'antiquité classique. Geneve: Vandoeuvres, 1972.
Soden, Wolfram von. "Die Unterweltsvision eines assyrischen Kronprinzen: nebst einigen Beobachtungen zur Vorgeschichte des Ahiqar-Romans." *Zeitschrift für Assyriologie* 43 (1936): 1–31.
Sokoloff, Michael. *A Syriac Lexicon*. Piscataway: Gorgias Press and Winona Lake: Eisenbrauns, 2009.
Stipp, Hermann-Josef. "Baruchs Erben: die Schriftprophetie im Spiegel von Jer 36." In *"Wer darf hinaugsteigen zum Berg JHWHs?" Beiträge zu Prophetie und Poesie des Alten Testaments*, edited by Hubert Irsigler, 145–170. Arbeiten zu Text und Sprache in alten Testament 72. Ottilien: EOS Verlag, 2002.
Stipp, Hermann-Josef. *Jeremia, der Tempel und die Aristokratie: die patrizische (schafanidische) Redaktion des Jeremiabuches*. Kleine Arbeiten zum Alten und Neuen Testament 1. Waltrop: Spenner, 2000.
Stipp, Hermann-Josef. "The Prophetic Messenger Formulas in Jeremiah According to the Masoretic and Alexandrian Texts." *Text* (1995): 63–85.
Stipp, Hermann-Josef. *Das masoretische und alexandrinische Sondergut des Jeremiabuches: textgeschichtlicher Rang, Eigenarten, Triebkräfte*. Orbis Biblicus et Orientalis 136. Göttingen: Vandenhoeck & Ruprecht, 1994.
Stipp, Hermann-Josef. *Jeremia im Parteienstreit: Studien zur Textentwicklung von Jer 26, 36–43 und 45 als Beitrag zur Geschichte Jeremias, seines Buches und judäischer Parteien im 6. Jahrhundert*. Athenäums Monografien 82. Frankfurt am Main: Hain, 1992.
Stolper, Matthew W. "The Governor of Babylon and Across-the-River in 486 B. C." *Journal of Near Eastern Studies* 48 (1989): 283–305.
Strawn, Brent A. "Comparative Approaches: History, Theory, and The Image of God." In *Method Matters: Essays on the Interpretation of the Hebrew Bible in Honor of David L. Petersen*, edited by Joel M. LeMon and Kent Harold Richards, 117–142. Resources for Biblical Study 56. Atlanta: Society of Biblical Literature, 2009.
Strugnell, John. "Problems in the Development of the Aḥîqar Tale." *Eretz-Israel* 29 (1999): *204–*211.
Suhr, Claudia. *Die ägyptische "Ich-Erzählung": Eine narratologische Untersuchung*. Göttinger Orientforschungen Ägypten 61. Wiesbaden: Harrassowitz Verlag, 2016.
Talmon, Shemaryahu. "The 'Comparative Method' in Biblical Interpretation—Principles and Problems." In *Essential Papers on Israel and the Ancient Near East*, edited by Frederick E. Greenspahn, 381–419. New York: New York University Press, 1991.
Tavernier, Jan. *Iranica in the Achaemenid Period (ca. 550-330 B.C.) Lexicon of Old Iranian Proper Names and Loanwords, Attested in Non-Iranian Texts*. Orientalia Lovaniensia Analecta 158. Leuven: Peeters, 2007.
Tavernier, Jan. "Multilingualism in the Fortification and Treasury Archives." In *L'archive des fortifications de Persépolis: état des questions et perspectives de recherches: actes du colloque organisé au Collège de France par la "Chaire d'histoire et civilisation du monde achéménide et de l'empire d'Alexandre" et le "Réseau international d'études et de recherches achéménides" (GDR 2538 CNRS), 3–4 novembre 2006*, edited by Pierre Briant, Wouter Henkelman, and Matthew W. Stolper, 59–86. Persika 12. Paris: De Boccard, 2008.

Thiel, Winfried. *Die deuteronomistische Redaktion von Jeremia 26–45*. Wissenschaftliche Monographien zum Alten und Neuen Testament 52. Düsseldorf: Neukirchener Verlag, 1981.

Tigay, Jeffrey, ed. *Empirical Models for Biblical Criticism*. Philadelphia: University of Pennsylvania Press, 1985.

Toorn, Karel van der. *Scribal Culture and the Making of the Hebrew Bible*. Cambridge: Harvard University Press, 2007.

Tov, Emanuel. *Textual Criticism of the Hebrew Bible*. Third revised edition. Minneapolis: Fortress Press, 2012.

Tov, Emanuel. *Scribal Practices and Approaches Reflected in the Texts Found in the Judean Desert*. Studies on the Texts of the Desert of Judah 54. Leiden: Brill, 2004.

Tov, Emanuel. *The Septuagint Translation of Jeremiah and Baruch: A Discussion of an Early Revision of the LXX of Jeremiah 29–52 and Baruch 1:1–3:8*. Harvard Semitic Monographs 8. Cambridge: Harvard University Press, 1973.

Ungnad, Arthur. *Aramäische Papyrus aus Elephantine*. Leipzig: J.C. Hinrichs'sche Buchhandlung, 1911.

Vayntrub, Jacqueline. "The Book of Proverbs and the Idea of Ancient Israelite Education." *Zeitschrift für die alttestamentliche Wissenschaft* 128 (2016): 96–114.

Veldhuis, Nick. "On Interpreting Mesopotamian Namburbi Rituals." *Archiv für Orientforschung* 42/43 (1995/1996): 145–154.

Venema, G.J. *Reading Scripture in the Old Testament: Deuteronomy 9–10, 31, 2 Kings 22–23, Jeremiah 36, Nehemiah 8*. Oudtestamentische Studiën 48. Leiden: Brill, 2004.

Waerzeggers, Caroline. "Babylonians in Susa. The Travels of Babylonian Businessmen to Susa Reconsidered." In *Der Achämenidenhof = The Achaemenid Court*, edited by Bruno Jacobs and Robert Rollinger, 777–813. Classica et orientalia, Bd. 2. Wiesbaden: Harrassowitz, 2010.

Wahl, Harald Martin. "Die Entstehung der Schriftprophetie nach Jer 36." *Zeitschrift für die alttestamentliche Wissenschaft* 110 (1998): 365–389.

Wanke, Gunther. *Untersuchungen zur sogenannten Baruchschrift*. Beihefte zur Zeitschrift für die alttestamentliche Wissenschaft 122. Berlin: Walter de Gruyter, 1971.

Webber, Sabra J. and Patrick B. Mullen. "Breakthrough into Comparison: 'Moving' Stories, Local History, and the Narrative Turn." *Journal of Folklore Research* 48 (2011): 213–247.

Weigl, Michael. *Die aramäischen Achikar-Sprüche aus Elephantine und die Alttestamentliche Weisheitsliteratur*. Beihefte zur Zeitschrift für die alttestamentliche Wissenschaft 399. Berlin: Walter de Gruyter, 2010.

Weinfeld, Moshe. *Deuteronomy and the Deuteronomic School*. Oxford: Oxford University Press, 1972.

Westenholz, Joan Goodnick. *Legends of the Kings of Akkade: The Texts*. Mesopotamian Civilizations 7. Winona Lake: Eisenbrauns, 1997.

White, Justin J. "Scribal Loyalty and the Burning of the Scroll in Jeremiah 36. A Response to Friedhelm Hartenstein." In *Jeremiah's Scriptures Production, Reception, Interaction, and Transformation*, edited by H. Najman and K Schmid, 1–21. Journal for the Study of Judaism in the Persian, Hellenistic, and Roman Periods Sup. 173. Leiden: Brill, 2016.

Widengren, Geo. *Literary and Psychological Aspects of the Hebrew Prophets*. Uppsala Universitet Arsskrift 10. Uppsala: Lundequistska bokhandeln, 1948.

Wigand, Ann-Kristin. "Politische Loyalität und religiöse Legitimierung: Überlegungen zur Textpragmatik der aramäischen Achiqarkomposition." *Die Welt des Orients* 48 (2018): 128–50.
Winner, Thomas G. "Literature as a Source of Anthropological Research: The Case of Jaroslav Hašek's Good Soldier Švejk." In *Literary Anthropology: A New Interdisciplinary Approach to People, Signs, and Literature*, edited by Fernando Poyatos, 51–62. Amsterdam: John Benjamins Publishing Company, 1988.
Whybray, Roger N. *The Intellectual Tradition in the Old Testament*. Beihefte zur Zeitschrift für die alttestamentliche Wissenschaft 135. Berlin: Walter de Gruyter, 1974.
Williamson, Hugh G. M. *Ezra, Nehemiah*. Word Biblical Commentary 16. Waco: Word Books, 1985.
Wills, Lawrence M. *The Jew in the Court of the Foreign King: Ancient Jewish Court Legends*. Minneapolis: Fortress Press, 1990.
Wills, Lawrence M. "Observations on 'Wisdom Narratives' in Early Biblical Literature." In *Of Scribes and Scrolls: Studies on the Hebrew Bible, Intertestamental Judaism, and Christian Origins Presented to John Strugnell on the Occassion of his Sixtieth Birthday*, edited by Harold W. Attridge, John J. Collins, and Thomas H. Tobin, S.J., 57–66. College Theology Society Resources in Religion 5. Lanham: University Press of America, 1990.
Wilson, Robert. "Exegesis, Explanation, and Tradition-Making in the Book of Jeremiah," In *Jeremiah's Scriptures Production, Reception, Interaction, and Transformation*, edited by H. Najman and K Schmid, 1–21. Journal for the Study of Judaism in the Persian, Hellenistic, and Roman Periods Sup. 173. Leiden: Brill, 2016.
Wright, David P. *The Disposal of Impurity: Elimination Rites in the Bible and in Hittite and Mesopotamian Literature*. Society of Biblical Literature Dissertation Series 101. Atlanta: Scholars Press, 1987.
Yardeni, Ada. "Maritime Trade and Royal Accountancy in an Erased Customs Account from 475 B.C.E. on the Ahiqar Scroll from Elephantine." *Bulletin of the American Schools of Oriental Research* 293 (1994): 67–78.
Young, Ian M. "Israelite Literacy: Interpreting the Evidence: Part I." *Vetus Testamentum* 48 (1998): 239–253.
Younger, K. Lawson. *A Political History of the Arameans: From Their Origins to the End of Their Polities*. Archaeology and Biblical Studies 13. Atlanta: SBL Press, 2016.
Zadok, Ran. "The Account of Nabû-Šuma-Iškun Revisited." *Altorientalische Forschungen* 44 (2017): 261–67.
Zamazalová, Silvie. "The Education of Neo-Assyrian Princes." In *The Oxford Handbook of Cuneiform Culture*, edited by Karen Radner and Eleanor Robson, 313–334. Oxford, UK: Ludwig-Maximilians-Universität München, 2011.
Zhakevich, Philip. *Scribal Tools in Ancient Israel: A Study of Biblical Hebrew Terms for Writing Materials and Implements*. History, Archaeology, and Culture of the Levant. University Park: Eisenbrauns, 2020.

Index of Ancient Sources

Italics indicates a reference only in a note.

Akkadian Sources

Adad Guppi 49

Amarna Letters *126*

BaAr 6
    no. 4 *6*

CTN 3
    no. 99 i 15 *49*
    no. 108 ii 38 *49*

CTN 4
    no. 202 68

CUSAS 10
    no. 14 (The Scholars of Uruk) 68
    no. 17 (Tribulations of Gimil-Marduk) 68

CUSAS 28
    no. 41 *6*

Epic of Gilgamesh *3*

Enuma Elish *3*

Idrimi 49

In Praise of the Scribal Art 83

K4347+16161
    ii 50–63 9, 67–68, 145

Marduk Prophecy 49

Ninurta-Pāqidāt's Dog Bite 83

RIBo 6
    Ash. no. 15
        ln. 7 74
RIBo Marduk-zakir-šumi no. 2 *74*
Nabu-šuma-iškun nos. 1–2 72
Nabu-šuma-iškun no. 1
    iii 26', 42'
    iii 32'–33' 72
Nabu-šuma-iškun no. 2
    i 17 72

RIBo 7
    Nab no. 24
        i 32 46

RINAP 1
    Tig-Pil III no. 42
        ln. 17' *70*

RINAP 3/1
    Senn no. 22
        v 17–vi 35 *72*
        vi 24–35 *72*
    Senn no. 109 *72*
    Senn no. 213
        ln. 33 *72*, 73

RINAP 4
    Esar no. 1
        i 8–16 141
        i 9–10 *141*
        i 14 82, 141
        ii 40–64 *72*
    Esar no. 48
        r. 70 45
    Esar no. 105
        iv 29–30 45

Ras-Shamra
    RS 16.142
        ln. 16

SAA 2
    no. 6 (Vassal Treaties of Esarhaddon)
        72, 82
    no. 8

ll. r. 18–27 70–71

SAA 3
  no. 32 (Underworld Vision of the Assyrian Prince) 9, 61, 145
    ln. r. 33 62
    ln. r. 35 62

SAA 4
  nos. 149–173 59

SAA 5
  no. 98
    r. 9'–10' 55

SAA 7
  nos. 1–7 65
  no. 1 7

SAA 8
  nos. 143–159 95
  no. 158
    ln. r. 4 95
    ln. r. 6 95

SAA 10
  no. 7 7
  no. 84 ln. r. 7–8 78
  no. 160 7, 53, 61, 81, 145
    ln. 4 53
    ln. 10 53
    ln. 13 53
    ln. 25 53
    ll. 32–33 61
    ln. 36 53
    ln. 45 53
  no. 175 58
  no. 182 77
  no. 205 95
  no. 222
    ln. 11 78
  no. 224 59
  no. 226
    r. 6–13 58, 59
  no. 227 59
  no. 228 59
  no. 294 8, 81, 145

ll. r. 16–17 59
ln. 21 77
ll. r. 21–22 59, 78
ln. 27 77
ln. r. 30 59, 61, 78
no. 307 77
no. 308 77

SAA 13
  no. 127 ln. 13 55
  no. 145 95

SAA 15
  no. 125 55, 65

SAA 16
  no. 21 70

SAA 17
  no. 2 166
    obv. 15–16 166

SAA 18
  no. 100 72, 147

Šimâ Milka
  ll. 1–7 53, 63
  ln. 146' 154
  Emar VI tome 2, no. 778–780 154
  KBo 12.70 154
  KUB 4.3 154
  RS 22.439 154
  RS94.2544+ 154
  RS 94.5028 154

Uruk List of Kings and Sages (W.20030)
  ln. 7 47

Arabic Sources

Alf laylah wa-laylah 3, 5

Quran
  Sura 31 3

Aramaic

1Q20
    ixx.24 74

Ahiqar (Pap. Ber. P. 13446 + Cairo EM JdE
    43502 = *TAD* C1 1; C3 7) vii, 10, 19,
    39
  Ar 48, *60*
    Ar.1–2 43–48
    Ar.1 139, 141
    Ar.2–7 48–56
    Ar.2 48, 76, 155
    Ar.3–4 62
    Ar.3 46, 49, 54, *79*
    Ar.4–5 140, 143
    Ar.4 51
    Ar.5–6 *48*, 50–51
    Ar.5 141
    Ar.6 48, 50, 69, 78, 143
    Ar.7–14 57–58
    Ar.7–Br.6 57–65
    Ar.7 51, 57, 143
    Ar.8–9 141
    Ar.8–10 143
    Ar.8 57, 143
    Ar.9 51, *54*, 71, 77
    Ar.10–12 143
    Ar.10 63, 69, 143
    Ar.11 58
    Ar.12 51, *54*, 59, 63
    Ar.13–14 *156*
    Ar.14–Br.1 144
    Ar.14–Br.2 60
  Av 40
  B (plate) *66*, 70
  Br *60*
    Br.1 51, 61, 78, *79*, 143–145
    Br.2 143
    Br.3 48, 54
    Br.6–14 65–69
    Br.6 65
    Br.8 44, 65, 71, 77
    Br.9–11 66
    Br.9 48, 65, 145
    Br.12 44, 51, 63
    Br.14 67, 147

  C (plate) *66*, 70
  Cr 41
    Cr.1–4 146
    Cr.1–8 70–75
    Cr.1 76
    Cr.2 74–75
    Cr.4–5 *45*
    Cr.5 65, 70, 145
    Cr.6 146
    Cr.8–Dr.i.15 75–80
    Cr.10 75, 146–148
    Cr.11 63, 71
    Cr.12 44, 63
    Cr.13 48, *70*, 75
    Cr.14–15 155
    Cr.14 75
    Cr.15–Dr.i.8 75
    Cr.15 75
    Cr.17–Dr.i.1 76, 148
  Dr 41
    Dr.i.1 71, *75*
    Dr.i.1–2 *76*
    Dr.i.5 59, 63, 145
    Dr.i.7 80
    Dr.i.7–8 63
    Dr.i.8 80
    D.i.8–13 75
    Dr.i.9 63
    Dr.i.12 44, 80
    Dr.i.12–13 63
    Dr.i.13 *78*
    Dr.i.13–15 *79*
    Dr.i.14 80
    Dr.i.14–15 146
    Dr.i.15 *41*, 79
    Dr.ii *76*
  Dv 40
    Dv.ii.1 40
  DVEx1 40
  E–H, J–L (plates) 140
  Fr
    Fr.i.12–13 *62*
    Fr.ii.1 40
    Fr.ii.5 40
  Gr
    Gr.ii.14 40
  Gv

Gv.iv 40
Gv$^{\text{upside down}}$ 44, 139–140
H (plate) 41
Hv^{pal}–Lv^{pal} 41
Jr
   Jr.i.1 40
Kr
   Kr.ii.22 40
L 41

Amherst 63
   xix ln. 7 44

Bactrian Documents (*ADAB*)
   nos. A1–8 166

Brooklyn Museum 16.99a-d *116*

Darius Inscription (*TAD* C2) 7, 19, 71, 82, 96

KAI
   no. 202
     A 2 *154*
   no. 216
     ln. 1 *154*
   no. 217
     1.1 *154*
   no. 222–224 (Sefire Inscriptions I–III)
     44–45, 65
   no. 222
     A 2.8 *43*
   no. 224 64
     ll. 9–11 64
     ll. 9–10 *75*
   no. 233 66
   no. 312
     A 1.1 *43*

Lemaire, *Nouvelle Tablettes Araméennes*
   no. 6
     r. 5' *54*

TAD
   A1 8 64
   A3 3 166
   A6 1 166

A6 2 166
A6 8–13 166
A6 8
   ln. 2 *54*
A6 10
   ln. 3 *46*
A6 15
   ln. 7 *78*
B1 1
   ln. 17 166
B2 3
   ln. 12 *78*
B2 3
   ln. 19 *78*
B4 3 *160*
   ln. 11 74
B4 4 166
B2 6
   ln. 2 *46*
C1 1 see Ahiqar
C3 7 see Ahiqar
D20 2
   ln. 5 *66*
D23 9
   ln. 6 *70*

Biblical Sources

Genesis
   Joseph Story 2
   LXX
     Gen 26:34 *109*
   MT
     Gen 26:34 *109*

Exodus
   MT
     34:1 *123*

Leviticus
   MT
     24:14 *119*

Numbers
   MT
     5:23 90

Deuteronomy 85
MT
- 6:1–10 *51*
- 17:9–12 90–91
- 31:9–11 90
- 31:10–13 91
- 32:36 *98*

Joshua
MT
- 2:1–8 *150*
- ch. 10 *150*

1 Samuel
MT
- chs. 19–20 *150*
- ch. 30 98

2 Samuel
MT
- 1:1 98
- 4:10 98
- 8:17 *127*
- 17:9 *119*
- 20:25 *127*

1 Kings
MT
- 4:3 *127*
- 10:8 *119*
- 12:9 112
- 14:10 *98*
- 16:9 *127, 128*
- ch. 17 *150*
- ch. 18 *150*
- 18:3 *127*
- 21:9 *100*
- 21:21 *98*

2 Kings
LXX
- 23:36–37 101

MT
- 9:8 *98*
- 10:5 *127*
- 12:11 *126, 127*
- 14:26 *98*
- ch. 17 *70*
- 18:18 127
- 18:26 127
- 18:37 127
- chs. 18–19 126
- 19:2 127
- 19:36–17 147
- 21:23 147
- ch. 22 126
- 22:3 127
- 22:8–10 127
- 22:12 127
- chs. 22–23 108, *109*
- 22:10 *116*
- 22:12–14 *108*
- 23:11 102
- 23:29 87
- 24:8 *108*
- 25:23 *115*
- 25:25 *115*

Isaiah
MT
- 1:26 *110*
- 8:16–18 *91*
- 22:15 127
- 22:15–25 128
- 36:3 127
- 36:11 127
- 36:22 127
- 37:2 127
- 40:14 111

Jeremiah
LXX
- 1:1 90
- 1:2 *158*
- 1:4 *89*, 153
- 1:11 *89*
- 1:13 *89*
- 8:8 *125*
- 11:1 *158*
- 13:3 *89*
- 13:8 *89*
- 14:1 *88–89, 158*
- 17:13 91

18:1 *158*
18:5 *88–89*
20:1–2 *110*
20:3 *110*
21:1 *158*
24:4 *89*
26:13 *158*
27:1 *158*
28:59 *158*
28:60 91
ch. 33 *158*
33:1 *158*, 159
34:2 *158*
35:12 *89*
36:30 *89*
37:1 91, *158*
38:33 91
ch. 39 160–161
39:1 *158*, 159–160
39:6–25 160
39:6 *158*, 159–160
39:8 160
39:9 160
39:10 160
39:11 160
39:12 *124*, 160
39:13 *124*, 160
39:16 94, *124*, 160
39:25 160, 161
39:26 *89*, 161
39:27 160
40:1 *89*, *98*, *160*
41:1 *158*
41:8 *158*
41:12 *89*, *158*
42:4 *102*
42:12 *89*
ch. 43 12, 14, 27, 84–85, *90*, 139, 160–161, *163*
43:1–8 87–99, 101, 121
43:1 *86*, 88, *89*, 121, 136, 139–140, 158–159, 162
43:2 88–90, 93, 95, *117*
43:3 *85*, 123
43:4 89–90, 93, *95*, 112, *117*, 122, *124*, 158
43:5 *124*, 143, 158

43:6 93, 98, *121*
43:7 85
43:8 *124*, 158
43:9–11 99–104
43:9 *86*, 99–101, *119*
43:10–11 *101*
43:10 99, 101, 103, 115, 117, 124–126, 145, 167
43:11 103–104, 112, 117, 167
43:12–19 104–113, *124*, *125*
43:12 103–104, 107, 109, 117, 124–126, 167
43:13 112–117, 124
43:14 103–104, 110, 115–116, *124*
43:15 94, *101*, 112, 117, *124*
43:16 111–112, 117, 147–148
43:17 112, *117*, *124*
43:18 *95*, 112–113, *117*, *121*, *124*
43:19 113–114, 120, *124*, 148
43:20–26 114–121, *124*
43:20 105, 114–115, 117
43:21 94, 105, 115, 117, *124*
43:22 115
43:23 99, *101*, 110, 115–116, 117, *125*
43:24 106, 116, *117*, 118–120
43:25 *107*, 108, 116, *118*, 120
43:26–32 121–129
43:26 119, *121*, 124, 126, 146, 148
43:27–31 123
43:27 *89*, 121, 124, 158
43:28 *101*, *117*, 121–124
43:29–31 101
43:29 99, i116
43:30–31 101
43:31 *85*, 119–120, 123
43:32 *101*, *117*, 122–124, 129, 162
44:6 *89*
44:15 *125*
44:17 *158*
44:20 *125*
45:27 *98*
46:15 *98*
47:1 *158*
49:7 *89*
50:3 *124*
50:6 *124*
50:8 *89*

51:1 *158*
51:31 *124*, *158*, *159*
52:25 *125*
MT
  chs. 1–45 *12*
  chs. 1–25 *12*
  1:1–4 *102*
  1:1 15, 90
  1:2 *90*, *158*
  1:4–9 *90*
  1:4 153, *158*
  1:18 106
  1:24 *91*
  2:8 *102*
  2:26 *102*, 106
  4:9 *102*, 106
  5:31 *102*
  6:13 *102*
  chs. 7–44 *12*
  7:1 *158*, 159
  8:1 *102*, 106
  8:8 15, 22, 25, *113*, 125, *132*
  8:10 *102*
  11:1 *158*, 159
  11:6 *158*
  11:20 *110*
  13:13 *102*
  14:1 *158*
  14:11 *158*
  14:18 *102*
  17:1 *91*
  17:13 *91*
  17:25 106
  18:1 *158*, 159
  18:3 *158*
  18:18 *102*
  ch. 20 98
  20:1–4 98
  20:1–2 *110*
  20:3 *110*
  21:1 *158*
  21:3 *158*
  23:11 *102*
  23:13 *102*
  23:16 94
  24:1 106
  24:8 106

25:18 106
chs. 26–29 *12*
ch. 26 *12*, 91, 98, 102, 106, *110*, *120*, 130, 133, 159
26:1 *89*, 97, *158*, 159
26:2 97
26:3 *87*
26:7 *102*, *158*
26:10 *110*
26:11 *102*
26:16 *102*
27:1 *89*, *158*, 159
27:2 *158*
27:16 *102*
ch. 28 *12*
28:1 *89*, *102*
28:5 *102*
ch. 29 *12*, 163
29:1 *102*
29:2 106
29:29 *102*
30:1 91, 96–97, *158*
ch. 31 163
31:33 91
chs. 32–45 *12*
ch. 32 *91*, 160–161, 163
32:1 *158*, 159–160
32:6–25 160
32:6 158, 159–160
32:8 160
32:9 160
32:10 160
32:11 160
32:12 *93*, 160
32:12–14 125
32:12–16 25
32:13 160
32:14 25
32:16–25 142
32:16 160
32:25 160, 161
32:26 161
32:27 160
32:32 *102*
32:33 106
33:1 *98*, *160*
34:1 *158*

34:6 *158*
34:8 *158*
34:21 106
35:2 102
35:4 102
chs. 36–44 *12*
ch. 36 12, 14, 20, 25–27, 84–85, *90–91*, *94*, 95, 98, *102*, 106, *107*, 108–109, *119*, 125–126, 128, 133–134, 139, 144, 147, *149*, *151–152*, 158–161, 163, 165
36:1–32 25
36:1–8 87–99
36:1–3 26
36:1 27, 88, *89*, 121, 136, 139–140, 158–159
36:2 88–90, 92–93, 95–96, *117*, 121, 141
36:3 85, *87*, 123
36:4 89–93, 95, 112, *117*, 122, 141, 158
36:5 97–98, 143–144, 158
36:6 92–93, *94*, 98–99, *113*, *121*, 131
36:7 85, *123*
36:8 *90*, *124*, 158
36:9–11 99–104
36:9 99–101
36:10–11 *101*
36:10 99, 101, 103, 115, 117, 124, *125*, 126, 145, 167
36:11 103–104, 112, 117, 167
36:12–19 104–113
36:12 103–104, 107, 109, 117, 124, *125*, 126, 167
36:13 112, 117
36:14 103–104, *109*, 110, 115–116
36:15 *101*, 112, 117
36:16 111, 117, 130–131, 147
36:17 *94*, 112, *117*, 148
36:18 28, *94*, 112–113, *117*, *121*, 131
36:19 113–114, 120, 131, 148
36:20–26 114–121
36:20 105, 114–115, 117, *125*
36:21 105, 115, 117, *119*, *125*
36:22–26 *130*
36:22 115

36:23 92, 95, 99, *101*, 110, 115–117, *125*
36:24 106, 112, 116, *117*, 118–120, *133*
36:25 *107*, 108, 116, *118*, 120
36:26–32 121–129
36:26 28, *90*, *113*, 119, *121*, 124, *125*, 126, 128, 131, 146, 148, 151
36:27–31 123, 140
36:27 *121*, 124, *139*, 158
36:28 90, *117*, 121–124
36:29 *91*, 99, *116*
36:31 85, 119–120, 123, 137
36:32 28, 90, *117*, 122–124, *125*, 128–129, 131, 162
chs. 37–44 *12*
37:3 *102*
37:15 *125*
37:17 *158*
37:20 *125*
38:27 *98*
39:15–18 *98*
39:15 *98*
40:1 *158*
40:2 *158*
41:1 *115*
43:3 25
44:1 *158*
44:15 *158*
ch. 45 *12*, 26, *159*
45:1–5 25
45:1 *158*
chs. 46–52 *12*
46:1 *158*
46:13 *158*
47:1 *158*
49:3 106
49:34 *158*
50:1 *158*
51:50 91
51:59 *93*, *158*
51:60 96
52:25 *125*
PESHITTA
20:1–2 *110*
20:3 *110*
26:1 159

26:3 *85*
26:13 *85*
36:1–8 *129*, *159*
36:4 *95*
36:9 *100*
36:10 *100*, *129*
36:20 114
36:24 *118*
Vulgate
36:4 *95*
36:20 114

Ezekiel
LXX
42:5 *102*
42:9 *102*
42:13 *102*
44:19 *102*
46:19 *102*
MT
2:9 *95*
40:17 *102*
40:44 *102*
42:3 *102*

Hosea
MT
4:6 90

Zechariah
MT
8:9 *119*

Psalms
MT
31:6 *115*
45:2 47
71:10 112
83:6 112

Proverbs 3
MT
22:29 47

Qohelet
MT
1:1 170

2:1 170

Esther 2
MT
3:12 *126*
8:9 *126*

Daniel 2
MT
2:5 44
2:22 149
3:8 66
5:1 74
6:25 66
7–12 29

Ezra
MT
4:22 *70*
7:6 47
7:14 63
8:29 *102*

Nehamiah
MT
8:8–9 91
10:37–39 *102*
13:4–5 *97*

1 Chronicles
MT
12:1 98
18:16 *127*

2 Chronicles
MT
19:8–11 91
24:11 *126*, *127*
30:23 112
34:8 *127*
34:15 *127*
34:18 *127*
34:20 *127*

Tobit 2, 5–6
4Q196 *6*
frag. 2.7–8 56

frag. 2.7 *46*
4Q198 *6*
Greek
  1:1 *170*
  1:3 *49, 170*
  1:14 *6*
  1:18–2:1 *149*
  1:22 *5, 44*
  2:10 *5, 6*
  14:10 *6, 44*

Sirah
  Greek
    50:27–29 *26*

Baruch
  Greek
    1:1 *124*
    1:3 *124*

Egyptian Sources

Ahiqar (Pap. Ber. P. 23729, P. 23730(?), P. 23829, P. 23830, P. 23831, and Cairo National Library 3122) *5, 154–155*

Eloquent Peasant *149*

Horus and Seth *69*

Instructions of Ankhsheshonqy *149*

Neferti *149*

Pap. Ber. P. 13540 (Pherendates Let.) *126, 166*

P.Rylands 9 *167*

Report of Wenamun *154*

Sinuhe (*COS* 1.38) *149, 154*
  b.1–15 *149*

Greek Sources

Democritus (via Clement of Alexandria)
  10, *154*

Herodotus
  I 137 *78*

Josephus
  Antiquities
    Ant 10.6.2 *95*
    Ant 10.9.1 *93*

Life of Aesop *3, 4, 65, 66, 154–155*
  Oxyrh. Pap 47 #3331 *155*
  Oxyrh. Pap. 53 #3720 *155*

Hebrew

Assessment Ostracon (Eshel, *IEJ* 53) *126*

Cairo Damascus Document
  CD-A
    x 4–6 *110*

E. Borowski Collection (Lemaire, *Eretz-Israel* 26)
  no. 22 *107*

Jeremiah Apocryphon
  4Q383
    frag. 1.1 *158*

KAI
  no. 200
    ln. 1 *127*
  no. 191 *128*

Lachish Ostraca *110*
  no. 3 *127*
  no. 6 *112, 127*
  no. 22
    ln. 4 *107*

Seals
  HaE II/2

no. 2.7 *107*
no. 4.3 *107*
no. 4.4 *107*
no. 5.21 *107*
no. 15.24 *107*

Avigad and Sass
  no. 4 *127*
  no. 21 *126*
  no. 22 *126*
  no. 23 *126*

Karshuni

Ahiqar
  Mingana 258 *154*
  Sachau 339 *154*

Jeremiah Apocryphon *109*, 138

Latin

Cicero
  De Oratore
    2.86.351–2.88.360 *96*
    2.88.360 *96*

Quintilian
  Institutio Oratoria
    2.4.27–41 *96*
    10.1.19 *96*
    11.2–6 *96*

Moabite

KAI
  no. 181
    ln. 1 *154*

Phoenician

KAI
  no. 24
    ln. 1 *154*

no. 26
  A.i.1 *154*

Sumerian

Sumerian Schooldays 52

Syriac (Ahiqar)

Ahiqar
  BM 7200 *3*
    fol. 144 r. 16–17 156
  BM Or. 2313 *3*
  BnF 422 *3*, 5
  Camb. Cod. Add 2020 *3*, 5, 66, *67*, 136
    1.1 *43*, *140*
    1.12 57
    1.13 60
    1.13–14 *57*
    1.14–15 157
    1.15 *66*, 156
    1.20 46
    2.75 157
    3.1 68, *144*, 157
    3.1–6 *67*
    3.6 68, 157
    3.7 *67*
    3.7–9 *67*
    3.8 46
    4.1 157
    4.4 *79*
    4.6 157
    4.9 *155*, 157
    4.10 78
    4.11 *79*
    5.1 157
    5.2 46
    7.7 157
    8.39 *154*
  Dayro d-Mor Gabriel 192 *3*
  Dom. Fr. Mosel 430 *3*
  Graffin *3*, *144*
    1.1 *5*
    2.3 57
    2.5 *58*

2.7 *66*
3.1 *157*
3.73 *157*
12.1 *155*
12.3 *155–156*
12.4 *78*
27.7 *46*
Houghton 80 *3*
 fol. 3 *156*
JerMkl 162 *3, 45*
Mingana 433 *3, 4*
Sachau 162 *3, 162*
 fol. 87a ln. 1 *58*
Sachau 336 *3*
Sachau 339 (Turoyo) *4*
Urmia 117 *3*
Urmia 230 *3*

Išodad of Merv
 CSCO 328, 29 *125*

Ugaritic

UD/KTU
 no. 1.3
  iii.11 *47*

Selected Terms Discussed

Italics indicates a reference only in a note.

Akkadian

lu2 (lu2šanû) 56

aḫḫū 71
alāku 55
– urumātu Elianda illiku 6
anāku 49
asû 7
āšipu 7

bārû 7
bēl
bēl pīḫāti 74
bēl ṭābtī 71

dāgil iṣṣūrī 7

ikkibu 77

kalû 7, 148
kunukku 54

māru 51
mašmaššû 51
milku 63

nāgir ekalli 64
narû 49

pīḫāti see bēl pīḫāti

qurbūte 55

rab 54
rab kiṣir 55
rab šaqê 56
rab ša-rēši 55
rab unqāti 46, 55–56, 164
rabiānu 74
rabû 73–74

rubû 72–75
rubû lā šanān 74
rubûtu 72, 73

sepēru 166
sēpiru 46, 165
– lu2sēpir ša bīt unqāta 55

ṣabātu 54
– ṭuppi ṣabātu 54

ša pî 94, 95
ša-rēši 79, 127
– see also rab ša-rēši
ša-ziqni 80, 127
šamallû 53
– lu2ŠAMAN.LÁ 53
šar šarri 74
šitimgalla enqūta 45

ṭābtu 77
ṭupšarru 7
– DUB.SAR 46
– lu2A.BA É DINGIR 95
ṭupšarru emqu 45–46

ummânu 7–9, 42, 47, 51, 79, 95, 148
ummânu emqu 45–47, 165
unqu 54–55
– lu2sēpir ša bīt unqāta see sēpiru
– ina nakkante bīt unqi 55

waṣābu 56

Aramaic

אבוה 80
א(ו)מן 46
אחד/אחז 54
– ואחז ספרא 54
אחרנן 80
אכל 66
אכל קרצ(י)א 66

[אנ]ה אחיקר 48, 155
ארדכל זי מלכא 46
אלהין 62

בב היכלא 164
בדא 67
בני 64
ברי זי לא ברי 67

גבר
גברין 80

הוית 44
המרכל 55

זיל 78

חבל
– יחבל מתא 70
חלף 49–50, 60
– יחלף 143
חלפה 58
חכם 142

טבתא 51, 71, 77

יוזף/י 56
יעט 42, 54, 63, 82, 164
יעט אתור 56

כהל
– לא אכהל 144
כן 40
כפם 94
כתב 166

מהיר 47, 82
מות
– תמות 57
מלה 44
– ומל[והי] 44
מלי 45
מילי יה[ו]ה 48
מלין 44, 139
מנדע
– כמנדע 59

נגד 42, 64
נגדוהי 63
נגדין 64–65, 75, 78, 79, 82, 164

ספר (document) 43
– ספר מלי 44
ספר (scribe) 165, 167
– ספרי אוצרא 166
– ספרא חכימא 45–47, 56, 63, 82, 164–166
– ספרי מדינתא 166
סריס 79, 82
סריסין 78

עלים 78, 82
עזקה 42, 49, 54, 82
– בית עזקה 46, 55
– רב [עז]קה see below
– רב עזקן see below
עטה 139
עטתה 44, 63
עם 80

צבות
– צבות ביתא 54

[צב]ית 54
צבת 54

פגר 79
פחה 74
[פ]קיד 64

רב 73–74
רב [עז]קה 56, 63, 164–165
רב עזקן 46, 164–165
רב [ש]קה 56
רבי 73–75, 164
רביא 42, 73, 82, 146
רחמה 58

שאל 57
שב 51, 78
שב אנה 144

תנין 56

Egyptian (Demotic)

šḥ 166

Greek

ακουσαντες *118*, 119
ἀναγινώσκω 94
ἀπέτεμνεν 116
ἄρχοντες
– πάντες οἱ ἄρχοντες 105

Βίβλος λόγων Τωβιθ 44

γένος
– τὸ γένος αὐτοῦ 119
γραμματεύς 124–129
γράψον 89, 90

δεδεμένος 98

Ἐγὼ Τωβιτ 49

καταρράκτην 110

λόγος
– τοὺς λόγους κυρίου 103

μαθητὴν 93

οἶκος 102
– ἐν οἴκῳ χειμερινῷ 115
– οἴκῳ/οἴκου Ελισαμα 105
– τὸν οἶκον τοῦ γραμματέως 105

παῖδας
– τοὺς παῖδας αὐτοῦ 119
παστοφόριον 102
περίπατοι 102
πρός 88

συνεβουλεύσαντο 111

υἱῷ τοῦ βασιλέως 106

Hebrew

אוּלַי 87
אָז
– בְּאָז 38, 99, 104, 115, 117
אָח 115
אֵלַי 89
אֲשֶׁר עַל־הַבָּיִת 127

בַּדָּיו 94
בוא
– הַבָּאִים 100
בֵּית הַחֹרֶף 115
בֶּן־הַמֶּלֶךְ 106, 119, 132–133, 146

דָּבָר 88
– הַדָּבָר 158
– יְהוָה דִּבְרֵי 103
– כָּל־דִּבְרֵי יְהוָה 104, 117
– כָּל־הַדְּבָרִים 90, 93, 95
דִּבְרֵי יִרְמְיָהוּ 103
דברים 51

זַרְעוֹ 119, 123, 133

חֲכָמִים 14, 23, 25, 113
חָצֵר 115

יְהוּדִי 110
יכל
– לֹא אוּכַל 144

כֹּהֵן
– הַכֹּהֵן 110
– הַכֹּהֲנִים 106
כּוּשִׁי 110
כָּלוּא 98
כתב 51, 92
– וְכָתַבְתָּ 89, 90

למד 51
לִשְׁכָּה 97, 102
לִשְׁכַּת אֱלִישָׁמָע הַסֹּפֵר 105
לִשְׁכַּת גְּמַרְיָהוּ 115
לִשְׁכַּת הַסֹּפֵר 105
לִשְׁכַּת הַשָּׂרִים 102

מְגִלַּת־סֵפֶר 90, 95
מהיר *47*
מהר *47*
מַהְפֵּכָה
– הַמַּהְפֶּכֶת *110*
מִפִּי 93–94, 124
מִפִּיו *94*

נָבִיא
– הַנָּבִיא *124*
– הַנְּבִיאִים *106*
נגד 112, 115, 117
נָגִיד *63, 65*

ספר 165–166
– הַסֵּפֶר 124–129, 131, 167
סְפָרִים 14, 25, *113*

עֲבָדָיו / עַבְדֵי הַמֶּלֶךְ 106, 119, 123, 132–133
עֶלְיוֹן
– הָעֶלְיוֹן 115
עָצוּר 97–98
– אֲנִי עָצוּר 144

קרא *94–95*, 117
– תִּקְרָאֵם *94*
קרע
– יִקְרָעֶהָ *116*

שב 111
שמע *51*, 86, 104, 111, 117, 123
– הַשֹּׁמְעִים 118
– לא שמע 38
שמע +כל הדברים 38
שפט *110*
שָׂרִים 14–15, 23, 86, 104–113, 131–132, 167
– כָּל־הַשָּׂרִים 105, 132

תוֹרַת יְהוָה 15, *113*

Old Persian

hamāra-kara 56

Sumerian

DUMU EDUBBA *52*

NIGIR *64*

Syriac

ܐܘܡܢ *46*
ܐܢܐ ܐܚܝܩܪ 157
ܐܓܪܬܐ ܚܬܝܡܬܐ 46
ܐܬܘܪܝܐ *47*

ܕܘܟܬܐ
– ܒܕܘܟܬܗ 58

ܫܕܪܬܐ *110*

ܡܐ̈ܢܝ ܐܘܡܢܘܬܐ *46*
ܡܗܦܟܐ *5*
ܡܗܝܪܐ *47*
ܡܗܪ *47*
ܡܗܡܝܢ *71*
ܡܬܠ *45*
– ܡܬܠܘܗܝ ܕܚܝܩܪ *45*

ܬܓܪܐ *63*

ܦܩܕܬܗ *66*

ܒܘܬܐ *46, 55*

ܦܘܐܠܐ ܕܡܠܟܐ ܣܢܚܪܝܒ *57*

ܬܫܒܘܚܬܐ *43*

Ugaritic

mhr
– *kp mhr* *47*
– *⸢y⸣d mhr* *47*

Selected Terms Discussed — 209

Persons

(Excluding Ahiqar, Nadin/Nadan, Jeremiah, and Baruch)

Aba-Enlil-dari 47
Achbor (Gk Akchobor) 108
Adad-šuma-uṣur 8–9, 52, 59–60
Ahiqam 108
Ahûqar (Gk Akchobor) 49
Amon 147
Arqu 49

David 150
Delaiah (Gk Dalaias) 105, *107* (Godolias), 108, *113*, 120

Eliashib 97
Elijah 150
Elishama (Gk Elisama) 105, *107*, 108, *115*, *124*, 125–126, 167
Elnathan 105, 108, *113*, 120
Esarhaddon 2, 82, 141, 147
– Esaraḫʾerîb 41

Gedaliah 115
Gemariah (Gk Gamarias) 102–103, 105, *113*, 120, *124*, 125–126, 167
Godolias see Delaiah.

Hananiah (Gk Hananias) 107
Hilkiah 134

Isaiah 127
Ishmael 115
Issar-šumu-ereš 51

Jehoiakim 11, 88, *119*, 141, 147
Jehoiakin 108
Jerahmeel 119–120, 146
Jonathan 150
Judith 109
Jehudi 87, 95, 105, 109–110, 116, 120

Mahseiah 93
Manzîpar 78

Marduk-apla-iddina II (Merodach-Baladan) 72–73
Marduk-šapik-zeri 53, 61–62
Meshullam 127
Micaiah 97, 103–105

Nabû-mušeṣi 95
Nabûsumiskun 2, 72–73, 75–77, 145–148
Nabu-šuma-iškun (son of Marduk-apla-iddina) 72–73.
Nabu-šuma-iškun (King of Babylon) 72–73
Nabûzardan 67
Nabu-zer-kitti-lišir 72
Nabû-zēru-iddina see Nabûzardan.
Nabu-zeru-lešir 51
Nehushta 108
Neriah 93

Pashhur 110

Sennacherib 2, 72–73, 141, 147
Seraiah 93
Shaphan (Gk Saphan) 28, 108, 126
Shebnah 126–128
Shemaiah (Gk Selemias) *107*, 108

Tabnî 77
Tobiah 97

Urad-Gula 8–9, 51–52, 59–62, 77, *78*, 82

Zakutu 70, 82
Zedekiah (Gk Sedekias) 105, *107*, 109

Abbreviations

AP	A.E. Cowley, *Aramaic Papyri of the Fifth Century B.C.* (Oxford: Clarendon Press, 1923).
BaAr 6	Babylonische Archive 6. Currently unpublished, but indexed in CUSAS 28.
BnF	Bibliotheque Nationale de France.
Brenton	English translation of LXX by Sir Lancelot C.L. Brenton according to the Accordance Bible Software Module, LXX (Brenton Translation).
CAD	Chicago Assyrian Dictionary.
CAL	Comprehensive Aramaic Lexicon. http://cal.huc.edu/
CUSAS 10	Andrew R. George, *Old Babylonian Texts in the Schøyen Collection*, Cornell University Studies in Assyriology and Sumerology (CUSAS) 10 (Bethesda: CDL Press, 2018).
CUSAS 28	Laurie E. Pearce and Cornelia Wunsch, *Documents of Judean Exiles and West Semites in Babylonia in the Collection of David Sofer*, Cornell University Studies in Assyriology and Sumerology (CUSAS) 28 (Bethesda: CDL Press, 2014).
DJD 19	Magen Broshi, Esther Eshel, Joseph Fitzmyer, Erik Larson, Carol Newsom, Lawrence Schiffman, Mark Smith, Michael Stone, John Strugnell, and Ada Yardeni, *Qumran Cave 4 XIV: Parabiblical Texts, Part 2*, Discoveries in the Judaean Desert 19 (Oxford: Clarendon Press, 1995).
DNWSI	Jacob Hoftijzer and K. Jongeling, *Dictionary of the North-West Semitic Inscriptions*, 2 vols, Handbuch der Orientalistik (Leiden: Brill, 1995).
Dom. Fr. Mosel	Dominican Friars of Mosul, Collection of the Dominican Mission.
DULAT	Gregorio del Olmo Lete and Joaquín Sanmartín, *A Dictionary of the Ugaritic Language in the Alphabetic Tradition*, Trans. W.G.E. Watson, 2 vols. (Leiden: Brill, 2003).
GKC	Wilhelm Gesenius, *Hebrew Grammar*, 2nd ed., ed. E. Kautzsch, trans. A.E. Cowley (Oxford, England: Clarendon Press, 1910 [Reprint 1985]).
Göttingen LXX	Joseph Zeigler, ed., *Jeremias, Baruch, Threni, Epistula Jeremiae*, Göttingen Septuaginta 15 (Vandenhoeck & Ruprecht, Göttingen, 2013). As found in Accordance, tagged by Rex A. Koivisto. OakTree Software, Inc. (2015).
HaE	Johannes Renz and Wolfgang Röllig, *Handbuch der althebräischen Epigraphik*, 4 vols. (Darmstadt: Wissenshaftliche Buchgesellschaft, 1995).
HMML	Hill Museum and Manuscript Library. https://www.vhmml.org/ (accessed 28.09.2021)
Joüon	Paul Joüon, *A Grammar of Biblical Hebrew*, trans. T. Muraoka, 2 vols. (Rome: Pontifical Biblical Institute, 1991).
KAI	Herbert Donner and Wolfgang Röllig, eds., *Kanaanäische und aramäische Inschriften*, vol. 1 fifth ed., vol. 2 third edition, vol. 3 second ed. (Wiesbaden: Harrassowitz, 2002, 1973, 1969).
KTU	Manfried Dietrich, Oswald Loretz, and Joaquín Sanmartín. *Die keilalphabetischen Texte aus Ugarit, Ras Ibn Hani und anderen Orten = The Cuneiform Alphabetic Texts from Ugarit, Ras Ibn Hani and Other Places*, third ed. (Münster: Ugarit-Verlag, 2013).

LXX	(the) Septuagint Textual (tradition) or (the) Septuagint Text as found in Göttingen LXX.
MT	(the) Masoretic Textual (tradition) or (the) Masoretic Text as found in BHS.
NETS	New English Translation of the Septuagint translation.
NJPS	New Jewish Publication Society translation.
Peshitta	The Old Testament In Syriac According to the Peshiṭta Version (Leiden: Brill, 1972–).
RLA	Reallexikon der Assyriologie.
SAA 7	Frederick Mario Fales and J. N Postgate, *Imperial Administrative Records*, State Archives of Assyria 7 (Helsinki: Helsinki University Press, 1992).
SAA 10	Simo Parpola, *Letters from Assyrian and Babylonian Scholars*, State Archives of Assyria 10 (Helsinki: Helsinki University Press, 1993).
Sélincourt	Herodotus, *The Histories*, trans. A. de Sélincourt, rev. ed., Penguin Classics (London: Penguin Books, 2003).
StaBi	Online digital collection held by the Staatsbibliothek zu Berlin. https://digital.staatsbibliothek-berlin.de/
TDNT	Theological Dictionary of the New Testament, ed. G. Kittel et al (Grand Rapids: Eerdmans, 1977–1978).
TDOT	Theological Dictionary of the Old Testament, ed. G. Johannes et al (Grand Rapids: 1997–2014).
UD	Jesús-Luis Cunchillos, Juan-Pablo Vita, and José-Ángel Zamora, eds., *Ugaritic Data Bank: The Texts* (Madrid: Laboratorio De Hermeneumática, 2003).

Sigla

‖	Content of two sources is the same.
≈	Equivalence between translations of two sources.
⌈ ⌉	Damaged letter.
[ ]	Restored letter.
{	}	Choice of reading due to ambiguous, damaged, or lost letter.
○	A single illegible or lost letter.